It is often said that marriage is a central or basic institution of society. This was perhaps more true in the past, or true in different ways, in periods when many marriages were arranged by parents, when brides were accompanied by dowries, and when marriage was used symbolically to represent the union of nuns to Christ or of rulers to their states.

This volume examines four of the main areas of importance in the history of marriage: first, the wedding itself, its economics and trappings; the laws that aimed to regulate aspects of marriage; intermarriage among social groups; and, finally, the consequences of marriage for women. A number of contributions to the book set out to challenge current historical assumptions about marriage as regards, for example, family marriage strategies or the effects of poverty and endogamy on marriage patterns in remote mountain communities.

Marriage in Italy, 1300–1650

Marriage in Italy, 1300–1650

Edited by

Trevor Dean

Roehampton Institute, London

and

K. J. P. Lowe

Goldsmiths' College, University of London

CAMBRIDGE
UNIVERSITY PRESS

PUBLISHED BY THE PRESS SYNDICATE OF THE UNIVERSITY OF CAMBRIDGE
The Pitt Building, Trumpington Street, Cambridge CB2 1RP

CAMBRIDGE UNIVERSITY PRESS
The Edinburgh Building, Cambridge CB2 2RU, United Kingdom
40 West 20th Street, New York, NY 10011–4211, USA
10 Stamford Road, Oakleigh, Melbourne 3166, Australia

© Cambridge University Press 1998

First published 1998

Printed in the United Kingdom at the University Press, Cambridge

Typeset in Plantin 10/12 pt [VN]

A catalogue record for this book is available from the British Library

Library of Congress Cataloguing in Publication data

ISBN 0 521 55402 0 hardback

Contents

Illustrations

Contributors

PATRICIA ALLERSTON is Lecturer in the Department of Modern History at the University of Glasgow

GIULIA CALVI is Associate Professor of Renaissance History at the University of Siena

STANLEY CHOJNACKI is Professor of History at the University of North Carolina at Chapel Hill

SAMUEL KLINE COHN, JR is Professor in the Department of Medieval History at the University of Glasgow

DAVID D'AVRAY is Professor in the Department of History at University College, London

TREVOR DEAN is Principal Lecturer in History at Roehampton Institute, London

GERARD DELILLE is Professor at the European University Institute in Florence and Directeur D'études at the Ecole des Hautes Etudes en Sciences Sociales in Paris

IRENE FOSI is Associate Professor in History at La Sapienza in Rome

LINDA GUZZETTI completed her doctoral research at the Technische Universität, Berlin

STEPHEN KOLSKY is Senior Lecturer in the Department of French and Italian Studies at the University of Melbourne

KATE LOWE is Senior Lecturer in History at Goldsmiths' College, University of London

JACQUELINE MUSACCHIO teaches in the Art History Department at Princeton University

PIET VAN BOXEL is Librarian and Lecturer at Leo Baeck College, London, and was for many years Lecturer in Rabbinics and New Testament at the University of Utrecht

MARIA ANTONIETTA VISCEGLIA is Professor of Early Modern History at the Terza Università of Rome

Acknowledgements

The following are thanked for kind permission to reproduce the illustrations: the British Library, London, for illustrations 1 and 2; the Ambrosiana Microfilm and Photographic Collection, University of Notre Dame, Indiana, for illustration 3; Soprintendenza per i beni artistici e storici delle provincie di Firenze e Pistoia, for illustration 4; the Biblioteca nazionale marciana, Venice, for illustration 5; Contessa Maria Pecori Giraldi Suardi for illustration 6; the Earl and Countess of Harewood and the Trustees of the Harewood House Trust, for illustration 7; the Trustees of the National Gallery, London, for illustration 8; the Philadelphia Museum of Art, for illustration 9; the National Galleries of Scotland, for illustration 10.

The articles by Giulia Calvi and Maria Antonietta Visceglia and Irene Fosi were translated by Anna Teicher; Gérard Delille's article was translated by Kate Lowe; and Linda Guzzetti's was translated by Trevor Dean.

Introduction: issues in the history of marriage

Trevor Dean and Kate Lowe

Why are historians interested in marriage? And why was marriage so important in past societies? Marriage is important because it heralded change: it brought the birth of a new family group (and often of a new household), involved the transfer of property, changed the status of the couple, attracted large amounts of legislation, implicated the wider kin, acted as an occasion for expenditure and consumption, facilitated social mobility, and served as an analogy in both the religious and political fields.[1] The history of marriage thus touches on demographic, legal, religious, economic and social history. This explains both the significance of marriage historically and its importance to historians.

Because marriage affected so many areas of life, historians approach it from many different perspectives. Among recent publications on marriage in Italy, for example, two collections of essays offer complementary approaches to those presented here: one edited by Michaela De Giorgio and Christiane Klapisch-Zuber and entitled *Storia del matrimonio*, in the series Storia delle donne in Italia published in 1996, and the other edited by Claudie Balavoine and entitled *Représentations et célébrations: le mariage à la Renaissance*, to be published in Tours. The former focuses in the main upon marriage in Italy between the eleventh and the twentieth centuries, being separated into sections on medieval, modern and contemporary times; it is thematic and aims to provide an overview. The latter, the proceedings of the annual Tours conference of 1995, addresses the subject by examining western Europe, rather than Italy alone, and by restricting its attention to the Renaissance; its especial concern is the iconography of marriage.

However, the present volume offers new material and arguments which

---

[1] S. Sogner and J. Dupâquier, 'Introduction' to *Marriage and Remarriage in Populations of the Past*, ed. J. Dupâquier *et al.* (London, 1981), p. 3; R. B. Outhwaite, 'Problems and perspectives in the history of marriage', in *Marriage and Society: Studies in the Social History of Marriage*, ed. R. B. Outhwaite (London, 1981), p. 11.

I

together suggest some new directions for research. We are concerned not just with marriage, but with underlying assumptions about it and the consequences of those assumptions. One of those assumptions relates to gender: marriage was understood to be a different act for women and men, and is therefore a fruitful point at which to investigate Italian Renaissance views on gender and on female and male roles. An attempt has been made to address questions arising from variations in social status and in local and regional conditions. Attention has also been focused on what kind of evidence, documentary, material and visual, is available for analysis. The four sections of this book correspond to four of the main areas of importance with regard to the historical study of marriage. With a subject as vast as this, there can be no notion of exhaustive inclusiveness. Instead we have commissioned articles on a variety of connected issues, from a range of disciplines, spread over a relatively long period of time and over the Italian peninsula. It should be stressed, however, that the majority of contributors are historians.

The first section contains articles on marriage ceremonies and festivities, which were often the most flamboyant part of the process. Before the strictures of the Council of Trent, most lay people perceived marriage as a social rather than a religious affair. They also knew it was a public rather than a private matter, and consequently weddings were celebrated in style whenever possible, both because they were thought of as an opportunity for entertainment and because publicity was vital. Family hospitality and repayment of old obligations sat happily with conspicuous consumption and lavish display at the top end of the social scale, but everyone with any means at all at their disposal celebrated after their own fashion. Patricia Allerston's piece here on wedding finery in sixteenth-century Venice makes this point more vividly by discussing the use of borrowing, hiring and buying second-hand as mechanisms that allowed a certain level of display at a smaller outlay than ordinary purchase. The components of a good wedding ranged from gastronomic treats and erudite drama to appropriate songs and music.

These customs of celebration were accompanied by the production of functional and artistic objects. These included jewellery, clothes, portraits, maiolica, silver and furniture; that is, they covered a large spectrum of type, but were restricted in detail and in iconographical subject matter. Some artists specialized in ornaments for weddings and made their names in this way. The best-known example is Apollonio di Giovanni, whose workshop produced a very large number of marriage-chests (*cassoni*),[2] but others, such as Andrea di Feltrini who was employed at the marriages of

[2] E. Callman, *Apollonio di Giovanni* (Oxford, 1974) and Callman, 'Apollonio di Giovanni and painting for the early Renaissance room', *Antichità viva*, 27 (1988).

Giuliano and Lorenzo de' Medici, worked only part-time on objects for marriage celebrations.[3] Jacqueline Musacchio's piece examines one theme portrayed on Tuscan marriage-chests and wainscoting in the fifteenth century, the rape of the Sabine women, in an attempt to unravel its message and popularity. In an article on the representation of Lucretia on similar objects, Cristelle Baskins found that the images reinforced 'cultural assumptions about the role of men and women'.[4] These paintings of rapes and their aftermaths were commissioned by men, either as fathers or husbands,[5] to adorn the bedchambers of their daughters or wives, and however beautiful their execution or scholarly their allusion, their main purpose must have been to reinforce a message of female submission. But the issue is not wholly straightforward, for the stories of the rapes of both Lucretia and the Sabine women resulted in decisive female reaction, a far cry from the stereotypical passive behaviour of a 'model' wife. What were women to make of this contradictory message?

Representations in art of weddings and marriage were relatively rarer than commemorative or exhortatory objects, although a few marriage-chests may have been decorated with wedding scenes.[6] The first place in terms of numbers of paintings goes to 'The betrothal [sposalizio] of the virgin' which was a popular subject for much of the fourteenth, fifteenth and sixteenth centuries.[7] Artists such as Giotto, Raphael and Rosso Fiorentino were all attracted by the subject, as were numerous others of lesser stature, so the demand for representations must have been great. It would be interesting to know if the commission of any of these paintings can be connected to contemporary Renaissance weddings or whether their religious content overrode other facets. Aspects of other biblical weddings, such as the wedding feast at Cana, and classical weddings, such as that of Dido and Aeneas, also found favour as themes. Representations of actual betrothals or weddings do exist but in smaller numbers (one famous example is the depiction by Pinturicchio in the Piccolomini Library in Siena Cathedral of the betrothal of the Emperor Frederick III and Leonora of Portugal in 1452) as do marriage scenes of unknown

[3] L. Monnas, 'The artists and the weavers: the design of woven silks in Italy, 1350–1550', *Apollo*, 125 (1987), p. 421.
[4] C. Baskins, 'Corporeal authority in the speaking picture: the representation of Lucretia in Tuscan domestic painting', in *Gender Rhetorics: Postures of Dominance and Submission in History*, ed. R. Trexler (Binghamton, 1994), p. 190.
[5] C. Klapisch-Zuber, 'Les femmes dans les rituels de l'alliance et de la naissance à Florence', in *Riti e rituali nelle società medievali*, ed. J. Chiffoleau, L. Martines and A. Paravicini Baglioni (Spoleto, 1994), pp. 6–8.
[6] But see B. Witthoft, 'Riti nuziali e loro iconografia', in *Storia del matrimonio*, ed. M. De Giorgio and C. Klapisch-Zuber (Rome and Bari, 1996), p. 138.
[7] S. Matthews Grieco, 'Matrimonio e vita coniugale nell'arte dell'Italia moderna', *ibid.*, pp. 258–9.

people in secular cycles. There are also curiously few examples of married couples without children where the accent is on the couple, as opposed to scenes involving well-known biblical and classical husbands and wives. An exception to this is Niccolò di Segna's *The Joys of Married Life* in the Palazzo Comunale in San Gimignano. Overall, Renaissance marriage scenes emphasized the historical at the expense of the contemporary.

On the other hand, images of symbolic marriages can be found in abundance. Their proliferation points to an ideology of marriage so central to the society that it was continually applied to other areas of life to describe or enshrine particularly important relationships. The metaphor of contractual relations based on consent, which supposedly existed between husband and wife, originally taken from the image of Christ and his church as bridegroom and bride, was then used to classify the relation of pope to church and bishop to diocese, where the pope and bishop were the head and husband in a mystical union with their flocks. Later in the Middle Ages it was extended to relations between secular rulers and their countries.[8] Kate Lowe's article looks at yet another form of symbolic marriage, that between Christ and nuns, and compares the wedding rituals for brides of Christ to those for secular brides, since complex rituals grew up around all these symbolic marriages.

Two of the clearest examples can be seen in the celebrations surrounding the marriage of the bishop of Florence to the abbess of S. Pier Maggiore, symbolizing his marriage to the Florentine church, and those surrounding the marriage of the doge of Venice to the sea, symbolizing his marriage to the republic. Both these ceremonies contained elements familiar from secular wedding ritual. The bishop of Florence, amid rich decorations, gave the abbess a ring, hosted an impressive banquet in the convent and originally spent the night there in a specially prepared bed.[9] The doge of Venice on board his ceremonial boat, the *Bucentaur*, threw a ring into the sea while repeating a formula of marriage: 'In signum veri perpetuique dominii' ('As a sign of true and perpetual dominion'); later he too gave the equivalent of a public wedding banquet.[10] Obviously the ideology of marriage contained within it the expression of a power relation which was convenient and pervasive in late medieval and early modern Italy, to the detriment of other configurations of partnership. There is never any doubt who is dominant in any of the relationships under discussion. From this, it can be deduced that the most important

[8] E. Kantorowicz, *The King's Two Bodies* (Princeton, 1957), pp. 207–18.
[9] G. Conti, *Fatti e aneddoti di storia fiorentina* (Florence, 1902), pp. 95–9; E. Viviani della Robbia, *Nei monasteri fiorentini* (Florence, 1947), pp. 43–6.
[10] E. Muir, *Civic Ritual in Renaissance Venice* (Princeton, 1981), pp. 119–34; A. Boholm, *The Doge of Venice: The Symbolism of State Power in the Renaissance* (Gothenburg, 1990), pp. 225, 236–7.

element of an ordinary marriage was thought to be the domination of one party, the female, by the other, the male. Alternative forms of symbolic marriage occasionally stress other features, it should be pointed out: for example, representations of St Francis marrying poverty, in which poverty is personified as a bride,[11] can be interpreted as expressions of choice over marriage partners.

The second section of the book includes various articles on intervention by church and state in the marriage process. This has traditionally been an area of strength in studies of marriage, as the legal basis of marriage ensured the keeping of records, and governments and relevant organs of the church generated their own paperwork. City statutes in late medieval Italy protected and promoted matrimony in various ways. For reasons of public order, they protected newly wed couples from physical and other injury. In order to curtail the costs to the parents or, later, to encourage more marriages to take place, they limited the size of dowries, wedding gifts and wedding banquets. They also created secular penalties for crimes against matrimony, that is for adultery, bigamy, abduction/fornication and clandestine marriage. Much time and energy was expended on sumptuary laws regulating excess in all forms, but especially luxury items. Some of this excess attached itself to marriage practices and celebrations which therefore became exposed to further legislation and interference.[12] Fourteenth- and fifteenth-century infractions which were later prosecuted included the giving of too many rings to the bride, failing to notify officials about a wedding banquet, serving forbidden foods and commissioning an over-expensive marriage-chest.[13] Stanley Chojnacki examines successive dowry laws in fifteenth- and sixteenth-century Venice and draws out the intimate connection between such legislation and definitions of nobility and propriety. These centuries also saw a successive tightening in the secular laws regarding matrimonial 'crimes', as investigated here by Trevor Dean. Extensive interference by the state in these areas ran counter to an ecclesiastical legal preserve and was perhaps partially responsible for the new level of church control of marriage promulgated at Trent.

Intervention by church authorities was another matter. Although revisionist histories exist which question the innovatory nature of much of the work of the Council of Trent, its pronouncements on marriage changed

---

[11] D. Gagnan, 'Typologie de la pauvreté chez St François d'Assisi: l'épouse, la dame, la mère', *Laurentianum*, 18 (1977), pp. 469ff.
[12] A. Esposito, 'Matrimoni "in regola" nella Roma del Quattrocento: tra leggi suntuarie e pratica dotale', *Archivi e cultura*, 25–6 (1992–3).
[13] C. Kovesi Killerby, 'Practical problems in the enforcement of Italian sumptuary law, 1200–1500', in *Crime, Society and the Law in Renaissance Italy*, ed. T. Dean and K. Lowe (Cambridge, 1994), p. 114.

the course of that institution by labelling it primarily ecclesiastical and by demanding exclusive church competence to regulate it.[14] The relevant texts of the council included a doctrinal preamble, twelve canons and a long decree entitled 'de reformatione matrimonii'. The most important canons declared marriage to be a sacrament, to be indissoluble, and that the church had exclusive competence over marriage cases. The decree regulated the norms for the celebration of marriage, most notably insisting upon the presence of the parish priest, upon prior publicity of the marriage by banns, upon witnesses and registration. Clandestine marriage received sharper definition, and public consent was required of the two main participants.[15] These changes both instigated the take-over of control of many aspects of matrimonial practice from the competence of the state or from nebulous dictates of local custom, and demanded strict enforcement of pre-existing regulations that had been allowed to lapse. David d'Avray's article investigates ecclesiastical requirements concerning the presence of a parish priest at marriages in northern Italy in the period after 1215 but before Trent. Much of the work carried out hitherto has focused on ascertaining whether the regulations promulgated at Trent represented a sea-change for the church or whether the council was exceptional in documenting the codification of already occurring behaviour.

What came to the fore at the Council of Trent was the struggle for control of the laity, exemplified here by contestation with secular authorities over the regulation of marriage. The kernel of this lay in the desire to administer and register marriages. In Italy prior to Trent, for example, notaries had registered marriages; after Trent, parish priests kept the books. Trent tightened the church's grip on lay behaviour regarding marriage in other ways too: the acquisition of dispensations in cases of marriage between the prohibited degrees, which theoretically had been a matter for the Penitentiary in the fifteenth and first half of the sixteenth centuries, but which had been dealt with effectively in Italy by the secular authorities, passed completely under church control.[16] This contest over control of marriage in a variety of situations intensified rather than died down in the course of the sixteenth and seventeenth centuries, peaking in the late eighteenth when the secular authorities scored notable triumphs.[17]

---

[14] J. Bossy, *Christianity in the West, 1400–1700* (Oxford, 1985), p. 25.
[15] A. Turchini, 'Dalla disciplina alla "creanza" del matrimonio all'indomani del concilio di Trento', in *Donna, disciplina, creanza cristiana dal xv al xvii secolo*, ed. G. Zarri (Rome, 1996), pp. 205–6.
[16] G. Brucker, 'Religious sensibilities in early-modern Europe: examples from the records of the Holy Penitentiary', *Historical Reflections*, 15 (1988), pp. 19–20.
[17] D. Lombardi, 'Intervention by church and state in marriage disputes in sixteenth- and seventeenth-century Florence', in *Crime, Society and the Law*, pp. 142, 156; Lombardi, 'Fidanzamenti e matrimoni dal concilio di Trento alle riforme settecentesche', in *Storia del matrimonio*.

Piet van Boxel's article, on the other hand, highlights some of the mechanisms employed by the church after Trent to coerce unbelievers (in this case Jews) into Catholic orthodoxy; here the struggle was between the Catholic authorities and Jews, and the reward for conformity was a reasonable dowry for an impecunious Jewish woman prepared to renounce her culture and religion in order to be able to marry. It is a welcome reminder of how wide the scope for intervention by unscrupulous parties in marriage was, when custom demanded the payment of a dowry, and it emphasizes yet again just how crucial marriage was for women. As one Renaissance legal writer in England declared, 'all women are understood either married, or to be married'.[18] Given this attitude, it is easier to see why desperate girls and women faced with a marriageless future might have felt compelled to forswear everything to obtain a husband.

The third section of the book examines patterns of intermarriage and views on the functionality of marriage. Sam Cohn's article examines endogamy and exogamy in the Tuscan countryside in the late fourteenth and fifteenth centuries, showing that mountainous areas were less inward-looking in their marriage patterns than is usually supposed. In addition to such questions, this section asks: in whose interests did marriage take place? Although the jurists believed the state of marriage to be more advantageous to women that to men,[19] there is little evidence to support the view that marriages were arranged for the benefit of women. The article by Irene Fosi and Maria Antonietta Visceglia answers this question decisively in the case of national groupings, and curial and papal families in Rome, by a rigorous investigation of the alliances contracted by them in the sixteenth and seventeenth centuries: marriage, they say, was conducted by men in the interests of family strategy, and not in the interests of individuals, male or female.

This is, however, a point of controversy among historians, between those giving emphasis to strategy and those giving emphasis to individual behaviour, and it deserves rather more extended treatment here. One of the firmest and most influential statements of the strategic point of view was made in the 1970s by Lawrence Stone, and although his focus was on early modern England, his outline is worth rehearsing for its general relevance and influence. For Stone, only in the eighteenth century did the modern family evolve, based on personal choice of partner and strong emotional ties within the nuclear family. In the later Middle Ages and early sixteenth century, by contrast, marriage was controlled by the wider kin in the interests of the family. Such 'family planning' had three objectives:

---

[18] Anon., 'The lawes resolutions of women's rights', p. 6, cited in I. Maclean, *The Renaissance Notion of Woman* (Cambridge, 1980), p. 75.

[19] Maclean, *The Renaissance Notion of Woman*, p. 75.

continuity of the male line, preservation intact of inherited property, and acquisition through marriage of further property or useful political alliances. Although these objectives were not, as Stone argues, always compatible, they had numerous consequences. First, families dictated the marriages and nuptiality of their children, delaying marriage for some, or denying marriage altogether for others, as nunneries absorbed unmarried women. Second, however, where property was absent as among the rural poor so was family strategy and control. Among the propertyless, parental control of marriage was weak, as children left home early to work as servants or apprentices. Third, the general emotional context, which both resulted from and partly explained controlled marriage, was one of coolness, of 'low affect'. This in turn was largely caused by demographic factors: marriages were concluded late in life and dissolved early by death, such that the conjugal family was short-lived and unstable, 'a loose association of transients'; childrearing was the main function of marriage, at the expense of elements of companionship; high infant mortality reduced parents' emotional commitment to their children; affection was spread thinly across the wider kin rather than concentrated in the conjugal unit; sentiment responded to social command.[20]

This has become a familiar interpretation. One Italian study of the 'models and rules for choice of marriage partner' uncritically took on the whole of Stone's interpretation.[21] However, elsewhere it has been criticized in many ways. Alan Macfarlane quickly responded, arguing for the existence of individualism and sentiment in marriage already by 1500; indeed, both Michael Sheehan and Judith Bennett have found couples already in the fourteenth century making personal choices of partner.[22] For the early modern period, Martin Ingram has argued that the family, far from overriding individual choice, carefully took account of it.[23] The notion that companionate marriage originated only in the Protestant Reformation has been systematically undermined.[24] Medievalists have demolished the idea that childhood and parental love for children were inventions of the early modern period.[25] Stone's limitation of strategy to

[20] L. Stone, *Family, Sex and Marriage in England, 1500–1800* (London, 1977), pp. 3–119.
[21] *Le funzioni sociali del matrimonio: modelli e regole della scelta del coniuge dal XIV al XX secolo*, ed. M. Buonanno (Milan, 1980), pp. 9–11.
[22] M. M. Sheehan, 'Choice of marriage partner in the Middle Ages: development and mode of application of a theory of marriage', *Studies in Medieval and Renaissance History*, new ser., 1 (1978), p. 18; J. M. Bennett, 'Medieval peasant marriage: an examination of marriage license fines in the *Liber Gersumarum*', in *Pathways to Medieval Peasants*, ed. J. A. Raftis (Toronto, 1981), pp. 212–14.
[23] M. Ingram, 'Spousals litigation in the English ecclesiastical courts, *c.* 1350–*c.* 1640', in *Marriage and Society*, ed. Outhwaite, pp. 49–50.
[24] K. M. Davies, 'Continuity and change in literary advice on marriage', *ibid.*
[25] S. Shahar, *Childhood in the Middle Ages* (London, 1990), pp. 1–4.

the propertied classes has also been challenged by those who perceive strategies even among the peasantry.[26] However, if some of the outer supports of Stone's interpretation have been stripped away, the essential core, of family strategies that controlled access to marriage, has remained largely in place, reinforced by the work of other influential historians such as Georges Duby.[27]

In Italy there is certainly plentiful evidence for parental control of children's marriages. Church court documents regarding disputed marriages often show parents promising their daughters contrary to their will, or imposing their will by force, or using beatings to persuade daughters to deny their own marriage promises of which parents disapproved.[28] This conforms to the picture elsewhere in Europe in which mothers, aunts and uncles threatened curses and physical harm to persuade daughters into marriages they did not want,[29] and parents thought that marriages concluded without their consent could be undone.[30] Even judicial practice in the ecclesiastical courts could favour parents, by construing a daughter's silence as tacit consent to a marriage, especially if accompanied by other signs such as the kiss and the ring.[31]

However, there is also evidence against parental control. At one level this comes, again, from church court records: individuals could persist in their choices against the pressure of parents and friends.[32] Girls could say no to proposals of marriage.[33] The proliferation of clandestine marriages in the later Middle Ages has been seen as evidence that, no matter what the church or secular authorities did, children's reaction against control could not be overcome.[34] One well-known Italian poem ('Mama, the time has come when I want to get married to a boy I like so much') thus portrays a mother unable to dissuade her daughter on the grounds of her young age, of the opposition of her friends and relatives, or of the risks.[35]

---

[26] G. Delille, 'Classi sociali e scambi matrimoniali nel Salernitano: 1500–1600 circa', *Quaderni storici*, 33 (1976), p. 991.
[27] G. Duby, *Medieval Marriage: Two Models from Twelfth-century France* (Baltimore, 1978).
[28] P. Rasi, 'La conclusione del matrimonio prima del Concilio di Trento', *Rivista di storia del diritto italiano*, 16 (1943), pp. 247–56; 'Documenti del secolo XIV tratti dall'Archivio notarile di Milano', *Bollettino storico della Svizzera italiana*, 12 (1890), p. 234.
[29] D. M. Owen, 'White Annays and others', in *Medieval Women*, ed. D. Baker (Oxford 1978), pp. 335–9.
[30] A. Wall, 'For love, money or politics? A clandestine marriage and the Elizabethan Court of Arches', *Historical Journal*, 38 (1995), pp. 520–1, 528–9.
[31] Rasi, 'Conclusione', pp. 260, 270, 289; G. Zanetti, 'La stipulazione del matrimonio a Trento nel sec. XIII', *Rivista di storia del diritto italiano*, 16 (1943), p. 30, n. 7.
[32] Rasi, 'Conclusione', pp. 241–2.
[33] *Ibid.*, pp. 242, 263; F. Fossati, 'Nuove spigolature d'archivio', *Archivio storico lombardo*, ser. 8, 7 (1957), p. 375.
[34] J. M. Turlan, 'Recherches sur le mariage dans la pratique coutumière (XIIe–XVIe s.)', *Revue historique de droit français et étranger*, ser. 4, 35 (1957), pp. 503–4.
[35] G. Carducci, 'Intorno ad alcune rime dei secoli XIII e XIV ritrovate nei memoriali

At another level there is the evidence of law and theology: the consensual theory of marriage had, it is argued by some legal historians, the consequence of recognizing women's capacity to act for themselves, as the marriage act had to be completed by them.[36] The exchange of consent was between two individuals, not between two families, and the woman was the subject, not the object of the contract.[37] A frequently heard maxim was that 'unwilling marriages usually have bad results',[38] and churchmen tried to redress the 'gender asymmetry' of medieval marriage through the ideas of consensual marriage and of the reciprocal conjugal debt.[39] Clerics stressed the importance of free will in marriage, on the argument that political marriages, and marriages by children too young to know what they were doing, led to wars.[40]

Both of these positions of parental control and of parental impotence are in themselves flawed. Examples of parents forcing children into marriage could just as well represent the exception as the rule, and the fact that cases came to court could be taken as evidence for the capacity of the victims to resort to the law.[41] On the other hand, too much attention to legal theory without an understanding of its social context can produce a distorted picture. In Florence, at least, the exchange of consent between the couple was firmly embedded within controlling contracts between the elder male kin of either side.[42]

It is also arguable, however, that marriage as family strategy fails to take account of other factors involved in deciding on marriage partners, astrology for example. Astrologers were consulted not only regarding the suitability of unions, but also regarding the most auspicious dates for weddings.[43] Then there is the activity of marriage brokers: did these

dell'Archivio notarile di Bologna', *Atti e memorie della Deputazione di storia patria per la Romagna*, ser. 2, 2 (1876), pp. 197–8.

[36] F. Brandileone, 'L'intervento dello stato nella celebrazione del matrimonio in Italia prima del concilio di Trento', *Atti dell'Accademia di scienze morali e politiche [di Napoli]*, 27 (1894–5), pp. 327, 335.

[37] A. Marongiu, 'Matrimonio medievale e matrimonio postmedievale: spunti storico-critici', *Rivista di storia del diritto italiano*, 57 (1984), p. 11.

[38] Sheehan, 'Choice of marriage partner', p. 9.

[39] J. W. Baldwin, 'Consent and the marital debt: five discourses in northern France around 1200', in *Consent and Coercion to Sex and Marriage in Ancient and Medieval Societies*, ed. A. E. Laiou (Washington, D.C., 1993), pp. 258–60.

[40] E.g. J. B. Williamson, 'Philippe de Mézière's book for married ladies: a book from the entourage of the court of Charles VI', in *The Spirit of the Court*, ed. G. S. Burgess and R. A. Taylor (Cambridge, 1985), p. 404.

[41] F. Pedersen, 'Did the medieval laity know the canon rules on marriage? Some evidence from fourteenth-century York cause papers', *Mediaeval Studies*, 56 (1994).

[42] C. Klapisch-Zuber, 'Zacharie, ou le père évincé. Les rites nuptiaux toscans entre Giotto et le concile de Trente', *Annales*, 34 (1979), pp. 1219–26.

[43] H. R. Lemay, 'Guido Bonatti: astrology, society and marriage in thirteenth-century Italy', *Journal of Popular Culture*, 17:4 (1984), pp. 82–5; A. Luzio, 'Isabella d'Este e

always operate within family strategies, or were brokers, as apparently alleged in a case from Udine in 1480, persons of low morality, who dishonestly persuaded people into matrimony, while living off the fees?[44] Moreover, 'family strategy' was clearly not an uncontentious issue. In Padua at the beginning of the sixteenth century, a grandfather instigated a court case, for nullity of his grandson's marriage, on the grounds that it had been imposed by the boy's mother.[45] In another case, the brother of a girl forced into marriage by her father refused to assent to it, or to stay in the same house as his new brother-in-law.[46] Relatives could thus differ over the marriage of children: the strategy often belonged to just one parent, not the whole family. One well-documented example of this is Francesco Guicciardini's marriage to Maria Salviati in 1506. Francesco married without his father's consent or approval, he recalls in his *Ricordanze*, but rather out of a different strategy, not out of love. His father had three objections to the Salviati marriage: close ties to the Salviati were dangerous given their enmity with the current political leader of Florence, Piero Soderini; Francesco's father needed him to obtain a larger dowry, as he had to find husbands for six daughters; and the Salviati had been brought up 'with too much pomp and indulgence'.[47] These objections were essentially political and financial: the political dangers of alliance to the Salviati outweighed any benefits; the marriage brought in too little in dowry, and would cost too much in expenditure. Francesco's reasoning was simpler and purely political: he wanted an alliance with the Salviati because their wealth, goodwill, reputation and in-laws from other marriages exceeded, in his view, those of all other Florentine families. Strategies were thus not always familial, but could be individual, just as, conversely, some families did not react with hostility to their children's individual choices based on love.[48] Strategy and individuality were thus not mutually exclusive; parents were not always opposed to love-matches. Marriages were concluded for a variety of reasons, and it does not always make sense to elevate a reason to the level of strategy.

The article by Gérard Delille discusses the use made of marriage alliance to dampen down or quell vendetta in Altamura in Apulia. His

---

Francesco Gonzaga, promessi sposi', *Archivio storico lombardo*, ser. 4, 9 (1908), pp. 61–2; G. Porro, 'Nozze di Beatrice d'Este e di Anna Sforza', *Archivio storico lombardo*, 9 (1882), p. 491.
[44] Rasi, 'Conclusione del matrimonio', pp. 242–3.
[45] *Ibid.*, pp. 284–5.
[46] *Ibid.*, pp. 279–81; Rasi, 'I rapporti tra l'autorità ecclesiastica e l'autorità civile in Feltre', *Archivio veneto*, ser. 5, 13 (1933), p. 104.
[47] Francesco Guicciardini, *Ricordi diari memorie*, ed. M. Spinella (Rome, 1981), p. 83.
[48] Boccaccio, *Decameron*, II.8, V.4; Rasi, 'Conclusione', p. 253.

reading reinforces the view that decisions over marriages were taken by the men in the family and that women were employed as 'objects' who were useful to the male lineage at certain junctures, notably marriage, when they could be given away or exchanged, but whose views (were they capable of having any) were of no importance. Men, too, could be 'objects' in this sense in marriage negotiations and contracts, but the difference lay in the fact that decisions were at least being taken in the interests of their gender and their family line, even if not in their own personal interests.

Doubt has also arisen regarding the value of marriage alliance to the two families concerned. Given the attention contemporaries paid to the political alignment and social standing of potential in-laws (and of their in-laws in turn), as in the Guicciardini case, it might seem natural to conclude that families joined through marriage became united in politics or business or other undertakings, and that this was the purpose of the marriage. This is certainly what they said. The doge of Genoa, for example, in commending the projected marriage of his sister to a son of Emanuele d'Appiano, lord of Piombino, wrote 'You have made *parentado* with persons who are not likely to cause you any burden, but rather will give you favour and increase in reputation among other states, which from now on will have more fear to do something that displeases you, than they have perhaps had up to now, because, when needed, we shall not omit anything pertaining to the duty of a good parent.'[49] Similarly, Francesco Sforza, lord of Milan, explained his proposed marriage alliance with the Gonzaga, lords of Mantua, by saying that they were already 'glued together in mind and mutual benefits', and sought to bind their descendants together in unity.[50] However, once married, in-laws do not always seem to have made much use of such relationships. Cammarosano has argued that the particular type of dowry system in Italy – in which dowry was seen as a form of credit, not a gift – limited the economic aspects of in-law-ship.[51] Klapisch-Zuber, in studying the memoirs and diaries of the Niccolini family of Florence, noted that most in-laws were mentioned only once, and that those mentioned more often had limited involvement with the Niccolini (acting as arbiters and pacifiers of their disputes, but not as lenders, guarantors or god-parents).[52] For Venice, Queller and Madden argue that the level of cooper-

[49] A. Pesce, 'Le trattative per il matrimonio di Battistina Fregoso con Iacopo III Appiani', *Archivio storico italiano*, 71:2 (1913), p. 140.
[50] A. Colombo, 'Nuovo contributo alla storia del contratto di matrimonio fra Galeazzo Maria Sforza e Susanna Gonzaga', *Archivio storico lombardo*, ser. 4, 12 (1909), p. 209.
[51] P. Cammarosano, 'Aspetti delle strutture familiari nelle città dell'Italia comunale (secoli XII–XIV)', *Studi medievali*, ser. 3, 16 (1975), p. 422.
[52] C. Klapisch-Zuber, ' "Parenti, amici e vicini": il territorio urbano d'una famiglia mercan-

ation among in-laws looks limited, and they wonder 'whether it is a mirage that political coalitions were bound together by marriage alliance'.[53] Similarly, Molho's study of Florentine marriages found that they bore no correlation to political alignments.[54] Such limited activation of their alliance raises a question over the extent of family strategy and control over marriage. Useful to remember in this context is an alleged southern Italian saying of the fifteenth century: 'that when lords want to make marriage alliances [*parentado*] together, they do so to cheat each other'.[55] Can it be that a strategy could aim not to acquire useful political allies, but to make political or economic gain at the expense of the in-laws?

Political strategy certainly seems to dominate marriage among Italian lords and princes. The matter of the dowry was easily settled in princely marriage alliances, because, as a Milanese ambassador said to the king of Naples in 1455, 'these affinities among lords are not made for the dowries, but in order to draw closer and unite'.[56] Indeed, haggling over dowry could lead to an accusation of behaving like a merchant.[57] Marriage negotiations were often started when girls were still children – at ages ranging from twelve years to less than two.[58] During the negotiations, girls were often referred to without name (*la putta*), such that their personality could be said to disappear.[59] One daughter could substitute for another in a marriage agreement.[60] Princely marriages were often concluded by proxy, thus avoiding personal exchange of consent, but with a long delay before the bride was finally delivered to her husband, in order to give the

tile nel XV secolo', *Quaderni storici*, 33 (1976), pp. 967–70. Cf. J. M. Bennett, 'The tie that binds: peasant marriages and families in late medieval England', *Journal of Interdisciplinary History*, 15 (1984), pp. 117–24, 126–7.

[53] D. E. Queller and T. F. Madden, 'Father of the bride: fathers, daughters and dowries in late medieval and early Renaissance Venice', *Renaissance Quarterly*, 46 (1993), pp. 700–4.

[54] A. Molho, *Marriage Alliance in Late-Medieval Florence* (Cambridge, Mass., and London, 1994), pp. 250–6.

[55] Antonio Minuti, *Vita di Muzio Attendolo Sforza*, ed. G. Porro Lambertenghi, *Miscellanea di storia italiana*, 7 (1869), p. 267. Cf. 'en mariage, il trompe qui peut': Turlan, 'Recherches', p. 499.

[56] C. Canetta, 'Le sponsalie di casa Sforza con casa d'Aragona (giugno–ottobre 1455)', *Archivio storico lombardo*, 9 (1882), p. 137.

[57] M. Bellonci, *Lucrezia Borgia, la sua vita e i suoi tempi*, second edn (Milan, 1939), p. 246.

[58] Luzio, 'Isabella d'Este', pp. 37–8; C. Santoro, 'Un registro di doti sforzesche', *Archivio storico lombardo*, ser. 8, 4 (1954), pp. 140, 157, 165; Colombo, 'Nuovo contributo' pp. 204–5; Canetta, 'Sponsalie', p. 137; G. Tabacco, 'Il trattato matrimoniale sabaudo-austriaco del 1310 e il suo significato politico', *Bollettino storico-bibliografico subalpino*, 49 (1951), p. 15, n. 32.

[59] Luzio, 'Isabella d'Este', p. 44; L. Rossi, 'Matrimonio di Sante Bentivoglio con Ginevra Sforza (8 marzo 1452)', *Bollettino della Società pavese di storia patria*, 6 (1906), p. 113; Canetta, 'Sponsalie', pp. 137–8.

[60] Colombo, 'Nuovo contributo', p. 205; A. Giulini, 'Un probabile progetto matrimoniale per Caterina Sforza', *Archivio storico lombardo*, ser. 4, 19 (1913), pp. 220–2.

family time enough to amass the large dowries agreed.[61] Dowry agreements often, though, included settlement of other outstanding debts between the two families, such that the real dowry was very much smaller (in the case of Caterina Cornaro's marriage to the king of Cyprus, 80 per cent of the dowry was discounted as existing debt).[62] Marriage agreements were also, of course, the occasion for significant transfers or assignments of property to satisfy political or territorial ambitions.

Despite all this, there is some evidence of love, affection and individual choice. Galeazzo Maria Sforza, betrothed to Dorotea Gonzaga, reported in 1463 to his father about his visit to Mantua, saying 'I know that nothing I could do would more please your Excellency than to comport myself decently with my wife [*sic*] and to give her caresses so that everyone knows that I love her.'[63] Ludovico Sforza, eagerly awaiting the arrival of his bride Beatrice d'Este, wrote that 'beside the natural desire to propagate our own blood, and to leave an image of ourselves to posterity, we could not have anything more welcome than the company and custom of our consort, as much for the pleasure and satisfaction which we hope of her virtues, as for having with us a perfect testimony of our love to the duke [her father]'.[64] Sforza thus gave his own version (reproduction, companionship, alliance) of the canonical three goods of marriage (faith, children and sacrament).

However, there would be strong grounds for rejecting professions of love and companionship as mere hypocrisy. When Francesco Sforza was trying to extricate his son, Galeazzo Maria, from his betrothal to Dorotea Gonzaga, in order to pursue a more prestigious French royal match, he had his envoy insist that the betrothal had been based on affection not politics, and 'if anyone should say that this alliance was made out of necessity of the war we were then waging against Venice, we say that this *parentado* was made to draw us closer in sincere love and good affection'.[65] Such protestation of course implies that common opinion regarded this marriage alliance to have been made merely in order to neutralize Sforza's eastern neighbour at a time of military threat.

Much of the evidence so far presented of princely marriages relates to

[61] Luzio, 'Isabella d'Este', pp. 44, 61; G. Romano, 'Valentina Visconti e il suo matrimonio con Luigi di Turaine', *Archivio storico lombardo*, ser. 3, 10 (1898), p. 19; Tabacco, 'Trattato matrimoniale', pp. 24–5; Rossi, 'Matrimonio di Sante Bentivoglio', pp. 111–12.

[62] 'Il matrimonio di Caterina Cornaro in due lettere di Gerardo Colli', *Archivio storico lombardo*, ser. 5, 1 (1914), p. 588.

[63] L. Beltrami, 'L'annulamento del contratto di matrimonio fra Galeazzo M. Sforza e Dorotea Gonzaga (1463)', *Archivio storico lombardo*, ser. 2, 6 (1889), pp. 130–1.

[64] Porro, 'Nozze di Beatrice d'Este', p. 488.

[65] Beltrami, 'L'annulamento', p. 128.

the Sforza family of Milan, and it may be that their unusual and precarious position – as not altogether legitimate successors to the Visconti
dukes led them into greater than usual utilitarian harshness when it
came to arranging marriages: this would certainly be suggested by the
marriage of the thirteen-year-old Elisabetta Sforza to the sixty-five-year-
old Guglielmo di Monferrato;[66] or their manipulation, in order to break
off Galeazzo Maria's betrothal, of Gonzaga reluctance to allow the
fourteen-year-old Dorotea Gonzaga to be inspected naked for physical
deformity;[67] or Francesco Sforza's alienation of his brother, Alessandro,
who was forced to take the public blame for a Sforza marriage that met
with hostility in Italian political circles, and who declared that he
wished his daughter had never been born or that she would drop
dead.[68]

However, the Sforza were by no means unique. Among their pre-
decessors as lords of Milan, Giangaleazzo Visconti was said to have forced
the marriage of his niece Lucia to the landgrave of Thuringia: following
Giangaleazzo's death, she declared on oath that she had uttered the
words of consent 'out of fear and reverence of Giangaleazzo, and at his
command', that he had told her 'Say yes', and had held her up to stop her
from fainting to the floor, and that she had been told 'If you do not do
what the lord pleases, he will destroy you'.[69] Against such powerful
patriarchs, the theoretical freedom of marriage consent was difficult to
sustain. But matriarchs could be just as bad, as the case of Queen
Giovanna of Naples and her niece, Giovanna duchess of Durazzo,
showed in the 1360s. Despite being over the canonical age to marry
without family consent, despite stating her objections to her aunt's candi-
date for her hand, despite making some sort of matrimonial promise to
her own lover, Aimon, son of the count of Geneva (she had been 'cap-
tivated at the sight of him'), Giovanna was detained in strict custody,
deprived of the use of her seal so that she could not write letters, and told
that her aunt would 'rather see her dead in a ditch than married to
Aimon'. Her aunt, the queen, successfully braved papal letters and bulls
supporting Giovanna's freedom to choose, in order to prevent this marriage.[70]

[66] P. Parodi, 'Le nozze di Guglielmo VII, marchese di Monferrato con Elisabetta Sforza',
     Bollettino storico-bibliografico subalpino, 25 (1923), p. 376.
[67] Beltrami, 'L'annulamento', pp. 129–32.
[68] Rossi, 'Matrimonio di Sante Bentivoglio', p. 111.
[69] G. Romano, 'Un matrimonio alla corte de' Visconti', *Archivio storico lombardo*, ser. 2, 8
     (1891), pp. 610–14. But note that it was now convenient (and safe) for her to make these
     declarations, and that, four years earlier, she had made what seems on paper an unforced
     choice: *ibid*.
[70] K. M. Setton, 'Archbishop Pierre d'Ameil in Naples and the affair of Aimon III of
     Geneva (1363–1364)', *Speculum*, 28 (1953).

The image, raised in the southern Italian proverb quoted above, of fathers competing to cheat each other leads naturally to the issue of a 'marriage market'. This is a very widely used metaphor for describing the way that marriages were arranged in the past. The metaphor is certainly supported by contemporary comments. The idea that people were mercenary in negotiating marriage was common.[71] San Bernardino of Siena accused women of 'displaying their daughters like wares on the market to prospective bidders'.[72] Leon Battista Alberti famously recommended, in his treatise on the family, that men should look over prospective brides as they would over farms that they were about to purchase.[73] A sixteenth-century writer remarked that 'a marriage seems like a sale of leather or clothes, there is so much bargaining'.[74] Marriage was even called a contract in canon law, and likened sometimes by lawyers to a contract of sale.[75] Modern historians commonly stress the commercial and business-like aspects of marriage negotiation. Klapisch-Zuber at one point refers to the woman as an 'object of trade'.[76]

This interpretation, of marriage as business transaction, has undergone two developments in recent years. First, Lorenzo Fabbri has attempted to apply the market metaphor in a more detailed and systematic fashion, in terms not just of supply and demand, but also of product and value, competition and exchange.[77] Thus the 'launch' of a daughter on the market was carefully prepared in advance.[78] The market was seasonal, with plague and political uncertainty depressing activity.[79] Information was gathered by parents on the state of the market and on eligible partners, by referring to lists drawn up by marriage brokers, and by engagement in daily discussions with friends and neighbours regarding betrothals and negotiations in progress.[80] Value on the marriage market was an amalgam of various elements: the amount of dowry (which 'in

---

[71] B. Cecchetti, 'La donna nel Medioevo a Venezia', *Archivio veneto*, 31 (1886), p. 309; B. Paton, *The Preaching Friars and the Civic Ethos in Siena, 1380–1480* (London, 1991), p. 220; A. Luzio, 'Isabella d'Este', p. 42; G. Le Bras, 'Mariage: la doctrine du mariage chez les théologiens et les canonistes depuis l'an mille', in *Dictionnaire de théologie catholique* (15 vols., Paris, 1908–50), IX, col. 2181.
[72] Paton, *Preaching Friars*, pp. 227–8.
[73] Leon Battista Alberti, *I libri della famiglia*, ed. R. Romano and A. Tenenti (Turin, 1969), p. 132.
[74] B. Witthoft, 'Marriage rituals and marriage chests in Quattrocento Florence', *Artibus et historiae*, 5 (1982), p. 44.
[75] Le Bras, 'Mariage', cols. 2182–4; D. Cecchi, 'Il matrimonio-contratto dall'Ostiense ai canonisti trecinquecenteschi', *Rivista di storia del diritto italiano*, 40–1 (1967–8).
[76] 'objet du négoce': 'Zacharie', p. 1220.
[77] L. Fabbri, *Alleanza matrimoniale e patriziato nella Firenze del '400: studio sulla famiglia Strozzi* (Florence, 1991).
[78] *Ibid.*, pp. 132–3.   [79] *Ibid.*, pp. 58–60.   [80] *Ibid.*, pp. 139–41.

good measure influenced family strategies, directing them towards this or that alliance'),[81] political implications, social considerations such as antiquity of lineage, friendship, neighbourhood and existing marriage alliances, and personal factors such as age, domestic virtues, physical attributes (including apparent childbearing capacity) and sexual reputation.[82]

However, this attempt to flesh out the market metaphor reveals only how unsatisfactory it is. As Klapisch-Zuber argued, this market, if it existed, did not function according to the law of supply and demand, for dowry levels did not vary like commodity prices.[83] In fact, dowry levels in Florence were often set years in advance, being determined by the size of parents' investments in the Dowry Fund. Moreover, Fabbri's attempt to incorporate political factors into market value fails adequately to take account of the fact (which he himself admits) that the very negotiation of marriage was often a political act, used by families to make political connections or to send out political messages, and used by rulers and leaders to extend their own influence or to curtail that of others.[84] Marriage as alliance cannot, thus, be contained within the market model: dowry is either the main determinant, or it is not; if marriages were political acts, it is difficult to see how they could constitute a market distributing a commodity by the price mechanism.

Furthermore, if marriage was a market, then it ought to be possible to find profit, in other words a surplus between what a family gave out and what it received, at the level of the individual transaction. This would be most noticeable in marriages between social unequals (so-called *mésalliances*), where the good name of an aristocratic daughter is traded for the coin of a socially ambitious merchant's son. But *mésalliances* were not frequent. According to Fabbri himself, putting unmarried girls into nunneries was considered by many preferable to 'marrying down'.[85] Molho has argued (though controversially) for the majority practice of endogamy within the Florentine patriciate, and the consequent marginal nature of exogamy. The Florentine elite tended not to marry their sons to the daughters of social inferiors.[86] Nor is Florence unique: no tendency to marry up has been found in Calabria or in

---

[81] *Ibid.*, p. 44.   [82] *Ibid.*, pp. 86, 97–129.
[83] C. Klapisch-Zuber, 'Le complexe de Griselda. Dot et dons de mariage au Quattrocento', *Mélanges de l'Ecole française de Rome*, 94 (1982), pp. 9, 19.
[84] Fabbri, *Alleanza matrimoniale*, pp. 86, 89, 145, 166–7.
[85] *Ibid.*, p. 44; and see T. Kuehn, 'Reading microhistory: the example of *Giovanni and Lusanna*', *Journal of Modern History*, 61 (1989), p. 521.
[86] Molho, *Marriage Alliance*, pp. 324–35; but see review by S. Chojnacki in *Journal of Social History*, 29 (1995–6), pp. 188–91.

Ragusa.[87] Preachers and moralists, we should note, stressed the importance of congruity between spouses, and in this they seem to have reflected social practice.[88]

Against the domination of the market model, Klapisch-Zuber has proposed a different interpretation: gift-exchange. This idea draws on Marcel Mauss's famous anthropological study, *L'essai sur le don*, of 1925, and resembles Claude Lévi-Strauss's *The Elementary Structures of Kinship*, first published in 1949. In developing the ideas of Mauss and Malinowski, Lévi-Strauss first pointed to the reciprocal giving, sometimes fantastically elaborate, that accompanied marriages. Such giving, he maintained, was cyclical and produced no nett gain: gifts 'are either exchanged immediately for equivalent gifts, or are received by the beneficiaries on condition that they will give counter-gifts, often exceeding the original gifts in value, but which in their turn bring about a subsequent right to receive new gifts'; but 'these gifts are not offered principally or essentially with the idea of receiving a profit or advantage of an economic nature'.[89] However, it is not just that marriages are accompanied by gifts, but that 'the woman herself is nothing other than one of these gifts, the supreme gift among those that can only be obtained in the form of reciprocal gifts'.[90] Having women to exchange is a precondition to obtaining a wife for oneself or one's sons.[91] In all the resulting cycles of bride-exchange, women are not exchanged for goods, but are exchanged for other women, either in the short or long term.[92]

In applying such ideas, Klapisch-Zuber is led to see the dowry as only one part of an extensive process of gift-exchange on the occasion of a marriage. The dowry was balanced by counter-gifts from the husband to the bride, or from the husband's family to the bride's.[93] Moreover, marriage itself is seen as a form of circulation of women: society did not tolerate female immobility or solitude, as a woman's very identity was

[87] G. Caridi, 'Capitoli matrimoniali, dote e dotario in Calabria (XVI–XVII sec.)', *Archivio storico per la Calabria e la Lucania*, 54 (1987), p. 36; D. B. Rheubottom, '"Sisters first": betrothal order and age at marriage in fifteenth-century Ragusa', *Journal of Family History*, 13 (1988), p. 369; S. M. Stuard, 'Dowry increase and increments in wealth in medieval Ragusa', *Journal of Economic History*, 41 (1981), pp. 797–8, 802; and see G. Laribière, 'Le mariage à Toulouse aux XIVe et XVe siécles', *Annales du Midi*, 79 (1967), p. 360; but cf. S. Carocci, 'Aspetti delle strutture familiari a Tivoli nel XV secolo', *Mélanges de l'Ecole française de Rome*, 94 (1982), pp. 60–1; J. B. Wood, 'Endogamy and *mésalliance*, the marriage patterns of the nobility of the *Election* of Bayeux, 1430–1669', *French Historical Studies*, 10 (1977–8).

[88] F. Brandileone, 'Nuove ricerche sugli oratori matrimoniali in Italia', *Rivista storica italiana*, 12 (1895), p. 623.

[89] C. Lévi-Strauss, *The Elementary Structures of Kinship*, second edn (London, 1969), pp. 52–3.

[90] *Ibid.*, p. 65.   [91] *Ibid.*, pp. 134–5.   [92] *Ibid.*, p. 238.

[93] Klapisch-Zuber, 'Le complexe de Griselda'.

determined by her movement relative to male households.[94] Klapisch-
Zuber, it must be said, rather holds back from the idea of cycles of
bride-exchange, but others have used the concept: it is men who give and
take in marriage; women are conduits of matrimonial ties, not partners.[95]
  One problem with such analysis is that reciprocal giving, as described
by Malinowski and Lévi-Strauss, has been imputed with gender bias by
feminist thinking. The 'norm of reciprocity', by focusing only on 'what
males exchange between one another', both ignores and objectifies
women: 'Women, though physically present, were seen but ignored as
active participants in their own right', and were denied 'motivation and
access to their own resources and strategies'.[96] 'What males exchange
between one another', it is argued, is only one part of a broader picture
which includes the production and control of resources by women, and
the creation of social stability through possessions that are inalienable and
not the object of gift-exchange. Though this theory is even more difficult
to apply to Renaissance Italy, it is reflected in the piece here by Stanley
Chojnacki, who has elsewhere commented on the increasing passage of
resources into female hands brought about by dowry inflation, and on the
possible changes this engendered in relations between husbands and
wives and in choice of marriage partners.[97]
  The fourth section of the book leads on naturally from these questions
and looks at the consequences and endings of marriage, two other fruitful
areas from which to gain understanding of assumptions underlying marriage. If women were in some senses 'objects' at the moment of their
marriage to men, did their situation ameliorate after the wedding day? As
Chojnacki has suggested, some noblewomen may have been able to
demand a different attitude from their husbands,[98] but for most women,
it is not clear that this was possible. Stephen Kolsky, however, has
examined collections of writings emanating from the courts of northern
Italy where, in contrast to the republics of Florence and Venice, he argues
that marriage did indeed offer new possibilities to the court wife. This is

[94] Klapisch-Zuber, 'La "mère cruelle". Maternité, veuvage et dot dans la Florence des
XIVe–XVe siècles', *Annales*, 38 (1983), p. 521.
[95] G. Rubin, 'The traffic in women: notes on the "political economy" of marriage', in
Toward an Anthropology of Women, ed. R. R. Reiter (New York and London, 1975), pp.
174–6; and see analysis of 'generalized' and 'restricted' systems of exchange in G. Delille,
Famille e proprietà dans le royaume de Naples (XVe–XIXe siècle) (Rome and Paris, 1985),
pp. 269–80.
[96] A. B. Wiener, *Inalienable Possessions: The Paradox of Keeping-while-Giving* (Berkeley,
1992), pp. 2–14.
[97] S. Chojnacki, 'Dowries and kinsmen in early Renaissance Venice', *Journal of Interdisciplinary History*, 5 (1975).
[98] S. Chojnacki, 'The power of love: wives and husbands in late-medieval Venice', in
Women and Power in the Middle Ages, ed. M. Erle and M. Kowaleski (Athens, Ga., and
London, 1992).

unusual: marriage may have been socially necessary for women, but the state of being married did not of itself bring advantages. Unfortunately, it is very difficult to find contemporary female opinions on this subject: married women in Renaissance Italy, of whatever social class, tended to leave few individual traces that related only to them, rather than to their husbands or their families. Collections of records presenting wives' points of view do not exist, though occasionally there are extant runs of personal letters, normally between husbands and wives when one of them was away. Women's wills are the exception to this rule, but women had to have goods or property at their disposal before they could make a will.[99] The ability of married women to act on their own behalf in legal matters depended on their place of residence, but in many cases their access to the law was through their husbands or their husbands' representatives though this is a matter of some debate.[100]

This absence of information about the married woman's point of view has led many to seek it in contemporary treatises on the behaviour of the good wife.[101] Models of wifely behaviour and wives' opinions about marriage are worlds apart, though an examination of the former is useful for what it reveals about the status of women in marriage and their capacity for independent action. The good wife obviously obeyed her husband at all times, and sometimes by fulfilling this role, her behaviour can be mistaken for that of an independent person. An interesting example of this is provided by what Christiane Klapisch-Zuber has called the ring game: established wives presented new wives with family rings on their marriage, but it was their husbands who took the decisions about the occasions and destinations of the rings.[102]

One of the most interesting aspects of marriage is that all marriages come to an end. Marriage is a finite state. Perhaps because of this, the possibility of failure always seems to have been built in and contingency plans for the end of marriages were available from the start. Ideally, the end should occur upon the death of either the husband or the wife, but other options were common enough in the period under discussion to

---

[99] I. Chabot, 'Risorse e diritti patrimoniali', in *Il lavoro delle donne*, ed. A. Groppi (Rome and Bari, 1996).

[100] T. Kuehn, '*Cum consensu mundualdi*: legal guardianship of women in Quattrocento Florence', *Viator*, 13 (1982); E. Rosenthal, 'The position of women in Renaissance Florence: neither autonomy nor subjection', in *Florence and Italy: Renaissance Studies in Honour of Nicolai Rubinstein*, ed. P. Denley and C. Elam (London, 1988).

[101] S. Vecchio, 'La buona moglie', in *Il Medioevo*, ed. C. Klapisch-Zuber (Rome and Bari, 1990); R. Ago, 'Maria Spada Veralli: la buona moglie', in *Barocco al femminile*, ed. G. Calvi (Rome and Bari, 1992).

[102] C. Klapisch-Zuber, 'The Griselda complex: dowry and marriage gifts in the Quattrocento', in *Women, Family and Ritual in Renaissance Italy*, ed. Klapisch-Zuber (Chicago, 1985), p. 234.

merit the attention of the secular and ecclesiastical authorities. Even if one spouse did die, the question of what the other spouse should do with regard to remarrying was a worrying one. The dilemma was especially severe for women, who were supposed not to be able to function effectively without being married. In fact, although women's lives may not have noticeably improved after their move from the unmarried to the married state, they took a definite turn for the better (in terms of the lifting of legal and social restrictions) when their husbands died. Two of the articles included here examine what happened after the failure or end of marriage. Linda Guzzetti analyses a set of separations in fourteenth-century Venice to see what had prompted the breakdown, whether relations were still amicable or not, what the options were for women, and what their legal position was. She believes that although families were involved in arranging marriages, they were not so clearly involved in interfering in the life of the couple after marriage. Giulia Calvi, on the other hand, investigates second marriages in late sixteenth-century Tuscany, shedding new light on the relationship between the government magistracy dealing with orphans and the mothers of the children.

Ceremonies and rituals of death are now seen to be similar in many respects to ceremonies and rituals of marriage, especially with regard to gender roles.[103] Recent work has suggested that the rituals were similar because they were both part of the same cycle that started with women as brides and ended with them in their widows' weeds.[104] However, some brides failed to live long enough to complete the second part of the equation as widows, and were participants in the twin rites of passage as bride and corpse.

To end on such a gloomy note might be thought inappropriate, but it is quite deliberate: it reminds us that the real possibilities for self-determination that marriage offered to some women were in practice limited by class either to the elite or to the lowest social groups.

[103] S. Strocchia, 'Death rites and the ritual family in Renaissance Florence', in *Life and Death in Fifteenth-century Florence*, ed. M. Tetel and R. Witt (Durham, N.C., and London, 1989).

[104] I. Chabot, 'La sposa in nero. La ritualizzazione del lutto delle vedove fiorentine (secoli xiv–xv)', *Quaderni storici*, 86 (1994), pp. 449–50.

Part I

Ceremonies and festivities

1   Wedding finery in sixteenth-century Venice

Patricia Allerston

Weddings in sixteenth-century Venice were reputed to be sumptuous affairs. Whereas writers such as Paolo Paruta extolled such splendour as a worthy expression of noble dispositions, government regulators of private expenditure criticized it as an unnecessary extravagance.[1] Historians have studied many different aspects of Venetian weddings, dwelling in particular upon the purposes they served among patrician families.[2] This article explores the events as opportunities for the ostentatious display of decorative material goods at various levels of society. It considers the finery exhibited at public and private celebrations in general and the items adapted to weddings, and it also suggests how and where such goods might have been procured. Although little documentary information regarding the acquisition of wedding finery in sixteenth-century Venice survives, much can be inferred from the methods of exchange which operated at the time and from sumptuary legislation. An understanding of the various means of obtaining luxury furnishings in the city suggests that wedding display was not necessarily as expensive as it appeared.

Weddings were important social events. In addition to supplying food and music for guests, an appropriately festive environment was created. When the eponymous hero of Alessandro Caravia's mid-1560s poem

I am grateful to Chris Black, Richard Mackenney, Dora Thornton and Kate Lowe for their valuable comments on earlier versions of this article.

[1] P. Paruta, *Della perfettione della vita politica* (Venice, 1579), pp. 185–6; J. Morelli, 'Delle solennità e pompe nuziali già usate presso li veneziani: dissertazione', in *Operette di Iacopo Morelli, bibliotecario di S. Marco* (3 vols., Venice, 1820), I, pp. 123–72; G. Bistort, *Il magistrato alle pompe nella Republica di Venezia: studio storico* (Venice, 1912; repr. Bologna, 1969), pp. 90–113; M. Newett, 'The sumptuary laws of Venice in the fourteenth and fifteenth centuries', in *Historical Essays by Members of the Owens College, Manchester*, ed. T. F. Tout and J. Tait (London, 1902).

[2] On the historiography of marriage in Venice, see S. Chojnacki, 'The power of love: wives and husbands in late medieval Venice', in *Women and Power in the Middle Ages*, ed. M. Erler and M. Kowaleski (Athens, Ga., and London, 1988), p. 127; also D. Romano, *Patricians and Popolani: The Social Foundations of the Venetian Renaissance State* (Baltimore and London, 1987), pp. 39–64.

Naspo bizaro resolves to marry Cate, a woman from the Biri (a Venetian workers' neighbourhood), he exhorts her to embellish the courtyard outside her abode: there, roasts, boiled meat and cake would be provided by the happy couple, and anyone who wished could dance the night away. A contemporary engraving of this scene (illustration 1) indicates how a popular wedding party might have appeared. An awning stretches above a cloth-covered table bearing napkins and flasks of drink, and the smartly dressed couple dances, as a musician, a cook and porters practise their trades.[3] Similar, though far more elaborate, preparations were made in September 1506 for the real-life wedding of Giustina, the second daughter of Zaccaria Freschi, a prominent *cittadino*, and her betrothed, Lodovico Bianco. The Freschi residence was sumptuously decorated 'according to convention' in readiness for the formal announcement of the betrothal and the gatherings of relatives, dignitaries and friends who came to pay their respects. It also provided a fitting setting for the lavish banquets, the dancing and the other entertainments which were hosted by the bride's father prior to his daughter's departure for her new home and the celebrations organized by the groom's family. As noted in the Freschi family documents, such ostentatious display at weddings was *de rigueur*.[4]

Owing to its traditional role as a trading entrepôt and its increasing importance as a centre of manufacture, sixteenth-century Venice boasted a sophisticated market in luxury furnishings. This market was remarkably flexible and operated at many levels, incorporating retail outlets and wholesale merchants, and accommodating domestic trade as well as business overseas.[5] A staggering variety of fancy goods suiting all pockets and tastes could be found in the city, yet residents of sixteenth-century Venice, in common with the inhabitants of many other European cities, were subject to legislation designed to limit their use of such items. They included restrictions aimed specifically at weddings.

Enacted for a perplexing mix of social, moral, economic and political reasons, sumptuary laws were intended to regulate ostentatious displays of wealth by private individuals. This type of legislation had been

[3] A. Caravia, *Naspo bizaro* (Venice, 1565), canto quarto, p. 42v, engraving p. 43r. See also P. G. Molmenti, *La storia di Venezia nella vita privata dalle origini alla caduta della Repubblica*, seventh edn (3 vols., Trieste, 1973), II, pp. 334–5, 340. On the artisan–poet Caravia, see R. Mackenney, *Tradesmen and Traders: The World of the Guilds in Venice and Europe, c. 1250–c. 1650* (Totowa, N.J., 1987), pp. 176–8; and J. Martin, *Venice's Hidden Enemies: Italian Heretics in a Renaissance City* (Berkeley and London, 1993), pp. 156–8.
[4] Venice, Biblioteca nazionale marciana (BMVe), MSS ital., cl. VII, 165 (8867), 'Memorie dell'illustre famiglia de' Freschi cittadini originarij veneti', fols. 43v–4v, 17–30 Sept. 1506; see also *Venice: A Documentary History, 1450–1630*, ed. D. Chambers and B. Pullan (Oxford, 1992), pp. 264–5 and Morelli, 'Delle solennità', p. 154.
[5] Mackenney, *Tradesmen*, pp. 81, 85–7.

1 Wedding party of Naspo bizaro and Cate, from A. Caravia, *Naspo bizaro*
   (Venice, 1565)

introduced long before the sixteenth century and it was widespread in Renaissance Italy. In comparison with cities such as Mantua and Milan, Venice developed a particularly extensive body of sumptuary regulations and, in 1515, a permanent magistracy was set up to see to their enforcement. The Venetian laws were stringent and they were often up-dated; so although Venetians had access to an abundant supply of luxuries they were meant to be abstemious in their use.[6] Unsurprisingly, the splendour displayed at weddings in Venice was a cause of great concern.

Regulations directed at wedding celebrations were issued in 1504, 1509, 1512, 1549 and 1557, and a particularly comprehensive set of sumptuary restrictions which included prescriptions for weddings was passed in 1562. These decrees relate mainly to marriage banquets; they focus on the number of meals offered, the variety of dishes and the quantity of guests, as well as the elaborate furnishings displayed which are detailed below. The value of gifts and the clothes worn at weddings were also regulated.[7] In spite of such legislation, sixteenth-century Venetian weddings continued to be sumptuous occasions.

Contemporary documents and literary works refer to the lavish display at patrician weddings. According to Francesco Sansovino, the famous eulogist of late sixteenth-century Venice, noble wedding banquets were conducted with 'pomp and great expense', involving up to 300 guests and a great variety of fine dishes.[8] Sansovino was careful to note that these festivities were regulated by laws, but other commentators of the same period, such as Cesare Vecellio and Giacomo Franco – who describe the

[6] See D. Owen Hughes, 'Sumptuary law and social relations in Renaissance Italy', in *Disputes and Settlements: Law and Human Relations in the West*, ed. J. Bossy (Cambridge, 1983); G. Fasoli, 'Lusso approvato e lusso riprovato', in *Memorial per Gina Fasoli: bibliografici ed alcuni inediti*, ed. F. Bocchi (Bologna, 1993), pp. 139–40; C. Kovesi Killerby, 'Practical problems in the enforcement of Italian sumptuary law, 1200 1500', in *Crime, Society and the Law in Renaissance Italy*, ed. T. Dean and K. J. P. Lowe (Cambridge, 1994); A. Liva, 'Note sulla legislazione suntuaria nell'Italia centro-settentrionale', in *Le trame della moda*, ed. A. G. Cavagna and G. Butazzi (Rome, 1995). On Venice, see Bistort, *Magistrato alle pompe*, pp. 9–10, 65 (volume and nature of laws), pp. 54–5 (permanent magistracy); Newett, 'Sumptuary laws'; P. Mometto, '"Vizi privati, pubbliche virtù": aspetti e problemi della questione del lusso nella Repubblica di Venezia (sec. XVI)', in *Crimine, giustizia e società veneta in età moderna*, ed. L. Berlinguer and F. Colao (Milan, 1989: La *'Leopoldina': criminalità e giustizia criminale nelle riforme del '700 europeo*, IX), pp. 237–70; *Venice: A Documentary History*, pp. 177–8.

[7] Venice, Archivio di Stato (ASVe), Senato, Terra (ST), reg. 14, fols. 196v–7r (second pag.), 3 Jan. 1503 *more veneto (mv)*; reg. 16, fols. 86v–7v, 16 Jan. 1508 *(mv)*; reg. 18, fols. 28r, 29r–30v, 8 May 1512; reg. 36, fol. 74v, 5 Jan. 1548 *(mv)*; filza 24, 9 Jan. 1556 *(mv)*; ASVe, Provveditori e soprapprovveditori alle pompe, busta 1, Capitolare primo, fols. 1r–v, 3r, 8 Oct. 1562. For a detailed discussion of these laws, see Bistort, *Magistrato alle pompe*, pp. 95–7, also pp. 378–93 (1562 laws published).

[8] F. Sansovino, *Venetia: città nobilissima et singolare*, rev. G. Martinioni (Venice, 1663), p. 401. See also Molmenti, *Venezia nella vita privata*, II, pp. 332–5.

rich apparel worn by the brides – were less punctilious.[9] Earlier patrician weddings described by Marino Sanudo were also splendid affairs. In May 1513, for example, the Foscari held an extravagant wedding lunch for more than 500 guests to celebrate a union with the Venier family. Everything at Ca' Foscari was beautifully arranged, and the banquet, which was followed by music, dancing and a theatrical entertainment, lasted into the early hours of the morning.[10]

Though they stress the overall sumptuousness of patrician wedding celebrations, Venetian commentators rarely detail the range of material goods on show. Sanudo records that silverware was used at a noble wedding banquet in August 1517 because, being wartime, it was unusual.[11] Visual records of these events are also rare. The Venetian sumptuary regulations on weddings do, however, refer to the array of luxury goods which were paraded on such occasions. These references correspond with items known to have appeared at other types of family celebrations as well as at public festivals, bearing out Giulio Bistort's assertion that sumptuary regulations are a useful source of information on Venetian private life.[12] In 1557, the Venetian authorities repeated complaints made in 1504 and 1512 about the elaborate decorations displayed when gatherings of relatives (*parentadi*) were held to celebrate a marriage, and additional criticisms were made in 1562. On such occasions, according to the legislators, the bride's and groom's houses were decorated, inside and out, with valuable furnishings. Expensive silk and wool hangings adorned rooms and entrances. Tapestries were hung on staircases and festoons embellished doors and windows. Decorative objects such as figurines, carvings and pictures were also displayed prominently to impress the guests. For the banquet itself, exotic table-carpets were deployed, protected by fine linen cloths.[13]

The association of expensive material goods with wedding banquets was not particularly unusual. Luxury furnishings and decorative objects were habitually displayed at private and public celebrations in Venice. The domestic receptions held after childbirth were also renowned for their

9 C. Vecellio, *Degli habiti antichi et moderni di diverse parti del mondo* (Venice, 1590), pp. 126v–7r, 128v–9r; G. Franco, *Habiti delle donne venetiane intagliate in rame nuovamente* (Venice, 1610; repr. Venice, 1877), nos. 5, 6.

10 M. Sanudo [Sanuto], *I diarii*, ed. R. Fulin *et al.* (58 vols., Venice, 1879–1903), XVI, cols. 206–7, 2 May 1513; other examples: VI, col. 225, 3 Sept. 1505; XXIV, col. 608, 26 Aug. 1517; XXXVII, col. 445, 16 Jan. 1525 (*mv*); LVII, cols. 525–6, 16 Feb. 1533 (*mv*).

11 *Ibid.*, XXIV, col. 608, 26 Aug. 1517.

12 Bistort, *Magistrato alle pompe*, p. 2.

13 ASVe, ST, filza 24, 9 Jan. 1556 (*mv*); reg. 14, fol. 197r (second pag.), 3 Jan. 1503 (*mv*) (wall-hangings); reg. 16, fol. 87r, 16 Jan. 1508 (*mv*); reg. 18, fol. 29r, 8 May 1512 (table-carpets); ASVe, Pompe, I, fol. 1v, 8 Oct. 1562 (festoons); see also Bistort, *Magistrato alle pompe*, p. 97. On the use of such items, see P. Thornton, *The Italian Renaissance Interior, 1400–1600* (London, 1991), pp. 44–8 (wall-hangings), pp. 48–51 (tapestries), pp. 216–19 (table-covers).

great ostentation. Sansovino's description of the rich decorations put on show at these events, including pictures, sculptures and precious metalwork, is confirmed by a rare sumptuary denunciation of 1605. Among the forbidden items spotted by officials in the house of Vincenzo Zuccato, a wool merchant, were large figurative silk tapestries and gilded wooden chests inlaid with bronze.[14] During the public celebrations held for the victory of Lepanto in 1571, the entire Rialto area, including the bridge, was adorned with tapestries, festoons and cloth of gold, together with pictures by famous Venetian painters such as Giovanni Bellini and Titian.[15]

People, as well as material goods, formed an important part of the rich tableau enacted at patrician weddings and this was a cause of additional concern to the Venetian authorities. Household servants were, for example, furnished with special garb (*drappi novizzali*). The sumptuary decree of 1562 stipulates that servants' clothing had to be plain (*schiettissimo*) and cheap, and this, together with a reference to wide stripes by Vecellio, indicates that elaborate, expensive livery tended to be the norm. The government also tried to restrict the large numbers of richly dressed female patricians who, like male relatives and friends, acted as attendants at weddings.[16] Grooms, like the other men present, attracted less criticism, but were equally well turned out: two early sixteenth-century examples wore costly black velvet.[17]

The focus of attention was the bride herself. Swathed in expensive fabrics and bedecked with jewels, she was the central element in the wedding display. Vecellio noted that 'Venetian brides make every effort to seem beautiful and to appear richly attired'.[18] In the text accompanying his engraving of an ornately dressed bride (illustration 2), he noted their use of finely worked, white silk and of elaborate lace collars and epaulettes, as well as of costly jewellery. Giacomo Franco praised such ostentation, likening these brides (whom he also depicted) to goddesses; he also maintained that the large number of valuable pearls worn by these women was worthy of foreign princesses.[19] Unsurprisingly, patrician brides were

[14] Sansovino, *Venetia*, p. 402; ASVe, Pompe, 6, Denuncie, 18 Jan. 1604 (*mv*).
[15] E. H. Gombrich, 'Celebrations in Venice of the Holy League and of the victory of Lepanto', in *Studies in Renaissance and Baroque Art presented to Anthony Blunt on his 60th Birthday* (London, 1967), pp. 63, 66.
[16] ASVe, Censori, busta 1, Capitolare 2, fol. 59, 16 Sept. 1595; ASVe, Pompe 1, fol. 3r, 8 Oct. 1562; see also Molmenti, *Storia di Venezia*, II, p. 333. ASVe, ST, reg. 14, fol. 196v, 12 Jan. 1503 (*mv*); reg. 18, fols. 28r–30r, 8 May 1512; see also Vecellio, *Degli habiti antichi*, pp. 126v–7r, 131r–v (stripes reference, p. 127r); Franco, *Habiti delle donne*, no. 7.
[17] Sanudo, *I diarii*, XXXVII, col. 445, 16 Jan. 1525 (*mv*); BMVe, 'Memorie dell'illustre famiglia de' Freschi', fol. 43v, 17–30 Sept. 1506.
[18] Vecellio, *Habiti antichi*, pp. 126r–7, 128v.
[19] Franco, *Habiti delle donne*, no. 5. On sumptuous brides, see also the poem 'Le berte, le truffe, i arlassi, e le magnarie, che usa le puttane a i so bertoni recitate da Nico Calafao da l'Arsenale', in *Delle rime piasevoli di diversi auttori nuovamente raccolte da M. Modesto Pino, & intitolate la caravana* (Venice, 1576), p. 19r; and Sansovino, *Venetia*, p. 401.

2 'Modern noble brides', from C. Vecellio, *Degli habiti antichi et moderni di diverse parti del mondo* (Venice, 1590)

a source of disquiet to Venetian sumptuary officials and a particularly severe decree, which centred on the use of cloth of gold, was issued in 1549. Although this type of fabric was cited by Franco in his description of noble Venetian brides, it had long been considered inappropriate wear for private individuals ('no[n] conveniente a privati cittadini'). The decree rebuked patrician fathers for dressing their daughters in such fabric and it also accused these nobles of adorning their offspring with an excessive quantity of jewellery, stating that 'they load the bride with jewels and pearls in every conceivable way'.[20]

---

[20] ASVe, ST, reg. 36, fol. 74v, 5 Jan. 1548 (*mv*): 'carricano la novizza di zoglie et perle in tutti quei modi ch[e] possono'; on blame attached to fathers in this way, see Newett, 'Sumptuary laws', p. 257; and Kovesi Killerby, 'Practical problems', p. 103; cf. S. Chojnacki, 'La posizione della donna a Venezia nel Cinquecento', *Tiziano e Venezia* (Vicenza, 1980), pp. 67–70.

32   Patricia Allerston

Paolo Paruta advocated such magnificence at patrician weddings to demonstrate noble qualities (*nobile virtù*).[21] Extravagant display was not, however, monopolized by high-born Venetians. The much-cited chronicle of the Freschi family reveals that Venetian *cittadini* (a privileged social group consisting of a small minority of the city's non-noble residents) were eager to emphasize their status within society by the same means. At the formal gathering to celebrate Giustina Freschi's wedding in 1506, the bride was dressed in crimson velvet and wore ornate jewellery, the residence was extravagantly decorated, and the family's coat of arms was prominently displayed – all traditional noble practices.[22] Though evidence is less extensive, parading costly material goods such as clothes and household furnishings was also important further down the social scale. In an anonymous poem published in 1576, Nico, a caulker in the Venetian Arsenal, describes the fine figure he had once cut with his velvet cloak and silver dagger, his rings, and his well-stocked abode.[23] Sentiments on largesse expressed by Naspo bizaro, the fictional character created by the artisan-poet Caravia, are, moreover, strikingly similar to the noble virtues expounded by Paruta: 'I derive no other pleasure in this life, except from spending and bestowing gifts with cheer.'[24] Since marriage was of crucial importance to all sectors of Venetian society in the sixteenth century, special efforts were, as Naspo bizaro and Cate's wedding suggests, no doubt also made to celebrate popular weddings.[25]

Accumulating the kinds of fine furnishings and precious decorative objects displayed at weddings was prevalent among sixteenth-century Venetians. Having a suitably appointed dwelling was immensely important for, as well as making domestic life more comfortable (a consideration

[21] Paruta, *Della perfettione*, pp. 185–6. See also Bistort, *Magistrato alle pompe*, pp. 5–9; and P. Burke, 'Conspicuous consumption in seventeenth-century Italy', in *The Historical Anthropology of Early Modern Italy: Essays on Perception and Communication* (Cambridge, 1987).
[22] BMVe, 'Memorie dell'illustre famiglia de' Freschi', fols. 42v–51r, 28 Dec. 1504–26 Jan. 1521 (*mv*) (1506 wedding, fols. 43v–4r); see also *Venice: A Documentary History*, p. 264; Morelli, 'Delle solennità', pp. 147–54. On Venetian *cittadini*, see A. Zannini, *Burocrazia e burocrati a Venezia in età moderna: i cittadini originari (sec. XVI–XVIII)* (Venice, 1993), pp. 11–13; U. Tucci, 'The psychology of the Venetian merchant in the sixteenth century', in *Renaissance Venice*, ed. J. R. Hale (London, 1973), pp. 360–6. On the Freschis' noble pretensions, see P. Fortini Brown, *Venetian Narrative Painting in the Age of Carpaccio* (New Haven and London, 1988), p. 26.
[23] 'Le berte, le truffe, i arlassi', p. 20v; on richly dressed Arsenal workers, see Caravia, *Naspo bizaro*, canto secondo, p. 15v.
[24] Caravia, *Naspo bizaro*, canto quarto, p. 41v; cf. Paruta, *Della perfettione*, pp. 184–5.
[25] G. Ruggiero, '"Più che la vita caro": onore, matrimonio e reputazione femminile nel tardo rinascimento', *Quaderni storici*, new ser., 66 (1987); R. Martin, *Witchcraft and the Inquisition in Venice, 1550–1650* (Oxford, 1989), pp. 103–6. See also Romano, *Patricians and Popolani*, pp. 56–64; G. Bernoni, 'Usi nuziali', in *Tradizioni popolari veneziani* (Venice, 1875), pt 4, pp. 114–18.

of increasing significance in the period), it was also a telling indication of refined habits and good taste.[26] In his book glorifying Venice in the late sixteenth century, Sansovino devoted a substantial section to the sumptuous objects contained within the city's noble houses. He described a scene of breathtaking luxury, citing, along with fine tapestries and various kinds of gilded furnishings (including leather wall-hangings, bedroom furniture and picture frames), buffets groaning with silver and other types of tableware.[27] Contemporary sources such as household inventories confirm that these types of luxury goods did belong, in spite of the restrictive sumptuary legislation, to Venetian patricians such as Paolo Barbo, a procurator of St Mark's (1509).[28]

Continuing with this theme, Sansovino claimed that similar furnishings, 'in proportion', also belonged to 'middling and lesser sorts' of Venetians: 'because there is no one with a furnished abode so poor who does not have walnut chests and bedsteads, green woollen wall-hangings, rugs, pewter and copper vessels, gold chains, silver forks and rings, such is the constitution of this city'.[29] Given the location of this famous excerpt within a chapter on palaces and its reference to people with adequately furnished houses ('con casa aperta'), one should naturally be wary of taking this statement at face value.[30] In addition, the last phrase reveals Sansovino's underlying concern in this passage (as elsewhere in his book), which was to portray an image of Venice as a perfectly organized and harmonious Republic. As in the case of noble Venetians' belongings, however, other sources do show that the kinds of costly material goods cited by Sansovino *were* amassed further down the social scale.

[26] Thornton, *Italian Renaissance Interior*, pp. 13–15; I. Palumbo-Fossati, 'L'interno della casa dell'artigiano e dell'artista nella Venezia del cinquecento', *Studi veneziani*, 8 (1984), p. 110; D. Thornton, 'The Study Room in Renaissance Italy, with Particular Reference to Venice, *c.* 1560–1620' (Ph.D. thesis, University of London, 1990), especially chs. 6–7.

[27] Sansovino, *Venetia*, p. 384.

[28] *Antichi testamenti tratti dagli archivi della congregazione di carità di Venezia*, ninth ser. (Venice, 1890), pp. 37–45, 1 Aug. 1509 (I owe this reference to R. C. Mueller). On the sumptuary laws, see ASVe, ST, reg. 18, fol. 29r, 8 May 1512; also Bistort, *Magistrato alle pompe*, pp. 239–42.

[29] Sansovino, *Venetia*, p. 385: 'il medesimo diciamo, de mediocri, & de bassi a proportione. Perché non è persona cosi miserabile con casa aperta, che non habbia casse & lettiere di noci, panni verdi, tapeti, peltri, rami, catenelle d'oro, forchette d'argento & anella, tale è la politia di questa città'. I am most grateful to Dora Thornton for introducing me to this passage and for notes of her lecture on 'furnishings and collections in the sixteenth-century Venetian palace'.

[30] See also Palumbo-Fossati, 'L'interno', p. 111. On the difficult term *casa aperta*, see *Grande dizionario della lingua italiana* (Turin, 1967), II, p. 824; cf. *Dizionario della lingua italiana*, ed. N. Tommaseo and B. Bellini (Turin, 1865), I, 2, '*casa*'. I am grateful for the helpful suggestions about this term made by Chris Black, Richard Goy, Deborah Howard, Dora Thornton and Jonathan Walker.

Wills and inventories recording movable property belonging to Venetian artisans and shopkeepers, do, for example, bear witness to the variety of furnishings that could be found in workers' homes in the sixteenth century. Commonly listed goods include household linen such as tablecloths, napkins and bedding, clothes, coffers and bedsteads. Goods bequeathed in 1538 by Domenico di Bernardo, a dealer in second-hand goods who also held two minor government posts, encompassed a well-dressed bed and a wide range of clothing, including furs, as well as money and stable property.[31] Even Nicolosa, a sick, widowed seamstress with 'very few goods' to her name, managed to supply three nieces and one nephew, in her will of 1569, with good household linen including tablecloths and bedding, as well as some shirts, and strongboxes (*forzieri*).[32] Items cited by Sansovino more usually associated with the upper echelons of Venetian society, such as gold jewellery, silver cutlery and wall-hangings, as well as mirrors, could also be found in artisans' houses. Nicolosa the widowed seamstress owned an 'antique' gold belt (*una centa d'oro di quelle antige*); in the late 1580s and early 1590s, the homes of Antonio Zuanelli, a carpenter, and Iseppo Locatelli, a fruitseller at Rialto, were both adorned with cloth hangings – in Locatelli's case, they included costly figurative draperies (*panni bergamaschi a colonne con figure*).[33] Late sixteenth-century records of movable property such as gold jewellery, clothing and household linen, stolen from similarly modest abodes, reinforce this notion that certain 'lesser' sorts of Venetians had reasonably furnished homes.[34]

In his recent study of the Venetian community of shipyard workers, the *arsenalotti*, Robert Davis argued that hoarding material wealth fulfilled important economic functions within this group; stocks of possessions, such as household linen and pewter plates, supplemented dowries, and they also served as a form of insurance in times of personal hardship.[35] The usefulness of material goods in this respect is indisputable: in emergencies, public auctions of personal effects were, for example, an important means

[31] ASVe, Sezione notarile, Testamenti, busta 95, notary Benzon, no. 170, Domenico fu Bernardo, 9 Sept. 1538.
[32] *Ibid.*, busta 36, notary Abramo, no. 55, Nicolosa sartora, relicta, 25 May 1569.
[33] The inventories of Zuanelli (1 June 1587), and Locatelli (20 Apr. 1591), are cited in Palumbo-Fossati, 'L'interno', pp. 142–3, 127, n. 39; see also pp. 121–38, 149, n. 68 (mirrors). For goods in inventories, see also P. Pavanini, 'Abitazioni popolari e borghesi nella Venezia cinquecentesca', *Studi veneziani*, 5 (1981), pp. 93–6, 111–12, 125–6.
[34] ASVe, Sant'Uffizio, busta 59, processo Marietta Greca, denunciation Agnesina, 23 Mar. 1587 (gold items, pearls, rings); busta 63, processo Franceschina, denunciation Elena, 17 May 1588 (clothing); busta 68, processo Angelica Romana, denunciation Michaela Dalmata, 4 Dec. 1591 (linen). I am indebted to Ruth Martin for references to witchcraft cases relating to stolen property.
[35] R. C. Davis, *Shipbuilders of the Venetian Arsenal: Workers and Workplace in the Preindustrial City* (Baltimore and London, 1991), pp. 99–103.

of realizing these assets.[36] By focusing solely on the economic utility of material wealth among the lower orders of Venetian society, however, the idea that, as among higher social groups, the likes of Nico, caulker in the Arsenal, derived pleasure and social benefits from having fine clothes and furnishings, is not given its due. In this regard, Fritz Schmidt makes an interesting contribution, contending that Venetian artisans and shop-keepers acquired increasing quantities of furnishings from the sixteenth century onwards because they developed closer ties to their homes.[37]

The luxury material goods displayed in Venetian houses were obtained from a wide range of sources. Imported items including tapestries and table-carpets could be bought direct from merchants. In the summer of 1586, for example, the *Ufficiali alle rason vecchie*, officials responsible for organizing public festivals and for providing sumptuous accommodation for visiting foreign dignitaries, purchased expensive cloth hangings and bench-carpets from two Flemings. For the same occasion, the *Ufficiali* commissioned two sets of ornate fabric hangings emblazoned with lions of St Mark from a certain Lorenzo, a specialist in decorative drapery (*conza razzi*) at Rialto, and a fine, red leather bench-cover fringed with gold, from another skilled tradesman, Cesare, a gilt-leather worker (*dai cuori d'oro*). This shows that buyers also had recourse to local artisans.[38] Wholesale and retail mercers, who were, as Richard Mackenney has shown, extremely successful traders in sixteenth-century Venice, also supplied furnishings and dealt in bridalwear. The principal shops along the Merceria, such as the Chalice (run by Bartolomeo Bontempelli, 1538–1616), were frequented by Venetian patricians and *cittadini* as well as by rich foreign visitors. They stocked lengths of luxury fabrics such as brocades worked with gold and silver, and costly braiding, suitable for making wall-hangings as well as sumptuous clothes. More modest mer-cers' shops could be found scattered throughout the city.[39]

In addition to new wares, there were numerous means of acquiring second-hand items in Venice. The second-hand market has tended to be

[36] P. Allerston, 'The market in second-hand clothes and furnishings in Venice, *c.* 1500–*c.* 1650' (Ph.D. thesis, European University Institute, Florence, 1996), pp. 234–50.
[37] F. Schmidt, 'Zur Genese kapitalistischer Konsumformen im Venedig der Frühen Neuzeit', in *Stadtgeschichte als Zivilisationsgeschichte: Beiträge zum Wandel städtischer Wirtschafts-, Lebens- und Wahrnehmungsweisen*, ed. J. Reulecke (Essen, 1990), pp. 33–6. I am grateful to R. C. Mueller for this reference.
[38] ASVe, ST, filza 98, 13 Aug. 1586; on such objects, see Thornton, *Italian Renaissance Interior*, pp. 48, 173, 85–6.
[39] Mackenney, *Tradesmen*, p. 86, figure 3.1, pp. 90–111. On luxury goods sold by mercers, see the demarcation dispute in ASVe, Corporazioni di arti e mestieri, ser. 45, Arte dei marzeri, busta 364, Processi, fasc. 102, Scuola di marzeri contro Ebrei che vendono merci e altro, nos. 7, 10, 23 July 1586, 11–12, 14, n.d. [1586] (furnishings); ASVe, Pompe, 1, fol. 58, 27 Oct. 1600 (silk trimmings). See also Vecellio, *Habiti antichi*, p. 139r.

disregarded by historians but, as I have shown elsewhere, it was an extremely important source of luxury goods.[40] The trade in used clothes and furnishings was a distinct sector within this market and it was an integral part of the Venetian urban economy. In Renaissance Venice as in other Italian cities, used luxury goods were not stigmatized and they were sought after by people from all walks of life, including patricians. In addition to the other furnishings bought in 1586, for example, the *Ufficiali alle rason vecchie* acquired a large, second-hand floor-carpet.[41] This indicates that top-quality furnishings were held in great esteem, irrespective of whether they were new or second-hand.

Simon, a Jewish trader from Padua, noted in 1585 that the fame of the Venetian second-hand market extended beyond the city's boundaries.[42] As well as shopping in the Merceria, noble foreign visitors to Venice also went to the city's main dealers in used goods, buying, as some of these traders reported in 1595, 'tapestries along with other sorts of goods'.[43] The Venetian market in second-hand clothes and furnishings was made up of a wide variety of outlets. A successful guild of second-hand dealers had existed in the city since at least the thirteenth century. Its members ranged from major retailers with shops at the heart of the city's commercial centre catering for wealthier sorts of clients, to pedlars hawking petty goods about the city's streets.[44] From around 1512 onwards a rival group of second-hand dealers made up of so-called 'German' Jews became established in the city.[45] They, like the members of the guild, dealt in different types of goods, but they developed a particular reputation for furnishings, supplying tapestries and wall-hangings to clients at the very top end of the market, such as the Venetian government, patricians and foreign ambassadors.[46] Alternative mechanisms of supply coexisted with

[40] See Allerston, 'The market'.   [41] AsVe, ST, filza 98, 13 Aug. 1586.

[42] *Ibid.*, filza 96, 31 Dec. 1585.

[43] ASVe, Ufficiali al cattaver (UC), busta 244, reg. 5, fol. 128, 27 Oct. 1594, fol. 165r, 19 Dec. 1595; see also C. Roth, *The History of the Jews in Venice* (Philadelphia, 1930), p. 175; B. Pullan, *Rich and Poor in Renaissance Venice: The Social Institutions of a Catholic State, to 1620* (Oxford, 1971), p. 478.

[44] Guild statutes of 1233 and 1264–65 are published in *I capitolari delle arti veneziane sottoposte alla Giustizia e poi alla Giustizia Vecchia dalle origini al MCCCXXX*, ed. G. Monticolo (3 vols., Rome, 1896–1914), I, pp. 135–8; II, 2, pp. 457–73. For traders, see Venice, Biblioteca del Museo Correr, Mariegola degli strazzaruoli, fols. 60–1 [13 July 1479]; fol. 100, 22 Sept. 1549.

[45] J. L. Bato, 'L'immigrazione degli Ebrei tedeschi in Italia dal Trecento al Cinquecento', in *Scritti in memoria di Sally Mayer (1875–1953)*, ed. U. Nahon (Jerusalem, 1956); and R. Bonfil, *Gli ebrei in Italia nell'epoca del Rinascimento*, transl. M. Acanfora Torrefranca (Florence, 1991), pp. 23–4. On their entry to Venice, see M. Ferro, *Dizionario del diritto comune, e veneto, che contiene le leggi civili, canoniche, e criminali* (6 vols., Venice, 1778–81), 'Ebrei'; Pullan, *Rich and Poor*, p. 478; and Allerston, 'The market', pp. 119–40.

[46] ASVe, ST, filza 98, 13 Aug. 1586; filza 118, 13 Dec. 1590; and ASVe, UC, 242, fols. 161v–3v, 10 Aug. 1594–8 June 1595. For mercers' complaints of being usurped by the Jews, see ASVe, Arte dei marzeri, 364, fasc. 102, no. 7, 23 July 1586.

these two sets of traders. Auctions of personal effects were, for example, traditional features of urban life and they played an important part in the circulation of used goods. Organized for a variety of reasons such as funding testamentary bequests and satisfying debts, these auctions were the means by which many different types and qualities of clothes and furnishings came on to the market.[47] Moreover, since rugs and drapery were displayed publicly at festivals and other celebrations, they were vulnerable to theft: items stolen in this way were sold and pawned and thus also fed into the second-hand market.[48]

Furnishings obtained by the variety of means listed above were either added to existing interior decorations (according to season) or were stored away, being brought out solely for special events such as weddings and births.[49] Vincenzo Zuccato, the wool merchant denounced for sumptuous display at the birth of his child in 1605, recorded that they were also produced during the main annual festivals celebrated by the household, probably occasions such as Carnival and Ascensiontide.[50] Venetian legislators complained about the cost of the fancy material goods exhibited at weddings, implying that they were also bought specifically for these events. In 1557, for example, the Senate lamented the 'large sum of money' that increased 'by the day', which was spent by families on the elaborate decorations displayed at *parentadi*.[51] Given the high cost of fine clothes and of quality furnishings such as tapestries, new *and* second-hand,[52] this type of expense accords well with the noble ideal of lavish expenditure proposed by Paolo Paruta. The second-hand rug bought by the *Ufficiali alle rason vecchie* in 1586 cost almost as much (85 ducats and 5 *soldi*) as the wall-hangings bought from the Flemish merchants (116 ducats, 5 *lire* and 8 *soldi*) for the same occasion.[53]

As Brian Pullan and others have shown, however, not all patricians, let alone other types of Venetians, had large sums of money available in the

---

[47] Allerston, 'The market', pp. 234–52. For inventories of goods sold at *commissaria* auctions, see Venice, Archivio delle istituzioni di ricovero e di educazione, Ospedale dei derelitti, busta 130, Angelica Leoncini, fasc. 4, 6 Dec. 1570; busta 68, Cristoforo Castigante, fasc. 4, fol. 23, 20 Apr. 1589. See also Sansovino, *Venetia*, p. 385.

[48] See ASVe, UC, 244, reg. 5, fol. 91v, 9 Sept. 1593; ASVe, ST, reg. 69, fol. 142v (second pag.), 9 Oct. 1599; also P. Fortini Brown, 'Measured friendship, calculated pomp: the ceremonial welcomes of the Venetian Republic', in *'All the World's a Stage': Art and Pageantry in the Renaissance and Baroque*, ed. B. Wisch and S. Scott Munshower (Pennsylvania, 1990), p. 142.

[49] Thornton, *Italian Renaissance Interior*, pp. 48, 192–204, 216.

[50] ASVe, Pompe, 6, Denuncie, 18 Jan. 1604 (*mv*): 'nelle feste principali dell'anno'.

[51] ASVe, ST, filza 24, 9 Jan. 1556 (*mv*); see also the decrees of 1504 and 1508 cited in footnote 7 above.

[52] Thornton, *Italian Renaissance Interior*, pp. 48–9.

[53] ASVe, ST, filza 98, 13 Aug. 1586. One Venetian ducat was worth 6 *lire* and 4 *soldi*, or 124 *soldi*.

sixteenth century.[54] In *L'amfiparnaso*, the harmonic comedy of 1597 written by Orazio Vecchi, Pantalone sends his servant Francatrippa to pledge an item in the Ghetto after deciding to hold a reception to celebrate his daughter's wedding.[55] In addition, Venetian patricians who did have capital were reluctant to fritter it away, preferring tangible investments to gratuitous prodigality.[56] Interestingly, in Venice, costly attire and furnishings did not necessarily have to be purchased for festive events, as there were various other means of obtaining such items.

Informal mechanisms existed whereby material goods could be borrowed and it would appear that this alternative supply system also functioned at weddings. In 1549, when the sumptuary regulators addressed the problem of bridal clothes made of cloth of gold, they complained that patricians defended themselves by saying that the cloth was on loan and had not been bought ('they say they had it on loan').[57] This excuse may simply have been, as the officials suspected, a ruse: such tricks devised to get around the laws are common in the history of sumptuary legislation.[58] It is equally true, though, that the practice of lending personal belongings for display did occur. In August 1593, for example, the patrician, Giulio Michiel, lent several household rugs to decorate the church of San Bartolomeo at Rialto for the celebration of its feast day.[59] Generosity was, like extravagant spending on special events, regarded as a noble quality and the importance of lending one's belongings to friends on festive occasions was emphasized by Pietro Aretino.[60] In addition to such informal mechanisms, there were other ways of procuring furnishings for special events. Like other Italian cities, such as Rome and Naples, Venice was renowned for magnificent religious festivals and elaborate public displays. Hosting these events required a large amount of specialist support, such as the decorators (*conzieri*) who adorned churches for special occasions with wall-hangings, tapestries and pictures.[61] There was also a flourishing

[54] B. Pullan, 'The occupations and investments of the Venetian nobility in the middle and late sixteenth century', in *Renaissance Venice*, ed. J. R. Hale (London, 1973); A. F. Cowan, 'Rich and poor among the patriciate in early modern Venice', *Studi veneziani*, new ser., 6 (1982).
[55] O. Vecchi, *L'amfiparnaso: comedia harmonica* (Venice, 1597), III.1.1, III.3.
[56] B. Pullan, 'Wage-earners and the Venetian economy, 1550–1630', *Economic History Review*, new ser., 16 (1964), pp. 421–2.
[57] ASVe, ST, reg. 36, fol. 74v (second pag.), 5 Jan. 1548 (*mv*): 'dicono haverla tolta ad imprestito'; also Bistort, *Magistrato alle pompe*, p. 97.
[58] Owen Hughes, 'Sumptuary law', pp. 69–70; Mometto, 'Vizi privati', p. 245; Kovesi Killerby, 'Practical problems', pp. 118–19.
[59] ASVe, UC, 244, reg. 5, fol. 91v, 9 Sept. 1593.
[60] P. Aretino, *Il primo libro delle lettere*, ed. F. Nicolini (Bari, 1913), p. 19, no. 12, 11 May 1529, p. 30, no. 23, 7 Jan. 1531 (*mv*); see also Paruta, *Della perfettione*, pp. 184–5.
[61] E. Muir, 'Images of power: art and pageantry in Renaissance Venice', *American Historical Review*, 84 (1979), pp. 36–7; Muir, *Civic Ritual in Renaissance Venice* (Princeton, 1981),

rental trade in decorative accoutrements. As well as selling their wares, artisans such as Lorenzo, *conza razzi*, and Cesare *dai cuori d'oro*, also hired them out. This trade operated at many levels. At the top, second-hand dealers and other traders supplied tapestries and rugs to the Venetian government to embellish accommodation provided for the duration of the stay of visiting dignitaries. In addition, hired goods graced the ducal palace during public festivities, official receptions and formal banquets, and they adorned the basilica of St Mark throughout the city's major religious festivals.[62] Patricians and *cittadini* also had rented tapestries in their homes and, given the cost of extensive rentals of these goods, this probably held true for one-off events such as weddings.[63] Further down the social scale, costly furnishings and fancy clothes were hired for business as well as pleasure: prostitutes rented these items to attract clients, while other poor Venetians rented clothes during festive periods.[64] Pietro Casola, visiting Venice during the celebrations held for Corpus Christi in 1494, noted that this was the case for some of the extravagantly clad Venetian women he witnessed at that time.[65]

In sixteenth-century Venice, then, there were various means of procuring the decorative finery required at private and public celebrations. Items could be brought out of store to be put on display or be brought in especially for the occasion. As well as commissioning luxury furnishings for a specific event, goods could also be purchased ready-made – new *and* second-hand – from a number of different sources. Friends might be prevailed upon to lend their belongings, and furnishings could also be rented. Most of these means of obtaining decorative objects had existed before the sixteenth century and they continued well into the early modern period. Of these, the supply of luxury goods on short terms is particularly interesting as it allowed Venetians, if they so wished, to supplement their existing stocks of household possessions for special

pp. 60–1; T. Garzoni, 'De' beccamorti, o pizzigamorti, o monatti, o sotterratori, & de' funerali, & de' conzieri', in *La piazza universale di tutte le professioni del mondo* (Venice, 1589), p. 446, discorso 43.
[62] See ASVe, ST, reg. 13, fol. 145r (second pag.), 4 Sept. 1500; reg. 69, fol. 142v, 9 Oct. 1599 (furnishings for visits); filza 118, 13 Dec. 1590; filza 141, 31 Jan. 1596 (*mv*); ASVe, UC, 242, fols. 161v–3v, 10 Aug. 1594–8 June 1595; 244, reg. 5, fols. 43v–4, 11 June 1592 (public occasions); ASVe, Ufficiali alle rason vecchie, busta 3, Capitolare, fols. 145v–6, 5 Jan. 1529 (supplying foreign ambassadors). See also Allerston, 'The market', pp. 176–8, 206–7.
[63] ASVe, UC, 244, reg. 5, fol. 134v, 14 Jan. 1594 (*mv*). On the high cost of renting for long terms, see London, Public Record Office, State Papers Venetian, bundle 17, pt 2, fol. 270r, Oct. 1614.
[64] Signori di notte al civil, busta 1, Capitolare A [ex-Capi di sestieri], fol. 129, 31 July 1533; fol. 139, 20 Dec. 1557; 'Le berte, le truffe', p. 19r; Fasoli, 'Lusso approvato', p. 139; also Newett, 'Sumptuary laws', p. 251.
[65] Casola, *Viaggio di Pietro Casola a Gerusalemme* (Milan, 1855), p. 15.

events requiring a really fine show: lacking sufficient hangings for the arrival of a special envoy at his palace in the early 1600s, the Tuscan resident in Venice, Niccolò Sacchetti, shrugged this off, explaining that 'the city is big and in two days those still lacking can be obtained for hire'.[66]

Weddings are excellent examples of occasions requiring a splendid show for a limited period of time. The availability of material goods on short terms for occasions such as these corresponds with the notion that, irrespective of sumptuary legislation, Venetians were shrewd regarding ephemeral magnificence. Yet the practice of renting out furnishings for *feste* was not limited to sixteenth-century Venice. In Florence, members of the second-hand dealers' guild provided household furnishings at short notice for festive events, whereas Jewish dealers in Rome rented out tapestries to cardinals and nobles for similar occasions.[67] The variety of means by which luxury furnishings could be obtained, not all of which required a considerable outlay, encourages a re-assessment of the splendour on show at important social events. The lavish pomp at weddings was certainly conspicuous, but it did not necessarily have to be consumed.

[66] Florence, Archivio di Stato, Archivio Mediceo del Principato, no. 3006, Carteggio Niccolò Sacchetti, residente in Venezia (1618–27), fol. 25v, 4 Aug. 1618: 'ma q[ue]sto poco importa, la città è grande et in due giorni quel' che manca si troverà a nolo'. On other benefits of short-term exchanges, see P. Allerston, 'L'abito come articolo di scambio nella società dell'età moderna: alcune implicazioni', in *Le trame della moda*, ed. A. G. Cavagna and G. Butazzi (Rome, 1995), pp. 119–20.

[67] ASF, Archivio delle Arti, Università dei linaioli, no. 2, Inserto contenente varie riforme di statuti (1561–75), fol. 18v, 31 Mar. 1561; G. L. Masetti Zannini, 'Ebrei, artisti, oggetti d'arte (documenti romani dei secoli XVI e XVII)' *Commentari*, new ser., 25 (1974), p. 285.

2 Secular brides and convent brides: wedding ceremonies in Italy during the Renaissance and Counter-Reformation

Kate Lowe

Marriage was considered essential in late medieval and early modern Italy, and an adult woman who had not experienced some form of 'marriage' was perceived as an aberration. If it was not possible for a young girl to marry a flesh-and-blood man, for whatever reason, the fiction was maintained that when she became a nun, which was the only respectable alternative, she was symbolically wedded to Christ or to God. This designation of the Christian virgin as a bride of Christ can be traced to Tertullian in the third century and was in common usage by the fourth century, when Ambrose was already reporting similarities between the rite for the consecration of virgins and the 'actual nuptial ceremony'.[1] The parallel nature of secular weddings and the 'weddings' of brides of Christ in Renaissance and Counter-Reformation Italy merits analysis, as the equivalence of the ceremonies was a prevalent perception much commented upon at the time. Both publicly signalled change in female status and the start of a new life. In biographies and life histories of nuns, rites of passage such as vestitions (when nuns put on the habit of their convent), professions[2] (when nuns made public vows) and consecrations[3] (when nuns were fully integrated into the convent) are crucial events, just as weddings are in the less frequent biographies of Renaissance wives.

This article will focus on the theory and practice of nuns' symbolic marriages and will investigate a range of views about the meaning and implications of the ceremonies involved. The terms 'wedding' and 'ceremony' will be taken here to include all the arrangements and wraparound

---

[1] I should like to thank Sabine Eiche for her help with vestition images, and Trevor Dean, Megan Holmes and Amanda Lillie for reading a draft of this article.
J. Bugge, *Virginitas: An Essay in the History of a Medieval Ideal* (The Hague, 1975), pp. 58, 66.
[2] See *Dizionario degli istituti di perfezione*, ed. G. Pelliccia and G. Rocca (8 vols. to date, Rome, 1974–), VII, cols. 916–71.
[3] *Ibid.* (Rome, 1975), II, cols. 1613–27.

which surrounded the series of central acts. Discussions of what was and was not suitable behaviour before, during and after vestition and profession ceremonies, and why it was or was not suitable, are to be glimpsed everywhere in the records. The problems of interpretation and significance associated with nuns' ceremonies can only be properly appreciated in the *longue durée* and by an investigation which touches on many parts of the Italian peninsula, in order to take account of change over time and local circumstances, but not to be wholly swayed by them. Because the Council of Trent is considered such a watershed in relation to norms of ecclesiastical behaviour, particular attention will be paid wherever possible to whether both rules and usages changed as a result of its decrees, or whether rules alone may have changed while usages remained the same.

I have argued elsewhere that just as the post-Tridentine church extended its control over 'ordinary' marriage arrangements, shifting the process from a social to an ecclesiastical one,[4] so too it tried to reinject the sacred into the 'wedding' ceremonies for its brides of Christ.[5] Here ceremonies of vestition, profession and consecration will be examined as complex and evolving cultural processes with radically different meanings for the many interested parties. It is also worth asking how much individual interpretation of events differed according to inclination, social class and locality, all questions which could equally be asked of participants in secular wedding processes. The ceremonies reveal the delicate power relationships among individuals, families, all-female institutions, secular local government, diocesan organization and the centralized church hierarchy, given that all of these had a stake in the ceremonies. Finally, analysing the ceremonies can also help to illuminate the variety of functions conceived of for women by men in their roles as fathers and heads of families, as participants in secular government and as guardians and legislators of the church. Marriage, either of secular women or of nuns, was an occasion for displaying women's functionality. Wedding ceremonies were public moments when the clash of male interests and most typically the complete disregard of female interests, or at best the subordination of female to male interests, can be most easily seen.

It should be made clear from the start that becoming a nun involved a series of ceremonies and was a gradual and cumulative process rather

---

[4] J. Bossy, *Christianity in the West, 1400–1700* (Oxford, 1986), p. 25; D. Lombardi, 'Intervention by church and state in marriage disputes in sixteenth- and seventeenth-century Florence', in *Crime, Society and the Law in Renaissance Italy*, ed. T. Dean and K. Lowe (Cambridge, 1994).

[5] K. Lowe, 'Resistance through ritual: familial customary behaviour versus church resacralization in the contest over nuns' ceremonies as brides of Christ in fifteenth and sixteenth-century Italy', in *Le mariage à la Renaissance: célébrations et répresentations*, ed. C. Balavoine (forthcoming, Tours).

than a single event signalling change of status. From this point of view, the different steps on the path to female monacation can be directly compared with the various stages of secular marriage.[6] Just as there are ambiguities which make it difficult to pinpoint the precise moment at which two people became married to each other in late medieval and early modern Italy, so too the transformation from non-nun to nun was both something that occurred over time and something that generated disputes. The necessary formalities that had to be observed by would-be brides of Christ could be drawn out or telescoped. At its most elongated, there could be four separate stages to the process of becoming a nun, necessitating four separate ceremonies: acceptance or entrance into a convent; vestition or the taking of the religious habit; profession; and consecration or veiling. At its most basic, there were only two stages to the process: vestition and profession, with veiling sometimes forming a part of profession. In theory, the ceremonies were supposed to be presided over by a bishop, but some abbesses, like the abbess of Sant'Onofrio di Foligno in Florence,[7] believed they had the right to carry them out, and occasionally cardinals and even popes took the matter into their own hands.[8]

The crucial point, however, is that while the church believed the liturgy not only to be the essential part of the ceremony but to comprise the whole of the ceremony, and believed that the presence of the bishop was mandatory, everyone else who was involved saw the liturgy as just one element in the process, and thought that the bishop's presence was not always necessary. For them there were many other considerations, ranging from the size of the dowry to the number of guests expected at the profession banquet. The extent of the display in each of these ceremonies would match the status and pockets of the individual postulant or novice, her family and the convent which she was entering, so that although the central 'religious' elements may have been roughly comparable, the exact combination of many of the other features (most of which had their own customary histories) varied considerably. It would be a mistake, however, to view these secular and social accretions merely as optional extras, because for the families concerned, and for some of the inmates of the

[6] On these stages, see C. Klapisch-Zuber, 'Zacharias, or the ousted father: nuptial rites in Tuscany between Giotto and the Council of Trent', in *Women, Family and Ritual in Renaissance Italy*, ed. Klapisch-Zuber (Chicago, 1985), pp. 181–96.
[7] M. Bartoli, 'Le antiche costituzioni delle monache di Foligno', in *La beata Angelina da Montegiove e il movimento del terz'ordine regolare francescano femminile*, ed. R. Pazzelli and M. Sensi (Rome, 1984), p. 125.
[8] See the drawing in the British Museum, London, by Francesco Solimena of circa 1705 of Pope Clement XI giving his niece her habit (1947.4.12.153), reproduced as plate 15 in *Alessandro Albani patrono delle arti*, ed. E. Debenedetti (Rome, 1993).

convents, they were as central to the process as the liturgy. This is conclusively shown by the peninsular-wide and at least two-century-long resistance proffered by nuns and their kin to the attempts by the church after Trent to sacralize the ceremonies.

The first section of this article will concentrate upon the ways in which secular and religious 'marriages' can be considered as related versions of the same act. These can be examined in a number of ways. At a conceptual level, there was a basic and obvious equivalence because both sets of wedding ceremonies celebrated the giving of a woman to a man. It says a great deal for the flexibility of Renaissance and Counter-Reformation ceremonies that one type of husband was not only absent but existed, if at all, in the spirit or imagination. It is probably therefore critical for the nuns' ceremonies that the prototype of the secular wedding existed, as it made their ceremonies familiar and comprehensible. A woman had to be married to a man; the actual presence of the husband was a formality that could be dispensed with, but the notion of a husband could not. Conceptually, there were also many difficulties with insisting that all respectable adult women be 'married', but these problems were not really addressed. The most obvious one is that marriage entailed the legitimation of sexual activity between the couple which led in turn to the production of children. Nuns, on the contrary, were supposed to be lifelong virgins and took vows of celibacy. The conjunction of the words nun and pregnancy or nun and baby signalled dysfunction and scandal. In what sense, therefore, could God or Christ be a husband?

One stark difference between the two types of wedding was that at vestitions, professions and consecrations there was often a bevy of brides, whereas secular weddings were celebrated one at a time. This was allied to a further conceptual problem that remained unaddressed about the provision of a spouse for nuns: why was God or Christ allowed to have more than one wife? Another difference is that marriage to God or Christ did not entail the acquisition of another family, additional kin and (for those above a certain social level) a new coat of arms; there was no new pairing of two families or creation of a new set of relatives, although new networks could be created through the convent. For the family of the nun this was an undoubted drawback to the arrangement and is probably one reason why it cost less to become a nun than to become a wife.

On the other hand, the idea of consent can also be seen to be pertinent to both ceremonies. Theoretically, the consent of the bride and groom was necessary for a valid marriage to take place, although in practice the decision to marry the couple was taken by the families involved. A nun's entrance into a convent also necessitated the consent of the relevant parties. First of all, the nun's relatives (in reality the nun's father if he was still alive) had to give their permission; second, in theory the nun herself had to be willing (but most girls would not have had the opportunity to refuse); and third, a majority of nuns in the chosen convent had to vote in chapter to accept the postulant. This was the case both before and after Trent. In the convent of S. Paolo in Milan, founded by Carlo Borromeo, the nuns took a secret vote on the entrant who had to be accepted by two-thirds or more of the voters.[9] In practice, 'real' consent may not have been forthcoming from the girls (this is true for secular marriage too) and convents could on occasion be collectively intimidated into giving consent when they wished to withhold it. At the Clarissan convent of S. Martino in Pisa, reserved for Pisan noblewomen, in a famous case in the 1570s, one faction of nuns led by Suora Giulia Ciampoli attempted to force the entrance of two Malaspina girls from the Lunigiana. When the vote went against them, Ciampoli resorted to more devious methods, which culminated in a vicious and ungodly battle between the two sides in the convent church during the ceremony of vestition itself.[10] This is a good example of the way in which vestitions and professions, like secular weddings, could be politicized and become sites of struggle. Theoretically, consent for both processes should also have come from the ecclesiastical authorities, but before Trent church consent to secular weddings remained a dead letter.

The intervention of the secular rather than the ecclesiastical authorities was much more uniform. A notary's presence was expected at weddings of both varieties, or rather at each stage of the two processes. The main reason for requiring a notary was that a contract involving financial exchange was being drawn up between two parties, but registration of a transaction by official record-takers meant that the secular authorities were in a position to exercise regulation if they so wished. Nuns' relatives also wanted to document the process of creating a nun, and convents wished to keep precise financial and administrative registers. Once again, there seems to have been a continuity in behaviour, and records of these ceremonies and transactions straddle the Tridentine divide. On 19 January 1554, the abbess and nuns of the convent of S. Ambrogio[11] in Rome gathered together at the grille of their convent church in the presence of the notary Curzio Saccoci de Sanctis to promise Lelio Sanguigni that they would receive his sister Teresa into the convent, and he in return prom-

[9] *Constitutioni e regole del monastero di S. Paolo di Milano, formate da S. Carlo cardinale arcivescovo* (Milan, 1626), p. 124.
[10] G. de' Ricci, *Cronaca (1532–1606)*, ed. G. Sapori (Milan and Naples, 1972), pp. 53–4. The Malaspina girls eventually gained entrance.
[11] For S. Ambrogio de Maxina, see M. Armellini, *Le chiese di Roma dal secolo IV al XIX* (2 vols., Rome, 1942), II, pp. 564–5.

ised to pay her dowry of 150 *scudi*.[12] On 23 May 1512 the act of profession of Suora Paola Vimercati at the convent of S. Apollinare in Milan was drawn up by Bonifortio Gira in the presence of the abbess and seventy-six named nuns.[13]

As far as the formal church ritual was concerned, there was also a straightforward twinning of sorts between the two sets of ceremonies. The liturgy for the consecration of virgins is indisputably linked to the liturgy of marriage, and the evolution of these two liturgical texts took place in a parallel fashion.[14] However, secular marriage took the lead in this, and the marriage liturgy influenced the ceremonial of 'the consecration of the virgins' rather than vice versa.[15] The fact that 'ordinary' marriage in Italy in the fifteenth century, for example, did not have to take place in a church or under the auspices of the church in any regard, and did not even require the presence of a priest, does not alter the central relationship between the two liturgies: the most important source for the liturgy for consecration was that of the marriage liturgy (although there were also several other sources, such as the liturgy for the ordination of priests and for baptism). The liturgies resembled each other in further ways: for example, during both sets of ceremonies the girls received rings[16] and wore bridal crowns.[17]

The use of music both at secular and at nuns' 'weddings', and the church's response to it, provides a good example of how there was a cross-over not only between the two liturgies, but also between nuns' liturgy and the practices associated with secular weddings. Music was a central feature of secular weddings, indisputably linked to social class, so that a tune played on bagpipes at a simple wedding in the countryside outside Lucca in the fifteenth century[18] was the equivalent at a different social level of the music commissioned for and played at the grand Medici weddings of the sixteenth century in Florence.[19] The point at issue is that

[12] Rome, Archivio di Stato (ASR), Collegio dei notari capitolini 1511, fol. 20r–v.
[13] P. Sevesi, 'Il monastero delle Clarisse in S. Apollinare di Milano (documenti, sec. XIII–XVIII)', *Archivum Franciscanum historicum*, 18 (1925), pp. 553–5.
[14] R. Metz, *La consécration des vierges dans l'Eglise romaine: étude d'histoire de la liturgie* (Paris, 1954), p. 363. For an interesting discussion of the consecration rite in the seventeenth century, see C. Monson, *Disembodied Voices: Music and Culture in an Early Modern Italian Convent* (Berkeley, Los Angeles and London, 1995), pp. 194–8.
[15] Metz, *La consécration*, p. 366.
[16] See Monson, *Disembodied Voices*, p. 195, and the entry on 'anello delle vergini' by V. Macca in *Dizionario degli istituti di perfezione*, I, cols. 628–9.
[17] At Le Murate in Florence, girls before Trent had been allowed home before the vestition ceremony to pick up these bridal crowns, Florence, Biblioteca nazionale (BNF), II II 509, fol. 154v.
[18] M. Bratchel, *Lucca, 1430–94: The Reconstruction of an Italian City-Republic* (Oxford, 1995), p. 175.
[19] See, for example, T. Carter, 'A Florentine wedding of 1608', *Acta Musicologica*, 14

music was expected at weddings, in the same way that other entertainment, such as plays, were.[20] Probably before Trent this was expressed at ceremonies for brides of Christ both in the sacred music in church that formed a part of the liturgy and in the more popular music that accompanied the feasting and dancing after the official ceremony. After Trent, when it became much more difficult to continue the celebrations in a noisy and joyous fashion, the musical part of vestition, profession and consecration ceremonies expanded disproportionately to allow the nuns a measure of creativity and a focus for emotional release.[21] So inspirational was the singing by the nuns of a dialogue between God and the soul at one entrance ceremony at S. Sisto in Rome in 1601 that Suora Cherubina Tiraboschi had a mystical experience and claimed to have been wounded by her heavenly husband.[22] This change in emphasis was greeted with yet more regulations by the church hierarchy banning any but the most basic musical accompaniment, either of voice or instrument, for convents in general and convent ceremonies (especially vestitions and professions) in particular.[23]

Marriage and profession shared a further, important correspondence – they both signalled the alteration in identity of the girl or woman by changing or adding to the name by which she had hitherto been known. Wives kept their Christian names but henceforth had to give their husband's name as well as their father's on any legal document, indicating not only the end of a particular phase of life, but also their more fluid status defined through their closest male relatives. This fluidity manifested itself through their ability to change allegiance from one family to another and from one man to another, simultaneously indicating the weakness and inconstancy of women and displaying their functionality. Their official form of address changed to Mona, a shortened form of Madonna. Nuns, in contrast, officially shed their surnames as they were supposed to sever ties to their families, and usually had their Christian names changed. In exchange, they received a formal title such as Suora or Madre, names which perhaps purposefully (but in some senses inappropriately) recognized and played upon relationships and status within a

(1974), A. Cummings, *The Politicized Muse: Music for the Medici Festivals, 1512–37* (Princeton, 1992) and J. Saslow, *The Medici Wedding of 1589* (New Haven and London, 1996).

[20] On plays at such ceremonies in the seventeenth century, see Monson, *Disembodied Voices*, p. 190.

[21] Nuns in the seventeenth century found another outlet in music by composing it themselves. See R. Kendrick, *Celestial Sirens: Nuns and their Music in Early Modern Milan* (Oxford, 1996).

[22] *Cronache e fioretti del monastero di San Sisto all'Appia*, ed. R. Spiazzi (Bologna, 1993), p. 505.

[23] M. Rosa, 'Le monache nella vita genovese dal secolo XV al XVII', *Atti della Società ligure di storia patria*, 27 (1895), pp. 99–100.

'normal' family. In practice, the family name of a woman's father remained in use for documentary purposes during the whole of her life. Within the two ceremonies there were differences related to these name changes. Wives did not have to say aloud their new name whereas nuns often did when they made their profession vow. So, for example, Suora Candida made her vow of profession at the Benedictine convent of S. Cecilia in Trastevere in Rome on 22 January 1578 and informed the witnesses to the ceremony that she had been known in the secular world ('chiamata al secolo') as Lucia.[24]

The non-religious customs associated with nuns' wedding ceremonies also showed dazzlingly clearly that their origins lay in the usages associated with secular marriage. Here too explicit comparisons between the two versions of a marriage abound. Even before patterns of behaviour are considered, the vocabulary of the customs proclaims their affinity. Nuns as well as brides took dowries (*doti*) to their 'husbands' (the convent acted as a substitute for men in this regard). Although the correct term for nuns' monetary offerings on 'marriage' was dotal alms (*elemosina dotale*) rather than dowry, that expression is found only rarely in the documents which everywhere talk of dowries. Another example is provided by the terminology of the trousseau. Not only are the same objects used by secular brides and brides of Christ but the same words are used for them; no distinction is made between them. Wedding baskets (*zane*) and holy dolls (*bambini*) are as much a part of convent life as of life in secular homes. The Dominican writer Suora Fiammetta Frescobaldi of the convent of S. Jacopo di Ripoli in Florence described the entrance ceremony of Beatrice di Bernardo della Casa in May 1577, which was heralded by the arrival of Beatrice's wedding baskets full of her clothes and necessities.[25] In 1505 Tommaso Guidetti's daughter Maddalena entered a convent in Florence and took with her the holy doll that her mother had been given in her wedding basket in 1482.[26] The trousseaux given to nuns may have been less ostentatious than those given to secular brides but, for nuns coming from families where other daughters would have received a trousseau, they were *de rigueur*. Apparently, like secular ones, they too contained family heirlooms and pieces passed down from mother to daughter regardless of which type of bride the girl was to be.

[24] ASR, Congregazioni religiose femminili, Benedettine Cassinensi in S. Cecilia in Trastevere 4091, busta 4, fol. 10r.
[25] G. Pierattini, 'Suor Fiammetta Frescobaldi, cronista del monastero domenicano di Sant'Iacopo a Ripoli in Firenze (1523–1586)', *Memorie domenicane*, 58 (Sept.–Oct. 1941), p. 231.
[26] C. Klapisch-Zuber, 'Holy dolls: play and piety in Florence in the *Quattrocento*', in *Women, Family and Ritual in Renaissance Italy*, ed. Klapisch-Zuber (Chicago, 1985), p. 312.

Aping the customs of secular brides was, it seems, common enough to be considered normal, although the connection was commented upon. Suora Eufroxina, the daughter of a notary, went on foot in November 1480 to enter the convent of Sant'Agostino in Ferrara and to meet her heavenly spouse, accompanied by noblewomen and preceded by young men, dressed in silver brocade with her hair loose to her shoulders, with a votive or devotional painting (*ancona*), a holy doll and white wax candles 'according to the custom of brides'.[27] The whole scene is redolent of a bride leaving home to go to an earthly husband.

Other non-religious usages were also popular and resistant to change, even in the face of church disapproval. Two of the most persistent were the giving of money to the nun and the feast with guests after the ceremony. Tommaso Rinuccini in 1665 described the old practice, later outlawed, of giving gifts or 'tips' to the 'bride', who had two servers on either side of her holding bowls to receive them.[28] At S. Zaccaria in Venice in the fifteenth century, a bowl was placed outside the grille on a carpet for donations from the public on the day that nuns were consecrated.[29] The ecclesiastical hierarchy had railed against such practices for years, but had difficulty implementing change at a local level. For example, a commission of cardinals deputed to look into the state of affairs in Neapolitan convents in October 1589 forbade the giving of presents or offerings to individual nuns at entrances, vestitions or veilings.[30] Conditions therefore differed between secular weddings and vestitions in this respect, but the usage of giving gifts to the bride was adapted to meet the changed circumstances: presents were still given, but in a standardized form and on a reduced scale.

The blatantly hedonistic entertainment of the after-ceremony meal or feast was targeted by the church as pernicious. The church believed that the ceremonies should be spiritual and serious, unencumbered by worldly matters. It emphasized sobriety and austerity as opposed to celebration and enjoyment. The Neapolitan regulations of 1589 are typical: feasts and sumptuous and splendid singing are forbidden, and only a sober recreation of mind and body is permitted, appropriate to sacred virgins.[31] But because the families and girls saw an equivalence of sorts between secular

---

[27] B. Zambotti, *Diario ferrarese dall'anno 1476 sino al 1504*, ed. G. Pardi, *Rerum italicarum scriptores (RIS)*, 2, XXIV, p. 83: 'segondo il consueto de le spoxe'.

[28] *Ricordi storici di Filippo di Cino Rinuccini dal 1282 al 1460 colla continuazione di Alamanno e Neri suoi figli fino al 1506*, ed. G. Aiazzi (Florence, 1840), p. 273.

[29] V. Primhak, 'Women in religious communities: the Benedictine convents in Venice, 1400–1550' (Ph.D. dissertation, University of London, 1991), p. 154.

[30] These *ordini* are published by C. Russo, *I monasteri femminili di clausura a Napoli nel secolo XVII* (Naples, 1970); the reference to presents is on p. 135.

[31] *Ibid.*, p. 136.

weddings and nuns' 'weddings', and because the banquet played such a vital role in secular weddings, and because big meals were fun, not much progress seems to have been made by the church, as is shown by its bleated repetitions of restriction. The eating of food in common was an integral part of almost any ceremony. The feast provided by the nuns (in lieu of the heavenly bridegroom) at convent banquets mirrors the food and sweets provided by secular husbands' families at wedding feasts. Angelo Peruzzi tried to limit the guest list for the post-profession meal to close family after his apostolic visitation to S. Chiara, the only female convent in Sarzana in 1584.[32] The constitution of the convent of S. Paolo in Milan prohibited any meal at all involving non-religious people after profession,[33] and Sienese decrees of 1575 set an upper spending limit on food for the 'banquet' of ten *scudi* for each nun playing a central part in the ceremonies.[34] A decree of 1666 in Genoa prohibited the handing out of any food or drink in the church itself or in the sacristy on vestition and profession days.[35] This was probably only echoing the bull promulgated by Alexander VII in 1657 which banned the offering of cakes and tarts at these occasions.[36]

The next section will attempt to unravel the processes at work in vestition, profession and consecration ceremonies and will analyse what the ceremonies meant or could have meant for the various parties involved. It should, however, be stressed that all parties recognized the importance of the ceremonies. When the nuns at four Benedictine convents in Lombardy refused to be relocated to Milan in 1578, Carlo Borromeo punished them by refusing to allow them to hold any vestition ceremonies (thereby cutting off their life-blood). The nuns and their families fought a rearguard action against the might of various popes, cardinals and bishops, and ten years later, in 1588, vestitions were finally permitted once again.[37]

The families of would-be nuns had radically different views from the church about the purpose of the ceremonies. The church focused on their religious and spiritual content. In addition, whereas the church saw the occasion as one in which female submission to the church was the primary objective, and at which a new recruit was shown her place and

---

[32] *La visita apostolica di Angelo Peruzzi nella diocesi di Luni-Sarzana (1584)*, ed. E. Freggia (Rome, 1986), p. 60.
[33] *Constitutioni di S. Paolo di Milano*, p. 135.
[34] G. Catoni, 'Interni di conventi senesi del Cinquecento', *Ricerche storiche*, 10 (1980), p. 203.
[35] Rosa, 'Le monache nella vita genovese', p. 100.
[36] *Bullarum privilegiorum ac diplomatum Romanorum pontificum amplissima collectio* (Rome, 1761), IV, part IV, p. 195.
[37] R. Beretta, 'Il monastero delle Benedettine di S. Pietro di Cremella', *Archivio storico lombardo*, 39 (1912), pp. 321–6.

publicly took vows to behave in a certain circumscribed fashion, families
of a certain social level saw the occasion as one in which display of family
honour was the primary objective, and at which a female member of the
family 'married' Christ and celebrated the passage from her home to a
new life in a respectable all-female organization. It was without doubt an
occasion for great celebration and enjoyment. The ceremony was an
opportunity for the family to become publicly identified with a particular
religious institution and partake of its merit. For the relatives and kin, the
emphasis of the ceremony was firmly centred on honour, and the status of
the family had to be upheld in exactly the same way as it would have been
at a secular wedding. Presents given to the convent by the family, for
instance, had to be in keeping with their social station. Fiammetta
Frescobaldi commented that, in accordance with the custom of the
convent, new entrants to S. Jacopo di Ripoli in Florence gave offerings to
the sacristy. On 10 May 1577 the seven girls who entered gave particularly
rich ones, thereby honouring and drawing attention to the status of their
families, because they belonged to the top echelon of Florentine society.[38]

Other ceremonies celebrating nuns' 'weddings' included elements
which actually publicized the family name, a commonplace occurrence at
secular weddings where the coats of arms of the two families making the
alliance would have been prominently displayed wherever possible. At
the turn of the sixteenth century, Cesare Speciano, the bishop of
Cremona, who carried out a comprehensive visitation of the female
convents in his diocese, criticized the decoration of convent refectories at
post-profession banquets: 'When a girl took her vows, neither pennants
nor silver plates[39] should be placed in the refectory, because this was in
imitation of secular brides, and was an example of vanity'.[40] Two points
make this a particularly fascinating comment for the purposes of this
study. First, both the pennants and the plates would probably have been
marked with the family coat of arms of the girl making her profession and
would have been part of the Renaissance culture of display. Thus the
decoration was directly related not to the religious event but to the
families taking part in it. Second, the bishop explicitly condemned this
practice on the grounds that it mirrored behaviour at secular weddings,
and was therefore unsuitable and inappropriate. After Trent, the church
attempted to separate the two types of 'wedding' and to make them
dissimilar by insisting upon the religious aspects of the experience of

---

[38] Pierattini, 'Suor Fiammetta Frescobaldi', p. 231.
[39] *Piatti* here refers to silver plate and not maiolica.
[40] M. Marcocchi, 'La riforma dei monasteri femminili a Cremona. Gli atti inediti della visita
del vescovo Cesare Speciano (1599–1606)', *Annali della Biblioteca governativa e libreria
civica di Cremona*, 17 (1966), p. 109.

becoming a nun and by outlawing all non-religious accretions. As this comment by Speciano shows, however, resistance was fierce on the part of the families who demanded a rite of passage for their daughters which above all else displayed the honour of their lineage.

The importance of vestition, profession and consecration ceremonies to the families of the girls is also acknowledged by the church authorities in the pre-Tridentine era. When all other access to the convent church was forbidden, as at S. Monaca in Florence in the 1440s and 1450s, the archbishop of Florence conceded that the public could go there on the feast day of the patron saint and for vestitions.[41] These two exceptions are indicative of the strength of feeling generated by the ceremonies.

Even for the central participants in the drama there was plenty of variation of meaning. For example, the political organization of the state or region in which the ceremony took place could have important implications for how the ceremony was perceived by those involved. On 9 September 1520 one of the daughters of Giovan Andrea Saluzzo, count of Castellar in Piedmont, called Giovanna Caterina and about to be re-named Lucia, made her profession at the Benedictine convent of Rif-reddo in the company of seven other girls.[42] Instead of recording the names or relationships of the kin who attended this ceremony, Saluzzo lists the representatives or officers from his estates and territories who were present, and also the size of offering that they donated. Saluzzo claims that they were invited expressly in order to give/show honour to the girl[43] (and through her, of course, to the family); they constituted, in effect, another form of hierarchical grouping akin to a family, for he was their feudal lord. Interestingly, the ceremony is here described by the father quite straightforwardly as a festivity or feast (*festa*), and the guest list, full of elected officers (*sindachi*), stewards (*castaldi*) and councillors (*consiglieri*), seems to have been exclusively male. Saluzzo at no point gives any indication that he considers the occasion to have been a religious one; rather the focus on family honour is given an added twist by the feudal structure. As well as swelling the ranks of kin who would normally be in attendance at vestitions and professions, these feudal vassals apparently boosted family honour by displaying the Saluzzo di Castellar coat of arms (topped by a gilded crown) painted on to their offertory torches.[44]

---

[41] M. Simari, 'Profilo storico-architettonico di un monastero fiorentino del Quattrocento: Santa Monaca', *Rivista d'arte*, 39 (1987), p. 173.

[42] 'Memoriale di Gio. Andrea Saluzzo di Castellar dal 1482 al 1528 edito da Vincenzo Promis', *Miscellanea di storia italiana*, ser. 8 (Turin, 1869), p. 557.

[43] *Ibid.*, pp. 557–8: 'fu honorare dita figlia et semosti [invitati] a venire a dita festa tute nostre terre'.

[44] *Ibid.*: 'Queste tute chomunità aviano chon la torgia nostre arme ben pente [dipinte] a colori fini et la chorona orpelata'.

This type of guest would never have been found at professions in, for instance, Florence or Rome, because the political structure and the ties of obligation and allegiance were completely different.

The future, present and past members of convents also had their own perceptions of what was happening at the ceremonies and why the various elements were included. The majority of the women may not have chosen to enter convents but for the duration of the ceremony they were the stars of the show. Nuns, too, clung to certain features, both religious and customary, and those in the convent and those about to enter (unless they were entering for religious reasons) all wanted the ceremonies to be as memorable and as enjoyable as possible. In a life centred on ritual, the omission of even minor parts was a cause for concern. In addition, in a monotonous, repetitive life, these ceremonies offered welcome relief from austerity. For the nuns, the ceremonies marked the entrance of new members of the female community, a swelling of the ranks and a re-inforcement of their position. The more senior nuns also recognized the importance of forging new links with local and non-local families which could be usefully achieved through the acceptance of their daughters into the community.

Some aspects were more important to the nuns than others. For the women themselves, music seems to have been an integral part of the process of becoming a nun, and particular music held particular memories which became stronger and more binding through repetition. Suora Domenica Salomonica in her dedication of the chronicle of S. Sisto in Rome to its first nuns reminded them that the church had sung particularly moving and apt words for each of them in the liturgy for their consecration.[45] The beauty or level of attainment of the music was also seen to redound to the honour of the convent. Customs grew up in individual convents connected with vestition and profession days, and some of these customs, if they were not too ostentatious or too worldly, became enshrined in the newly written rules and constitutions which emerged after Trent. For example, at S. Bernardo di S. Susanna in Rome, the nuns had to wear a special item of clothing, a type of hood (*cocolla*), on these special days to mark them off from the ordinary round.[46]

This divergence in understanding about the meaning of nuns' wedding ceremonies between the organization of the church, the individual nuns submitting to these rites of passage, the members of all-female communities and the families involved in them is additionally reflected in visual

---

[45] *Cronache e fioretti*, ed. Spiazzi, p. 27.
[46] *Regola del santissimo padre Benedetto con le constitutioni quali si debbano osservare nel monastero delle monache et collegio delle zitelle di S. Bernardo in S. Susanna di Roma* (Rome, 1594), pp. 73–4.

representations of these events. Rather different types of image appear to have been produced for each of the four interested parties, with artists adopting the partisan arguments of their patrons and emphasizing very different elements in the 'wedding' ceremonies through their compositions. The images under discussion have been chosen specifically for this purpose. So far only visual representations of the ceremonies which took place inside the convent church have been located.

The church's view that the occasion was first and foremost a religious event ensured that images commissioned by it or for its use focused on this aspect, normally to the exclusion of all others. These images were produced for a devotional and didactic purpose. A good example of this category of image is provided by an early fifteenth-century Venetian miniature on the first folio of 'the benediction and consecration of virgins' in a manuscript of the rule of St Benedict, now in the Biblioteca ambrosiana in Milan (illustration 3).[47] The manuscript was owned by the nuns of S. Lorenzo in Venice,[48] and the miniature has been attributed to the Venetian miniaturist Cristoforo Cortese.[49] Only four figures are included in this sober scene. Seated on the right on a chair of office, wearing his mitre and holding his crosier, the bishop is larger and weightier than the others. With his right hand, he gives a 'wedding' ring to one of a pair of nuns, who are bowed in positions of humility and are on their knees in front of him. One of the nuns is stretching out her right hand so that the appropriate finger is positioned to receive the ring; her left hand and both the hands of the second nun remain crossed on their chests. Both nuns are wearing Benedictine habits and are sporting Benedictine head-dresses. Above them hovers what may be a representation of their heavenly husband, who holds a crown in each hand over the nuns' heads and also has his arms crossed. Nothing in the image refers to any previous life the nuns may have had – there are no marks of individuality or distinguishing signs, let alone any family members witnessing the event. Nor does the image allow of any interpretation other than a traditionally religious one. A male invested with the full power of the church is engaged in transforming the status of the two women at his feet, and the material emblems of

[47] See Milan, Biblioteca ambrosiana, A 125 sup., fol. 90r, *Inventory of Western Manuscripts in the Biblioteca Ambrosiana, part one, A-B superior*, ed. L. Jordan and S. Wool (Notre Dame, 1984), pp. 52–3, and R. Cipriani, *Codici miniati dell'Ambrosiana* (Milan, 1968), p. 5.

[48] On San Lorenzo, see *Monasteri benedettini nella laguna veneziana*, ed. G. Mazzucco (Venice, 1983), pp. 40–3, U. Franzoi and D. Di Stefano, *Le chiese di Venezia* (Venice, 1976), pp. 466–77 and *S. Lorenzo*, ed. F. Gaeta (Venice, 1959). It had previously been thought that the manuscript belonged to the Benedictine convent of S. Lorenzo di Ammiana in Venice, rather than to the richer and more famous Benedictine convent of S. Lorenzo martire; but see Milan, Biblioteca ambrosiana, A 125 sup., fol. 101v.

[49] C. Huter, 'Panel paintings by illuminators. Remarks on a crisis of Venetian style', *Arte veneta*, 28 (1974), pp. 13–14.

ne nō cōfecrare æ ccōanr
tnali.nel ectam name an
pfertrur er uirgines ben

3 Cristoforo Cortese (attrib.), *Benediction and consecration of virgins*

the transformation, the ring and the crowns, seem able to summon up the
ethereal but necessary spouse. The notional husband of the nuns' wedding ceremony takes form in this representation. This image also stresses
the church's view that nuns' roles were essentially submissive, and that
nuns gained their heavenly husband through the intervention and inter-
cession of male members of the church hierarchy. The nuns are presented

in a vacuum, and there is no sign either of an abbess or of any other members of a female community. Nor is there any sense of place. Images commissioned by individual nuns, convents or relatives could portray an entirely different kind of event, reflecting their perception of what was taking place. The veiling and consecration (mislabelled vestition) of Suor Antonia in the Cistercian convent of S. Donato in Polverosa[50] near Florence at the beginning of the sixteenth century (illustration 4) was recorded by an unknown miniaturist,[51] and is the most detailed visual representation of one of these ceremonies to have been found so far. S. Donato was a relatively well-off convent[52] and some of its inmates came from the higher echelons of Florentine society. It had previously been suggested that this miniature was the work of Suor Antonia, a daughter of Paolo Uccello, who was a Carmelite nun in S. Frediano in Cestello, and who was also a known artist;[53] whatever the identity of the artist s/he had an in-depth knowledge of convent life and ceremonies. It is conceivable that the San Donato Suor Antonia painted the scene herself, as she has either written or caused to be written around the image an inscription in the first person singular, giving details of the occasion.[54] The miniature may have been an early and elaborately idiosyncratic equivalent of what became a common practice in the seventeenth century: the writing and illuminating by hand by the nun herself of her own profession note.[55]

However, whether or not Suor Antonia painted this busy and full scene, she undoubtedly commissioned it. The image here serves a commemorative function and may have been the frontispiece of a *libro di donna* kept by Suor Antonia. The trappings of an ordinary wedding ceremony are very

---

[50] On the history of S. Donato in Polverosa or S. Donato a Torri, see E. Repetti, *Dizionario geografico, fisico, storico della Toscana* (6 vols., Florence, 1833–46), v, pp. 544–5, and M. Marini, 'S. Donato in Polverosa: storia e archaeologia in un monastero alle porte di Firenze' (*tesi di laurea*, University of Florence, 1994–5).

[51] This miniature is now in Florence, Gabineto dei disegni degli Uffizi (Inv. 1890, no. 3335); it is labelled 'Vestizione di un monaco'.

[52] It had a gross property value of 5,615 gold florins in 1427–38; see G. Brucker, 'Monasteries, friaries and nunneries in *Quattrocento* Florence', in *Christianity and the Renaissance: Image and Religious Imagination in the Quattrocento*, ed. T. Verdon and J. Henderson (Syracuse, 1990), p. 49.

[53] A. Parronchi, *Paolo Uccello* (Bologna, 1974), pp. 65–6.

[54] The inscription reads:' [E]go soror Antonia pro [. . .] secundum regulam sancti Benedicti abbatis coram deo et omnibus sanctis eius quorum reliquie hic habentur in hoc loco qui vocatur / S. Donatus cisterciensis ordinis constructo in honorem beatissime [. . .] / virginis Marie nec non at beati Donati martiris in presenti anno domini Severi abbatis et domine Domitille abbatisse [. . .]'. It is published in *La chiesa e la città a Firenze nel XV secolo*, ed. G. Rolfi, L. Sebregonda and P. Viti (Florence, 1992), p. 179.

[55] See ASR, Congregazioni religiose femminili, Santa Maria della Concezione in Campo Marzio, 4 (professioni delle monache benedettine, 1571–1740), e.g. fol. 79r (1628) and fol. 115r (1666).

4 Anon., *Veiling and consecration of Suor Antonia degli Albizzi*

much more in evidence than in the earlier scene but the notion of the heavenly husband has been dispensed with. Although the religious cere- mony is taking place in the top centre stage, there are multiple areas of activity and a whole troupe of players. Three points in particular stand out: the first is the attention to detail in everything from dress to window coverings, the second is the number of people portrayed at the ceremony and the third is the prominence given to the two coats of arms.

The scene is set in the interior of a Renaissance church with a paved floor and rosette-coffered ceiling. Not much is known about the architec- ture of the convent church or churches of S. Donato at this date.[56] The image could represent the real Renaissance interior of the convent church at S. Donato or it could be just located in time by being set in a precise but generic early sixteenth-century architectural setting. There are three win- dows: a small round window behind the altar and two tall oblong win- dows to left and right. Under the one on the right is an elegant carved stone doorway. The ecclesiastical trappings are rich: the altar is adorned with a cloth-of-gold altar frontal, a cross and four candlesticks. The sense of place is almost palpable. The people are dispersed around the sides of a triangle in four distinct groups. At the top of the altar steps the veiling of a single nun is in process, requiring the attention of three tonsured clerics and the participation of an altar boy. At the base of the triangle, other already veiled sisters, clustered around a solid wooden lectern topped by another cross, sing from a choirbook placed upon it. On the right are the female spectators to this event, both lay and ecclesiastical, and on the left are the male spectators, including representatives from the main male orders. A couple of children complete the guest list. Two coats of arms are prominently displayed in the top left and top right of the church, that on the left belonging to the degli Albizzi, and that on the right to the Vecchietti. The strong composition, refined technique and convincing use of portraiture all suggest the image was executed by an accomplished and reputable artist or miniaturist. Although the artist has clearly not mastered the rules of mathematical perspective, the construction of the church interior and the proportionality of figures in space are successfully rendered and contribute towards the accurate description of place.

The spatial arrangement of this scene emphasizes the importance of order, hierarchy and sexual segregation in the church. But while they probably record faithfully the position of the abbot at the apex of the spectacle, the two groups composed solely of members of the church are counterbalanced by two large mixed groups, representing the variety of civil states. The spectators and the decorations are included because they

---

[56] But see M. Marini, 'S. Donato in Polverosa' for further information.

are a vital ingredient of the process, and within them family members and coats of arms create an alternative sphere of influence to the Catholic church, its personnel and its signs and symbols. Here too the sense of an ordered and flourishing female community is very evident, and the nun receiving her veil at the altar is about to join her sisters at the lectern; she will move from one group to another. The scene does not take place in a vacuum but in the rather beautiful church which is only one part of the material plant of the female organization to which the nun belongs.

The nun at the centre of this image was Cassandra degli Albizzi, the daughter of Paolo di Piero degli Albizzi and his second wife, Ginevra di Marsilio Vecchietti.[57] Under one year old at the time of her father's *catasto* return in S. Giovanni, Chiave, in Florence, in 1480,[58] she was received into the convent and given her habit on 22 November 1501, at which point she was given the name Suor Antonia.[59] The abbess at the time was Suora Domitilla Guasconi,[60] but the act of veiling in the image was carried out, according to the inscription, by an abbot called Severo. In fact, the abbot and monks involved in the ceremony were from the brother Cistercian convent of S. Salvatore di Settimo, whose abbot at this time was called Marco, but Severo, an abbot of Modena, was staying in Settimo because the congregation had a system of sending abbots around abbeys in rotation to 'oversee' other abbeys.[61]

The emphasis on family and kinship made manifest by the inclusion of two coats of arms belies the abnormality of the scene. At secular weddings, two coats of arms were displayed because two sets of families were considered to be involved, the patrilineages of the fathers. Here the coat of arms of Cassandra's mother, Ginevra Vecchietti, is displayed in a conscious or unconscious attempt to mimic secular wedding practice. What happens as a concomitant of this is that the female ancestors of the nun in the scene receive an unexpected boost in status. In fact, it is also clear that nuns' relationships with their female relatives and in particular with female members of their matrilineages were closer and of greater

[57] P. Litta, *Celebri famiglie italiane* (Milan, 1819–74, Naples 1902–3), Albizzi di Firenze, *tavola* XIII. Marino Marini has also independently tracked down the identity of this nun.
[58] Florence, Archivio di Stato (ASF), Catasto 1022, 189v. Fifteen *bocche* are listed in this *catasto* return: her father, her mother and thirteen children from her father's two marriages. Her father, who is described as 'vecchio e infermo' pleads great poverty, but lives on until 1490. He states that none of his five daughters (Cassandra was the youngest) has a dowry of any description.
[59] ASF, Corporazioni religiose soppresse dal governo francese, 233, 104, fol. 56r.
[60] Both she and Suor Antonia are recorded as present in the convent on 24 June 1513; see ASF, Corporazioni religiose soppresse dal governo francese, 233, 62, fol. 51v.
[61] At the top of a list of the monks of S. Salvatore in Settimo in chapter of 1 March 1501 (i.e. 1502) are the abbot Marcus and the abbot of Modena Severus: ASF, Notarile antecosimiano 9647, fol. 417r.

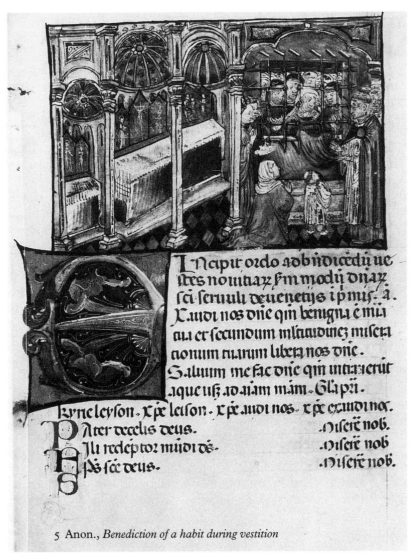

5 Anon., *Benediction of a habit during vestition*

importance than wives' relationships, so that this very unusual display of a mother's coat of arms can also be seen as a reflection of normative behaviour for nuns.

Presenting the point of view of the female community inside the convent is a rare fifteenth-century image of a vestition taking place through a grille (illustration 5). This too is a miniature, from a Benedictine ritual handbook (*rituale*)[62] commissioned by the nuns and convent of S. Servolo in Venice.[63] The handbook has three sections, on the benediction of habits during vestition, on profession and on the benediction and consecration of virgins. The miniature is effectively separated into two halves: on the right is the vestition scene, crowded with people, and on the left is a detailed representation of the interior of an empty Renaissance church. The ceremony on the right has the convent grille as its backdrop. On one side of it, in the external church, a tonsured priest wearing a long blue cloak with a large gold clasp, aided by a tonsured altar boy, blesses the new habit of the postulant which is being passed through the grille. The postulant is on her knees in front of him, and two women in secular dress stand on the left. Behind the priest on the right is at least one other tonsured priest and at least one other non-tonsured man. Segregation of the sexes is thus also recorded at this ceremony.

On the other side of the grille, in the internal church, a whole crowd of nuns waits to receive the new inmate into their midst; an abbess is not discernible but the representation is of a thriving community. The nun who passes the habit through the grille wears the white head-dress of a Benedictine novice,[64] and one of the bars of the grille has not been painted to allow her face to be observed uninterruptedly. This is also the case with another nun to her left, and other nuns' faces have been positioned so that the whole face fits into a grille partition. Thus framed, the nuns appear individualized and central to the scene. As the commissioners of this image were the nuns themselves, it probably represents the theoretical norm for vestitions in enclosed or reformed convents. Vestitions were supposed to take place at the grille to emphasize the separation between the outside world and life in the convent, but it is known that many did not. Many convents did not even have a grille. S. Servolo, however, had been reformed in the 1430s when three Observant nuns from the convent of Santa Croce della Giudecca were sent to set an example to the four remaining nuns at S. Servolo whose behaviour and observance had become lax,[65] which makes the reality of the location more likely. The miniature may well be a fairly accurate representation of fifteenth-century practice at S. Servolo after this date.

It is also possible that the convent church depicted is that of S. Servolo, which may have been rebuilt before 1470 when it was consecrated by

[62] Venice, Biblioteca nazionale marciana, cod. lat. III, 72 (3402), fol. 2r. On it, see G. Valentinelli, *Bibliotheca manuscripta ad S. Marci Venetiarum* (6 vols., Venice, 1868–73), II, pp. 322–3. The image is reproduced in *Monasteri benedettini*, ed. Mazzucco, p. 35 and in Primhak, 'Women in religious communities', p. 7.
[63] On San Servolo, see *Monasteri benedettini*, ed. Mazzucco, pp. 34–5.
[64] *Dizionario degli istituti di perfezione*, I, cols. 1235–6.
[65] G. Cappelletti, *Storia della chiesa di Venezia* (Venice, 1855), IV, pp. 85–6.

Urbano dei Vignati, the bishop of Sebenico (Šibenik) in Dalmatia.[66] Pride in their new church and a desire to preserve a record of it could have been additional reasons for commissioning the handbook and miniature. The church has three naves, divided by pilasters and ending in semicircular apses painted spectacularly in blue and gold. Various works of art are visible including three altarpieces with sparse figures painted in white on a blocked gold background. A triptych of a crucifixion with two saints hangs above the main altar, while the other two appear to have diptychs, one with a madonna and child with a saint and the other with two saints. The altar cloths are of white damask and have fringes. The floor, which extends across both scenes and provides a sense of continuity, is patterned with green and black diamond-shaped lozenges. Once again, the sense of place and vibrant community are notable and there is no husband, however notional, on display. If the representation is of the interior of S. Servolo, the artist must have spent time in the exterior church in order to take note of the details. Convent visions of the rituals of their communities are unusual and are especially valuable as they emanate from an all-female institution. This 'view from the other side' of a nun's ceremony is rather paradoxical because although the artist may have been on the outside, his patrons were inside.

The fourth image under consideration is complicated because it does not purport to lead to devotion, to teach by example or to record an event, either for an individual or an institution. Instead, by inflating the role in the ceremony of secular elements and worldly display, it can be said to represent the point of view of the nun's relatives. It is an illustration of probably the most common type of vestition scene, that of the imagined vestition of a saint (illustration 6). Vestition images are especially associated with saints Clare,[67] Catherine of Siena[68] and Humility.[69] The purpose of the image under discussion was, however, different from that of most imagined vestition scenes, for the patrons of it were attempting to acquire piety through visual association with sanctity. Although the image had a religious theme, it was approached from a secular point of view, and

[66] F. Correr, *Ecclesiae Venetae antiquis monumentis nunc etiam primum editis illustratae* (13 vols., Venice, 1749), V, p. 100.
[67] For vestitions of St Clare in Italy, see, for example, G. Kaftal, *Iconography of the Saints in Tuscan Painting* (Florence, 1952), col. 272, fig. 314 (a Giovanni di Paolo *predella* formerly in the Fuld Collection in Frankfurt) and Kaftal, *Iconography of the Saints in the Painting of North-East Italy* (Florence, 1978), col. 228, fig. 271 (a Paolo Veneziano panel in the Accademia in Venice).
[68] G. Kaftal, *Iconography of the Saints in the Painting of North-West Italy* (Florence, 1985), col. 193, in fresco cycles by Giovanni Donato da Montorfano in S. Maria delle Grazie in Milan and of the Ligurian school in S. Maria di Castello in Genoa.
[69] Kaftal, *Iconography of the Saints in Tuscan Painting*, col. 493 and fig. 573, a fourteenth-century Florentine school altarpiece in the Uffizi in Florence.

6 Lorenzo Lotto, *St Bridget and the miracle of the dry wood*

portraits of the patrons and their families highlight the fact that the saint's face is hidden from view. The image is one of a cycle on the miracles of St Bridget[70] commissioned from Lorenzo Lotto by two members of the Suardi family[71] of Trescore near Bergamo circa 1525 for their family oratory.

Once more the scene unfolds in a chapel (which might have existed) and a sense of place is pervasive. The bishop stands at the apex of the composition, at the top of the altar steps, below an altarpiece of the crucifixion, in front of a cross and four candlesticks, reading the liturgy from a large book held aloft by an altar boy. To the left is a window and a door leading to the sacristy, while to the right, through a gaping hole in the wall, St Bridget can be seen giving food and drink to the needy. In the vestition scene, Bridget is kneeling at the bottom of the altar steps,

---

[70] F. Cortesi Bosco, *Gli affreschi dell'Oratorio Suardi: Lorenzo Lotto nella crisi della riforma* (Bergamo, 1980), pp. 106, 108–10, 112.
[71] On the Suardi family, see Bonoreno Corbella, *De genealogia illustrissimae Soardorum familiae brevis epitome* (Bergamo, 1612).

prostrating her forehead on the top one, and causing grass and flowers to spring up. This is the rationale for the inclusion of this image in the cycle for it represents the so-called miracle of the 'regreening' of the dry wood. Bridget is dressed in yellow. In addition to the bishop and the altar boy, there are three priests present (one holding the bishop's crosier) to stress that this rite of passage required the intervention of the ecclesiastical hierarchy. But the religious contingent is far outnumbered by non-religious representatives. Ranged to either side of Bridget are the various members of Maffeo Suardi's nuclear family, carefully segregated with men on the left and women on the right. It is as though the Suardi family are standing in for St Bridget's own family as witnesses to her vestition; they wear elaborate and expensive secular clothes displaying their own status. Although the saint provides the focus of the story, the Suardi, through proximity and participation, have positioned themselves so that they are a necessary and expected element of the process. As the patrons of this image, even if they are not strictly the relatives of the 'nun', the Suardi show what purpose a vestition ceremony would have served for them. Perhaps because they had no nun in the family, the image omits any mention of the female community: St Bridget is a lone postulant, unguided by an abbess and unwelcomed by her peers.

These four images can be interpreted as representing their commissioners' points of view about what was happening at 'wedding' ceremonies for nuns. Each group emphasized the centrality of their own contribution. The church's view that this was a spiritual moment of union with a heavenly husband is counterbalanced by the individual nun's knowledge that the rite of passage constituted the most important moment of her life, by the convents' attitude that it was a solemn but joyous occasion when new members joined their community, and by the relatives' belief that the ceremonies honoured their status through their daughters and were moments for display and fun. These conflicting views can probably be summed up best by Alexander VII's prohibition in 1657 of fireworks at these ceremonies, which must have seemed grossly inappropriate to the church but presumably were just the latest fad in a long line of social customs deployed by the families and convents to express and experience pleasure.[72] Quite obviously, the social class of the nun and the wealth and social status of the convent were all-important in the jockeying for position between these four sets of interested parties, and local conditions (including the state of diocesan organization) and usages also played their part. But beyond these considerations, there does seem to have been some sort of recognizable form for these ceremonies.

[72] *Bullarium privilegiorum collectio*, IV, part IV, p. 195.

The parallel nature of the 'wedding' ceremonies for nuns and brides adds to the evidence that the ceremonies themselves were occasions when women's functionality was publicly on display. Women served a variety of functions by being displayed as secular brides and a variety of others by being displayed as brides of Christ. The decisions about what the women should do were taken by their relatives, in practice mainly by their fathers, and except in a small minority of unusual cases, the women were not consulted: their interests were subordinated to those of their families or individual members of them. The fight between the ecclesiastical and secular authorities over control of and access to nuns which intensified after Trent was the next step in this process of perceiving nuns as passive instruments of male policy, and it illustrates how there was often a clash of male interests over manipulation of females. Wedding ceremonies of whatever sort can profitably be viewed against this backdrop.

3 The rape of the Sabine women on Quattrocento marriage-panels

Jacqueline Musacchio

In this examination of Renaissance marriage imagery, we shall begin with a long and narrow panel in the collection of Harewood House in West Yorkshire (illustration 7). It was painted circa 1465, by the Florentine artist Apollonio di Giovanni. Diminutive, carefully executed figures are scattered throughout the panel, in an undulating rhythm that moves chronologically from the top right to the bottom left. They span three different but related scenes that range from a court area hung with festive drapes, to a town with fanciful Romanesque architecture, to the mountainous countryside directly outside the crenellated town walls. On the far right, a man sits on a dais, his hand raised over the crowd of revellers dressed in Renaissance costume who gather at his feet. Other men, tumblers in parti-coloured clothing, perform in the foreground, and lutists serenade the elaborately attired women and men who watch from the sidelines. The coy gestures and cocked heads of these spectators signify that they are engaged in intimate conversations. Opposite the enthroned figure, however, there is a sense of disorder. A bench is tipped over, serving as a barrier for the figures and delineating the interior and exterior space. A woman at the far end of the bench glances to her right and realizes that something is amiss; she reaches out a hand to alert her companion. The men and women to the left of this bench form seven struggling pairs. Further to the left, passing through the city gate into a mountainous landscape, these couples are echoed by pairs of soldiers engaged in hand-to-hand combat.

The composition is enigmatic. The figures roam across the panel, distracting the viewer with a profusion of rich details which transform the struggling groups at the centre and the far left into decorative patterning. This embellishment belies the violence inherent in the actual subject, which is the Roman foundation myth of the rape of the Sabine women.[1] What we see in this panel, and in others like it, is the abduction that preceded what twentieth-century viewers would actually consider the rape. However, during the Renaissance, the term was used in a more general manner to signify violent abduction and its consequences, making the tradition of referring to the ancient myth as a rape valid.[2] The representation of such a scene is obviously intriguing. In a recent study, Margaret D. Carroll examined the implications of mythological rape scenes in sixteenth- and seventeenth-century art and their connections to authoritarian rule.[3] She concluded that images of mythological rapes were especially appropriate in princely contexts as a way of justifying claims to absolute sovereignty. In this article I hope to demonstrate that this theory can be further extended to the private and domestic context of the Renaissance patrician's home, where such images encapsulated the contemporary beliefs regarding marriage and the role of women in the private sphere.

The abduction, and subsequent rape, of the Sabine women was described in several ancient sources known in the Renaissance, such as Livy's *Ab Urbe Condita* (I.9–13), Ovid's *Fasti* (3.199–228) and Plutarch's biography of Romulus in his *Vitae* (II.14–19). With the humanist interest in classical literature, these texts were circulated widely in manuscript form and in printed Italian and Latin editions during this period. There were, for example, printed editions of Livy and Plutarch by 1470, and such books can be found in contemporary household inventories.[4] Their popularity is difficult to determine, but the fact that Renaissance artists utilized the story indicates that at least the basic facts of the myth were common knowledge for much of the art-buying public.

These basic facts were extremely suggestive. According to classical sources, the Sabine story was set in the eighth century BC, shortly after Rome had been founded and encircled by walls. As the ruler of this new city, Romulus tried to make alliances with neighbouring states to secure brides for his population. The Romans had few women to marry and bear their children, and they faced extinction within a generation. But no man would send his daughter to them, fearing the great power developing under Romulus. As a result, the Romans had to turn to trickery and force.

[1] J. Poucet, *Recherches sur la légende Sabine des origines de Rome* (Louvain, 1967); G. B. Miles, 'The first Roman marriage and the theft of the Sabine women', in *Innovations of Antiquity*, ed. R. Hexter and D. Selden (New York, 1992).
[2] N. Davidson, 'Theology, nature and the law: sexual sin and sexual crime in Italy from the fourteenth to the seventeenth century', in *Crime, Society and the Law in Renaissance Italy*, ed. T. Dean and K. J. P. Lowe (Cambridge, 1994), pp. 83–4; and see T. Dean's contribution to this volume, pp. 85–106.
[3] M. Carroll, 'The erotics of absolutism: Rubens and the mystification of sexual violence', *Representations*, 25 (1989), especially pp. 19–20.
[4] A. F. Verde, 'Libri tra le parete domestiche. Una necessaria appendice a *Lo studio fiorentino, 1473–1503*', *Memorie domenicane*, 18 (1987).

7 Apollonio di Giovanni, *The rape of the Sabine women* (*cassone* panel)

Romulus declared a festive celebration and invited the nearby tribes to a day of games. This celebration is the setting for most of the representations of the legend, exemplified here by a fragment from a late fifteenth-century panel by Domenico Morone in the National Gallery, London (illustration 8).[5] The story is shown at the moment of the prearranged signal from Romulus, which prompted the Romans to seize the Sabine daughters for their brides. Plutarch described how the Romans, 'drawing their swords and falling on with a great shout ravished away the daughters of the Sabines'.[6] In Morone's panel, the Romans' festive cloaks are tossed aside and men rush to action over barriers and on ladders, their acrobatic leaps disguising the real violence of their acts. The Sabine women helplessly protest, but their male relatives can offer no resistance in the face of this onslaught.

With no other choice, the Sabine women gradually resigned themselves to their fate and began to produce children for their new husbands, ensuring the future success and prosperity of the city of Rome. After a period of several years, the Sabine men rose up to battle the Romans and reclaim their daughters. But at the very moment when combat was

---

[5] Another fragment, probably from the same panel, depicts the scene immediately prior to the rape, establishing the festive and deceptive setting that lured the Sabines into complacency before the attack began: see C. Baker and T. Henry, *The National Gallery. Complete Illustrated Catalogue* (London, 1995), p. 475.

[6] Plutarch, *Lives*, transl. B. Perrin (Cambridge, Mass., 1914), p. 131.

imminent, the Sabine women, trailed by their new children, ran into the midst of the battle. They begged the soldiers to end the fighting between their natal families and their new husbands for the sake of their new descendants. Their importance to the reconciliation is clear; Livy noted that the women 'dared to go amongst the flying missiles, and, rushing in from the side, to part the hostile forces and disarm them of their anger, beseeching . . . that fathers-in-law and sons-in-law should not pollute with parricide the suppliants' children, grandsons to one party and sons to the other'.[7] In the late fifteenth-century panel by Jacopo del Sellaio from the Philadelphia Museum of Art illustrated here, the battlefield is clearly divided between warring factions, who stand poised within striking distance (illustration 9). Their pikes are raised and their banners are flying. The scene follows standard battle iconography, except for the insertion of the pleading women and their small children in the midst of the action.

The three Sabine panels examined thus far were originally part of domestic furnishings that celebrated and commemorated marriage. An understanding of the original function of these furnishings is necessary to situate the particular iconography of Sabine panels within Renaissance family life. For example, the panel by Apollonio once formed the front of a marriage-chest, or *cassone*.[8] Pairs of these marriage-chests

[7] Livy, *From the Founding of the City*, transl. B. O. Foster (Cambridge, Mass., 1919), p. 49.
[8] The only monographic treatment of Italian painted furnishings is the monumental but

8 Domenico Morone, *The rape of the Sabine women* (*after the signal*)
(*cassone* panel, fragment)

were presented to the new bride, and were used to transport her dowry
goods in a ceremonial procession through the city streets. This public
procession signified the bride's removal from her father's home and
arrival at her new husband's residence.[9] There is no consensus regarding which man – father, husband or father-in-law – provided her with
the chests, although one of them must have, since few women had
much disposable income of their own. Today's difference of opinion
regarding the original purchaser of Renaissance marriage-chests is
understandable, as the often arbitrary documents provide no single

outdated P. Schubring, *Cassoni. Truhen und Truhenbilder der italienischen Frührenaissance*
(Leipzig, 1915 and 1923); see also E. Callmann, 'Apollonio di Giovanni and painting for
the early Renaissance room', *Antichità viva*, 27 (1988).
9   C. Klapisch-Zuber, 'Zacharias, or the ousted father: nuptial rites in Tuscany between
Giotto and the Council of Trent', in *Women, Family, and Ritual in Renaissance Italy*, ed.
Klapisch-Zuber (Chicago and London, 1985).

answer.[10] But all these male relatives would have agreed on correct female behaviour, which, we shall see, was often reflected in the iconography of these marriage-panels. All parties were concerned with making politically and economically advantageous marriage alliances, which were carefully negotiated and extravagantly celebrated.

Both Brucia Witthoft and Christiane Klapisch-Zuber have described the public procession of the bride and her dowry as a triumph, with the captured woman escorted to her husband's home surrounded by excessive displays of wealth and power.[11] Such processions were also depicted on marriage-panels of the time.[12] When the bride arrived at her new home, she was led into the set of rooms newly furnished for the marriage, sometimes at great expense.[13] Her chests would be kept in these rooms for seating and storage. During the second half of the fifteenth century, the chests were complemented with, or sometimes replaced by, painted wainscoting panels, or *spalliere*, set high into the walls of the rooms.[14] Both the panel by Sellaio and the fragment by Morone seem to have been *spalliere* panels.

Contemporary inventories indicate that marriage-panels were relatively common in patrician and merchant homes. However, their cost, at roughly 34 florins for a pair of chests in the mid-fifteenth century, was the equivalent of an unskilled labourer's annual earnings, putting them out of the reach of many in the lower classes.[15] Nevertheless, these panels were so common that they were usually described simply as painted, or, at the most, historiated, with no mention of their specific iconography.[16] The popularity of both *cassoni* and *spalliere* made them a part of the daily experience of a significant percentage of the population. However, only a small amount of the original output survives. The placement of *cassoni* on

[10] See the many examples cited in C. Klapisch-Zuber, 'Les femmes dans les rituels de l'alliance et de la naissance à Florence', in *Riti e rituali nelle società medievali*, ed. J. Chiffoleau, L. Martines and A. Paravicini Baglioni (Spoleto, 1994).

[11] B. Witthoft, 'Marriage rituals and marriage chests in Quattrocento Florence', *Artibus et historiae*, 5 (1982); Klapisch-Zuber, 'Zacharias'.

[12] *Le tems revient 'l tempo si rinuova. Feste e spettacole nel tempo di Lorenzo il Magnifico*, ed. P. Ventrone (Florence, 1992), p. 152.

[13] J. K. Lydecker, 'The domestic setting for the arts in Renaissance Florence' (Ph.D. thesis, Johns Hopkins University, 1987).

[14] On *spalliere* panels in general, see A. B. Barriault, *Spalliera Paintings of Renaissance Tuscany. Fables of Poets for Patrician Homes* (University Park, Pa., 1994).

[15] E. Callmann, *Apollonio di Giovanni* (Oxford, 1974), p. 25; R. Goldthwaite, *The Building of Renaissance Florence* (Baltimore, 1980), pp. 429–37.

[16] For example, there was 'uno paio di forzieri storiati' in Paolo di Ghuglielmo's estate in 1429: Florence, Archivio di Stato (ASF), Magistrato dei pupilli avanti il principato, 166, fol. 55v. A rare but more specific reference was to 'uno forziere dipinto di storia di Lucrezia' in the estate of Bartolomeo di Ghabriello in 1450: ASF, Magistrato dei pupilli, 171, fol. 183r. For a marriage-panel with this subject, see J. Miziolek, 'The story of Lucretia on an early Renaissance *cassone* at the National Museum in Warsaw', *Bulletin du Musée National de Varsovie*, 35 (1995).

9 Jacopo del Sellaio, *The reconciliation of the Romans and the Sabines* (*spalliera* panel)

the floor and their use as seating often harmed the painted panels. In fact, they were occasionally described as damaged in their own time; in 1418, Bardo da Spicchio's estate included a pair identified as *cactivi*, or 'bad'.[17] As a result, while we often have the front panel of a chest, which was the most elaborately painted part (and therefore carefully preserved), we rarely have an entire chest. To get a sense of what is lost, it is useful to recall that Ellen Callmann identified approximately fifty known chest panels as from Apollonio di Giovanni's workshop, although his notably incomplete workshop record listed 170 chest pairs.[18] *Spalliere*, on the other hand, were less mobile and more protected by their integral location high on a wall, but were perhaps more often destroyed when ownership of the building changed.

The iconography of this group of marriage-panels is of especial interest here. The rape of the Sabine women seems, at first, a rather surprising image to decorate a gift to a bride. Yet we shall see that it was eminently

---

[17] ASF, Magistrato dei pupilli, 29, fol. 108r.
[18] Callmann, *Apollonio*, pp. 4–6, 25–6, 76–81.

appropriate within the context of Renaissance marriage. It appears on several complete *cassoni* and *spalliere* panels, as well as on other fragments, from the second half of the fifteenth century.[19] Other panels depict the intervention of the Sabine women in battle and the ensuing reconciliation between the Romans and the Sabines.[20] And we must remember that every surviving panel represents many more that have been destroyed.

[19] See C. Huelsen, 'On some Florentine *cassoni* illustrating ancient Roman legends', *Journal of the British and American Archaeological Society of Rome* (1911), pp. 477–8. Among the surviving examples are *cassoni* in Harewood House, discussed in Callmann, *Apollonio*, pp. 72–3, and Malahide Castle, *ibid.*, p. 38; *spalliere* in the Palazzo Colonna, discussed in *Catalogo sommario della Galleria Colonna in Rome. Dipinti*, ed. E. A. Safarik (Rome, 1981), pp. 28–9, and the Museo del Prado, in *Inventario General de Pinturas I. La Colección Real* (Madrid, 1990), p. 247; and fragments in the Ashmolean Museum, discussed in C. Lloyd, *A Catalogue of the Earlier Italian Paintings in the Ashmolean Museum* (Oxford, 1977), pp. 10–11, the National Gallery of Scotland, in H. Brigstocke, *Italian and Spanish Paintings in the National Gallery of Scotland* (Edinburgh, 1993), pp. 21–3, and the National Gallery, London, discussed in Baker and Henry, *The National Gallery*, p. 475.

[20] See the companion *spalliera* to the Palazzo Colonna panel included in Safarik, *Catalogo sommario*, pp. 28–9, and the Philadelphia panel in B. Sweeny, *John G. Johnson Collection. Catalogue of Italian Paintings* (Philadelphia, 1966), p. 70.

The Sabine myth as a subject should first be considered within the general category of domestic furnishings. The elaboration of furnishings for the home during this period expanded the artistic possibilities beyond traditional religious painting and sculpture with a strictly devotional or didactic intent. This does not mean that sacred images declined in popularity; if anything, their range also expanded. For example, Cardinal Giovanni Dominici recommended that young children be provided with images of the Christ child and exemplary saints to strengthen their devotion.[21] This tenet was adhered to quite well; we need only read Neri di Bicci's workshop record to get a sense of the great numbers and variety of workshop-produced and mass-consumed devotional works of art that existed at this time.[22] But with the growing secularism of the Renaissance, the scope of non-religious iconography also widened. The domestic setting became the place for a variety of objects and the subjects painted on them often reflected contemporary ideologies. In fact, Leon Battista Alberti advocated interior decoration for private dwellings that illustrated, as he described it, 'tales that poets make for moral instruction'.[23] Alberti was writing at mid-century; surely he knew of marriage-panels, which were especially strong at that moment and which put particular emphasis on exactly these poets' stories. This is not to say that the use of these secular narratives as didactic tools appealed to everyone. Girolamo Savonarola complained about the use of pagan tales instead of biblical narratives on marriage-chests.[24] But he was not as knowledgeable about these marriage-panels as he professed. Stories of virtuous Old Testament women, such as Esther, Susanna and the queen of Sheba, were adapted as appropriate subjects for many panels, perhaps destined for the homes of Florence's prosperous Jewish population.[25]

Nevertheless, painted *cassoni* and *spalliere* utilized only a limited range of literary, biblical and ancient subjects.[26] A century after the peak in popularity of these marriage-panels, Giorgio Vasari characterized their iconography as tales from Greek and Latin texts, and his iconographic

[21] G. Dominici, *Regola del governo di cura familiare*, ed. D. Salvi (Florence, 1860), pp. 131–2.
[22] N. di Bicci, *Le ricordanze*, ed. B. Santi (Pisa, 1976); M. Gregori, A. Paolucci and C. Acidini Luchinat, *Maestri e botteghe. Pittura a Firenze alla fine del quattrocento* (Florence, 1992).
[23] L. B. Alberti, *On the Art of Building in Ten Books*, transl. J. Rykwert, N. Leach and R. Tavernor (Cambridge, Mass., 1988), p. 299.
[24] Schubring, *Cassoni*, p. 19.
[25] M. Haraszti-Takács, 'Fifteenth-century painted furniture with scenes from the Esther story', *Jewish Art*, 15 (1989), pp. 23–4.
[26] P. F. Watson, *The Garden of Love in Tuscan Art of the Early Renaissance* (Philadelphia, 1979); C. L. Baskins, '"La festa di Susanna": virtue on trial in Renaissance sacred drama and painted wedding chests', *Art History*, 14 (1991); E. Fahy, 'The Tornabuoni-Albizzi panels', in *Scritti di storia dell'arte in onore di Federico Zeri*, ed. M. Natale (Milan, 1984).

analysis accords well with surviving objects.[27] Although early panels focused on decorative patterning, courtly motifs or contemporary romantic literature, by the mid-fifteenth century, which is when these Sabine panels were produced, a definite shift was evident. There was a decided turn from amatory scenes to images of ancient battles.[28] This shift was noticed by Paul Schubring early this century, but it was articulated most clearly and more recently by Callmann. In her various studies on *cassoni*, Callmann observed that panels from the second half of the fifteenth century focused on the themes of ancient heroics or personal humility, and linked this change both to new artistic conventions and to growing tensions within family life.[29] For the purposes of this article, it is important to note that many of these factors were affected by the demographic catastrophes of the preceding decades, beginning with the first outbreak of the bubonic plague in 1348. In this way, the procreative emphasis of the Sabine myth found a distinct counterpart in Renaissance society, since both were driven, as we shall see, to enlarge their population.

Sabine panels tended to focus on the key distinguishing elements of the Roman myth. The use of a continuous narrative often opened the panel to the depiction of several scenes at once. Invariably, Romulus' signal and its immediate aftermath were depicted. While dealing with this rather circumscribed group of scenes, the artists used several motifs to draw the viewer into the panels. In many cases, both the Romans and the Sabines are in Renaissance dress, encouraging a close identification with the viewer.[30] The scenes are often placed in a recognizable ancient Roman setting. This is especially evident in the *spalliera* panel by Bartolomeo di Giovanni of circa 1488, now in the Galleria Colonna in Rome, where the action travels in waves around an ancient amphitheatre, set in front of the Torre delle Milizie, the Pantheon and the Column of Trajan.[31] The addition of children in the scenes of the reconciliation brings an almost comic element into the otherwise intense battlefield, and forces the viewer to trace the movements of the stumbling children as they weave in

[27] G. Vasari, *Le vite de' più eccellenti pittori, scultori ed architettori*, ed. G. Milanesi (9 vols., Florence, 1878–85), II, pp. 148–9.
[28] Following this iconographic change, inventories occasionally listed chests painted with unspecified antique scenes; see Ser Giuliano del Rosso's estate of 1481, which included 'uno paio di forzieri dipinti all'anticha da spose' (ASF, Magistrato dei pupilli, 177, fol. 158v).
[29] Callmann, *Apollonio*, p. 40; Callman, 'The growing threat to marital bliss as seen in fifteenth-century Florentine paintings', *Studies in Iconography*, 5 (1979). Related reasoning can be found in Witthoft, 'Marriage rituals', p. 54.
[30] As observed by D. O. Hughes in 'Representing the family: portraits and purposes in early modern Italy', in *Art and History: Images and their Meaning*, ed. R. I. Rotberg and T. K. Rabb (Cambridge, 1986), p. 11. Some contemporaries condemned it: see *Filarete's Treatise on Architecture*, transl. J. R. Spencer (New Haven, 1965), p. 314.
[31] This panel is illustrated in Safarik, *Catalogo sommario* pp. 28–9.

and out of the horses and soldiers. Visual conventions like these emphasized the link between ancient Rome and Renaissance times, and encouraged the viewer to see them as similar situations.

The need for such a connection was important. With the growing humanist interest in classical antiquity, ancient stories were considered ideal models for Renaissance life, and the Sabine story was no exception. Roman men would have been praiseworthy for their heroism and for their concern for the future of the city. In the same manner, Sabine women would have been extolled for their submissiveness to the needs of husbands and city. A connection can also be made to the larger, civic desire to equate the Renaissance city with the glory of ancient Rome. This founding story could be a useful didactic tool in the ongoing search for ancient justification of contemporary ideology. As such, its depiction on marriage-panels fulfilled a necessary role in family life, by providing a narrative worthy of emulation.

But the popularity of the Sabine myth in the art associated with Renaissance marriage cannot be explained solely in these terms. Other marriage-panels incorporated ancient stories that likewise served as ideal examples.[32] What made the Sabine legend, in particular, so appealing? Contemporary marriage-panels did not illustrate every ancient story; each was carefully chosen from among the hundreds of possibilities. We therefore need to allow for a more nuanced reading of each individual subject depicted on these detailed panels. Renaissance women were not Sabines and fifteenth-century Italy was not the early Roman empire. But these images could have served as a more subtle impetus to society in general. Through their brilliantly painted and carefully gilt compositions, figurative marriage-panels presented the reality of marital expectations to the new bride in a manner that rendered the harshness of marriage more palatable. Yet the figurative scenes on the panels were obviously more emphatic about these expectations than a simple decorative pattern could have been. The subject of the Sabine myth was particularly blatant: like the Sabine women, Renaissance brides were required to obey their new husbands and bear their children. A marriage-panel painted with such a scene emphasized this message. The close relationship between iconography and function, and the presence of these panels in the home itself, point to their overall didactic intent.[33]

But why was this particular message so critical at this particular time?

---

[32] Callmann, *Apollonio*, pp. 38–9; Witthoft, 'Marriage rituals', pp. 53–4.
[33] On the other hand, some scholars emphasized the decorative role of these panels over the didactic: A. Schiaparelli, *La casa fiorentina e i suoi arredi nei secoli XIV e XV*, ed. M. Sframeli and L. Pagnotta (Florence, 1983), p. 294; K. Christiansen and J. Pope-Hennessy, 'Secular painting in fifteenth-century Tuscany: birth trays, *cassone* panels and portraits', *Metropolitan Museum of Art Bulletin*, 38 (1980), p. 12.

One reason for the popularity of the Sabine myth may have been demographic: it had surprising resonance with the real situation in post-plague Italy. Both ancient Rome and Renaissance Italy were under extreme practical and ideological pressure to increase their populations. During the period under discussion, the Italian city-states were only slowly recovering from the devastation of the plague, which hit at least a dozen times between 1348 and 1600.[34] In 1348 alone it killed between one-third and one-half of the population and caused both political and economic chaos throughout the Italian peninsula. The city of Florence, where many of the Sabine panels were painted, can serve as an example of the catastrophic population decline: in 1338 the population was estimated at 120,000 inhabitants, but by 1441 it had sunk to 37,000.[35] These recurring epidemics must have created an overwhelming awareness of mortality in Renaissance society, which was in turn manifested in many aspects of life.[36]

In addition, this same period witnessed an alarmingly high death rate among young married women that seems closely linked to childbearing, as well as a significant number of stillbirths, miscarriages and early infant deaths.[37] It was not until the late fourteenth century, after several outbreaks, that the true impact of the plague was evident in a variety of areas. For example, Samuel Cohn has demonstrated how testators changed the overall emphasis of their bequests after the second plague outbreak.[38] And Katharine Park has shown the dramatic effects of the recurring epidemic on public health policy during this time.[39] By the late fourteenth century, in view of their drastically reduced populations, the dangers inherent in childbirth and infancy, and the constantly returning plague itself, both individual families and the city-states must have felt a certain urgency towards increasing their numbers. In solely practical terms, both needed a large population to survive, as well as to fight wars, rent homes and shops, maintain low wages and pay taxes.

Post-plague society placed great emphasis on the continuation of the husband's lineage through the conception and safe delivery of healthy male heirs. Under ideal circumstances, this required the wife's acquies-

---

[34] M. Ginatempo and L. Sandri, *L'Italia delle città. Il popolamento urbano tra Medioevo e Rinascimento (secoli XIII–XVI)* (Florence, 1990).

[35] D. Herlihy and C. Klapisch-Zuber, *Tuscans and their Families: A Study of the Florentine Catasto of 1427* (New Haven and London, 1985), pp. 60–92.

[36] A. Molho, *Marriage Alliance in Late Medieval Florence* (Cambridge, Mass., 1994), pp. 2–3. See also P. Binski, *Medieval Death. Ritual and Representation* (London, 1996).

[37] Herlihy and Klapisch-Zuber, *Tuscans*, pp. 257–79.

[38] S. K. Cohn, *The Cult of Remembrance and the Black Death. Six Renaissance Cities in Central Italy* (Baltimore and London, 1992).

[39] K. Park, 'Medicine and society in medieval Europe, 500–1500', in *Medicine in Society. Historical Essays*, ed. A. Wear (Cambridge, 1993), pp. 87–8.

cence, as well as her good health and her maternal capabilities. Writers as disparate as Leon Battista Alberti, Alessandra Strozzi and Cherubino da Spoleto emphasized childbearing as a primary reason for marriage, undoubtedly taking their cue from a long-standing classical and Christian tradition.[40] Sumptuary laws also reveal this contemporary stimulus to childbearing. In 1433, one law declared that women were ignoring their duty to bear children and demanding costly clothing and accessories, therefore causing great financial hardships for their husbands.[41] The image of Rome replenishing its population through the rape of the Sabine women, considered by ancient writers to be a purely practical and necessary event that ensured the future of the city, may therefore have appealed both to the Renaissance city as a civic entity and to men as family members. The images of the Sabine story on marriage-chests therefore illustrated and advocated control over childbearing as a way to achieve success in the state and in the family.

This use of the Sabine story as a plague-related *topos* has not been sufficiently acknowledged. The development of the Sabine myth as an independent image comes about only after the mid-fifteenth century. Conveniently, this was concurrent with the burgeoning interest in ancient history, the development and elaboration of new art forms like marriage-panels, and the effects of multiple plague outbreaks. There were few reasons to depict this distinctly pagan subject in the Middle Ages, and earlier images of the myth were relatively limited; they tended to be within the context of illuminated manuscripts of Augustine's *City of God*, where, interestingly, the incident is condemned by Augustine as a tragedy.[42] But suddenly, in the late fifteenth century, the story became popular on its own, as the subject of secular domestic furnishing panels.

In the past, art historians have associated the plague with significant changes in the style and iconography of monumental sacred art from the second half of the fourteenth century through the fifteenth century and beyond.[43] However, as Sabine imagery should make clear, plague icono-

---

[40] L. B. Alberti, *The Albertis of Florence: Leon Battista Alberti's Della Famiglia*, ed. G. Guarino (Lewisburg, 1971), pp. 27–8, 121; Alessandra Macinghi Strozzi, *Lettere di una gentildonna fiorentina del secolo XV ai figliuoli esuli*, ed. C. Guasti (Florence, 1877), pp. 527–31; Cherubino da Siena (*sic*), *Regole della vita matrimoniale*, ed. F. Zambrini and C. Negroni (Bologna, 1888), pp. 61–2. Cherubino's book, originally published in 1490, was a popular guide to married life: in 1502, the dowry of Caterina Bongianni included 'uno libro di Fra Cherubino in forma coperto di cordovano azuro' (ASF, Acquisti e doni, 302, insert 1, unnumbered folio).

[41] R. E. Rainey, 'Sumptuary legislation in Renaissance Florence' (Ph.D. thesis, Columbia University, 1985), p. 479.

[42] D. Wolfthal, "'A hue and a cry": medieval rape imagery and its transformations', *Art Bulletin*, 75 (1993), pp. 39–40.

[43] P. Heitz, *Pestbl—tter des XV. Jahrhunderts* (Strasbourg, 1901); R. Crawfurd, *Plague and Pestilence in Literature and Art* (Oxford, 1914); M. Meiss, *Painting in Florence and Siena*

graphy did not have to focus solely on mortality. Grim Last Judgement scenes, images of the triumph of death, or cycles of suffering plague saints such as Sebastian or Roch were not the only options available to Renaissance artists who wanted to comment on the impact of the plague. And, perhaps most importantly, monumental art was not the only type of art influenced by the plague. Domestic art, which surrounded people every day in their own homes, was also affected. Within this setting, the epidemics inspired specific iconography and particular objects to help offset the omnipresent mortality. The very development of painted marriage-panels as an art form to encourage, celebrate and commemorate marriage is closely linked to the contemporary importance attached to marriage. Without this emphasis, the production of marriage-panels would have faltered quickly. Childbirth, too, had its own attendant objects, ranging from figuratively painted wooden trays and maiolica vessels to special clothing and accessories.[44] These also remained popular as long as they were deemed necessary; surviving objects and documentary evidence indicate a significant drop in the production and possession of marriage and birth objects by the late Cinquecento, conveniently contemporary with the beginning of steady demographic recovery in the Italian peninsula.

Although late fifteenth-century writers do not seem to state the explicit connections between contemporary marriage and the Sabine myth, the presence of these panels makes it clear that the links were there in the viewers' minds. It was only articulated later: direct links between the implications of the Sabine legend and marriage were made by Marcantonio Altieri and Baldassare Castiglione in the early sixteenth century. Klapisch-Zuber has shown how Altieri, whose text emphasized the rape of the women, believed that every aspect of the marriage ritual recalled the Sabine myth.[45] Castiglione, on the other hand, emphasized the reconciliation effected between Romans and Sabines by the women as a noteworthy act, worthy of praise.[46] Both Altieri and Castiglione saw the Sabine women as exemplary for their role in uniting, strengthening and populating Rome. And, significantly, both ignored the violent nature of the founding story.

Many modern scholars have followed this tradition of interpreting the

after the Black Death (Princeton, 1951); Cohn, The Cult of Remembrance, pp. 271–80; L. Marshall, 'Manipulating the sacred: image and plague in Renaissance Italy', Renaissance Quarterly, 47 (1994).

[44] I have examined the wide range of these childbirth objects in 'The art and ritual of childbirth in Renaissance Italy' (Ph.D. thesis, Princeton University, 1995).

[45] M. Altieri, Li nuptiali, ed. E. Narducci (Rome, 1873); Klapisch-Zuber, 'An ethnology of marriage in the age of humanism', in Women, Family, and Ritual, pp. 254–5.

[46] B. Castiglione, The Book of the Courtier (Harmondsworth, 1987), pp. 233–4.

10 Apollonio de Giovanni, *The rape of the Sabine women* (*cassone* panel,
fragment)

Sabine story positively.[47] And we have already noted that the fifteenth-
century painted marriage-panels similarly disguised the violent act with
their charming compositions, bright colours and gilt details. In fact, this
sort of deception was similar to the manner in which the Romans originally disguised the impending violence from the visiting Sabines in a
carnival-like setting. During the sixteenth century, for reasons that have
yet to be determined, marriage-panels were more obvious in their violence and it is therefore easier to identify their subjects.[48] But in the
fifteenth century elaborate display often hid the true subject so completely that the panel was misidentified. This was clearly the case with a
fragment from a marriage-chest now in Edinburgh, which went by the

[47] See E. Gombrich, who called the Sabine story an 'auspicious topic' in 'Apollonio di
Giovanni: a Florentine *cassone* workshop seen through the eyes of a humanist poet',
Journal of the Warburg and Courtauld Institutes, 18 (1955), p. 27; A. Arikha, who referred to
the rape as a 'heroic act' in *Nicholas Poussin: The Rape of the Sabines* (Houston, 1982), p.
14; and A. Bagnoli, who referred to the subject's 'matrimonial implications' in *Domenico
Beccafumi e il suo tempo* (Milan, 1990), p. 328. Particularly problematic is N. Bryson,
'Two narratives of rape in the visual arts: Lucretia and the Sabine women', in *Rape*, ed. S.
Tomaselli and R. Porter (Oxford, 1986), incisively reviewed by S. Kappeler, 'No matter
how unreasonable', *Art History*, 11 (1988).
[48] See the Sabine panels by Bartolomeo di David of circa 1540, in Bagnoli, *Domenico
Beccafumi*, p. 329, and by Girolamo della Pacchia of circa 1520, in B. B. Fredericksen,
Catalogue of the Paintings in the J. Paul Getty Museum (Malibu, 1972), p. 28.

mysterious misnomer 'The Venetian Brides' until identified by Ernst Gombrich in 1955 (illustration 10).[49] The festive costumes of the crowded scene disguised its actual iconography. The violence is only evident upon close examination, which makes the flailing arms and distressed expressions of the women apparent. The central couple in the foreground who seem to be dancing are instead engaged in a dramatic lunge as the woman falls to the ground in her urgency to escape her pursuer.

Panels like this clearly indicate that the Sabine legend is, at its most basic retelling, blatantly violent. Of course, violence was not unique to marriage-panels with the story of the Sabine women; the story of Nastagio degli Onesti from Boccaccio's *Decameron* was also a popular, and even bloodier, subject for marriage-panels.[50] Most myths have some basis in reality, and the reality of ancient Rome must have been violent indeed for such a tale to be accepted as the norm in the canon of its founding legends. Transplanted to the post-plague world of Renaissance Italy, the ancient myth had particular resonance. Despite their charming facades, these painted panels emphasized the husband's rule over his wife and his right to resort to force to ensure her submission to the needs of his lineage. The repopulation of the family and the city was critical, and the depiction of the Sabine myth on marriage-panels provided a subtle yet omnipresent impetus to this.

The connection of this violent myth to Renaissance marriage was not without some precedent. The criminal act of rape was, on occasion, a precursor to legitimate marriage in the pre-modern era. In many cities, 'rapists' of unwed women faced relatively trivial punishments for their crimes, although these punishments could increase according to the social position and age of the violated woman.[51] In most cases, punishment was meted out to compensate the woman's father for his loss of valuable (and betrothable) property rather than to console the victim.[52] One solution to the crime that could find favour with both the father and the 'rapist' was to offer the girl in marriage to her assailant. In these cases, the father protected his honour and freed himself of his now-spoiled goods with minimal expense and publicity, the dangerously tainted

---

[49] Gombrich, 'Apollonio di Giovanni', p. 27; T. Henry, 'The subject of Domenico Morone's "Tournament" panels in the National Gallery, London', *Burlington Magazine*, 136 (1994).

[50] C. Olson, 'Gross expenditure: Botticelli's Nastagio degli Onesti panels', *Art History*, 15 (1992).

[51] U. Dorini, *Il diritto penale e la delinquenza in Firenze nel secolo XIV* (Lucca, 1923), pp. 67–9; *Statuta populi et communis Florentiae publica auctoritate collecta castigata et praeposita anno salutis MCCCCXV* (3 vols., 'Friburgi', 1778–83), II, p. 318; G. Ruggiero, *Violence in Early Renaissance Venice* (New Brunswick, 1980), pp. 156–70.

[52] See the famous case of Artemisia Gentileschi, sensitively analysed in M. D. Garrard, *Artemisia Gentileschi* (Princeton, 1989).

woman got a husband and the 'rapist' got a wife, which allowed him to engage in his violent behaviour within the sanctioned bonds of matrimony. The use of Sabine iconography on marriage-panels, then, served as tacit approval of violence before and within marriage when it led to the desired outcome.

The role of the Renaissance bride as childbearer was emphasized by both social convention and demographic necessity. This role was critical in the post-plague society, where the severely reduced population created unprecedented political, economic and social difficulties. In this setting, a *cassone* or *spalliera* panel illustrating the rape of the Sabine women and their subsequent acceptance of their roles as wives and mothers could be a direct exhortation to childbearing. The panels did not serve as simple ancient examples, and their meaning did not depend upon a complex reading and understanding of classical literature. The Roman foundation myth had a more basic appeal in this demographically depressed and lineage-obsessed society. These panels, whether paraded through the streets as announcement of the bride's future role, or seen every day as decorative, functional and didactic furniture and decoration in her bedchamber, would serve constantly to reinforce a woman's own perception of her identity as wife and mother.

Part II

Intervention by church and state

4 Fathers and daughters: marriage laws and marriage disputes in Bologna and Italy, 1200–1500

Trevor Dean

The role of the church courts in late medieval Europe in reinforcing parental authority over children's marriage choices has recently been the object of some academic debate.[1] On the one hand, it is argued that the pattern of activity in the French church courts, when compared to the English, suggests that French parents 'co-opted' the courts into their struggle to prevent their children from breaking arranged betrothals. On the other hand, it has been objected that the activity of the courts cannot be read solely in terms of the needs of parental authority, especially as there is evidence, even from France, of parents acting contrary to the court's wishes, and as the church had its own powerful reasons for prosecuting irregular unions. This article is concerned with civic law and secular courts, not canon law and the church courts, but it raises many of the same issues: how did fathers, through law and its enforcement, seek to control the institution of marriage, and especially the theoretical freedom of children to make their own marriage choices?

The history of secular law on matters such as adultery, clandestine marriage and other crimes against matrimony has of course been studied and surveyed by legal historians in the past. However, the standard authorities on Italian legal history are unsatisfactory in their treatments. Salvioli skipped over the whole issue, asserting that the city-states surrendered competence to the church in cases of adultery, rape, bigamy, concubinage and so on.[2] Pertile is considerably inaccurate in his generalizations regarding these laws: though noting the differences of law and penalty

---

[1] C. Donahue, 'The canon law on the formation of marriage and social practice in the later Middle Ages', *Journal of Family History*, 8 (1983); A. J. Finch, 'Parental authority and the problem of clandestine marriage in the later Middle Ages', *Law and History Review*, 8 (1990); C. Donahue, '"Clandestine" marriage in the later Middle Ages: a reply', *ibid.*, 10 (1992); F. Pedersen, 'Did the medieval laity know the canon law rules on marriage? Some evidence from fourteenth-century York cause papers', *Mediaeval Studies*, 56 (1994).
[2] *Storia del diritto italiano*, ed. P. Del Giudice (3 vols., Milan, 1923–7), II, pt 2, p. 84.

among various cities, he sees these only as legal differences, not historical or regional ones.[3] His reliance on statutes from only a few of the major cities, and rather more on minor or marginal areas, combined with a tendency to blend barbarian lawbooks, communal statutes and Enlightenment codes into a synthesis, produced a text in which chronological development is often obscured. Some trends are therefore muted or even inverted, as in the case of adultery.[4] The first part of this article will therefore seek to establish a more secure historical development of the criminal laws on adultery, bigamy, rape and marriage.

Thirteenth-century statutes are largely silent on adultery, but in the early fourteenth they move quickly, first to impose financial penalties on the man,[5] then to impose them on the woman also (fine and loss of dowry).[6] From the mid-fourteenth century, more severe, corporal penalties were introduced for the woman, ranging from shaving and whipping, or imprisonment, to death.[7] Boccaccio's story in the *Decameron* (VI.7), in which the city of Prato abolished the death penalty for a wife's adultery in response to one adulteress's clever pleading, runs entirely counter to the historical trend, but may, of course, have been intended as a fictional discussion of the appropriateness of this penalty. Conversely, for a husband keeping a mistress the financial penalty was set much lower, and corporal penalty was rarer.[8] The double standard of these laws is immedi-

---

[3] A. Pertile, *Storia del diritto italiano*, second edn (6 vols., Turin, 1892–1900), III, pp. 285–302; V, pp. 514–38.

[4] *Ibid.*, V, pp. 524–6. For another example of such confusion, see III, pp. 301–2.

[5] C. D'Arco, *Studi intorno al municipio di Mantova* (7 vols., Mantua, 1871–4), II, p. 78; *Statutum lucani communis an. MCCCVIII* (Lucca, 1991; repr. of Lucca, 1897), p. 136; and perhaps *Il costituto del comune di Siena*, ed. A. Lisini (2 vols., Siena, 1903), II, p. 355.

[6] *Statuto di Arezzo (1327)* ed. G. Marri Camerani (Florence, 1946), p. 212; *Statuto del comune di Montepulciano (1337)*, ed. U. Morandi (Florence, 1966), p. 189; *Statuti di Perugia dell'anno MCCCXLII*, ed. G. Degli Azzi (2 vols., Rome, 1913–16), II, p. 115; *Gli statuti del comune di Treviso (sec. XIII–XIV)*, ed. B. Betto (2 vols., Rome, 1984–6), I, pp. 429–30; *Statuti di Verona del 1327*, ed. S. A. Bianchi and R. Granuzzo (Rome, 1992), p. 467; *Statuta civitatis Mutine anno 1327 reformata* (2 vols., Parma, 1864), II, p. 398.

[7] *Statuta Cremonae* (Brescia, 1485), p. 30v; *Statuta communis Vincentie* (Vicenza, 1490), p. 89v; *Statuta et decreta communis Genuae* (Genoa, 1498), pp. 9–v; *Statuta Carpi MCCCLIII* (Modena, 1887), p. 68; *Statuti della terra del comune della Mirandola e della corte di Quarantola riformati nell'anno MCCCLXXXVI* (Modena, 1885), p. 93; *Statuta patavina* (Venice, 1528), pp. 114v–5 (law of 1399); *Leges Brixianae* (Brescia, 1490), cl. 71; *Statuta civitatis Cesene* (Venice, 1494), II.45; *Statuta et ordinamenta civitatis Laude* [1390] (Milan, 1537), p. 100.

[8] *Statuti di Ascoli Piceno dell'anno MCCCLXVII*, ed. L. Zdekauer and P. Sella (Rome, 1910), p. 125; *Lo statuto di Bergamo del 1331*, ed. C. Storti Storchi (Milan, 1986), p. 173; *Statuti di Bologna dall'anno 1245 all'anno 1267*, ed. L. Frati (3 vols., Bologna, 1869–77), I, p. 264; *Statuta comunis et populi civitatis Camerini*, ed. F. Ciapparoni (Camerino, 1977), p. 244; *Statuta Faventiae*, ed. G. Rossini, *RIS*, second edn, XXVIII, pt 5, p. 165; *Statutum lucani communis*, pp. 227–8; *Costituto di Siena*, II, p. 252; *Statuta communis Parmae* (4 vols., Parma, 1855–9), I, p. 290; III, p. 254; *Statuta civitatis Cesene*, III.51; *Decreta Sabaudie ducalia* (Turin, 1477), p. 133.

ately obvious: the contrast is one between increasing severity towards the extra-marital affairs of the married woman and stable penalty for those of the married man.[9] The view that women were more at fault than men in adultery was, of course, a common one, shared for example by late medieval preachers.[10]

Laws on bigamy, though less common, followed the same evolution, from lighter financial penalties,[11] to heavier ones accompanied by loss of dowry,[12] and eventually in the fifteenth century to capital punishment.[13] The latter penalty was, however, incurred only in specific circumstances: fifteenth-century laws distinguished, in ways that earlier ones did not, between bigamous betrothals (*sponsalia*) and bigamous matrimony, the difference between the two being copulation. The really serious crime, in the eyes of the law-makers, was the consummation of a second marriage while living in a consummated first marriage.

Rape was dealt with less straightforwardly by many statutes. Often it appears in catch-all clauses, misleadingly headed 'de adulteriis', regarding a variety of sexual offences with virgins, wives and widows. The words used in these statutes do not always mean 'rape' in the modern sense: the Latin word *raptus* meant abduction or theft (property too was 'raped');[14] while *stuprum* cannot securely be translated as rape either, meaning violent sex without consent, given that some statutes talk of *stuprum* with consent.[15] Such uncertainty might almost be said to have authority: one Roman-law text (*Digest*, 48.5.6) admitted that the terms 'stuprum' and 'adulterium' were used 'promiscuously', and that 'properly adultery is committed with a married woman, stuprum on a virgin or widow'. Baldus too had to explain the difference between adultery and *raptus*.[16] To the modern mind, the defining difference between adultery and rape lies in the issue of consent or force; to Roman lawyers it lay in the matrimonial

---

[9] Cf. *Digest*, 48.5.14.5: 'periniquum enim videtur esse, ut pudicitiam vir ab uxore exigat, quam ipse non exhibeat'.

[10] B. Paton, *Preaching Friars and the Civic Ethos: Siena, 1380–1480* (London, 1992), pp. 260–1.

[11] *Statuti di Bologna 1245–1267*, I, pp. 263–4; *Gli statuti veronesi del 1276*, ed. G. Sandri (Venice 1940), p. 427; *Statuta antiquissima Saone (1345)*, ed. L. Balletto (2 vols., Genoa, 1971), II, p. 34 (clause dated 1260); *Statuti del comune di Vicenza MCCLXIV*, ed. F. Lampertico (Venice, 1886), p. 196.

[12] *Statuto di Montepulciano*, p. 189; *Statuto di Arezzo*, p. 212; *Statuti di Verona*, p. 468; *Statuti di Treviso*, I, pp. 430–1; *Statuta Camerini*, p. 245; *Statuta civitatis Tridenti* (Trent, 1528), III.38.

[13] *Statuta Vincentie*, p. 93; *Statuta Carpi*, pp. 105–6 (addition of 1446); *Volumen magnum capitulorum civitatis Ianue a. MCCCCIII–MCCCCVII*, in *Historiae patriae monumenta* (20 vols., Turin, 1836–1955), XVIII, col. 922.

[14] 'Rapere est de loco ad locum trahere cum vi': Baldus, *Consilia* (5 vols., Venice, 1575), I, p. 116, *consilium* 357.

[15] *Statuta Cremonae*, p. 30v; *Statuti di Verona*, p. 467; Pertile, *Storia*, V, p. 516.

[16] *Consilia*, IV, p. 41v, *consilium* 171.

status of the woman. This does not mean that force was ignored: both rape and adultery could be committed, in this way of thinking, with consent or with force; and the use of violence carried a heavier penalty. 'Rape is a crime of many dimensions',[17] and city statutes on 'rape' usually comprise a number of elements – abduction, the use of force, sexual violation, the possibility of consent – which were considered in various combinations, with distinct penalties. Italian law was not like English, in which the law of rape was, in the later Middle Ages, completely confused with the law of abduction, to the point that it provided remedy only to fathers prosecuting elopements, and not to women prosecuting sexual violence.[18] Laws on rape/abduction followed the same path towards severity taken by other sex-crimes. The earlier laws provided only financial penalties (often much lighter if the victim was a lower-class woman or a prostitute);[19] those after the mid-fourteenth century provided a much graver penalty (death).[20] In this it might be tempting to see the city legislators bringing their statutes into line with Roman law, which prescribed death for *raptores*.[21] But in fact civic statutes tempered the severity of Roman law, for, almost invariably, those which ordained capital punishment for

[17] G. Ruggiero, *The Boundaries of Eros: Sex Crime and Sexuality in Renaissance Venice* (New York and Oxford, 1985), p. 89.

[18] R. D. Groot, 'The crime of rape *temp.* Richard I and John', *Journal of Legal History*, 9 (1988); J. B. Post, 'Ravishment of women and the Statutes of Westminster', in *Legal Records and the Historian*, ed. J. H. Baker (London, 1978); Post, 'Sir Thomas West and the Statute of Rapes, 1382', [*Bulletin of the Institute of*] *Historical Research*, 53 (1980); E. W. Ives, 'Agaynst taking awaye of women: the inception and operation of the Abduction Act of 1487', in *Wealth and Power in Tudor England*, ed. E. W. Ives, R. J. Knecht and J. J. Scarisbrick (London, 1978).

[19] *Statuti inediti della città di Pisa dal XII al XIV secolo*, ed. F. Bonaini (3 vols., Florence, 1854–7), I, p. 363; *Statuti di Treviso*, I, pp. 429–30; *Codex statutorum magnifice communitatis atque dioecaesis Alexandrinae* (Alessandria, 1547) (1297 statutes), p. 65; *Il codice osimano degli statuti del secolo XIV* [1308], ed. D. Cecchi (2 vols., Osimo, 1991), I, p. 250; *Costituto di Siena*, II, p. 355; *Statutum lucani communis*, p. 136; *Statuti della repubblica fiorentina* (2 vols., Florence, 1910–21), II: *Statuto del podestà dell'anno 1325*, ed. R. Caggese (Florence, 1921), p. 229; *Statuto di Bergamo*, p. 173; *Statuto di Arezzo*, p. 212; *Gli statuti di Sarzana del 1330*, ed. I. Gianfranceschi (Bordighera, 1965), p. 110; *Statuti di Ascoli*, p. 89. For the same attitude in prosecution, see Ruggiero, *Boundaries of Eros*, p. 99.

[20] *Statuta Saone (1345)*, II, p. 14; *Statuto di Forlì dell'anno MCCCLIX*, ed. E. Rinaldi (Rome, 1913), p. 217; *Statuti della Mirandola (1386)*, pp. 93–4; *Statuta Cremonae* (1387), p. 30v; *Statuta patavina*, p. 112v (law of 1390 (*sic*, but 1290?) partially anticipated by one of 1329: p. 114); *Statuta et ordinamenta civitatis Laude*, p. 100; *Statuta varia civitatis Placentiae* [1391] (Parma, 1860), p. 379; *Statuta Faventiae* (1410), p. 165; *Statuta Vincentie* (1425), p. 89v; *Statuta civitatis Verone* (Vicenza, 1475), III.42; *Statuta lucensis civitatis* (Lucca, 1490), IV.83; *Leges Brixianae*, cl. 66; *Statuta civitatis Cesene*, III.48–9; *Statuta civitatis Tridenti*, III.67–8; *Statuta et novae reformationes urbis Romae* (Rome, 1523), II.54; IV.2.21; *Statuta civitatis et principatus Papiae* (Pavia, 1590), p. 187. Cf. Pertile, *Storia*, V, pp. 516–18.

[21] *Codex Iustinianus*, 9.13, *De raptu virginum*.

abduction also allowed the matrimonial option:[22] if both the *raptor* and his victim were unmarried, and if the victim consented to matrimony, he could marry and endow her and thus avoid penalty. The stricter Roman-law rule (that such marriage was impossible)[23] was thus put aside in favour of the canon-law rule (inspired by the Bible) that the rapist/seducer should marry his victim and/or grant her a dowry.[24] That a 'rapist' should marry his victim seems ghastly to modern eyes, but this is because the modern crime of rape has shed all connection with abduction, and because 'normal' sexuality has become less violent.[25] In the past the figure of the rapist was an ambiguous one: abduction might be followed by sexual violence, or it might be consented to by the woman, as a prelude to marriage. If many abductions were in fact elopements, then matrimony was the objective from the start, and the law merely had the effect of transferring the obligation to provide dowry from the father to the 'abductor'.

Most cities also had laws requiring parental consent to daughters' marriages.[26] There was, however, great variety among these, and some significant limitations. Cities set differently the age below which consent was required: fifteen at Vercelli,[27] sixteen at Ascoli and Todi,[28] eighteen at Padua,[29] twenty at Arezzo, Brescia, Pisa, Sarzana, Vicenza,[30] twenty-five at Piacenza, Perugia, Mirandola.[31] Penalties were almost always financial and rarely involved loss of dowry rights.[32] Above those ages, women were sometimes explicitly allowed to marry without consent. At Treviso this permission was enacted to remedy negligent delay by parents in marrying their daughters: after a woman reached twenty years, two close kinsmen could give her in marriage and award her a dowry.[33] Similar permissions were more often issued to deal with the problem of the fatherless girl:

[22] This was also sometimes found where the penalty was pecuniary: *Statuti di Treviso*, I, p. 428; *Statuti di Sarzana*, pp. 110–1; *Il codice osimano*, I, p. 250.
[23] See *Codex Iustinianus*, 9.13: 'Nec sit facultas raptae virgini vel viduae vel cuilibet mulieri raptorem suum sibi maritum exposcere, sed cui parentes voluerint, excepto raptore, eam legitimo copulent matrimonio'.
[24] Pertile, *Storia*, III, pp. 290–1; V, pp. 514–15; Paton, *Preaching Friars*, p. 222.
[25] Ruggiero, *Boundaries of Eros*, p. 102.
[26] Pertile, *Storia*, III, p. 278.
[27] *Statuta communis Vercellarum ab anno MCCXLI*, in *Historiae patriae monumenta*, XVI, col. 1131.
[28] *Statuti di Ascoli*, p. 89; *Statuta civitatis Tudertine* (Todi, 1549), p. 92.
[29] *Statuta patavina*, p. 115v.
[30] *Statuti di Pisa*, I, p. 362; *Statuti di Sarzana*, p. 140; *Statuto di Arezzo*, p. 243; *Leges Brixianae*, cl. 72; *Statuti del comune di Vicenza*, pp. 119–20.
[31] *Statuta Placentiae*, p. 372; *Tertium volumen civitatis populique Perusini statutorum* (Perugia, 1523), pp. 33–4; *Statuti della Mirandola*, pp. 121–2.
[32] At Lodi, unusually, the woman was disinherited: *Statuta et ordinamenta civitatis Laude*, p. 39.
[33] *Statuti di Treviso*, I, p. 376.

when the brothers or other kinsmen delayed her marriage beyond the age of fourteen (Osimo), fifteen (Camerino) or eighteen (Parma, Faenza, Lodi), she was allowed to marry without their consent and without penalty.[34] There were, though, some conditions attached: at Faenza there had to be at least ten witnesses to the marriage from the girl's neighbourhood; at Camerino the marriage had to take place in a city church (very unusual), in the presence of the *podestà* (chief judge) and civic councillors. Some cities allowed the mother to consent, if there was no father living; others created a hierarchy of consenting kin in which mothers were placed after paternal grandfathers or brothers,[35] or were excluded altogether if they had remarried.[36]

Even more significant is the geographical variety in the incidence and type of such legislation on matrimonial consent. There was little legislative concern in these matters (or regarding other crimes against marriage) in Piedmont.[37] In Tuscany too it appears markedly attenuated. The laws on consent at Lucca and Arezzo were relatively short and simple.[38] At Siena a statute penalized only matrimony without two or three suitable witnesses.[39] Most surprisingly of all, there was no law on consent at Florence: the city that legislated more volubly than most on so many other aspects of social life was silent here.[40] Is this silence, which conforms to other archaic features of marriage practices in Florence, to be explained by the persistence there of the Lombard institution of the *mun-*

---

[34] *Statuta Camerini*, p. 250; *Statuta Faventiae*, p. 166; *Statuta communis Parmae* (4 vols., Parma, 1855–9), I, p. 290 (law of 1241); *Il codice osimano*, I, p. 228; *Statuta et ordinamenta civitatis Laude*, p. 39.

[35] *Statuta Vincentie*, p. 89v; *Statuti della Mirandola*, p. 121; *Statuti di Ascoli*, p. 89; *Statuta patavina*, p. 115v.

[36] *Statuti di Pisa*, I, p. 362; *Tertium volumen*, p. 33.

[37] *Statuti del comune di Ivrea*, ed. G. S. Pene-Vidari (3 vols., Turin, 1968–74); *Gli statuti del comune di Torino del 1360*, ed. D. Bizzari (Turin, 1933); *Codex statutorum Alexandrinae*; *Statuta communitatis Novariae anno MCCLXXVII lata*, ed. A. Ceruti (Novara, 1879); *Statuta civitatis Novariae* [1460] (Novara, 1583); 'Statuti del comune di Chieri', in L. Cibrario, *Delle storie di Chieri libri quattro* (2 vols., Turin, 1827), II; *Decreta Sabaudie ducalia*.

[38] *Statuto di Arezzo*, p. 243; *Statutum lucani communis*, p. 137.

[39] *Costituto di Siena*, I, p. 252. Though later jurists referred to a Sienese law imposing a penalty on those who married women under twenty-five without the consent of two agnates (Nicolaus de Tudeschis, *De sponsalibus et matrimoniis* (*Lectura quarti libri decretalium*) (Venice, 1473), p. 2v), this does not appear to be included in *L'ultimo statuto della repubblica di Siena (1545)*, ed. M. Ascheri (Siena, 1993).

[40] *Statuto del podestà*; *Statuti populi et communis Florentiae anno salutis MCCCCXV* (3 vols., 'Friburgi', 1778–83). And see D. Lombardi, 'Intervention by church and state in marriage disputes in sixteenth- and seventeenth-century Florence', in *Crime, Society and the Law in Renaissance Italy*, ed. T. Dean and K. J. P. Lowe (Cambridge, 1994), p. 151, n. 17. Note that Klapisch-Zuber's assertion that Florence issued decrees regarding marriage (that *sponsalia* take place in church) is not borne out by the texts quoted: C. Klapisch-Zuber, 'Zacharie, ou le père évincé. Les rites nuptiaux toscans entre Giotto et le concile de Trente', *Annales*, 34 (1974), p. 1225, n. 53.

dualdus (a protector or tutor of women, without whose consent they could not enter into any legal contract)?[41] By contrast, outside Tuscany laws on consent were made harsher and stricter in the fifteenth century. At Padua a new law was issued in 1420 appointing as penalty on the woman a loss of dowry and thirty days' imprisonment on bread and water, and on the man a fine and a year in prison.[42] At Verona, the penalties, having been fixed and financial in the 1276 statutes, were made discretionary and mixed (that is, corporal and pecuniary) in 1475.[43] At Belluno, another city under Venetian rule, a new law, apparently of 1424, remarked that the previous financial penalty gave 'incentive to do wrong', and provided a new penalty of death for abductors and their accomplices.[44] The duke of Ferrara responded to complaints about the many marriages 'that are made secretly and dishonestly', by making prosecution easier: no longer was it possible only through the father's accusation, but it could be instigated also through denunciation or inquisition.[45] This was to make clandestine marriage a matter of public and official concern. At Ferrara's subject town of Adria, the statutes of 1442 directed that the penalty for abduction should be that for sexual violence, namely death and confiscation of property.[46] Finally, at Bologna, the new statutes of 1454 declared that 'we know from experience that under the pretext of ample dowry or hoped-for inheritance or succession, marriages are contracted in great number by young men without the consent of their kinsmen, from which it often happens that grave disorders are raised up, and even enmities and homicides follow'. To prevent these evils, the new law required all marriages to women under twenty-two years to have the consent of fathers or other kinsmen (or the mother, in their default), and set penalties on the groom (death if the woman was forced), the bride (loss of dowry), the marriage broker (L. 500), recording notary (L. 200) and witnesses (L. 100).[47] This trend towards severity then flowed into Emperor Charles V's legislation, which punished such marriages with death and confiscation.[48]

There was also anxiety over the consequences of broken betrothals. The same Bolognese statutes asserted that enmities, woundings and

---

[41] *Ibid.*; T. Kuehn, '*Cum consensu mundualdi*: legal guardianship of women in Quattrocento Florence', *Viator*, 13 (1982).
[42] *Statuta patavina*, pp. 115–v. The same law was issued at Brescia: *Leges Brixianae*, cl. 72.
[43] *Statuti veronesi*, p. 426; *Statuta Verone*, III.44.
[44] *Statutorum magnificae civitatis Belluni libri quatuor* (Venice, 1747), p. 227 (III.41). The statutes are dated to 1456 in Del Giudice, *Storia del diritto*, I, pt 2, p. 591.
[45] Ferrara, Archivio di Stato, Archivio storico comunale, Libro delle provvigioni statutarie 1457–91, fol. 45v.
[46] Pertile, *Storia*, v, p. 518, n. 26.
[47] Bologna, Archivio di Stato (ASBo), Comune, Statuti, XVI, fols. 45–v.
[48] Pertile, *Storia*, III, p. 295.

killings resulted from multiple betrothal of girls by their parents: henceforth, a girl, once promised as bride to one man, could not be promised to
another.[49] This concern was shared too at Modena and at nearby Carpi.
This was more clearly stated at Carpi, where additions to the law in 1446
instituted penalties for clandestine marriage and for the breaking-off of
'sponsalia de futuro', with the aim of supporting honesty and good mores,
avoiding 'contentions and scandals', and of ensuring that betrothals be
made more cautiously and unmade less easily.[50] For Modena, Borso
d'Este approved in 1454 the local draft of a new law that penalized
abduction with hanging, 'even if, before the abduction, the woman contracted per verba de futuro with the abductor, with the consent of her
father or other kinsmen unless, after the abduction, she contracted matrimony per verba de presenti or carnally consummated it' (and in that case
a fine was still payable for the abduction).[51] The Modenese city government thus sought to prevent the irregularity of betrothal and abduction
not followed by matrimony: a once-betrothed and abducted daughter was
an offence both to her father's authority and to that of her intended
husband.

In northern Italy, these statutes seem to cluster in the middle decades
of the fifteenth century, and we must doubtless look to the specific
social and economic conditions of those years to explain them. However, it is worth noting that all these laws were preceded by a full
century by legislation in the south. For in 1332 King Robert of Naples
issued an edict eloquently forbidding 'lascivious and insolent young
men' of the city of Naples from the 'abominable corruption' of abducting young girls from their fathers' houses, or kissing them in public
places, by which they subverted the proper procedure, divinely ordained
and parentally controlled, for arranging marriage. Like the duke of
Ferrara later, King Robert ordered that judges prosecute offenders ex
officio, even if no accusation was laid. His penalties were severe: loss of
property or inheritance, for the man; loss of dowry and inheritance, for
the woman.[52]

All these examples show how marriage and its discontents were charac-
teristically treated as a public order matter by the secular authorities, in

[49] *Ibid.*, p. 236, quoting 1454 statutes, I.136. Cf. *Digest*, 48.5.12.7: 'Quaerebatur an iure
mariti possit accusare vir eam feminam quae, cum ei desponsa fuisset, alii in matrimonium a patre fuisset tradita'.
[50] *Statuta Carpi*, pp. 105–7.
[51] *Statuta criminalia* (Modena, 1487), fol. 197 (10 Jan. 1454). Cf. *Codex Iustinianus*, 9.13,
which specified that the death penalty applied to 'etiam eum, qui saltem sponsam suam
per vim rapere ausus fuerit'.
[52] *Capitula regni Siciliae* (Naples, 1551), pp. 71–2; A. Marongiu, 'La forma religiosa del
matrimonio nel diritto del regno di Napoli', in Marongiu, *Byzantine, Norman, Swabian
and later Institutions in Southern Italy* (London, 1972), pp. 8–9.

contrast to the moral concerns of the church. Such secular legislation also ran counter to the canon law of marriage, according to which matrimony was contracted by free consent of the couple. No other consent was necessary to form a valid union; the formation of marriage should be free of any restriction imposed by parents, lords or governments. Yet within a few decades of the full enunciation of this principle by Popes Alexander III and Innocent III, Italian cities began to row in the opposite direction, to preserve or recover some parental control,[53] and as the decades passed, those efforts against the canonical current intensified. No sooner had the period of ecclesiastical legislation on these matters closed, with the *Decretals* of 1234,[54] than the period of secular legislation began. Such insistence on the requirement of parental consent was supported too by the academic civil lawyers: by the early thirteenth century, they had reinterpreted their Roman-law texts to allow for the canonical position that consent alone made a marriage, but still insisted that such consent include that of the parents, as well as that of the couple.[55] In the late fourteenth century, the renowned jurist Baldus opined that statutes punishing those who married without paternal consent were valid, because such action was 'against good mores' and 'creates capital hatred'.[56]

The validity of such statutes – and specifically that at Bologna – was in fact a matter of academic debate in the mid-fourteenth century. 'By statute of the city of Bologna, a penalty is imposed on anyone who contracts matrimony with a daughter in her father's power [*filiafamilias*] without her father's consent', one treatise on betrothal and matrimony expounds, in asking whether an ecclesiastical judge could stop a secular judge from proceeding in such a case.[57] At Bologna the conclusion was that the ecclesiastical judge could not, and that such statutes were indeed valid. The debate, however, continued elsewhere. Baldus, making what was a common distinction between substance and form, argued for validity on the grounds that the statute did not prevent the substance of matrimony, but merely punished bad behaviour [*malos mores*] and the

---

[53] As, too, early thirteenth-century *coutumes* in southern France: J. M. Turlan, 'Recherches sur le mariage dans la pratique coutumière (XIIe–XVIe s.)', *Revue historique du droit français et étranger*, ser. 4, 35 (1957), p. 488, n. 34.

[54] G. Le Bras, 'Mariage', *Dictionnaire de théologie catholique* (Paris, 1926), IX, col. 2163.

[55] C. Donahue, 'The case of the man who fell into the Tiber: the Roman Law of marriage at the time of the Glossators', *American Journal of Legal History*, 22 (1978); M. Bellomo, *La condizione giuridica della donna in Italia. Vicende antiche e moderne* (Turin, 1970), pp. 53–4.

[56] *Tractatus illustrium . . . iuris consultorum* (alias *Tractatus universi juris*) (18 vols., Venice, 1584), II, p. 103; but cf. p. 130v where he acknowledges that political prohibition of marriage (for example, the Florentine statute forbidding marriage with certain hostile Tuscan families) 'might seem to go against the freedom of matrimony'.

[57] 'Tractatus . . . de sponsalibus et matrimoniis . . . Ioannis Brunelli', in *Tractatus*, IX, p. 20v, no. 4 (rehearsing the debate as reported by Johannes Andreae).

sowers of delinquency.[58] Numerous civil lawyers concurred, arguing 'that
more trouble [*inconvenientia*] can come from the contrary opinion than
from this one'.[59]

However, not all jurists agreed. The influential canon-lawyer Johannes
Andreae (d. 1348) was opposed; so too later was Johannes Brunelli.[60] The
latter, drawing on the opinion of Johannes Andreae, thought that the
arguments used to support such law were 'not very convincing' (*parum
urgentia*). These were: that the statute was in agreement with civil law;
that it applied not to the substance of matrimony, but only to its form;
that divine law can be limited by human law; that the father can take
advice for his children, especially as women often act against their own
interests; and that it is possible to legislate in 'prohibited matters', by
strengthening the common law with added penalty. Canon lawyers would
of course have had little difficulty in proving that divine law could not be
limited by human law, while most of the other arguments failed in face of
the rule that matrimony should be free of restriction. The opinion of
Johannes Andreae seems to have become a classic statement, used and
repeated by later commentators: 'such statutes are not valid, as by them
matrimony, which must be free, is inhibited and because laymen cannot
legislate regarding matrimony'.[61]

Some lawyers acknowledged defeat. Baldus's own brother, Angelus,
admitted that 'matrimony is a spiritual thing, and civil law does not
determine the substance of spirituality'; and though in the imperial past
civil law had done so, 'today determination in spiritual matters belongs
to the church alone, therefore all civil laws on the substance and essence
of matrimony, which are contrary to canon law, are abrogated'.[62] The
same objection had been made to Emperor Frederick II's various laws
on matrimony (prohibiting secret, informal marriage, or baronial marriages without his consent, or inter-racial marriages):[63] Andrea de Isernia
(d. circa 1316), responding to apologists for such legislation, commented
that 'some others say, and more accurately, that the secular prince cannot legislate at all regarding matrimony, whether of the substance or of
incidentals'. Frederick's attempt, he continued, to prohibit matrimony,
which was made in heaven, would ensure the destruction of his own

[58] 'Baldi perusini . . . tractatus . . . de statutis', in *Tractatus*, II, p. 103.
[59] 'Tractatus . . . Ioannis Brunelli', p. 20v.
[60] 'Tractatus'; Marongiu, 'La forma religiosa del matrimonio', pp. 9–10.
[61] Nicolaus de Tudeschis, *De sponsalibus et matrimoniis*, p. 2v; Nicolaus de Tudeschis, *Consilia* (1474), *consilium* 12.
[62] *Consilia D. Angeli de Ubaldis perusini* (Frankfurt, 1575), p. 17v, *consilium* 29; and see p. 60, *consilium* 92. See also J. Kirshner, '*Mulier alibi nupta*', in *Consilia im späten Mittelalter*, ed. I. Baumgärtner (Sigmaringen, 1995), pp. 164–5.
[63] *Constitutiones regni Siciliae per Andream de Ysernia comentatae* (Naples, 1552), pp. 296, 298–9, 300.

soul; and matrimony had to be free, and could not in any way be impeded, even indirectly.[64]

Through all these laws, on adultery, bigamy, 'rape' and marriage, social factors were present in the determination of penalty. It was not envisaged that the laws be applied equally to all, or be open to all to use. Three distinctions are especially noticeable: between city and countryside, between respectable and low society, and between interested parties and outsiders. Penalties were much reduced for adulteries, abductions and fornications when committed by peasants, rather than by citizens.[65] Peasant marriages were worth less and required less protection from the law. Second, women were commonly differentiated: between those leading 'honest' and those leading 'indecent' lives, with virgins, wives and widows in the former category, and servants, slaves and prostitutes in the latter.[66] The definition of 'honesty' was, of course, the restriction of a woman's sexuality to a matrimonial relationship: 'a woman is to be understood to be of good life, if she lives in the same house as her husband';[67] the definition of a 'dishonest' woman given in one statute-book was the same as the definition of a public prostitute in another (being 'known' by two or more men).[68] Last, prosecution of these crimes was often limited to those cases in which injured parties (principally the woman, or her husband or father) presented an accusation; and prosecution ex officio and by inquisition was sometimes specifically excluded.[69] However, the tendency seems to have been for these distinctions and restrictions to fall away: the lesser penalties for rural crimes occur in earlier statutes; the path to prosecution was sometimes opened up to denunciations by other parties or to official action.[70] This tendency was also present in actual prosecution, as we shall see.

In Bologna, the new law on parental consent to marriage had three levels of justification. First, experience: in other words the law purported to address a perceived contemporary problem. Second, the motivation of

---

[64] *Ibid.*, pp. 296, 298.
[65] *Statuti di Bologna 1245–1267*, I, pp. 264–5; *Statutum lucani communis*, pp. 136, 138–9; *Statuti di Treviso*, I, pp. 427, 430.
[66] *Statuta Carpi*, p. 68; *Statuto del podestà*, p. 229; *Statuta Genuae*, p. 9v; *Statuti di Pisa*, p. 363; *Statuto di Montepulciano*, pp. 189–90; *Statutum lucani communis*, pp. 138–9. Cf. Pertile, *Storia*, v, pp. 518–19.
[67] *Statuta patavina*, pp. 187–8.
[68] *Statuti della Mirandola*, p. 93; *Statuta Cremonae*, p. 30v.
[69] *Statuto di Arezzo*, p. 212; *Statuta Camerini*, p. 255; *Statutum lucani communis*, p. 136; *Statuti di Sarzana*, p. 111; *Statuta Saone*, p. 15; *Statuta Cremonae*, p. 30v; *Leges Brixianae*, cl. 67; *Aegidianae constitutiones* (Venice, 1605), p. 299 (IV.69); *Statutorum Belluni libri*, p. 228. Cf. Pertile, *Storia*, v, p. 527, who advances this as a general rule on the basis of the Belluno statutes.
[70] As in Ferrara and Naples, above; also *Aegidianae constitutiones*, p. 300 (IV.70); *Statuta civitatis Ast.* (n.p., n.d., but 1534) [1379], p. 29v.

young men: they were contracting marriages secretly in the hope of large dowry or inheritance. Third, there was the danger of enmities and homicides that followed such disobedient and incontinent behaviour. Similar reasoning supported similar laws elsewhere: at Camerino, 'avarice and inordinate appetite to possess' led men into marriages 'which cannot be thought equal and suitable';[71] in the March of Ancona, men, 'impelled by lust or drawn by cupidity for property', harassed single women, 'under the pretext of matrimony', and provoked parents into violent revenge;[72] at Trent, young girls with expectations of a 'good, fat patrimony', were abducted and married by men acting 'not out of heat for their persons or *parentelle*, but for their patrimonies, in contempt of *parentelle* and of superiority'.[73]

Such thinking needs to be put into a number of different contexts. First, legislators were not alone in seeing marriage choices as a source of conflict and disorder. Chroniclers, too, presented major episodes of fighting within cities and between families as arising from disputes over marriage, especially broken marriage promises.[74] Second, these new laws represented an attempt by states and regimes to bolster paternal authority and to discipline what they saw as the fickle and mercenary attitudes of young males to matrimony. How far the law-makers were acting at the behest of fathers, though, is a difficult question. Fathers had a dual, and often contradictory role: their interests as parents of daughters were different from their interests as parents of sons. It would also be wrong to interpret these new laws solely as the product of tension between parents and children. There were other stimuli to lawmaking: it is well known, for example, that itinerant preachers of the fifteenth century often incited city councils to issue fresh enactments in important moral areas.[75] The special mention of lust and avarice in preambles, and of the need for parity between the couple, certainly suggests a clerical influence,[76] and attunes with some preachers' attitudes to the 'marriage market'.[77] But would preachers really recommend

---

[71] *Statuta Camerini*, p. 249.

[72] *Aegidianae constitutiones*, pp. 301–2 (law of 1510).

[73] *Statuta civitatis Tridenti*, III.68.

[74] See T. Dean, 'Marriage and mutilation: Italian medieval vendetta', forthcoming in *Past and Present*.

[75] See, for example, A. Rizzi, 'Il gioco fra norma laica e proibizione religiosa: l'azione dei predicatori fra Tre e Quattrocento', and C. Cardinali, 'Il santo e la norma: Bernardino da Siena e gli statuti perugini del 1425', in *Gioco e giustizia nell'Italia di Comune*, ed. G. Ortalli (Treviso and Rome, 1993).

[76] San Bernardino da Siena warned those intending to marry to avoid three bad intentions, namely *cupiditas*, *carnalitas* and *malignitas*: 'Tractatus de nubere volentium doctrina ex sermonibus beati Bernardini Aquilani': *Tractatus*, IX, p. 113v. He also argued for parity of age and social rank.

[77] Paton, *Preaching Friars*, pp. 219–20, 227–8.

something so obviously uncanonical as restriction of the *libertas matri-monii?*

The turn towards severity in legislation on sex-crime and matrimony might have another origin. With a few exceptions (Naples, Savona), severity is a feature of new laws issued in the long period of social and economic 'crisis' that followed the Black Death of 1348. It is tempting to argue that law-makers were responding to adolescent male impatience caused by economic and demographic instability: economic difficulty forced men to delay marriage; the rising ages at first marriage, compounded by gender imbalances in the population, increased the pool of women available for marriage; dowry inflation whetted the appetites of unmarried youths. The ruling classes as husbands and fathers reacted by hedging their daughters with new penal laws. Certainly the laws' depiction of young men rushing into marriage at the prospect of large dowry connects with rising levels of dowry. However, modern study of these pressures, of rising marriage ages, dowry inflation and gender imbalance, has so far largely limited itself to the major cities of the peninsula, and in particular to Florence: the one city where, as we have seen, there was no law requiring parental consent.[78] Moreover, increasing severity of penalty, the decline of accusation and the rise of official prosecution were general phenomena in late medieval legislation and law-enforcement.[79] And, of course, the period of post-plague crisis can hardly be stretched as far as to catch new laws of the second half of the fifteenth century.

A further possible explanation lies in the growth of state power and of bourgeois officialdom. Such factors have been drawn in evidence to explain new legislation in sixteenth-century France that first required parental consent to marriage, on pain of disinheritance, and then threatened children who disobeyed with the new capital offences of *rapt de violence* or *rapt de séduction*. Such laws, it is suggested, served the interests of the new class of law-trained office-holders allowing them to consolidate their family property.[80] The similarity of this mid-sixteenth-century legislation in France to that of mid-fifteenth-century Italy is manifest. It is not clear, however, that the explanation is satisfactory, even

[78] D. Herlihy and C. Klapisch-Zuber, *Les Toscans et leurs familles: une étude du catasto florentin de 1427* (Paris, 1978), pp. 195–6, 204–9, 394–418; R. M. Smith, 'The people of Tuscany and their families in the fifteenth century: medieval or Mediterranean?', *Journal of Family History*, 6 (1986).
[79] T. Dean, 'Criminal justice in mid-fifteenth-century Bologna', in *Crime, Society and the Law*, pp. 17–20, 30–2.
[80] S. Hanley, 'Family and state in early modern France: the marriage pact', in *Connecting Spheres: Women in the Western World, 1500 to the Present*, ed. M. J. Boxer and J. H. Quataert (New York, 1987).

for France: it ignores the tradition of local customary law, which also prescribed disinheritance for clandestine marriage;[81] it presumes that an office-holding elite was the creation of the sixteenth century; it supposes that such an elite was the main motivator and beneficiary of such legislation; and it offers an overly materialistic reading of juristic ideology, and of the reasoning in favour of such laws.

If neither preaching, nor demography, nor office-holding seem to offer satisfactory explanations for increased legal severity regarding clandestine marriage, perhaps more might be revealed through study of the activity of the secular courts in a single city. Here it is proposed to examine the development of prosecutions in Bologna. If we look in the long term at the incidence of prosecutions related to marriage, in the central criminal court, we find a fairly consistent number of cases of bigamy, incest, rape and mistress-keeping, but the figures for adultery and abduction go through an interesting inversion between the late fourteenth and mid-fifteenth centuries. In the 1390s, in addition to prosecutions for rape, bigamy, incest, keeping a mistress and spouse-killing, there are twelve cases of adultery, but only one case of abduction.[82] A similar pattern emerges for the 1380s.[83] By contrast, in the 1440s, there were again some cases of rape, bigamy and wife-killing, but now thirteen prosecutions of abduction, and only one of adultery.[84] The following decade presents

---

[81] Turlan, 'Recherches'.
[82] All following manuscripts are in ASBo, Comune, Curia del podestà, Inquisitiones, unless otherwise stated. One case of incest (Inq., 275, reg. 6, fol. 61), one of abduction (267, reg. 2, fol. 108v), three of bigamy (261, reg. 6, fol. 57; 267, reg. 1, fol. 67; 267, reg. 2, fol. 165), three of husband-killing (257, reg. 1, fol. 36; 259, reg. 4, fol. 42; 274, reg. 1, fol. 54), six of mistress-keeping (257, reg. 1, fol. 54; 261, reg. 6, fol. 29; 267, reg. 1, fol. 30; 268, fol. 109; 269, reg. 1, fol. 78; 274, reg. 6, fol. 152), seven of rape (262, reg. 1, fol. 118; 264, reg. 1, fols. 20, 51; 266, reg. 1, fol. 263; 267, reg. 1, fol. 34; 273, reg. 1, fol. 102; 274, reg. 6, fol. 122), eleven of wife-killing (257, reg. 2, fol. 8; 258, reg. 3, fol. 59; 259, reg. 2, fol. 53; 261, reg. 2, fol. 53; 261, reg. 4, fols. 34, 44; 266, reg. 1, fol. 55; 267, reg. 2, fol. 95; 269, reg. 1, fol. 1016 [*sic* ‡ 116]; 274, reg. 1, fol. 131; 275, reg. 3, fol. 44; 275, reg. 6, fol. 2), and twelve of adultery (257, reg. 5, fols. 2, 19; 258, reg. 3, fol. 45; 263, reg. 4, fol. 74; 264, reg. 1, fol. 43; 266, reg. 2, fol. 30; 269, reg. 2, fol. 84; 270, reg. 1, fol. 103; 273, reg. 1, fol. 64; 273, reg. 3, fol. 38; 274, reg. 2, fol. 67; 274, reg. 5, fol. 28).
[83] One case of incest (253, reg. 4, fol. 108), one of abduction (254, fol. 37), two of rape (238, reg. 8, fol. 79; 241, reg. 1, fol. 230), four of mistress-keeping, two of which involve abduction (237, reg. 5, fol. 104; 239, reg. 2, fol. 151; 239, reg. 3, fol. 136; 244, reg. 2, fol. 169), eight of wife-killing (238, reg. 9, fols. 132, 138; 239, reg. 2, fol. 111; 239, reg. 4, fol. 59; 241, reg. 1, fol. 142; 241, reg. 3, fol. 105; 242, reg. 2, fol. 30; 244, 1 June), and eight of adultery (236, reg. 4, fols. 83, 107; 240, reg. 2, fol. 82; 240, reg. 6, fol. 188; 245, reg. 2, fol. 59; 249, reg. 4, fol. 118; 253, reg. 4, fols. 31, 36–7).
[84] One case of bigamy (353, reg. 1, fol. 32), three of incest (346, reg. 2, fol. 71; 352, reg. 1, fol. 156; Capitano del popolo, reg. 867, fol. 9), two of rape (348, reg. 1, fol. 37; 349, reg. 2, fol. 110), five of spouse-killing (348, reg. 2, fols. 3, 89; 349, reg. 3, fol. 4; 353, reg. 2, fol. 68; 347, reg. 2, fol. 15), thirteen of abduction (345, reg. 1, fol. 40; 347, reg. 2, fols. 2, 16, 29; 349, reg. 1, fol. 73; 349, reg. 2, fols. 78, 81; 352, reg. 1, fol. 33; 353, reg. 1, fols. 51, 108; 353, reg. 2, fols. 110, 224; 353, reg. 2 (II), fol. 20), and one of adultery (346, reg. 1, fol. 82).

similar figures.[85] It might be objected that this difference is merely one of labelling, that adultery was likely to involve the removal ('extraction') of the wife from the matrimonial home, and that the same type of criminal action was prosecuted as adultery in one decade and as abduction in another. These objections do not stand: first because most adulteries, according at least to the indictment, took place *in* the matrimonial home, while the husband was absent; second, because abductions in the mid-fifteenth century usually had as their object the daughter, not the wife. The difference is clear: the court was acting to punish injuries to husbands at the end of the fourteenth century, and injuries to fathers in the mid-fifteenth.

It might also be objected that the court and its jurisdiction changed between the late fourteenth and the mid-fifteenth century. Were adultery cases dealt with in a different tribunal in the later period? The only other secular court was that of the *Capitano del popolo*, but this mainly dealt with more physical and direct affronts to public security (conspiracy, brigandage and so forth) and with adultery cases only when compounded with murder.[86] The obvious alternative tribunal was the episcopal court, but little is known about the activity of ecclesiastical courts in Bologna or elsewhere in Italy.[87] However, it seems unlikely that the episcopal court would lay claim to adultery cases without also laying claim to bigamy. In fact, although the bishop's vicar did claim one difficult bigamy case in 1448,[88] only three years later the cardinal legate put aside an episcopal claim to two other cases on the grounds that 'the secular judge, by both common law and the municipal law of Bologna, can punish adulterers and bigamists, and that the *podestà* preceded the ecclesiastical judge in prosecuting, and consequently should not be prevented from exercising his office'.[89] There is no indication that the pattern of prosecution in the court of the *podestà* had any relation to the activity or inactivity of the bishop's court.

Four examples of abduction, all from the 1440s, will help explore the

---

[85] One case of incest (361, reg. 1, fol. 73), one of rape (363, fol. 225), two of bigamy (357, fols. 81, 83), two of mistress-keeping (355, reg. 1, fols. 80, 117), three of spouse-killing (361, reg. 1, fols. 78, 128; 361, reg. 2, fol. 119), three of adultery (361, reg. 1, fol. 193; 362, reg. 2, fol. 55; 355, reg. 2/3, fol. 146) and seven of abduction (355, reg. 1, fols. 85, 92, 135; 355, reg. 2/3, fols. 26, 59, 88; 360, reg. 1, fol. 114; 361, reg. 2, fol. 195; 362, reg. 1, fol. 68).
[86] Giudici del Capitano del popolo, regs. 821–43 (1384–96) and 866–9 (1441–6), *passim*. For rare adultery cases: reg. 838, fols. 39, 43.
[87] Cf. G. A. Brucker, 'Ecclesiastical courts in fifteenth-century Florence and Fiesole', *Mediaeval Studies*, 53 (1991), pp. 245–5.
[88] The twice-married woman argued that her first husband had deceived her – he was a professed friar and soon left her – and that she had taken learned advice before remarrying: Inq., 353, reg. 1, fols. 32–4.
[89] Inq., 357, fols. 81–5.

nature of this crime. In the first, from 1441, four men were prosecuted for abducting a girl from outside her father's house in the *contado*, and for bringing her to the city where, against her father's will, she married one of them. This prosecution was, however, annulled by the government on receipt of (allegedly) more truthful information: that the indicted men were her relatives, that they were acting to her benefit, that she had called them to defend her, that they acted with the consent of her mother.[90] It is difficult to see which version contains more of the truth: evidently the girl had been removed from her father's control, but the combined forces of her mother and male kin persuaded the government that this was not truly a case of abduction. In the second case, from 1442, three men, including one Biagio, went to a field, where they found Chelda, described in the trial record as a virgin: she was at a well, while her father was in an adjacent vineyard. One of the three said to the father, 'It seems to me that you don't intend to fulfil what you promised, to give your daughter as wife to Biagio, who is here.' 'No', replied the father, 'I don't want to, as I have heard ill of him.' Upon which reply, the three men seized Chelda, and took her to another village, where she married Biagio.[91] Here we clearly have the father's control of his daughter being successfully challenged after he tried to renege on a promise of marriage. Marriage also occurs in the third case, also from 1442, in which a group of four men from Minerbio, including one Benedetto, seized a fatherless woman called Margarita, against her will, hitting her with their hands. They took her to a house, where Benedetto hit her twice across the face and 'violently and by force married her and placed the ring on her finger'. She, refusing to consent, took off the ring and threw it to the floor.[92] This case is clearly different: there is no father, the woman does not consent, and violence is used against her. She really was abducted in the modern understanding of the term. In the fourth prosecution, two men, the sons of craftsmen, were accused of going at night to the city house of Matteo Garsendini, in which a young girl, Caterina, lived as Matteo's servant. They 'seduced and extracted' her, with her consent, 'raped' her and kept her for several days. At the same time, they stole from Matteo's house a long list of bed-linen, house-linen, women's clothes and jewels.[93] In this case, the nature of their plunder – the typical contents of a bride's trousseau – suggests that this is not rape, but clandestine marriage in the absence of the father.

These four cases contain most of the essential typological elements of abduction prosecutions. In some there is a previous, unfulfilled marriage-promise by the father, and a band of men, sometimes perhaps looking like a wedding party, take the daughter away by force for the marriage to be

---

[90] Dean, 'Criminal justice in Bologna', p. 34.   [91] Inq., 349, reg. 1, fol. 73.
[92] Inq., 349, reg. 2, fol. 81.   [93] Inq., 353, reg. 1, fol. 51 (1448).

contracted.[94] This is clearly stated in one prosecution in 1462, in which thirteen armed men seized a young girl at night and presented her to another man: 'I have brought you Lucia, your betrothed', said their ring-leader, 'promised to you by Niccolò Aldrovandi and his kinsmen, because we intend that the promises made to you should be observed.'[95] In other cases, the abduction happens with the girl as a willing, even perhaps organizing, party, and either to escape her father, or to make (or make public) a clandestine marriage. 'You have married me in secret. I want you to marry me in public before these people', said one young woman (*domicella*), taken by her 'abductor' to his father's house.[96] In one case a witness stated that the girl had resolved to go with her abductor, or with anyone else, 'as it best turned out'.[97] Sometimes, girls were the objects of rivalry, even fighting, between sets of relatives.[98] These could be closely or distantly related.[99] When an age is mentioned for abducted girls, it is always thirteen or fourteen, the very moment when they entered marriageability.[100] Such contention for control of a girl's marriage suggests a relative shortage of nubile females.

The scene in these abduction cases is most often the countryside, not the town.[101] The case comes to the *podestà*'s court not through accusation by the father, but through official denunciation or inquisition. The few cases of abduction of a wife are swamped by the majority of prosecutions for abduction of daughters.[102] These girls are mostly peasants, not the daughters of citizens. The father is often an absent figure: the girl lives with her mother or is a servant in the house of her uncle or of some other man.[103] 'The role of uncles in the life of the poor should not be underestimated.'[104] The abductors too are usually inhabitants of the *contado*, or come from just over the border with Bologna's neighbouring cities.[105] In

[94] Inq., 349, reg. 2 (II), fol. 20 (1449).   [95] Inq., 364, reg. 1, fol. 54.
[96] Inq., 353, reg. 1, fols. 108–9v (1448).
[97] 'prout sibi melius accidisset': Inq., 353, reg. 2, fol. 114.
[98] Inq., 355, reg. 2/3, fol. 59 (1450).
[99] *Ibid.*, fol. 110.
[100] Inq., 354, reg. 2 (II), fol. 20; 347, reg. 2, fol. 16; 1468–9, fol. 138; Dean, 'Criminal justice in Bologna', pp. 33–4.
[101] *Contado*: Inq., 237, reg. 5, fol. 104; 239, reg. 2, fol. 151; 267, reg. 2, fol. 108v; 341, reg. 1, fol. 72; 349, reg. 2, fols. 78, 81; 353, reg. 2, fols. 110, 224; 354, reg. 2 (II), fol. 20; 347, reg. 2, fols. 2, 29; 355, reg. 1, fols. 92, 135; 355, reg. 2/3, fol. 59; 360, reg. 1, fol. 114; 364, reg. 1, fols. 54, 58; 1468–9, fols. 115, 138. City: 352, reg. 1, fol. 33; 353, reg. 1, fols. 51, 108; 347, reg. 2, fol. 16; 361, reg. 2, fol. 195; 362, reg. 1, fol. 68; 364, reg. 2, fol. 80; 373, fol. 207.
[102] Wife: 237, reg. 5, fol. 104; 239, reg. 2, fol. 151; 254, fol. 37; 267, reg. 2, fol. 108v; 362, reg. 1, fol. 68; 364, reg. 1, fol. 58.
[103] Inq., 347, reg. 2, fols. 16, 29; 353, reg. 1, fol. 51; 353, reg. 2, fols. 110, 224; 355, reg. 1, fols. 92, 135; 355, reg. 2/3, fols. 59, 88; 361, reg. 2, fol. 195; 373, fol. 207; 1468–9, fol. 115.
[104] L. Stone, *Family, Sex and Marriage in England 1500–1800* (London, 1977), p. 76.
[105] From the territories of Modena or Imola: 354, reg. 2 (II), fol. 20; 355, reg. 2/3, fol. 59; 1468–9, fol. 115.

other words, these prosecutions are part of the city's attempt to discipline the inhabitants of the *contado*,[106] and part of the state's attempt to increase the authority of fathers or, where absent, to replace it.

A similar pattern arises from prosecution of other, related crimes. Thirteen cases of sexual violation survive in the trial records of the late fourteenth century and the mid-fifteenth. Of the six late fourteenth-century trials, four concerned the rape of married women.[107] In contrast, five of the seven mid-fifteenth-century cases related to sexual assault on young girls.[108] A similar pattern seems to have occurred in late medieval Venice.[109] Most of these prosecuted rapes had happened in the *contado*. Trials of rapes committed in the city usually involved outsiders: men from Germany or Milan; Jews.[110] In the case of bigamy trials, the predominance of foreigners is even more marked: of ten cases, six concerned foreigners, men or women from neighbouring cities (Reggio, Pistoia, Florence and so on), who left spouses there and remarried in Bologna.[111] For these crimes, the courts were thus used mainly to control and punish the misdemeanours of the non-citizen world of *contadini* and migrants.

In looking for explanation of these features of the prosecution of sexual/matrimonial offences, we might turn to the history of prostitution in Bologna. For the rise in prosecutions of abduction coincides with a heavier legislative hand set over the public brothel. In 1439, the Bolognese government came under pressure from the officials of the fabric of the new church of San Petronio to remove prostitutes from streets near the church, so as to end the offensive sight of their 'fetid and abominable public displays'. Preachers had often warned, the officials recalled, of God's revenge on the city if the brothel was not removed. The government responded by reiterating a previous order for prostitutes to stay within the bounds of the public brothel, and for the closer regulation of the inns and alleyways surrounding it.[112] This effort to control and enclose prostitutes, by roughly coinciding with moves to discipline extra-marital sexual activity in both town and countryside, allows us to connect the changes in law, giving more power to fathers, to the action of

---

[106] According to S. Cohn, sexual offences were at the forefront of Florentine judicial efforts to 'civilize' its peasantry: 'Sex and violence in the Renaissance', in his *Women in the Streets: Essays on Sex and Power in the Italian Renaissance* (Baltimore, 1996).

[107] Inq., 238, reg. 8, fol. 79; 241, reg. 1, fol. 230; 264, reg. 1, fol. 51; 266, reg. 1, fol. 263; 267, reg. 1, fol. 34; 273, reg. 1, fol. 102.

[108] Inq., 333, reg. 2, fol. 109; 334, reg. 2, fol. 123; 340, reg. 1, fol. 65; 341, reg. 1, fol. 75; 348, reg. 1, fol. 37; 349, reg. 2, fol. 110; 363, fol. 225.

[109] Ruggiero, *Boundaries of Eros*, pp. 96–108.

[110] Inq., 341, reg. 1, fol. 75; 348, reg. 1, fol. 37; 349, reg. 2, fol. 110.

[111] Inq., 238, reg. 8, fol. 51; 244, reg. 2, fol. 41; 248, reg. 4, fol. 55; 261, reg. 6, fol. 57; 267, reg. 1, fol. 67; 267, reg. 2, fol. 165; 341, reg. 2, fol. 43; 353, reg. 1, fol. 32; 357, fols. 81, 83.

[112] Comune, Liber Fantini, fols. 77v–9.

the courts, enforcing a stricter sexual morality against peasants and migrants.

Increasing official prosecution of abduction, sometimes involving clandestine marriage, led eventually to the new legislation of 1454. The new statute may well have been a response to particular cases, or to their quickening rhythm, in the early 1450s. In December 1451 eleven men were prosecuted for making an armed break-in to a house in Anzola and abducting two young girls.[113] In March 1452, eighteen men of Piumazzo and Calcaria were prosecuted for the armed and violent abduction of one girl, and the attempted abduction of another (the alleged fiancée of the gang-leader).[114] In June of the same year, a citizen, Niccolò Procacini, was prosecuted for clandestine marriage with a fatherless girl living with her uncle. 'Driven by carnal desire', the indictment alleged, he had secretly contracted marriage with Dorotea Codebo, a 'domicella intacta', 'not promised or married to any man', and then consummated the marriage, without the knowledge or consent of her uncle or brothers, 'contrary to divine and human laws, without any religious formality, and contrary to the statutes'.[115] The most interesting part of this case is Niccolò's defence. Of his two witnesses, one merely reported hearsay that the marriage had been carried out legitimately, and that Dorotea's uncle had in fact consigned her to Niccolò's mother as his wife, while the other also maintained the opinion that the marriage was done legitimately, adding that, even if what the indictment alleged were true, nevertheless 'statute-law was obviated by the custom that obtained in the city of Bologna, because many women marry without the consent of their kins-men and this can be proved by . . . many citizens who, privately and secretly married their wives'.[116] It was precisely to obliterate such custom that the new statute of 1454 strengthened the legal arm of fathers against sons and daughters; but prosecutions continued to arise, as before, more from the difficult relations between fatherless daughters and the uncles with whom they lived, as one final case shows.

In 1473 Bassotto de' Baciacomari was prosecuted by inquisition for abducting Nicolosia di Giacomo da Minerbio from the house in the city of her uncle, a spicer named Marco di Bartolomeo. Bassotto had allegedly taken her to his father's house nearby and there married her, against Marco's wishes and to his injury and ignominy.[117] Here is the familiar figure of a fatherless country woman, living with her uncle in the city. Though this woman was, according to witnesses for the defence, aged twenty-seven, her uncle still claimed to have 'custody and control' of her and her marriage choice. Her own choice looks rather unequal: Bassotto

[113] Inq., 358, reg. 1, fol. 58.   [114] Ibid., fols. 121–2.   [115] Inq., 358, reg. 2, fol. 37.
[116] Ibid., fol. 38.   [117] Inq., 373, reg. Nov. 1472–Oct. 1473, fol. 207.

was the son of a long-established citizen family;[118] she was an orphan, the niece of an immigrant trader.

Bassotto duly appeared before the *podestà* to deny the charge, and he presented his witnesses.[119] Two of these had been with him on the night of the alleged abduction, and their version of events was significantly different from the indictment: Nicolosia had not been abducted by Bassotto, but had turned up at a neighbour's house and asked him to send for Bassotto to come. 'What are you doing here?', Bassotto asked when he arrived. 'My uncle has chased me out of the house and told me that if I wait until tomorrow morning, he will kill me', she replied. She had earlier told the neighbour's wife a similar tale: 'I have left my uncle's house because I cannot stand it. They are always threatening to beat me, and I can't do anything that pleases them.' Unfortunately, Bassotto was not outwardly pleased to see her, according to this testimony: 'What do you want me to do? Why don't you go to your *parenti*?' he asked her. 'I don't have any', she cried tearfully, 'For the love of God, put me with your mother and sister.' Moved to pity, Bassotto did as she wished, sending her to his mother, where she stayed. But she was ill and infirm and after a week she died. What caused her death is not clear: it was rumoured in the neighbourhood that she had left her uncle because of 'beatings and threats'; but one witness also heard her say that she was pregnant by Bassotto. We might surmise that her uncle had always objected to her friendship with Bassotto, that the fact of her pregnancy had become known to him, and that he had responded by hitting her and expelling her from his house.

At this point Nicolosia's aged step-mother, Lucia, was brought forward to testify, and more of her daughter's unfortunate past was brought to light.[120] Nicolosia's father had died six years previously, entrusting her to his wife's custody. At the time, Lucia promised never to abandon Nicolosia, and to treat her as if she was her own daughter. Her husband told Nicolosia to stay with Lucia and not to stay with any others, warning her 'that if the dead can learn about the living, and you ignore Lucia's orders, I will come to chase you away [*fucare*] with my own hand.' Fear of a ghostly beating had little hold on her, however, for within a few weeks Marco asked if Nicolosia would like to go for a month to a spa with him and his family; her step-mother refused, but when Nicolosia 'began to cry', she consented. Nicolosia obviously at first found her uncle's family more congenial: his daughters were more of her own age and presumably provided livelier company than her lone step-mother. Within time too,

[118] *Corpus chronicorum bononiensium*, ed. A. Sorbelli, *RIS*, second edn, XVIII, pt 1, vol. II, pp. 187, 202, 362; vol. III, pp. 34, 319, 332–3.
[119] Inq., 373, reg. Nov. 1472–Oct. 1473, fols. 222–3v.   [120] *Ibid.*, fol. 242–v.

her step-mother remarried, and Nicolosia quickly moved permanently into her uncle's household. Lucia, though, did not lose contact with Nicolosia, and, according to her own deposition, gave Bassotto permission to marry her, just a few weeks before her alleged abduction. How well Nicolosia had been treated by Marco remained an unresolved issue. One witness produced by Bassotto claimed that Marco and his wife had treated her badly, and that for some months they had been saying they would expel her; whenever he went to eat with them, they insulted and threatened her (*puctana, gaioffa, ribalda*).[121] This was, however, contradicted by other witnesses summoned by the court: Marco and his wife had treated her as they did their own children, 'viz in making her clothes of good cloth, with velvet sleeves'.[122] The quality of parental love of a daughter was thus measured by some in the cloth of her sleeves.[123]

The *podestà* eventually acquitted Bassotto of the charge of abduction.[124] There was insufficient testimony to convict: no witness had actually seen the alleged crime; the most the witnesses could offer was hearsay.[125]

Nicolosia's sad story has elements in common with other cases and other life-histories.[126] Her father had moved to the city when she was a child; no mother is mentioned, presumably she was already deceased. Her father had perhaps failed to find a husband for her, and on his deathbed he tried to ensure that the two women, his new wife and his daughter, stayed together. But piety alone could not keep them: they both looked for husbands. The widow Lucia was more successful, presumably because she reclaimed her dowry. Nicolosia had only her uncle to turn to, but his initial welcome eventually turned to violence and jealousy, when she 'shamed' him by becoming pregnant.[127] What really happened remains unclear: either he threatened to kill her and she ran away to Bassotto, or Bassotto took her, and her uncle lodged a complaint with the *podestà*. As in other cases, relatives rivalled to give consent to the woman's marriage: Lucia had already given hers, but Marco claimed injury when Nicolosia married without his. Fatherless daughters in households appar-

---

[121] *Ibid.*, fol. 245v.   [122] *Ibid.*, fol. 244v–5.
[123] Cf. the means used to recruit women into prostitution: *The Society of Renaissance Florence*, ed. G. Brucker (New York, 1971), pp. 196–8; M. S. Mazzi, 'Il mondo della prostituzione nella Firenze tardo medievale', *Ricerche storiche*, 14 (1984), p. 353.
[124] Inq. 373, reg. Nov. 1472–Oct. 1473, fol. 248v.
[125] *Ibid.*, fol. 245.
[126] C. Klapisch-Zuber, 'La "mère cruelle". Maternité, veuvage et dot dans la Florence des XIVe–XVe siècles', *Annales*, 38 (1983).
[127] See the case of 'Bernardo Machiavelli's pregnant servant', in *Society of Renaissance Florence*, pp. 218–22; T. Kuehn, 'Dispute processing in the Renaissance: some Florentine examples', in Kuehn, *Law, Family and Women: Toward a Legal Anthropology of Renaissance Italy* (Chicago, 1991), pp. 83–8.

ently burdened with girls awaiting marriage were tempted into affairs and clandestine marriage; but not for that did their male relatives allow them freedom to choose.

Thomas Kuehn has warned us that we should use trial records to reconstruct not the history of a love-affair, but rather the history of a trial.[128] The story of Bassotto's trial can help us to connect the two halves of the analysis so far: the issue of new laws by city fathers, and their enforcement largely against non-citizens. For whatever we might try to deduce about the affair between Bassotto and Nicolosia, the signal facts about this prosecution are that it involved a citizen, which was rare, and that it clearly failed. There is thus a distinction to be made between legislation and prosecution. If we look only at the legislation, we might agree with Donahue that the law was being used to strengthen parental, and especially paternal, authority over children's marriages. However, if we look at the pattern of prosecution, we notice, first, that it is country-folk, not citizens, who are mostly prosecuted for abduction/clandestine marriage; second, that the sort of cases that came to court involved not the reinforcement of paternal authority but its replacement (the father was absent, the uncle was not an effective substitute); and third, that the cases came to court not by accusation of the injured party, but by official action, inquisition ex officio. This all means that there was more to prosecution than simple enforcement of the law or parents co-opting the courts in their struggle against self-willed children. Issues of city control of the countryside and of public concern over moral disorder disturb such a neat picture.

It must be added that the evidence of legislation, of prosecution, and of at least one Bolognese witness suggest that there is a problem in the concept of 'family marriage strategies', so frequently espoused by modern historians. If 'marriages are contracted in great number by young men without the consent of their kinsmen', if the custom – even among citizens – was for 'many women' to marry without the consent of their kin, then in what sense did family strategies for the marriage of children exist? Were they really restricted only to the upper classes?

[128] T. Kuehn, 'Reading microhistory: the example of *Giovanni and Lusanna*', *Journal of Modern History*, 61 (1989), pp. 518, 532–3.

5 Marriage ceremonies and the church in Italy after 1215

David d'Avray

They liked to begin a paper with some formula like, 'I want to raise some questions about so-and-so', and seemed to think they had done their intellectual duty by merely raising them. This manoeuvre drove Morris Zapp insane. Any damn fool, he maintained, could think of questions; it was *answers* that separated the men from the boys (David Lodge, *Changing Places*).

Pace Lodge's Morris Zapp, one must sometimes prove that there is a problem before progress can be made. When excellent scholars contradict each other and even themselves on a major issue, without realizing, apparently, that a question is being disputed, then the unconscious argument needs to be brought into the open, even if provisional solutions only can be proposed.

So the question: was the presence of a priest required at a marriage under pain of sin by the general law of the western church after the Fourth Lateran Council (1215)? Note that this is a question about legality and sin, not about validity. It is well known that a simple exchange of consent was enough to make a valid marriage in this period, until the Council of Trent. The marriage could be validly contracted behind a hedge, in a bedroom, in a brothel, or anywhere. Though the church recognized such 'clandestine' marriages, it regarded them as sinful. The problem is: was a marriage clandestine if it was not held in church (or at the church door)? Was it clandestine if no priest was present?

According to Jean Dauvillier, perhaps the leading pre-war historian of medieval marriage law, an ecclesiastical ceremony was obligatory after 1215: 'the celebration of marriage is reserved to the priest, and not to any priest, but to the parish priest'.[1] In the same year, the neglected scholar G. H. Joyce argued that in areas of Italy which came under Lombard law,

---

The whole structure of this paper's argument was recast in the light of suggestions by Dr Kate Lowe, to whom thanks.

[1] J. Dauvillier, *Le mariage dans le droit classique de l'église depuis le Décret de Gratien (1140) jusqu'à la mort de Clement V (1314)* (Paris, 1933), p. 105.

'it was customary to celebrate the wedding with a considerable gathering of friends and acquaintances, but without ecclesiastical ceremony', and that 'This, it was held, might justly be regarded as a marriage *in facie ecclesiae*'.[2]

Joyce implies that outside these parts of Italy the words *in facie ecclesiae* ordinarily signified that the union should be solemnized with the church's ritual.[3] Brundage's extremely learned recent study of the medieval law of marriage draws a similar contrast (adding a class dimension):

Fourteenth- and fifteenth-century English synods insisted that marriage ought to take place in church, which was also the common practice in France. In northern Italy . . . nuptials were usually celebrated in the home, and it was not common for couples to receive the nuptial blessing as part of the wedding rite . . . Clergymen typically played more prominent roles in the weddings of lower-class North Italian couples, for example, than they did in weddings among the upper classes. Wealthy and prominent persons usually had their marital consent witnessed by a notary; their humbler neighbours were much more likely to exchange consent in the presence of a priest.[4]

Whereas Joyce is suggesting that non-ecclesiastical marriages in the parts of Italy he specifies were not breaking any law of the church, Brundage elsewhere says explicitly that 'Canon law . . . did require . . . that the wedding take place publicly, *and that a priest be present to witness their vows and bestow a nuptial blessing on them*'[5] (my italics). Another recent authority, Gaudemet, takes the contrary view for granted. He refers to a later twelfth-century papal decretal which accepts the practice of certain regions by which the couple give their consent in the presence of a notary rather than a priest.[6] Of course, this decretal of Alexander III antedated decree 51 on clandestine marriages of the Fourth Lateran Council. However, Gaudemet seems to assume (rightly, as will be argued below) that the latter decree did not require an ecclesiastical marriage ceremony.[7]

A study by Klapisch-Zuber,[8] which deals specifically with marriage ritual in late medieval Italy, fails to take a clear position on the question posed above. A principal argument of her important paper is that priests

[2] G. H. Joyce, *Christian Marriage: An Historical and Doctrinal Study* (London and New York, 1933), pp. 109–10.
[3] *Ibid.*, p. 109.
[4] J. A. Brundage, *Law, Sex, and Christian Society in Medieval Europe* (Chicago and London, 1987), pp. 502–3.
[5] J. A. Brundage, *Medieval Canon Law* (London and New York, 1995), p. 73.
[6] J. Gaudemet, *Le mariage en Occident. Les moeurs et le droit* (Paris, 1987), pp. 231–2; Joyce also noticed this decretal: *Christian Marriage*, pp. 64, 109 n. 3.
[7] Cf. Gaudemet, *Le mariage*, p. 233.
[8] C. Klapisch-Zuber, 'Zacharie, ou le père évincé. Les rites nuptiaux toscans entre Giotto et le concile de Trente', *Annales*, 34 (1979). The discussion which follows implies no disrespect for a fine historian.

did not normally preside over the marriages of the Tuscan families which she knows so well. Ecclesiastical ritual was conspicuous by its absence. But was this omission a violation of the church's law? Klapisch-Zuber does not say or, rather, she sends out apparently contradictory signals.

On the one hand, she implies that synodal legislation endorsed the practice of letting a notary, rather than a priest, officiate at a marriage.[9] On the other hand, she says that Antonino of Florence, in his *Summa* and in his constitutions of 1455, stresses the obligation to hear mass at a first marriage.[10]

These contradictory pieces of evidence require scrutiny. The evidence for synodal approval of marriage by a notary rather than a priest does not in fact stand up to closer examination. The passage she quotes (from the 1517 Council of Florence) says that no-one shall contract *sponsalitii* either in the future tense or in the present tense without first calling their priest or notary, who will have them exchange a form of words.[11] Taken by itself, this seems to imply that a notary, instead of a priest, could officiate at the exchange of consent which made the couple man and wife. The words which come next in the decree, and which Klapisch-Zuber does not quote, in fact suggest that the ceremony for which priest and notary were interchangeable was not the one at which present consent was exchanged.[12] It was the latter which mattered most. Before it, there was no marriage in the eyes of the church, but after it the marriage bond had been created. (Since the church claimed the authority to define what was a marriage and what was not, and since by the late Middle Ages the laity had on the whole come to recognize this authority, in terms of power the

[9] 'Je ne peux citer qu'une exception à l'absence de prêtre, et cette exception confirme largement la règle! Le 19 septembre 1477, Filippo Strozzi épouse en secondes noces, à la campagne, Vaggia Gianfigliazzi. Le notaire invité à poser les questions et à recueillir les consentements demeure introuvable. Alors, Filippo se rabat sur un prêtre qui se trouve là. On ne saurait mieux dire: le prêtre n'est ici qu'une solution de remplacement. Encore en plein XVIe siècle, les textes statutaires et *législation synodale* chargeront le notaire de ces importantes fonctions' (my italics): Klapisch-Zuber, 'Zacharie', p. 1226.
[10] *Ibid.*
[11] 'Nessuno ardisca contrahere sponsalitii ne de futuro ne de presenti se prima non chiama el prete suo o vero un notaio, el quale faccia le parole tra loro in questa forma' (Concilium Florentinum, 1517, cap. I; J. D. Mansi, *Sacrorum Conciliorum . . . Collectio*, xxxv, col. 247) cit. Klapisch-Zuber, 'Zacharie', p. 1241, n. 55.
[12] 'Antonio, prometti tu alla M. qui presente, che ogni volta che da lei o da suoi sarai richiesto, tu la piglierai per tua moglie; & esso risponda! messer sì. Et dipoi il detto prete o notajo, chiami dua testimonj come cóstoro hanno contracto sponsalia de futuro, il quali si possono dissolvere di consetimento delle parti con la auctorita dell'ordinario. Et acciò che queste cose si habbino ad osservare, condanna in dieci ducati li sposi, la madre, & padre, & tutte quelle persone che si intrametteranno in detti sponsalitii senza questa solennità': Mansi, *Sacr. Conc.*, xxxv, col. 247; cf. R. C. Trexler, *Synodal Law in Florence and Fiesole, 1306–1518* (Vatican City, 1971: Studi e Testi, 268), p. 125.

church's view counted even if lay concepts were less clear-cut.) In short, this passage from the Florentine synod's statutes does not answer our question either way.

Some at least of the contrary evidence to which Klapisch-Zuber refers (perhaps without averting to the tension within her presentation) is also inconclusive. The reference to Antonino's *Summa* is hard to follow up, because incomplete.[13] A couple of passages suggest that, for Antonino, the essential thing from the church's point of view was to be able to prove that the marriage had taken place: if not, a mortal sin was committed.[14] On much the same lines, he implies elsewhere that the presence of witnesses was the crucial thing.[15] These passages do not really contradict others in which he implies that in some regions a first marriage had to be blessed at some point between consent and consummation: he seems to be indicating that this is not a universal obligation.[16]

Klapisch-Zuber also cites synodal statutes. It is clear that Antonino of Florence tried hard through his legislation to make the conjugal mass a part of every first marriage; in particular, he refers to ignorant people who enter into a first marriage without the blessing or the 'messa dil congiunto

---

[13] Klapisch-Zuber, 'Zacharie', p. 1241 note 56, refers to '*Summa*, III, tit. i, *De statu conjugatorum*, fo. 6 et 32 vo.'. She gives no chapter number, so it is difficult to trace the passages she has in mind unless one is using the same edition. She uses the Venice 1582 edition. I have used the following edition: *Sancti Antonini . . . Summa theologica*, ed. P. Ballerinius, 4 pt (Verona, 1740).

[14] 'Septimo nota quod contrahens matrimonium clandestine, ita scilicet quod non possit probari; peccat mortaliter, quia contra praeceptum ecclesiae agit': Antonino, *Summa*, 3. tit. 1, cap. xix, col. 80.

[15] '*De diversis vitiis conjugatorum in genere.* Ex notatis in praecedentibus capitulis, & para-graphis nota summatim vitia tam virorum quam mulierum conjugatorum quae concer-nunt conjugium, & quae mortalia sunt . . . Quarto, quum quis contrahit matrimonium clandestine sine praesentia saltem testium, & quousque manifestum faciat sufficienter, semper est in mortali': Antonino, *Summa*, 3. tit. 1, cap. xxiv, col. 114.

[16] From the same section: 'Undecimo, quando consummant matrimonium ante benedic-tionem nuptiarum, quum benedici debeant, ut quia primum matrimonium' (col. 115); cf. the following passage: 'Dicit etiam Guillelmus, quod in illis locis, ubi consuetum est, quod prius adhibeatur benedictio nuptialis ante consummationem matrimonii, si absque dispensatione hoc utatur conjugio ante ipsam benedictionem & sine justa caussa [*sic*], peccat mortaliter. Sed Richardus in 4 magis declarans dicit, quod quamvis actus conju-galis regulariter sit licitus; tamen aliquo modo vel tempore per accidens potest esse illicitus, & hoc propter scandalum populi, ut in clandestino matrimonio, antequam ecclesiae innotescat, vel propter ecclesiae prohibitionem, quae alicubi [= in some places?] prohibet, conjuges carnaliter commisceri ante solemnitatem matrimonii; quam tamen solempnitatem quidam dicunt observandam, & contrarium faciens prohiberi respectu actus petendi debitum, non respectu reddendi; unde peccaret tunc exigens & non reddens: & licet ante benedictionem huiusmodi exigens mortaliter peccet; tamen pos-tquam semel exigit, non peccabit ulterius secundum quosdam, nisi novo exigat con-temtu. Etiam Thomas in 4 distinct. 33 quaest. 2 ad 3. dicit, quod si sponsa admittat sponsum ad actum conjugalem ante benedictionem, credens eum velle matrimonium consummare; non peccat, nisi signa appareant fraudis expressa, ut sit conditio multum distans propter nobilitatem uel divitias; tamen non tenetur reddere de necessitate': Antonino, *Summa*, 3. tit. 1, cap. 20, col. 90.

secondo à ordinato la sancta chiesa'.[17] This phrase might be taken to imply a general rule for western Christendom, but that might be to lay too much weight on it. It might mean that the church has ordained a special liturgy for a nuptial mass – 'the mass which the holy Church has ordained for marriage'. Or again, it does not have to imply a *general* rule: in his *Summa*, Antonino uses the words 'the church' in connection with what appear to be local rules.[18] Nevertheless, this phrase is the nearest thing I have yet found to evidence for an obligation to be married in front of a priest.

Antonino's attempt to enforce this obligation (or, if there was no pre-existing general obligation, as seems to me more probable, to introduce it) may have been quite untypical. Antonino's legislation was abolished in the early sixteenth century and until recently nearly all of it appeared to have been lost.[19] Trexler, who discovered and edited it, made the following interesting comments:

the constitutions themselves do not permit us to lose sight of the individual prelate, the force of Antoninus' personality in his time. That very quality . . . may provide a clue as to why his legislation has remained unknown until now, and why even now vestiges of this body of law remain so difficult to find. The very directness and inflexibility of Antoninus' legislation, its massive intervention in governmental process and in festive procedures, may have caused its demise . . . Perhaps after Antoninus' death in 1459 the Florentine government took steps to make his law unenforceable . . . The evidence for such an hypothesis remains to be found. But one thing is clear: Florence wanted its great bishop canonised; it did not want his law.[20]

[17] The passage cited by Klapisch-Zuber reads as follows in full: '58. Item perchè abiamo inteso in alchuno luogo in contado della nostra diocesi da alchuno ignorante farsi le nozze prime senza la benedictione overo messa dil congiunto secondo à ordinato la sancta chiesa, comandiamo strettamente a'sacerdoti parochiali che comandino sotto pena di scomunicatione ai loro parrochiani, dov'è tale difetto, che se ne debino da questo guardare per l'avenire. Altrimenti saranno punito allo albitrio nostro. Ma ad quelgli che si congiungono per secondo matrimonio, non dicano tale messa': R. C. Trexler, 'The episcopal constitutions of Antoninus of Florence', *Quellen und Forschungen aus italienischen Archiven und Bibliotheken*, 59 (1979) pp. 271–2. (Klapisch-Zuber gives wrong page numbers.) Cf. also the following provision of another of Antonino's constitutions: 'E similemente che non si faccino le nozze o consumi il matrimonio primo che odino la messa dil congiunto lo sposo e la sposa, se sono le prime nozze, però ch'alle siconde non si dice la messa. E i sacerdoti di contado questo più volte annunctino a lloro popolani. E siano tenuti di notificare a nnoi sotto pena di £V chi fa il contrario nella parochia sua' (no. 3, Trexler, 'Episcopal constitutions', p. 257).
[18] 'vel propter ecclesiae prohibitionem, quae *alicubi* prohibet' (my italics) (cited above, footnote 16).
[19] Trexler, 'Episcopal constitutions', at pp. 244–5.
[20] *Ibid.*, pp. 255–6. These remarks seem to refer to the first part of the constitutions, addressed to the laity and applying only to the diocese of Florence. The constitutions in the second part were addressed to the clergy and applied to the whole province, the bishops of Fiesole and Pistoia giving their counsel and consent (*ibid.*, p. 247). The later decree abolishing Antonino's legislation, referred to in the previous note, is phrased in comprehensive language and would seem to apply to both parts. Of the decrees on the marriage ceremony quoted above (footnote 17) one (no. 3) comes from the first part, the other (no. 58) from the latter.

Perhaps Antonino's effort to make every first marriage into an ecclesiastical ceremony should be interpreted as an instance of his extremism.[21]

In summary, Antonino leaves us with some tricky and conflicting evidence, one piece of which (the phrase 'secondo à ordinato la sancta chiesa') perhaps suggests, but by no means conclusively, that an ecclesiastical marriage ceremony was required by the church. Powerful evidence pointing in the opposite direction is found in the law commentary of perhaps the greatest canon lawyer of the thirteenth century, Henry of Segusio or 'Hostiensis'.[22] He says that there are various sorts of clandestine *sponsalia* (he seems to mean or at least include marriages by present consent, not just betrothals), and then gives an account of the first kind:

Firstly because certain solemnities are omitted which are required there for respectability, viz. that the benediction be given before the church,[23] and that the bride should be sought and received from those under whose dominion and power she is and given a dowry by them, and, when she has been brought home as a wife, that the bride and bridegroom should devote themselves to prayer and keep chastity for two or three days; for otherwise the marriage contracts are believed to be adulterine. However, *it is not a sin if all these things do not take place* [my italics], as [Gratian, *Decretum*] 30.5.1, 2, 3 and throughout.

Primo quia omittuntur solempnitates quedam que ibi requiruntur de honestate, scilicet quod benedictio detur[24] in facie ecclesie, et ut sponsa ab hiis sub quorum dominio et potestate est petatur et recipiatur et dotetur, et cum ducta fuerit biduo uel triduo sponsi orationibus uacent et castitatem custodiant. Aliter enim sponsalia contracta adulterina creduntur. *Non tamen est peccatum si omnia hec non intervenerint*, ut xxx.q.v.c.i. ii. et iii. et per totum.[25]

Hostiensis is following Gratian 30.5.1, more or less, but the words I have italicized do not seem to have come from this canon,[26] though they may echo the famous letter of Nicholas I to the Bulgarians which is included as chapter 3 in the same *quaestio* of Gratian.[27] What Hostiensis seems to

---

[21] It would obviously not seem extreme in an English context, but I am suggesting that it may have been extreme for Italy.

[22] On Hostiensis see K. Pennington, 'Henry of Segusio (Hostiensis)', in his *Popes, Canonists and Texts, 1150–1550* (Aldershot, 1993) and Brundage, *Medieval Canon Law*, p. 214.

[23] The phrase 'before the church' is ambiguous. It might mean 'in front of the church', in the sense of an actual edifice, or it might mean 'with the open knowledge of the church' as community. The following passage about marriages of the great, also from the commentary in Hostiensis's *Summa aurea* on X.4.3 of the *Decretals* of Gregory IX, suggests that the latter interpretation is right: 'non sit necesse banna proponi quando uocat uxorem a remotis partibus et publice nuntios mittit. Sic enim in facie ecclesie contrahi poterit matrimonium inter ipsos, nec offendetur mens istius constitutionis' (I have used British Library, MS Royal 10.E.VIII, fol. 168va).

[24] *detur*: MS adds *s* (probably in error, i.e. not abbreviation for *scilicet*).

[25] *Summa aurea* on *Decretals* X.4.3 (MS Royal 10.E.VIII, fol. 168ra).

[26] Cf. *Corpus iuris canonici*, ed. E. Friedberg (2 vols., Leipzig, 1879–81, repr. Graz, 1955), I, col. 1104.

[27] 30.5.3, Friedberg edn, col. 1105.

make explicitly clear is that the blessing by the priest could be omitted without sin. Later on in this part of his commentary he almost, but not quite, qualifies this, by saying that it is the general custom of the church to have a solemn blessing or to make an offering in church before consummating a marriage, so it is a sin of a kind to omit this.[28] The casual 'or' seems significant here: a money offering would apparently suffice. In a rather similar way, the late medieval canonist Nicolaus de Tudeschis or 'Panormitanus' (1386–1445)[29] says that a priest ought to take part in a marriage contract *or it should at least be contracted with his knowledge* (*conscientia*).[30]

To recapitulate: we have a division of opinion among historians about a question which most of them hardly avert to as a problem, we have a weak piece of evidence on one side from Antonino of Florence, and we have a strong piece of evidence for the other hypothesis, viz., that there was no general official church rule that priests should conduct marriages. It is surely this second hypothesis that should hold the field until some contrary evidence be forthcoming. The evidence of Hostiensis converges with other canonical evidence cited by Joyce, the only one of the scholars discussed at the start of this paper to address our problem squarely and back up his view with solid evidence.[31] Furthermore, if there was a duty to get married before a priest, where is the papal or conciliar decree which lays down the obligation?

[28] 'Quam penam patiantur clandestine contrahentes et sui presentiam exhibentes? Et quidem si primo modo peccent aliqui sed tribus ultimis non ostendant [*read:* offendant?], non est peccatum per omnia, ut patet supra . . . Ideo dixi 'per omnia' quia si sine benedictione sollempni uel oblatione in ecclesia more solito facta sponsus sponsam suam carnaliter cognouerit [*MS adds and expunges* carnaliter] utique [uterque *MS?*] peccat, quia uenit contra generalem consuetudinem ecclesie, et contemptor consuetudinis ecclesiastice sicut preuaricator legis diuine punitur, ut xi.d. *In hiis* [*Decretum Gratiani* D.11 c.7]': Hostiensis, *Summa aurea*, on X.4.3, British Library, MS Royal 10.E.VIII, fol. 169ra. (I must admit that the meaning of the preceding context, from 'Quam penam' to 'non ostendant', of the remark discussed, is not fully clear to me.) The authority from Gratian states that 'In his rebus, de quibus nihil certi statuit diuina scriptura, mos populi Dei et instituta maiorum pro lege tenenda sunt. Et sicut preuaricatores legum diuinarum, ita contemptores consuetudinum ecclesiasticarum cohercendi sunt' (*Corpus*, ed. Friedberg, I, col. 25).
[29] Brundage, *Medieval Canon Law*, p. 180.
[30] 'Item quod in contractu matrimonii debet interuenire presbiter uel saltem cum conscientia ipsius contrahi': MS Royal 9.F.IX, fol. 17rb (he is commenting on X.4.3.3 of the *Decretals* of Gregory IX).
[31] One of Joyce's notes is worth quoting in full: 'Panormitanus in c. 3, X, IV, iii, n. 9. Et licet verbum Ecclesiae sumatur multipliciter, ut nota glossam in c. finali *Ne Praelati* [c. 4, X, V, iv] tamen in proposito sumitur Ecclesia pro collectione fidelium, facit *De Consecr.*, dist. i, c. eccl. [c. 8] "Contrahens ergo coram multitudine secundum patriae consuetudinem non dicitur clandestine contrahere." The canonist Sebastian Sapie adds the following note: "Adde quod contrahens coram pluribus testibus matrimonium dicitur clandestine contraxisse si de consuetudine palam et publice contrahi debebat"' (*Christian Marriage*, p. 110, n. 1).

It is certainly not decree 51 on clandestine marriages of the Fourth Lateran Council, though this decree would seem to lie behind Dauvillier's claim that Lateran IV reserved the celebration of marriage to the parish priest.[32] This is simply an error, for the decree says nothing of the kind.[33] Its purpose is different. It follows immediately after the one which reduces the forbidden degrees of consanguinity and affinity to manageable limits, and precedes one which tightens up the laws of evidence in cases turning on the forbidden degrees. In the preceding period, the law on forbidden degrees had been used as a way of getting easy annulments.[34] All three decrees seem to be designed to stop this. The set of degrees is reduced to an enforceable limit (canon 50), the standard of evidence required to annul a marriage on the grounds of consanguinity or affinity is set at a higher level (canon 52), and, in canon 51, the decree which concerns us, the system of banns is introduced to make sure that any impediment would come to light before the marriage, rather than after it. Here a clandestine marriage is not a marriage without a priest: it is a marriage which has not been publicly announced beforehand through the system of banns. There is no hint that a couple who exchanged the words in a secular setting, say before a notary, without any ecclesiastical presence, were committing a sin or were at variance with canon law.

Nor can it be argued that the canon simply presupposed some preceding law. As noted above, a late twelfth-century papal decretal accepts that in some regions a notary rather than a priest could officiate.[35] One must therefore suppose that this state of affairs was left unchanged by the Fourth Lateran Council.

It is conceivable that some later papal or conciliar decree might come to light, making it illegal and sinful to be married without a priest. A definitive answer to the question posed at the beginning of this paper would require a trawl through all the main decretalist commentaries, priests' manuals and handbooks for confessors, and this task has not been attempted here. The aim has been to bring the problem out into the open and to suggest the solution which seems most likely after a preliminary survey of some key pieces of evidence. It may be added, since evidence for

[32] See above, at footnote 1.
[33] For the text of the decree, see *Conciliorum oecumenicorum decreta*, ed. J. Alberigo et al., third edn (Bologna, 1973), p. 258. For a discussion of the decree and its aftermath, see P.-J. Kessler, *Die Entwicklung der Formvorschriften für die kanonische Eheschliessung. Ein Beitrag zur kirchlichen Rechtsgeschichte* (Bonn dissertation; Borna-Leipzig, 1934), pp. 46–51.
[34] J. W. Baldwin, *Master, Princes, and Merchants: The Social Views of Peter the Chanter and his Circle* (2 vols., Princeton, 1970), I, p. 335.
[35] See above, footnote 6. Joyce, *Christian Marriage*, p. 64, n. 1, raises and solves a relevant problem with the lucid scholarship that is typical of this book. See also Kessler, *Die Entwicklung*, p. 41: 'oder von einem Notar'.

a general obligation to get married before a priest has proved so elusive to twentieth-century scholars, that it cannot have been very obvious in the period after Lateran IV even if it does exist. But most probably it does not. A couple of further reflections may be permitted. Getting married was a crucial rite of passage in the lives of the majority of the population. If we are right to suspect that there was absolutely no general church law requiring a religious ceremony, that is a striking fact. It is easy to picture canon law in the age of the Papal Monarchy as a monolithic system. The preceding discussion should remind us how much room could be left for regional variation. Where no dogmatic issue was involved, the church's law of marriage could be flexible and sensitive to differences in custom. These differences in marriage customs have only been mapped in the most impressionistic way. We know that an ecclesiastical marriage ceremony was more of a norm in England and France than in Italy in this period, but there is much work to be done on regional variation in Italy. How unusual was the attempt of Antonino to make a nuptial mass the rule for first marriages? Pursuing this line of reflection in a more negative direction, one may speculate that the requirements of local canon law may have been vague or ambiguous in some places. One suspects that both in Florence after Antonino and at other times and places people may have been genuinely unclear about what was required of them. Secondly and finally, if the church allowed priests to be left out of wedding ritual, that is a reminder that in this period orthodox religion could be quite unecclesiastical. This final conclusion can be applied beyond the immediate topic of wedding ritual. For instance, it has often been remarked that the role played by priests and clerics in Wolfram von Eschenbach's *Parzifal* is insignificant; yet this is an extremely religious poem, and not at all unorthodox.[36] Lay religion could be unclerical without being anticlerical.

[36] See the illuminating comments in B. Mockenhaupt, *Die Frömmigkeit im Parzival Wolframs von Eschenbach. Ein Beitrag zur Geschichte des religiösen Geistes in der Laienwelt des deutschen Mittelalters* (Darmstadt, 1968), ch. VI.2, esp. p. 270.

Additional note: That there was no universal obligation to get married in church is confirmed by a passage in a manuscript sold at Sotheby's on 17 June 1997, after this paper went to press: 'si duxit uxorem in interdicto ecclesie *vel ante benedictionem ubi est consuetudo quod nuptie benedicantur*' (my italics) (Michael of Belluno, Speculum conscientie, section *ad coniugatos*; the manuscript, which is still unfoliated, will be accessioned as Trinity College, Dublin, MS. 10994. My thanks to the Board of Trinity College, Dublin, and to Dr C. de Hamel of Sotheby's for a preview).

6 Dowry and the conversion of the Jews in sixteenth-century Rome: competition between the church and the Jewish community

Piet van Boxel

At the beginning of the Counter-Reformation the church authorities, on the defensive, implemented various disciplinary measures to stem the dissemination of heretical doctrines. At the same time they took the offensive – in the form of intensive conversionary action against unbelievers – in order to compensate for the loss of faithful members of the church.[1] The founder of the Order of the Jesuits, Ignatius Loyola, was foremost among those concerned with the conversion of Jews resident in Rome.[2] It was due to him that the efforts to convert Jews to the Christian faith acquired an organized set-up. From 1538 onwards he offered accommodation to Jews, using the premises occupied by the Jesuits themselves, first near Torre del Melangolo and subsequently on Piazza Altieri. Here they were given religious instruction in preparation for their baptism. However, the restricted space available and the difficulties the order had in meeting the expenses involved forced Ignatius to give up this task so dear to him. Other possibilities were looked for in order to carry on the missionary activity among the Jews. New premises, located on Piazza d'Aracoeli, in the church of San Giovanni di Mercato, were provided by the parish priest Giovanni di Torano who took over full responsibility from the Jesuits. That the initiative was highly appreciated by the church authorities is proved by the fact that on 19 February 1543 these arrangements were given official papal approval. Pope Paul III (1534–49) author-

---

[1] For the policy of the church regarding mission among the Jews in the Middle Ages and the Counter-Reformation, see P. Browe, *Die Judenmission im Mittelalter und die Päpste* (Rome, 1973).

[2] For Ignatius's interest in mission among the Jews in Palestine, see K. Hoffmann, *Ursprung und Anfangstätigkeit des ersten päpstlichen Missionsinstituts. Ein Beitrag zur Geschichte der Katholischen Juden- und Mohammedanermission im sechzehnten Jahrhundert* (Münster, 1923), p. 2.

ized 'the founding of a convent for Jewish women and girls who had been baptized or wished to be baptized, and also the establishment of a house for the same categories of Jewish males'.[3] The institution, which now was called Casa dei catecumeni, was also granted the right to choose a cardinal protector and thus acquired the official status of a papal mission-ary institution.[4] The undertaking was conducted by the Confraternita dei catecumeni, a body of twelve priests, who one year later were replaced by twelve laymen (*deputati*) under the chairmanship (*praepositus*) of Giovanni di Torano.[5] The female section, arranged in a monastic format, was supervised by a Roman widow. The personal interest Pope Paul III showed in missionary activity in general was undoubtedly an important impetus to the establishment of the Casa dei catecumeni, and he was particularly gratified at the development of organized missionary activity amongst the Jews.[6]

From all indications this activity was in no small measure successful. The number of potential converts who came to stay in the hospice and the 'convent' increased steadily. Moreover, female converts were allowed to stay until they had found a suitable Christian marriage partner and those who did not marry became nuns and continued to live in the section reserved for female converts. The premises became overcrowded: already in the pontificate of Paul IV, the female section lacked necessary space, for forty women were accommodated in the convent and fourteen were living elsewhere.[7] This section was therefore transferred in 1558 from San Giovanni di Mercato to Piazza Margana.[8] In 1562 it was given papal recognition as a convent in the canonical sense of the word.[9] Thus a proper place was created for converts who wanted to live as nuns under monastic vows, but who, because of their Jewish descent, had been rejected by other convents.[10] In 1568 the convent was, again for reasons of space, moved, this time to the *praeceptoria* of the Knights of Saint John near the church of San Basilio, but it kept its name, derived from its former premises belonging to the archconfraternity of SS. Annunziata sopra Minerva, and was henceforth known as SS. Annunziata in San Basilio.[11]

The archives of the Casa dei catecumeni, which are kept in the Archivio storico del Vicariato in Rome, contain a wealth of information regarding Jewish converts, which also sheds light on the relationship between the Jewish community of the Roman ghetto and the church. The earliest

[3] Hoffmann, *Ursprung und Anfangstätigkeit*, pp. 1–11.   [4] *Ibid.*, pp. 12–15.
[5] For the later scandals involving Giovanni di Torano, see *ibid.*, pp. 35–7.
[6] *Ibid.*, p. 12.   [7] *Ibid.*, p. 83.
[8] *Ibid.*, pp. 83–4; Rome, Archivio storico del Vicariato (ASVR), Libro delle memorie della chiesa, fol. 12.
[9] Hoffmann, *Ursprung und Anfangstätigkeit*, pp. 84–6.   [10] *Ibid.*, p. 83.
[11] *Ibid.*, pp. 87–8; ASVR, Libro delle memorie, fols. 26–8.

documents in the archives are dated 1562. One specific category of documents preserved there are marriage certificates which contain dowry regulations. As will be shown, they illustrate the way in which the church authorities attempted to attract members of the Jewish community in Rome by offering them tempting conditions for matrimonial life which the Jewish community was rarely able to provide.

The documents of the Archivio storico del Vicariato should be read in the light of the dowry practice in Christian-ecclesiastical and Jewish traditions.[12] The practice of giving a dowry to the bride was designed to guarantee maintenance to the woman in case her marriage was annulled or her husband died. In Greek and Roman law the dowry had initially been either a moral or a social obligation for the father of the bride, but later it became a legal duty.[13] From the twelfth century onwards it was a wide-spread practice in Italy. Throughout late medieval Italy, and in many parts of Europe, marriage and dowry were twin institutions.[14] Among church authorities the question was even discussed whether this legal obligation could be considered an essential condition for the validity of the sacrament of holy matrimony. The basis of the discussion was the late medieval instruction inserted in the *Decretum Gratianum*: 'no marriage should be without a dowry' ('nullum sine dote fiat coniugium'). In the legal decisions of the thirteenth century, this rule was considered to be applicable to so-called clandestine marriages, for which a dowry would present the only evidence. However, since it did not function as a proof for marriages which were contracted in church in the presence of witnesses, the dowry was finally not considered an essential element for validating the marriage.[15] Not being an indispensable part of the marriage contract, the dowry remained a highly commended practice in the church. In the sixteenth century it was a generally accepted custom, as appears from the discussion during the Council of Trent regarding the abuse of marriage. As far as the clandestine marriages of under-aged couples were concerned, that is, those marriages contracted without parental approval, it was suggested that boys (under twenty-two) should be disinherited and that girls (under twenty) should be deprived of their dowry.[16] The church authorities expected the deprivation of the dowry, which invariably accompanied a

---

[12] For dowry in Jewish and Roman law, see B. Cohen, *Jewish and Roman Law. A Comparative Study* (New York, 1966), pp. 348–76.

[13] *Ibid.*, p. 359.

[14] A. Molho, *Marriage Alliance in Late Medieval Florence* (Cambridge, Mass., and London, 1994), p. 18.

[15] A. Esmein, *Le mariage en droit canonique* (Paris, 1929), I, pp. 209–11; *Enciclopedia del diritto* (Varese, 1965), XIV, pp. 9ff.

[16] H. Jedin, *Geschichte des Konzils von Trient* (4 vols., Freiburg, Basel and Vienna, 1949–75), III, pp. 157–61, especially p. 158.

marriage, to be an effective means of combating the practice of clandestine marriage. The influential theologian Tomas Sanchez (1550–1610) in his treatise on marriage published in 1630 formulated his high esteem for the dowry as follows: 'Even though a marriage can exist without a dowry, it is not dignified and decent when the dowry is lacking.'[17] It is therefore not surprising that the church considered the donation of dowries to the poor and orphans one of its *opere pie* (pious works), which were meant to rebuild the church during the Counter-Reformation (the practice had started only in the fifteenth century).[18]

The dowry was an essential part of Jewish matrimonial law too. Although early Jewish law does not indicate a standard amount of dowry and allowed a father to give according to his generosity and means, a minimum was fixed. In the Mishnah, the second-century compilation of Jewish law, it is stated: 'If a man gives his daughter in marriage without prescribed conditions, he may not assign to her less than fifty *zuz* . . . If an orphan is given in marriage she shall be assigned not less than fifty *zuz*; if there is more in the poor-funds they should provide for her according to the honour due to her'.[19] The same conditions can be found in the *Arba'ah Turim*, the great code by Jacob ben Asher (d. 1340), which became a major textbook of Jewish law and was first printed in 1475. In the *Arba'ah Turim* no standard amount is fixed apart from the mishnaic minimum of 50 *zuz*, but it is established that this amount should be paid 'in the local currency'.[20] That the dowry was paid in cash only began to show up from the fifteenth century onwards, probably under the influence of Christian tradition.[21] The regulations are repeated in the *Shulhan Arukh*, the code compiled by Joseph Karo (1488–1575) and first printed in Venice in 1565. In the *Shulhan Arukh* the obligation is laid down that the poor should be provided with a dowry from the general fund.[22] The administrators[23] are even bound to take out a loan when there are not enough funds available.[24]

---

[17] 'Licet matrimonium constare possit sine dote, non tamen decus et honestum est, ut dote privetur', T. Sanchez, *De sancto matrimonii sacramento* (Venice, 1737), I, 60.2; see also IV, 26 and VI, 9.

[18] *Handbuch der Kirchengeschichte*, ed. H. Jedin (6 vols., Freiburg, Basel and Vienna, 1962–75), IV, pp. 453–5; A. Esposito, 'Le confraternite del matrimonio. Carità, devozione e bisogni sociali a Roma nel tardo Quattrocento (con l'edizione degli Statuti vecchi della Compagnia della SS. Annunziata)', in *Un'idea di Roma. Società, arte e cultura tra Umanesimo e Rinascimento* (Rome, 1993), pp. 7–51, especially p. 7.

[19] Ketuboth, 6:5.

[20] *Arba'ah Turim*, Yoreh De'ah, 250, par. 2.

[21] S. D. Goitein, *A Mediterranean Society. The Jewish Communities of the Arab World as Portrayed in the Documents of the Cairo Geniza*, iii: *The Family* (Berkeley, Los Angeles and London, 1978), pp. 130, 180.

[22] Yoreh De'ah 249, par. 15.

[23] On community organization in Rome and elsewhere in Italy, see R. Bonfil, *Rabbis and Jewish Communities in Renaissance Italy* (New York, 1990), pp. 100–86.

In accordance with the Mishnah the minimum amount was declared to be 50 *zuz*, and if there were sufficient funds available the bride should be given an amount in accordance with her dignity.[24]

According to one estimate, the number of Jews living in Rome rose from 1,800 in 1527 to 3,500 in 1591.[26] The situation of the Jewish community in the ghetto of Rome during the second half of the sixteenth century was one of great poverty due to economic restrictions and financial burdens laid upon the community by the church.[27] The rather desperate financial situation is reflected in an enactment regarding the dowry to be given to poor brides issued by the administrators in 1618. It was agreed that annually not more than twelve girls could benefit from a dowry.[28] This restriction was apparently caused by the number of poor brides who asked the administrators for a dowry. It is interesting to note that during the pontificate of Pope Gregory XIII (1572–85), there were about twenty-two Jewish marriages per year, and this figure fell to nineteen during the pontificate of Pope Sixtus V (1585–90).[29] If the same situation also pertained in 1618, which is more than likely, the girls requiring a dowry constituted more than half of the total number of brides in one year. The percentage of marriages which were contracted with the assistance of the administrators and the unknown number of those from whom a dowry was withheld show how desperate the situation was for prospective Jewish spouses – this, and not the lack of physical space in the ghetto as Stow suggests, was the reason why so many were forced to relinquish their marital plans.[30] It was furthermore established that no financial support whatsoever should be given by the community in cases where a girl had promised her future bridegroom a dowry that exceeded 200 *scudi* which turned out at the wedding to be unavailable. At the same time the amount of dowry for poor girls was fixed at 50 *scudi*.[31] All these enactments show

---

[24] Yoreh De'ah 257, par. 5.   [25] Yoreh De'ah 249, par. 15.
[26] A. Toaff, *Il ghetto di Roma nel Cinquecento. Conflitti etnici e problemi socioeconomici* (Hebr.) (Jerusalem, 1984), pp. 14–15.
[27] H. Vogelstein and P. Rieger, *Geschichte der Juden in Rom* (2 vols., Berlin, 1895–6), II, p. 145; A. Berliner, *Geschichte der Juden in Rom* (2 vols., Frankfurt am Main, 1893), II, pp. 8, 12, 16; A. Milano, *Il ghetto di Roma* (Rome, 1964), pp. 129–53. On papal policy towards the Jews during the Counter-Reformation, see K. Stow, *Catholic Thought and Papal Jewry Policy* (New York, 1977).
[28] Berliner, *Geschichte der Juden*, II, pp. 57ff.
[29] K. Stow, 'The consciousness of the closure', in *Essential Papers on Jewish Culture in Renaissance and Baroque Italy*, ed. D. Ruderman (New York and London, 1992), pp. 386–400, especially p. 396.
[30] Stow, 'The consciousness', p. 397.
[31] Berliner, *Geschichte der Juden*, II, pp. 57ff.; Vogelstein and Rieger, *Geschichte der Juden in Rom*, II, p. 314. The enactment was still in force in 1682 as is apparent from a financial report of the community which mentions 600 *scudi* (=12 × 50 *scudi*) spent on dowries for poor girls: Milano, *Il ghetto*, p. 151.

the financial conditions of a community which had apparently great difficulties in keeping to its halakhic obligations. The 50 *scudi*, though greatly exceeding 50 *zuz* in value,[32] may be considered to be the halakhic minimum to which the community had to adhere. Having restricted the number of dowries, the administrators would not have given more than the halakhic minimum to each bride.

Although not a missionary tool in itself but part and parcel of Christian marriage tradition, the dowry seems to have played an important role in the conversionary activities of the church from the very beginning of the Counter-Reformation. Ignatius Loyola speaks of dowries given to a widow and two girls who had converted to Christianity in 1542.[33] Only two years after the Casa had been given papal approval in 1543, the cardinal of the *Camera apostolica*, Guido Ascanio Sforza, issued the decree *Mandatum catecumenorum pro helemosinis colligendis*, in which he requested all the ecclesiastical and secular local authorities to incite the members of the church to support the missionary activity. This appeal was a reaction to the request for financial support by the deputies of the Casa dei catecumeni, because they had spent huge amounts of money, among other things to grant the mandatory dowry to Jewish converts for their marriage. In the future these kinds of expenses were to need the support of members of the church.[34]

The practice of giving the dowry to converted Jewish brides was carried on in the following years as can be illustrated by the Casa's financial report from January 1565 to April 1568, which also contains information about the average amount of the dowry: 'for nine dowries given to nine spinsters during that period, some more some less, a total of 462.80 *scudi*'.[35] This comes to an average of just over 50 *scudi* per person.

Full details of the average of 50 *scudi* as a dowry for converted Jewish brides are provided by the archives of the Casa dei catecumeni. The *Atti ufficiali*, of which the first volume runs from 1565 to 1587, are preserved in these archives. A significant number of documents in this volume concern the dowry of the Jewish female converts who lived in the convent, the female section of the Casa dei catecumeni. The dowry assigned to the Jewish converts was, however, only partially paid by the Casa dei

---

[32] Fifty silver *scudi* have a weight of 1,470 grams (J. Delumeau, *Vie économique et sociale de Rome dans la seconde moitié du XVIe siècle* (Paris, 1957), pp. 396, 399); 50 *zuz*, each being one-fourth of a shekel with an average weight of 14.2 grams, are 177.5 grams in weight (M. Jastrow, *A Dictionary of the Targumim, the Talmud Babli and Yerushalmi, and the Midrashic Literature* (New York, 1971), under 'zuz'; *Encyclopaedia Judaica* (16 vols., Jerusalem, 1971–2), XIV, pp. 1347ff. and VI, p. 185).

[33] Hoffmann, *Ursprung und Anfangstätigkeit*, p. 24.

[34] *Ibid.*, p. 41.

[35] Vatican, Biblioteca apostolica, MSS Vat. Lat. 6792, I, fol. 96a.

catecumeni. The normal practice was that the archconfraternity of SS. Annunziata sopra Minerva also contributed considerably.[36] SS. Annunziata sopra Minerva was the first confraternity which had as its specific goal the provision of a dowry to poor girls. The condition for receiving a dowry was a good reputation: the converted girls supported by the Casa dei catecumeni were apparently considered to have such a reputation.[37] The fact that the confraternity contributed to the dowries of female Jewish converts shows a genuine interest in this missionary activity. In one of the documents the contribution of the confraternity is called 'usual': 'which the venerable society of the SS. Annunziata is accustomed to give to the neophyte girls'.[38] The sum in question amounted to 35 *scudi*, to which usually 15 *scudi* were added by the Casa dei catecumeni: 'which the society of the Catecumeni usually gives to the neophyte girls'.[39] In a number of documents the respective contributions of the two institutions ('*domus catechumenorum* 15 *scudi*, SS. Annunziata 35 *scudi*') are explicitly mentioned.[40] Sometimes a more specified division of contributions is given: $35\frac{1}{4}$ *scudi* for SS. Annunziata and 15 *scudi* less a quarter for the Casa dei catecumeni.[41]

The participation of the archconfraternity in arranging dowries for converted Jewish girls is confirmed by its own archives. In the records regarding among other things the assignments and conditions of dowries the names of neophytes also appear.[42] A comparison between the two archives shows that the two institutions worked together in a number of cases,[43] and therefore proves the involvement of the archconfraternity in

[36] In addition to allowing it to rent out the house on Piazza Margana which had been used as a convent for the neophytes until they moved to the *praeceptoria* of the Knights of Saint John: Hoffman, *Ursprung und Anfangstätigkeit*, pp. 83–4.
[37] Esposito, 'Le confraternite', pp. 7ff.
[38] 'Quae est solita dare venerabilis Societas Sanctae Annuntiatae supra Minervam puellis neophytitis', ASVR, busta I, fol. 1209 (31 July 1566). A copy of this document is in I, fol. 1242.
[39] 'Quas Societas Catecumenorum dare solet puellis neophytis', ASVR, busta I, fol. 1038 (25 Feb. 1571). The Casa was also called the Società, Monastero or Confraternita dei catecumeni: Hoffmann, *Ursprung und Anfangstätigkeit*, pp. 12, 83.
[40] See ASVR, busta I, fols. 203 (444, 1132); fols. 296 (315); fol. 597; fol. 698; fols. 702 (709); fols. 962 (963); fol. 1012; fols. 1039 (1241c). The numbers in brackets refer to documents which deal with the same people as those in the preceding number.
[41] ASVR, busta I, fol. 702; fols. 1011 (237); fols. 1012 (1011b).
[42] Rome, Archivio di Stato (ASR), SS. Annunziata 246, Doti, quietanze e anniversarii generali dall'anno 1475–1726. Since this record is arranged in alphabetical order and lacks consecutive pagination, I shall refer to the letter and the folio of the alphabetical section.
[43] The same dowries are referred to in ASVR, busta I, fol. 1011 and ASR, Ann 246, D, fol. 6; ASVR, busta I, fol. 1039 and ASR, Ann 246, F, fol. 14; ASVR, busta I, fol. 296 and ASR, Ann 246, A, fol. 15; probably also ASVR, busta I, fol. 1012 and ASR, Ann 246, D, fol. 6; ASVR, busta I, fol. 597 and ASR, Ann 246, V, fol. 6; ASVR, busta I, fol. 698 and ASR, Ann 246, V, fol. 8.

this aspect of missionary activity. The amount of 50 *scudi* is, however, not always specified as described. Sometimes the 50 *scudi* are recorded as donated wholly by the Casa dei catecumeni.[44] But even to dowries entirely ascribed to the Casa, the same formula probably applies: converts who were said to be provided with a dowry of 50 *scudi* by the *domus catecumenorum* received *de facto* a contribution from the archconfraternity.[45] In one case the dowry of 50 *scudi* is registered as given by the Casa dei catecumeni, to which a note is added that this also comprises the dowry given by SS. Annunziata de Urbe.[46] Although in a few cases the total sum of the dowry did not amount to 50 *scudi*,[47] the documents of both institutions give us enough evidence to conclude that there was a fixed policy of providing converted Jewish girls with a dowry of 50 *scudi*. The usual amount given by SS. Annunziata to Christian brides in the sixteenth century was 45 *scudi*.[48] That the dowries given to converted girls were rounded up to 50 *scudi* was apparently due to the halakhic minimum.

The distribution of dowries to Christian brides was one of the main functions of the institutions of the *opere pie*. Sometimes it even became their only objective. An enumerative description of some of these institutions, which were set up during the first decades of the Counter-Reformation and were thus contemporary with the Casa dei catecumeni, will enable a comparison to be made between their dowry policy and that of the Casa.

The Confraternita del santissimo sacramento e di S. Maria mater Dei carmine (founded in 1543) provided four to six girls every year with a dowry of 30 *scudi*.[49] Santa Maria del pianto (founded in 1546) had fixed the amount at 25 *scudi*.[50] The Confraternita del santissimo sacramento e del nome del dio (from 1565) gave 25 *scudi* every year to twenty girls.[51] S. Apollonia in S. Agostino (from 1565) provided six girls yearly with a dowry of 30 *scudi*.[52] Santissimo rosario (from 1576) used the donation of Giovanni Battista Marini Barone di Bomba to provide two girls per year

---

[44] ASVR, busta I, fol. 148; fols. 293 (756, 763, 1133); fols. 524 (516); fol. 1016. In some cases only the 15 *scudi* actually given by the Casa are registered, see ASVR, busta I, fol. 451; fols. 659 (396, 725, 934, 1214).

[45] ASVR, busta I, fol. 148 and ASR, Ann 246, C, fol. 25; ASVR, busta I, fol. 293 and ASR, Ann 246, P, fol. 9; ASVR, busta I, fol. 524 and ASR, Ann 246, C, fol. 17. According to one document in the ASVR (busta I, fol. 524), Caterina Neophita received 50 *scudi* from the Casa dei catecumeni whereas another document (busta I, fol. 1015) speaks of 35 *scudi* given to her by SS. Annunziata.

[46] ASVR, busta I, fol. 1046c.

[47] In one case the Casa gave only 9 *scudi* instead of 15, whereas SS. Annunziata provided the bride with the usual 35 *scudi* (ASVR, busta I, fol. 719 and ASR, Ann 246, L, fol. 19). In another case the total amount was 40 *scudi* (ASVR, busta I, fols. 586, 300, 749).

[48] Esposito, 'Le confraternite', p. 15.

[49] C. Fanucci, *Trattato di tutte l'opere pie dell'alma città di Roma* (Rome, 1601), p. 57.

[50] *Ibid.*, p. 265.   [51] *Ibid.*, p. 280.   [52] *Ibid.*, pp. 290ff.

with a dowry of 40 *scudi*.[53] Santissimo sacramento in S. Giovanni Scossa
Cavalli (from 1578) supplied six girls every year with a dowry of 25 *scudi*.[54]
The Confraternita delle sante stigmate (from 1594) gave 25 *scudi* each
year to three girls.[55] Besides the confraternities, various guilds provided
daughters of their members with dowries, e.g. S. Lorenzo delli spetiali
(from 1448), S. Marta dei serventi nel palazzo del papa (from 1537), S.
Giuseppe dell'arte dei falegnami (from 1539) and Sant'Eligio dei ferrari
(from 1550). These guilds gave respectively 50, 40 and 30 *scudi*;[56] however, as they were not institutions for the poor or orphans, their policy is
less suitable for comparison. From this survey it becomes clear that the
dowries given to Jewish converts do not reflect a general practice. The
other institutions provided their brides usually with a much smaller
amount, whose average was only 25 to 30 *scudi*.[57]

The average based upon the amounts as laid down by the statutes of the
various institutions is confirmed by the practice of an institution which
bears comparison with the Casa dei catecumeni. The Confraternita della
rosa o dei Funari founded during the pontificate of Paul III in 1536 was
established to provide for girls who were mainly daughters of prostitutes
or criminals or women of abject poverty.[58] Since this confraternity tried to
make these girls into devoted and true members of the church through
Christian marriage that had the approval of the confraternity, the comparison with the Casa dei catecumeni is appropriate.[59] Both institutions
were involved in conversion activity, albeit of a different type. The actual
dowry policy of the Confraternita della rosa can be established with great
precision. In its archives there is a list of about 300 dowries which were
distributed between November 1578 and March 1582.[60] Although there
are some extremes,[61] more than 83 per cent (250 dowries) consisted of 25
scudi.[62] The difference in treatment of converted Jewish girls is illustrated

[53] *Ibid.*, p. 223.   [54] *Ibid.*, p. 243.   [55] *Ibid.*, p. 312.
[56] Fanucci, *Trattato*, pp. 382, 393, 406.
[57] Cf. C. Black, *Italian Confraternities in the Sixteenth Century* (Cambridge, 1989), pp. 165–6,
178–84.
[58] C. B. Piazza, *Opere pie di Roma, descritto secondo lo stato presente* (Rome, 1679), p. 158. On
this institution, see A. Camerano, 'Assistenza richiesta ed assistenza imposta: il conserva-
torio di S. Caterina della rosa di Roma', *Quaderni storici*, 82 (1993).
[59] For a comparable treatment of prostitutes and Jews by the church, see Stow, 'The
consciousness', pp. 392ff.
[60] See ASR, S. Caterina della rosa 60, fol. 2.
[61] The smallest dowry is 20 *scudi*, the largest 600. Between those two extremes the following
amounts are given: 28 *scudi* (once); 30 *scudi* (five times); about 40 *scudi* (three times); 50
scudi (twenty-five times); 70 *scudi* (once); 100 *scudi* (nine times); 200 *scudi* (once); 300
scudi (once); 500 *scudi* (four times).
[62] Piazza indicates that the usual dowry for the girls of S. Caterina de' Funari was 60 *scudi* 'più
o meno secondo la possibilità del luogo' (*Opere pie*, p. 159), and Fanucci mentions 80 *scudi*
(*Trattato*, p. 167) but for the years 1578–82 these amounts do not represent the average.

by the case of 'neophyta Enilia' who was provided with 50 *scudi* by the Confraternita.[63]

Apart from promoting missionary activities by their authoritative approval, the popes also contributed their own money. Pius V showed his concern for the work of the Casa by giving considerable financial support when the institution moved to the *praeceptoria* of the Knights of Saint John.[64] Various documents prove a much more personal involvement on the part of the pope, who, apart from leaving a lump sum at the disposal of the Casa, provided individuals with a dowry on more than one occasion. Pio Ghislerio was in charge of its distribution. Before his conversion, Pio Ghislerio was Moses, the son of Elia Corcos, one of the leading figures of the Jewish community in Rome. Both father and son were baptized by Pius V, whose family name of Ghislieri they adopted at their baptism. Moses also took the pope's chosen papal name and was called Pio Ghislerio.[65] That he, the son of the former leader of the community, was in charge of the papal donations to Jewish converts shows the tactical implementation of the pope's personal interest in this missionary activity. Successful conversion stories such as these would have been very useful to the church, and placing Jewish converts in high-profile positions *vis-à-vis* their own communities was a clever strategy for winning more converts. According to a statement of Pio Ghislerio, Pius V donated money personally to particular converts.[66] It is remarkable that, of the donations listed, only the dowries are fixed at 50 *scudi*. The other papal donations are either not specified (a lump sum to be divided among the members of a family) or they amount to less than 50 *scudi*. The Casa dei catecumeni was also assisted by papal support in individual cases.[67] Whether these papal donations were a sign of particular interest in specific converts and intended as an inducement to the Jews is difficult to say. One papal dowry does certainly yield such an impression. A certain Gratiosa Austicurtia received a papal dowry of 100 *scudi* at her marriage with the neophyte Pascatius Sirletus.[68] A dowry given by the pope to a Christian bride who

---

[63] ASR, S. Caterina della rosa 60, fol. 2, 17 Apr. 1582. See Esposito, 'Le confraternite', p. 16, who points to the overall policy of the Roman confraternities of providing girls with a dowry according to the needs and customs of the various social groups.

[64] Hoffmann, *Ursprung und Anfangstätigkeit*, p. 88.

[65] For a full discussion of this disputed identification, see P. van Boxel, 'Het getto van Rome en de doop van Elia Corcos', in *Ter Herkenning*, 20 (1992), pp. 215–25.

[66] ASVR, busta I, fol. 1216: 'Dominus Pius Ghislerius neophitus romanus de pecuniis Sanctissimi Domini Nostri Pii Papae Quinti et de eius mandato et commissione pro elemosina dedit consignavit et manualiter exbursavit infrascriptas pecunias infrascriptis neophitis'.

[67] ASVR, busta I, fol. 65; busta I, fols. 293 (1133). Sometimes the two contributions amounted exactly to 50 *scudi* as in busta I, fols. 203 (444); busta I, fol. 962.

[68] ASVR, busta I, fol. 33.

married a neophyte is quite remarkable. The most plausible explanation is that the pope took special interest in this marriage: Pascatius Sirletus was apparently a protégé of Cardinal Sirleto, the protector of the Casa dei catecumeni whose name he adopted at his baptism. Papal dowries must have been regarded as a special honour and must have played a special role in this missionary activity.

The most generous of the church leaders in the period we are dealing with was certainly Pope Gregory XIII. He was known for his magnanimity to institutions and individuals. Immediately after his coronation he placed 15,000 *scudi* at the disposal of the various charitable institutions.[69] The missionary activity among the Jews was also substantially supported by him. In the course of his pontificate, he spent 24,000 *scudi* on the convent and the Casa dei catecumeni.[70]

During the greater part of his pontificate (from 1572 to 1582) Gregory followed the standard policy of the Casa dei catecumeni. But by the end of his pontificate the amount of a papal dowry had increased to 100 *scudi* or even more.[71] In the same period, the dowries of the Casa and the Confraternita showed an increase as well.[72] No official explanation is given as to why this dowry policy changed from 1581 onwards. It is, however, probably not pure coincidence that in 1581 a series of anti-Jewish regulations were promulgated by Pope Gregory XIII which were meant to defend and promote the Christian faith.

In the bull *Antiqua Judaeorum impietas* of 1 June 1581 the pope granted full power to the Inquisition to take action against various forms of heresy, blasphemy and demonism of which the Jews were suspected. The Inquisition was furthermore entitled to take measures against any kind of activity that threatened promulgation of the faith.[73] On 27 May of that year the bull *Accepimus multos* was promulgated, in which the persecution of the *marranos* (Spanish Jews converted to Christianity) was announced.[74] The sequestration of all Hebrew books was also imposed on 1 July 1581 and the expurgation of any statement against the Christian faith which they might contain.[75] The increase of the amount of dowry may be

[69] Hoffmann, *Ursprung und Anfangstätigkeit*, p. 152.
[70] M. Ciappi, *Compendio delle heroiche et gloriose attioni et santa vita di papa Gregorio XIII* (Rome, 1591), p. 38.
[71] ASVR, busta I, fol. 129 (19 Dec. 1581); busta I, fol. 129b (19 Dec. 1581); busta I, fols. 120 (993) (10 Feb. 1582); busta I, fol. 65 (3 Feb. 1584); busta I, fol. 99 (10 Sept. 1584).
[72] To 100, even 160 *scudi*: ASVR, busta I, fol. 56 (19 Mar. 1583); busta I, fols. 992 (67) (27 Aug. 1583). For SS. Annunziata sopra Minerva two dowries of 40 *scudi* are registered: ASVR, busta I, fol. 65 (3 Feb. 1584); busta I, fols. 157 (167) (16 May 1585), and in 1600 SS. Annunziata increased the dowry to 80 *scudi*: Fanucci, *Trattato*, p. 214. This increase may be seen as part of the same policy.
[73] Hoffmann, *Ursprung und Anfangstätigkeit*, pp. 135ff.   [74] *Ibid.*, p. 139.
[75] Berliner, *Geschichte der Juden*, II, p. 18. On censorship of Jewish literature during the pontificate of Gregory XIII, see P. van Boxel, *Rabijnenbijbel en Contrareformatie. Kerkelijk toezicht op de Joodse traditie onder Gregorius XIII (1572–1585), getoetst aan drie manuscripten*

connected with these anti-Jewish ordinances and regarded as an intensified missionary assault on the Jewish community. In its quest to win recruits from the Roman Jewish community, the church authorities pursued a policy which aimed to compete with traditional Jewish practice. Jewish converts were given special treatment and offered dowries of not less than 50 *scudi* which were double the amount usually given to Christian brides by the charitable institutions. This amount constituted the halakhic minimum for a dowry which later, as a result of the financial straits of the community, became the maximum amount. The church was therefore careful to ensure that the conditions it offered to prospective converts were not less favourable than those of the ghetto.[76] From 1581 the amount of dowry offered to converts was increased considerably and this increase coincided with the promulgation of several anti-Jewish decrees. It would appear then that the dowry became a tool of conversion whereby Jews were enticed out of the ghetto with the assurance of favourable matrimonial conditions. In 1618 the number of applicants for a dowry and the straightened financial situation forced the administrators of the ghetto to issue an enactment which restricted the number of dowries given to poor girls to twelve per year, and the maximum amount was fixed at 50 *scudi*. One can only wonder how many girls from whom a dowry was withheld by the administrators of the Jewish community succumbed to the temptation of becoming Christian brides rather than remaining Jewish but unmarried.

uit de Biblioteca Vaticana (Hilversum, 1983).

[76] A similar concern shows in the regulation regarding the inheritance of converts. Immediately after their baptism an inventory of the possessions of the Jewish parents had to be made in order to safeguard the convert's inheritance; thus conversion could not cause any financial loss. See Hoffmann, *Ursprung und Anfangstätigkeit*, pp. 145ff.

7 Nobility, women and the state: marriage regulation in Venice, 1420–1535

Stanley Chojnacki

In July 1457 two Venetian nobles, Jacopo Gabriel and Pasquale Malipiero, appeared in the court of the patriarch of Venice to defend Gabriel's son, Giovanni, against a breach-of-promise suit brought by the noblewoman Orsa Dolfin.[1] She claimed that in March 1455 Giovanni had married her by touching her hand in the presence of witnesses, but had failed to follow through by taking her (*transducere*) to live with him; now she petitioned Venice's highest ecclesiastical tribunal to compel him to complete the marriage.[2] The defence strategy of Gabriel and Malipiero was to impeach Orsa's suitability as a wife. 'No one of sound mind', they declared, would credit such a marriage, since the two parties were 'unequal in every respect'.[3] They claimed that at the time of the purported touching of hands she was thirty years old 'and more', while Giovanni was only eighteen. Worse, she was 'not of good or chaste life and reputation'. If Giovanni frequented her, it was not 'to contract marriage but to have sexual relations with her, as young men do', and 'if he made the marriage – and we have no knowledge of it, indeed we find it impossible to believe that he did so – it was because he was seduced and tricked'.[4]

---

[1] Portions of this essay were presented to the Annual Meeting of the American Historical Association, Washington, D.C., in 1992; the Middle-Atlantic Renaissance and Reformation Seminar, Charlottesville, in 1993; and the European History Seminar, Syracuse University, in 1995. The author expresses his appreciation for valuable suggestions and criticisms received on all three occasions, with special thanks to Barbara J. Harris for invaluable advice.
Venice, Archivio storico della Curia patriarcale, Sezione antica (hereafter APV), Causarum matrimoniorum, busta 2, fasc. 1, doc. 5 (27 July 1457).

[2] For marriage rituals in Florence, see C. Klapisch-Zuber, 'Zacharias, or the ousted father: nuptial rites in Tuscany between Giotto and the Council of Trent', in *Women, Family, and Ritual in Renaissance Italy* (Chicago, 1985), pp. 183–7.

[3] 'Non debet cadere in mente alicuius sane mentis, cum dictum matrimonium esse ac fuisse inequale omni respectu': APV, Causarum matrimoniorum, busta 2, fasc. 1, doc. 2 (5 May 1457).

[4] 'Si forte frequentasset ipsam domum illud fecisset non causa contrahendi sed causa habendi eam carnaliter ut faciunt iuvenes cum ipsa sit inh[on]este vite'; 'si Johannes illud matrimonium fecisset fuisset seductus et circumventus non autem asseveravimus id quod ignorabamus imo quod nullo modo credimus': *ibid.*, doc. 4.

Above all, they stressed Orsa's and Giovanni's social and economic inequality. Giovanni's paternal great-grandfather had left his two sons, Zaccaria, Giovanni's grandfather, and Zaccaria's brother, also named Giovanni, an estate worth 50,000 ducats, which would have put them jointly among the richest 1.5 per cent of Venetians.[5] Moreover, the elder Giovanni had married the daughter of none other than Doge Antonio Venier (1382–1400). Though less illustriously married, Zaccaria had left his three sons an estate worth probably more than 80,000 ducats;[6] and, equally importantly, had negotiated prestigious marriages for them: Marco marrying Doge Antonio Venier's granddaughter; Girolamo, marrying a woman from the Mocenigo lineage, with three Quattrocento doges; and '*ego Jacobus*', marrying the daughter of his partner on the defence team, Pasquale Malipiero, young Giovanni's maternal grand-father, who would himself be elected doge the following year. These marriages were illustrious not only because of the paternity of the brides, but also because of their marriage portions: Marco received 3,000 ducats, Girolamo and Jacopo 2,500 ducats each. These were exceptionally – and, as we shall see below, illegally – large dowries.

In stark contrast with those glittering credentials, Gabriel and Malipiero dismissed Orsa's paternal grandfather, Luca Dolfin, as a pau-per and pointed out that her father, Antonio Dolfin, and his brother, Nicolò, had married commoners (*non nobilem sed plebeiam*). The Dolfin brothers had 'always lived in poverty', been elected to few offices in the government, and lacked the means to pay government imposts. Consist-ent with this sorry profile was Orsa's alleged dowry. 'It is unthinkable', Jacopo Gabriel declared, 'that the dowry donna Orsa promised my son Giovanni, 350 ducats, is suitable for a noble of respectable status such as my son; indeed, it would hardly be appropriate for an artisan.'[7] Indeed, such a meagre dowry was itself evidence that Orsa and her allies 'thought to gull him owing to the youth's childish innocence'.[8] Altogether, 'this alleged marriage is anything but equal with regard to the age, status,

---

[5] This estimate is based on calculations in G. Luzzatto, *Storia economica di Venezia dall'XI al XVI secolo* (Venice, 1961), pp. 129–32; and F. C. Lane and R. C. Mueller, *Money and Banking in Medieval and Renaissance Venice*, I: *Coins and Moneys of Account* (Baltimore, 1985), pp. 290–1.

[6] Extrapolated from figures of interest and rent stated in APV, Causarum matrimoniorum, busta 2, fasc. 1, doc. 5.

[7] 'Item quod fuit et est absque eo quod dos quam dicit d. Ursia promisisse ipsi Johanni filio meo de ducatis 350 sit conveniens viro nobili bone conditionis qualis est filius meus, ymo talis dos non esse ferre conveniens inter cerdones.' Compare similar scorn of Alessandra Macinghi Strozzi: G. Brucker, *The Society of Renaissance Florence: A Documentary Study* (New York, 1971), p. 38.

[8] 'Item ex quantitate dotis, ex qua constaret de puerilitate istius iuvenis ut sic voluerint eum decipere': APV, Causarum matrimoniorum, busta 2, fasc. 1, doc. 2.

nobility, wealth, influence, experience and other such characteristics of Giovanni and Orsa; on the contrary, it is of great disparity and inequality, as anyone aware of their respective circumstances would conclude'.[9]

How the patriarch's court decided Orsa's suit is not known, but the interest of the case lies less in its disposition than in the contrast between Orsa and Giovanni painted by the young man's father and grandfather. They depicted a patrician marriage model based on worldly maturity in grooms, chaste youth in brides – values shared by the Gabriels' counterparts in Florence – and, most emphatically, the wealth and prominence of both contracting families, qualities conspicuously lacking in the Dolfins.[10] The critical indicator of socio-economic status was thus a record of marriages with distinguished noble (and preferably ducal) families and generous marriage portions. For Jacopo Gabriel and Pasquale Malipiero, to be noble was to marry nobly, that is, richly and prestigiously.

Yet, their patrician ideal was not the only one current in Quattrocento Venice. Despite their strenuous arguments to the contrary, Orsa Dolfin also was a patrician.[11] Indeed, for all that Jacopo Gabriel sought to portray his family as more noble than hers, another gauge reversed that ranking. A roster of Venice's ruling class compiled a century earlier – during the dogeship of Giovanni Dolfin (1356–61), coincidentally – had included the Dolfins among the twelve 'noblest' houses, Venice's founders in the distant past and its rulers during the intervening centuries.[12] By contrast, the Gabriels were merely listed among the noble rank and file, with no mention of great deeds or even origins.[13] These differences reveal very different conceptions of nobility: one based on distinction over many centuries, the other on wealth, connections and political prominence in the present. In the fifteenth century they collided. The supremacy of the Dolfins and twenty-three other ancient houses, called the *case vecchie* or *longhi*, was challenged by a new noble elite, less ancient and historically

---

[9] 'Item quod fuit et est absque quod dictum assertum matrimonium foret equale etate, genere, nobilitate, divitiis, potentia, annorum, et similibus, inter dictum Johannes [*sic*] et dictam Ursiam, ymo omnimodo disparitas et longa inequalitas et ita quilibet sciens utrasque condiciones comuniter judicaret': *ibid.*

[10] S. Chojnacki, 'Measuring adulthood: adolescence and gender in Renaissance Venice', *Journal of Family History*, 17 (1992), pp. 373–5, 378–9; D. Herlihy, and C. Klapisch-Zuber, *Tuscans and Their Families: A Study of The Florentine Catasto of 1427* (New Haven, 1985), pp. 203–7; A. Molho, 'Deception and marriage strategy in Renaissance Florence: the case of women's ages', *Renaissance Quarterly*, 41 (1988), pp. 194, 204–10, and *passim*; J. Kirshner, *Pursuing Honor while Avoiding Sin: The Monte delle Doti of Florence*, Quaderni di *Studi Senesi* XLI (Milan, 1978), pp. 6–10.

[11] 'dominam Ursiam filiam quondam domini Antonii Dolfino ex nobilibus Venetiarum': APV, Causarum matrimoniorum, busta 2, fasc. 1, doc. 3.

[12] *Venetiarum historia vulgo Petro Iustiniano Iustiniani filio adiudicata*, ed. R. Cessi and F. Bennato (Venice, 1964), pp. xviii–xxv, 258, 276.

[13] *Ibid.*, p. 272.

illustrious, but more aggressive and wealthy. The symbol of the change was the newer houses' capture of the ducal throne.[14] Whereas all but one of the doges elected in the two centuries before 1382 belonged to the *case vecchie*, after that year they would not see one of their number on the ducal throne until 1612. Thus when Jacopo Gabriel and the doge-to-be Pasquale Malipiero documented the inferiority of Orsa Dolfin's family, they were asserting criteria of nobility that represented a change in the sociopolitical culture of the patriciate, proudly proclaimed in Jacopo's recitation of the doges in his family's recent marriages.

But ducal politics, criteria of nobility, and the culture of matrimony in fifteenth-century Venice are not reducible to contention between a wealthy, new power-elite and the older status-elite. Surrounding both those groups was a more miscellaneous element, the 150 houses that constituted the noble majority. Including some families of venerable lineage as well as relative newcomers, its members were united by dependence on the economic benefits of noble status and a determination to tighten their monopoly of them.[15] For the men and women of this group, the ancient prominence of the Dolfins and the wealth and connections of the Gabriels were irrelevant or unattainable or both. What they possessed, beyond material need, was the capacity to press their interests in government councils. Their deployment of it between 1420 and 1535 turned the attention of the state to dowries and the women they accompanied, as the chief determinants of nobility.

The complex interactions between the *case vecchie*, the new 'ducal' houses and the patrician rank and file shaped the structure of patrician society and regime from the later Trecento into the Cinquecento. They were played out at the boundaries between government authority, social interaction and family interest, blending into one encompassing dynamic the meanings of nobility, government and the role of women. These were matters of contention in their own right; the persistent refashioning of each with reference to the others gives Venetian society and regime from the fourteenth to the sixteenth century wide-ranging dynamism behind its familiar façade of stasis. The principal thoroughfare through this shifting landscape is legislation on marriage. In increasingly precise enactments,

---

[14] 'Distinzioni segrete che corrono tra le casate nobili di Venezia', Venice, Biblioteca marciana, MSS ital., cl. VII, 1531 (7638), fols. 2v–3r. See S. Romanin, *La storia documentata di Venezia*, third edn (10 vols., Venice, 1972–5), IV, pp. 305–6; R. Finlay, *Politics in Renaissance Venice* (New Brunswick, 1981), pp. 92–6. On the number of patrician houses, see S. Chojnacki, 'Social identity in Renaissance Venice: the second Serrata', *Renaissance Studies*, 8 (1994), pp. 345–6.

[15] S. Chojnacki, 'Political adulthood in fifteenth-century Venice', *American Historical Review*, 91 (1986), pp. 797–9; F. C. Lane, *Venice, A Maritime Republic* (Baltimore, 1973), pp. 196–7, 201.

the government refined its definition of nobility and extended the purview of its authority by prescribing the ways in which families were to reproduce themselves and the ruling class. Because of the pivotal role of women, the legislation focused on them. Examining it reveals conflicting interests, public and private, among nobles, within families, and between men and women. The stakes and the discourse framing them changed over the decades, and the government's evolving responses reveal that the most consistent characteristic of 'the state' in Venice was its mutability, reflecting unsettled ideas in noble society about daughters, wives and mothers. To follow the regulation of marriage during those years is thus to follow change and contestation in the relationships between regime and ruling class, government and family, and men and women.

The take-off point was the first third of the Quattrocento, when a cluster of laws defined noble marriage. In 1422, the Great Council acted to deny noble status to the sons, even legitimate, of noble fathers and mothers of servile or otherwise 'vile' status.[16] The stated purpose of the legislation, to prevent 'denigration' of the Council by unworthy members, was overwhelmingly endorsed, gaining the votes of 422 of the 473 council members present.[17] That near-unanimity is in striking contrast with the vote on a forerunner measure of 1376, prohibiting nobles' bastards from inheriting their fathers' status. Though also premised on the need to avoid 'denigration of the honour and reputation of our regime [*dominii*]', it prevailed only on the third reading, and then with a majority of only two votes.[18] In 1376 there had been no consensus on marriage as the medium of the class's reproduction, or on the mothers of the next generation of nobles. It was expressly to repair this deficiency that the new legislation was proposed in 1422.[19] By instituting a requirement that all claimants to noble status document their mothers' identities along with their fathers', it made maternity a determinant of nobility.

Two years earlier, in August 1420, the more restricted and powerful Senate had also moved on marriage, enacting the first limit on dowries.[20]

---

[16] Venice, Archivio di Stato (ASVe), Maggior Consiglio, reg. 22, Ursa, fols. 47v–48r (26 May 1422).
[17] 'Quod ullo modo denigraretur nostrum maius consilium': *ibid.*
[18] ASVe, Maggior Consiglio, reg. 19, Novella, fol. 171v (28 Dec. 1376).
[19] 'Et dicta pars fuerit et sit non tantum utilis': ASVe, Maggior Consiglio, reg. 22, Ursa, fol. 47v.
[20] ASVe, Senato, Misti, reg. 53, fol. 70r–v (22 Aug. 1420). The preamble is printed in G. Bistort, *Il Magistrato alle Pompe nella Repubblica di Venezia* (1912; repr. Bologna, 1969), p. 107. For discussion, see S. Chojnacki, 'Marriage legislation and patrician society in fifteenth-century Venice', in *Law, Custom, and the Social Fabric in Medieval Europe: Essays in Honor of Bryce Lyon*, ed. B. S. Bachrach and D. Nicholas (Kalamazoo, 1990); Chojnacki, 'Social identity', pp. 350–1. Bistort (pp. 106–7) considers laws of 1334 and 1360 to have been aimed at restraining dowries, but they actually concern trousseaux and wedding gifts.

Alarmed by the 'wicked practice that has arisen' of ambitious matchmaking fathers pushing dowry levels so high 'that many of our nobles cannot get their daughters married', while others compromised the inheritance prospects of their sons, the act's proponents urged imposing a ceiling of 1,600 ducats, two-thirds to count as dowry, the other one-third as *corredo*. The distinction is important. The dowry strictly so-called was a daughter's share of the patrimony, to be returned to her or to heirs designated by her at the end of the marriage.[21] But the *corredo*, originally the trousseau brought by the bride, had evolved by the early Quattrocento into a gift to the husband, retained by him or his estate when the dowry was returned to the wife.[22] Underscoring the distinction, the preamble noted that fathers were earmarking more of the marriage settlement for the *corredo* at the expense of the dowry, with the result that daughters were losing the inheritances they would otherwise have enjoyed. Limiting marriage settlements thus had two purposes: to prevent fathers from squandering family wealth on their daughters' marriages, and to restrain the tendency toward de-emphasizing dowries in order to inflate the *corredo* premiums with which fathers attracted desirable sons-in-law.

Like the Gabriel–Dolfin litigation, the 1420 dowry law revealed divisions among nobles on marriage and the role of government. Proponents urged state intervention to save, and deter, fathers from the ruinous pressures of the marriage market, because 'otherwise these corruptions cannot be extirpated'.[23] But others saw government standards as an

[21] M. Bellomo, *Ricerche sui rapporti patrimoniali tra coniugi* (Milan, 1961), pp. 131–85; S. Chojnacki, 'Dowries and kinsmen in early Renaissance Venice', *Journal of Interdisciplinary History*, 5 (1975), pp. 575–80; F. Ercole, 'L'istituto dotale nella pratica e nella legislazione statutaria dell'Italia superiore', pt. 1, *Rivista italiana per le scienze giuridiche*, 45 (1908), pp. 197–232; D. O. Hughes, 'From brideprice to dowry in Mediterranean Europe', *Journal of Family History*, 3 (1978), pp. 278–85; J. Kirshner, 'Wives' claims against insolvent husbands in late medieval Italy', in *Women of the Medieval World: Essays in Honor of John H. Mundy*, ed. Kirshner and S. F. Wemple (Oxford, 1985), pp. 256–65; C. Klapisch-Zuber, 'The "cruel mother": maternity, widowhood, and dowry in Florence in the fourteenth and fifteenth centuries', in *Women, Family, and Ritual*, pp. 121–4; T. Kuehn, 'Some ambiguities of female inheritance ideology in the Renaissance', in Kuehn, *Law, Family and Women: Toward a Legal Anthropology of Renaissance Italy* (Chicago, 1991), pp. 238–41.
[22] S. Chojnacki, 'From trousseau to groomgift in late medieval Venice', in *Venice: Society and Crusade. Studies in Honor of Donald E. Queller*, ed. T. F. Madden and E. E. Kittell (Urbana, Ill., forthcoming). See also A. Caso, 'Per la storia della società milanese: i corredi nuziali nell'ultima età viscontea e nel periodo della Repubblica Ambrosiana (1433–1450), dagli atti del notaio Protaso Sansoni', *Nuova rivista storica*, 65 (1981), pp. 523–7; J. Kirshner, 'Materials for a gilded cage: non-dotal assets in Florence, 1300–1500', in *The Family in Italy from Antiquity to the Present*, ed. D. I. Kertzer and R. P. Saller (New Haven and London, 1991), pp. 192–5; C. Klapisch-Zuber, 'Les corbeilles de la mariée', in *La maison et le nom: Stratégies et rituels dans l'Italie de la Renaissance* (Paris, 1990), pp. 216–20.
[23] Bistort, *Magistrato alle Pompe*, p. 107.

unwarranted intrusion into private matters. In contrast to the Great Council's overwhelming endorsement two years later of the law excluding low-status women from patrician motherhood, the dowry limitation measure passed the Senate with fifty-one votes in favour, twenty-seven against and twenty abstentions. Four months later the opponents acted to repeal the law, claiming that its unprecedented usurpation of the rights of fathers had thrown the entire marriage market into 'such confusion that no marriages are being contracted'.[24] Worse, it had caused a 'significant loss of honour and freedom for our state and citizens'. The word *libertas* appears four times in the repeal bill, whose proponents declared that only one thing could right the wrong: to nullify the August law, thus 'restoring to all our citizens and subjects [*fideles*] their customary liberty in matters of marriage and dowry'.[25] Despite the support of 45 of the 126 senators present, the repeal measure failed, but its premises presented a powerful challenge to government regulation of marriage. Against state action to aid embattled fathers, unmarriageable daughters and sons with bleak inheritance prospects, it claimed the high ground of honour, freedom and Venetian tradition – as well as orderly matrimonial practice now thrown into disarray by government meddling.[26]

Two contending patrician ideologies were mobilized over government regulation of marriage. On one side were libertarians, invoking Venice's most sacred traditions in opposition to restrictions on the use of their matrimonial capital. Among them were wealthy and well-connected families for whom large dowries were a means of gaining or consolidating social prominence. Indeed, if Jacopo Gabriel's boasting about the dowries his kinsmen commanded is accurate, such families had a compelling motive for opposing dowry limits: Jacopo and his brother Girolamo were in violation of the law of 1420, both having received 2,500-ducat dowries in the 1430s.[27] Joining them on the libertarian side were *case vecchie* men loath to lose the dowry–*corredo* pay-off from their marketability as prestigious sons-in-law (although poorer *case vecchie* fathers, such as Antonio Dolfin, welcomed restraints on dowry standards). Finally, wealthy and socially ambitious newcomers also had good reason to resist restrictions on the free marriage market. The father of the bride who brought 3,000 ducats in 1419 to Jacopo Gabriel's eldest brother, Marco, would have

---

[24] ASVe, Senato, Misti, reg. 53, fol. 94v (30 Dec. 1420).
[25] *Ibid.*
[26] On 'liberty' see E. Crouzet-Pavan, '*Sopra le acque salse': Espaces, pouvoir et société à Venise à la fin du Moyen Age* (2 vols., Rome, 1992), II, pp. 980–1; A. Tenenti, 'The sense of space and time in the Venetian world of the fifteenth and sixteenth centuries', in *Renaissance Venice*, ed. J. R. Hale (London, 1973), pp. 35–7.
[27] Marco Barbaro, 'Libro di nozze patrizie', Biblioteca marciana, Venice, MSS ital., cl. VII, 156 (8492), fol. 96v.

chafed under the limit of 1,600 passed the following year.[28] Whether as purveyors or as recipients of large marriage settlements, whether members of distinguished ancient houses or of newly wealthy families striving for status and connections, men with the means and will to advance their family's interest by advantageous marriages had no sympathy with the levelling aims of dowry limitation. For them, the salient mark of nobility was wealth, antiquity or preferably both, displayed in the marriage market by dowries and *corredi* conveyed and commanded. Their spokesmen in the Senate, urging repeal, could clothe their interests in the sacredness of the traditional freedom of Venetians to conduct private affairs without governmental interference.

Yet they were greatly outnumbered by noble families hard-pressed to keep up with steadily rising dowry standards, who advanced a statist ideology premised on governmental responsibility for the well-being of private citizens. For them, 'customary freedom' counted for less than protection from economic distress, and the only agency capable of warding it off was the government. In the language of the August law, the inflation in dowries and *corredi* 'had to be corrected by *regimen nostrum*, since otherwise it cannot be stopped'. The appeal to government intervention built on recent precedent. Starting in the 1380s the statist ideology had produced new programmes of economic relief for hard-pressed nobles and new procedures for proving patrician status, in order to prevent men of dubious credentials from claiming relief.[29] The convergence of state and nobility tightened as needy patricians assigned to the government the authority to define and attribute noble status and the responsibility of assuring them its tangible benefits.

Those earlier initiatives targeted men, defining noble credentials in the male line, the masculine role in government, and men's responsibility for providing for their families.[30] In contrast, the marriage laws of the 1420s emphasized the importance of women, in the determination of noble status and in the ominous consequences of dowry competition. In this they gave legislative voice to ideas that the young patrician humanist Francesco Barbaro had expressed only a few years earlier in his treatise *De re uxoria* (1415–16). Barbaro's emphasis on maternal lineage in breeding worthy patricians and his disapproval of large dowries in favour of wifely virtue prefigured the legislation of the 1420s.[31] The law of 1422 dictating

---

[28] *Ibid.* (for date of the marriage).
[29] Chojnacki, 'Political adulthood', pp. 797–8; Chojnacki, 'Social identity', pp. 343–8.
[30] A law of 1392 raised stipends of offices usually occupied by 'poor nobles' 'unable to live or support their families on the basis of them': ASVe, Maggior Consiglio, reg. 21, Leona, fol. 61v.
[31] F. Barbaro, *De re uxoria liber in partes duas*, ed. A. Gnesotto (Padua, 1915), pp. 42–4, 50–3.

status requirements for the mothers of nobles was premised on a class-based notion of female honour. By accrediting only women of a certain economic and social substance as mothers of nobles, it explicitly fortified the bastard-exclusion law of 1376, since respectable women could be relied on not to conceive bastards who, subsequently legitimized, might 'denigrate' the Great Council.[32] Other legislation of the time intensified scrutiny of the paternal credentials of claimants to patrician status.[33] Now in 1422 it was deemed just as necessary for officials to ascertain 'who is or was the mother' of every would-be noble. Government supervision of marriage was the means of safeguarding the exclusiveness of the patriciate, with the status and virtue of mothers now joining paternal descent as an essential gauge of nobility.

Women also preoccupied the framers of the dowry-restraining law of 1420. Curtailing matrimonial *laissez-faire* was a way of saving fathers from themselves: not only from the peril into which their alliance-seeking threw family finances, but from the morally dangerous effects on their daughters. Large dowries for some girls entailed imprisoning their sisters in convents or, worse, keeping them unmarried at home, an expedient so 'dangerous and shameful [that it] was practised nowhere else in the world'.[34] Even women who did marry suffered from their fathers' avidity for desirable sons-in-law, owing to the inflation of the *corredo* at the expense of the dowry. These were the '*corruptiones*' into which the pressures of the marriage market were leading fathers desperate to meet the ruinous standards set by wealthy families. The measure of the corruption was its effect on the women of the class, whose need was offered as justification for government regulation. This was the first time, but would not be the last, that the state overrode the domestic authority of fathers, asserting its concern for patrician daughters and legislating measures designed to protect their interests.

On the same day as the Senate passed the dowry-limitation law, it adopted three companion measures. One waived the 1,600-ducat limit for *popolane* girls 'who contract marriage ties with nobles'; they could bring portions of 2,000 ducats.[35] This was a concession to needy nobles such as Orsa Dolfin's father, Antonio, who had gladly negotiated his *casa vecchia* credentials for the 2,000-ducat dowry his 'plebeian' wife brought him.[36] Despite the scorn of men like Jacopo Gabriel and Pasquale Malipiero, the prospect of large dowries from hypergamous brides had wide appeal among nobles: though the 2,000-ducat limit prevailed, one-

[32] ASVe, Maggior Consiglio, reg. 22, Ursa, fol. 47v.
[33] Chojnacki, 'Social identity', pp. 344, 347.
[34] Bistort, *Magistrato alle Pompe*, p. 107.
[35] 'Parentelam contrahentibus cum nobilibus': ASVe, Senato, Misti, reg. 53, fol. 70r.
[36] ASVe, Giudici del proprio, Diiudicatum, reg. 2, fol. 55v.

third of the senators favoured setting no limit on them at all. The rival proposals for the dowries of *popolane* express different patrician conceptions of wifely desirability, one emphasizing birth, the other dowry wealth. They parallel the contrast between the ancient but impoverished Dolfins and the rich, well-connected, but until recently undistinguished Gabriels – with an interesting twist. For it was the Dolfins whose status outweighed their current straits and who could thus marry women of the populace without fear of losing it.[37] For newly prominent families such as the Gabriels, however, prestigious alliances, preferably with families with ducal lustre and forged by means of large dowries, were necessary advertisements of recently attained status.

The Senate's debate on marriage displayed a range of patrician interests. Setting a limit on settlements protected rank-and-file noble families from the derogatory effects of unrestrained dowry inflation.[38] The higher ceilings extended to *popolane* brides legitimated fortune-hunting outside the patriciate by families down on their luck. And the effort to repeal the newly legislated dowry limit reveals the keenness of the wealthy to benefit from their advantage on the marriage market. But on one thing all interests converged: whether libertarian or statist, they pressed their objectives in the legislative councils of the government, now the arena of debate on noble marriage, on the mothers of nobles, and on nobility.

But the Quattrocento state's concern with women was not confined to their parentage and marriage portions. Another law enacted at the session of 22 August 1420 took up inheritances by married women which exceeded the 1,600-ducat dowry limit. In such cases, the excess, if liquid, was to be invested in the woman's name in the state funds (*Camera degli Imprestiti*), there to remain until her marriage ended; if immovable property, it was not to be sold until the end of the marriage.[39] The stated purpose of the law was to prevent women's non-dowry wealth from serving as disguised dowry supplements or otherwise falling under their husbands' control. Although her capital had to remain unredeemed for the duration of the marriage, 'a married woman in this situation is at all times free to make whatever use she chooses of the interest income from her *prestiti* or the rental income from her real estate holdings'.[40] Confirming women's economic rights – and protecting non-dowry female inheritance, often

[37] Antonio Dolfin's brother, Nicolò, received a dowry of 1,200 with a *corredo* of undetermined size from his wife, daughter of a man described by Jacopo Gabriel and Pasquale Malipiero as 'a *popolano* soap-maker': APV, Causarum matrimoniorum, busta 2, fasc. 1, doc. 5. The dowry is in ASVe, Giudici del proprio, Vadimoni, reg. 4, fol 10v.

[38] This interpretation corrects Chojnacki, 'Marriage legislation', pp. 172–7.

[39] ASVe, Senato, Misti, reg. 53, fol. 70r–v.

[40] *Ibid.* The thirteenth-century statutes had already given married women freedom to make use, as they pleased, of all their property, except dowry and bequests received during marriage: *Volumen statutorum, legum, ac iurium d. venetorum*, ed. Jacopo Novello (Venice, 1564), Lib. I, cap. 39, p. 19v.

overlooked in scholarship – was the means by which the government sought to set the terms of the economic relationship between families that came together in marriage. That aim surfaced again in 1449 in an act of the Great Council requiring notaries to submit a copy of every dowry receipt they notarized to the government chancery, there to be recorded, with the date of the receipt, in a 'large parchment book'.[41] The stated reason for the measure was that too often widows lost track of receipts notarized decades earlier, with the result that property rightfully theirs remained in their husbands' estates. The new registration requirement would provide widows with documentation in government records, thus enabling them to recover their dowries without 'great effort' (*labore magno*).

The government's sensitivity to the varied circumstances of womanhood is evident in other marriage legislation of the 1420s. A third supplemental measure passed on 22 August exempted widows and unmarried women aged twenty-four and over from the dowry ceilings just enacted.[42] Fathers and brothers themselves, the senators knew that women past adolescence had more difficulty attracting husbands and thus required larger dowries.[43] The same was true of widows. Whether in the famous typology of the 'cruel mother' framed by Christiane Klapisch-Zuber,[44] the young widow quickly forced to abandon her children and remarry for the benefit of her brothers, or in the equally likely case of a widow voluntarily seeking security and companionship for herself and her fatherless children,[45] women entering second marriages had to add a premium to their dowries in order to compete for husbands with girls unencumbered by ties to earlier marriages. By tailoring marriage regulation to the phases of the female life cycle, the senators displayed awareness of the nuances of women's roles in relations between and within families. As if to help families avoid the stain of over-age female wantonness with which Jacopo Gabriel and Pasquale Malipiero would seek to taint Orsa Dolfin in the 1450s, the Senate amended its dowry regulations to enable families to avoid the perils to male interest and honour associated with mature, unmarried female relatives living outside convent walls.[46]

---

[41] ASVe, Maggior Consiglio, reg. 22, Ursa, fol. 176r–v (28 Dec. 1449).
[42] ASVe, Senato, Misti, reg. 53, fol. 70v.
[43] Chojnacki, 'Measuring adulthood', pp. 373–5; Molho, 'Deception and marriage strategy', pp. 194, 204–10 and *passim*.
[44] Klapisch-Zuber, 'The "cruel mother"', pp. 120–7.
[45] E.g. ASVe, Procuratori di San Marco, Commissarie miste, busta 307, Nicolò Vitturi, fasc. 2, 1 June 1430.
[46] Compare Klapisch-Zuber, 'The cruel mother', p. 123; Molho, 'Deception and marriage strategy', pp. 206–10; Kirshner, *Pursuing Honor*, pp. 6–10; G. Ruggiero, *The Boundaries of Eros: Sex Crime and Sexuality in Renaissance Venice* (New York, 1985), pp. 16–44; D. E. Queller and T. F. Madden, 'Father of the bride: fathers, daughters, and dowries in late medieval and early Renaissance Venice', *Renaissance Quarterly*, 46 (1993), pp. 704–5.

With another law five years later, the government further tailored its marriage rules to distinctions among women. On 22 March 1425 the Senate directed the state attorneys, the *avogadori di comun*, to prosecute evasions of the new limits, ordering any husband who received a dowry larger than 1,600 ducats to return the excess to his wife's family and also pay a fine in the same amount.[47] There was one exception: men who married blind women were not held to the legal limit. Eighteen years later, that exemption was extended to husbands of physically misshapen women.[48] These two laws balanced the need to restrain dowries against the importance of marriage for all women, among whom, the Senate recognized, there were distinctions that impinged on their marriageability. The preamble to the latter measure declared its concern for the 'subvention' of women with physical disabilities, in order that 'those women may also marry who are physically insulted by nature but economically embellished by fortune'.[49]

The legislation of the early Quattrocento reveals the centrality of marriage in manoeuvres over the meaning of nobility, the issue on which status, prominence and material well-being of all patricians hinged. For all segments of the ruling class, the political and social importance of marriage was immense, fuelling private and public tensions over the assembling of dowries, to which government councils responded with aggressive new initiatives to regulate patrician marriage. The stakes were vital: to prevent the most vulnerable nobles from being priced out of the noble marriage market, with all the dangers to social and political order that might follow from their loss of status and connections, a concern expressed in other legislation in the same years which underscored the importance of conducting government business 'in the most equitable way possible, in order to prevent divisiveness among the nobles of Venice'.[50] The means of defusing such problems was to deepen the state's involvement in the business of marriage, which entailed bringing into focus the distinctive characteristics of women, who emerge in this legislation as the articulating medium of governmental direction of social relations, both within the patriciate and between patriciate and *popolo*. The early years of the following century saw a further escalation of marriage legislation, bringing a new ideological significance to the mediating role of women in the state's evolving definition of nobility.

The first decades of the Cinquecento witnessed the blossoming of the

---

[47] ASVe, Senato, Misti, reg. 55, fol. 101v.
[48] ASVe, Senato, Terra, reg. 1, fol. 115v (21 Jan. 1443/4).
[49] 'quod etiam ipse que naturaliter sunt in membris offense et accidentaliter sunt in pecuniis ornate possint maritari': *ibid.*
[50] ASVe, Maggior Consiglio, reg. 21 Leona, fol. 169r (5 July 1407).

'myth of Venice', the body of celebratory writing which attributed
Venice's exceptional political stability to a combination of divine favour,
constitutional perfection and the patriciate's wise government.[51] The
promulgation of the myth was a response to economic and political blows
suffered in the decades around 1500: losses of eastern possessions to the
Ottoman Turks; news of the navigation of non-Mediterranean routes to
the East; and, most devastating of all, the shattering defeats of the War of
Cambrai.[52] In the face of these reverses, adulatory treatises by learned
nobles fashioned an ideology that celebrated Venice's long history of
prosperity and stability as evidence of the divinely inspired justice that
uniquely marked the government and its custodians.[53] The myth's ideological application was also displayed in legislative language which to the
early Quattrocento linkage between the honour of the regime and the
genealogical purity of the patriciate added a new element: the divinely
mandated and historically proven governing mission of the ruling class.
The language appears in a 1497 law of the powerful Council of Ten,
which claimed as its mandate 'to ensure justice and uniformity [equabili-
tate] among all those who participate in providing peaceful and secure
government for our republic, which thanks to God's grace and mercy is
prospering'.[54]

The chief means of carrying out the mandate was once again regulation of marriage. The best-known measure of the period is the law passed
by the Council of Ten in 1506 instituting the famous Libri d'Oro, registers
of male noble births.[55] Its main provision was to require nobles to notify
the avogadori di comun of the birth of sons, whose names were then
officially recorded. The rationale resembled that of the law of 1422
disqualifying sons of low-status women: to protect the Great Council
from 'contamination, blemishing, or any other denigration'. But there
was something new as well. Keeping out interlopers was now declared to
be critical to the 'preservation of the peaceful union' as well as of the
'glorious reputation' of the state – a goal that 'our most wise forefathers'

[51] E. Muir, *Civic Ritual in Renaissance Venice* (Princeton, 1981), pp. 13–61; Finlay, *Politics in Renaissance Venice*, pp. 27–37; G. Silvano, *La 'Republica de' Viniziani': Ricerche sul repubblicanesimo veneziano in età moderna* (Florence, 1993).
[52] E.g., Tenenti, 'The sense of space and time', pp. 22–33; F. Gaeta, 'L'idea di Venezia', in *Storia della cultura veneta*, III: *Dal primo Quattrocento al Concilio di Trento*, ed. G. Arnaldi and M. Pastore Stocchi, pt 3 (Vicenza, 1981), pp. 632–41; but cf. Crouzet-Pavan, *Espaces, pouvoir et société*, II, pp. 970–83.
[53] Muir, *Civic Ritual*, p. 57.
[54] ASVe, Consiglio dei Dieci, Misti, reg. 27, fol. 171v.
[55] *Ibid.*, reg. 31, fols. 109v–110r (31 Aug. 1506). See S. Romanin, *La storia documentata di Venezia* (10 vols., 1853–69; third edn, Venice, 1972–5), II, p. 250; H. Kretschmayr, *Geschichte von Venedig* (3 vols., 1905–34; repr. Aalen, 1964), II, pp. 75–7; and G. Maranini, *La costituzione di Venezia* (2 vols., 1927–31; repr. Florence, 1974), II, pp. 62–5.

had 'zealously' pursued in their diligent concern for the 'common good'.[56] The common good was thus construed as resting on concord among the nobles entrusted with the government of Venice, a principle now dignified by the invocation of the past. Crucial to realizing it were the identities of the mothers who bore the sons. Henceforth, an official noble birth certificate would include not only the patrilineal qualification but also 'the birthplace and surname of the mother', in order to ensure that she met the criteria established in the law of 1422. Those requirements put the highest value on mothers born of noble families, whose pedigree and virtue was recognizable to all, and whose inscription in an official register would be a permanent document of the bilateral patrician bloodlines of their sons, whether born in Venice or abroad.

Uniformity within the ruling class was thus tied more tightly than ever to respectable parentage on both sides. That principle, already institutionalized in 1422, required reaffirmation in the early Cinquecento because of the large number of male nobles prevented from marrying respectably in the competitive matrimonial climate. Despite the official ceiling set in 1420, dowries had continued to grow, sparking new efforts at restraint in the early Cinquecento, as will be noted shortly. Dowry inflation limited the number of patrician girls who could marry, inevitably excluding men from the patrician marriage market in the same proportion, which may have exceeded 40 per cent.[57] However, whereas unmarriageable girls most often ended up in convents, permanent bachelorhood left men at large, to enter informal liaisons outside their own class or to satisfy their sexual urges in more disorderly ways.[58] Marino Sanuto reported in his famous *Diarii* the 'shame to the Venetian nobility' brought by the marriage in 1526 between the noble Andrea Michiel and the 'sumptuous and beautiful prostitute' Cornelia Grifo.[59] It was to counter the insistent efforts of fathers to insinuate the offspring of such *mésalliances*, legitimate or not, into the patriciate that newborn sons and their mothers were now required to be registered in the *Libri d'Oro*.

The effect was further to refine the definition of nobility. The *Libro d'Oro* law sharpened the distinction between men who reproduced the ruling class in the officially prescribed way, newly reaffirmed by the Council of Ten, and others who were denied, or who rejected, the generative

[56] ASVe, Dieci, Misti, reg. 31, fol. 109v.
[57] S. Chojnacki, 'Subaltern patriarchs: patrician bachelors in Renaissance Venice', in *Medieval Masculinities: Regarding Men in the Middle Ages*, ed. C. A. Lees (Minneapolis, 1994), pp. 78–9.
[58] Ruggiero, *Boundaries of Eros*, pp. 35–7, 90–1, 97–8; Ruggiero, *Binding Passions: Tales of Magic, Marriage, and Power at the End of the Renaissance* (New York, 1993), pp. 3–7.
[59] *I diarii di Marino Sanuto*, ed. R. Fulin *et al.* (58 vols., Venice, 1879–1903), XLI, col. 166 (11 Apr. 1526).

patriarchy which constituted the fullness of male noble status. The measure of difference was in the origins and surnames of the women with whom nobles fathered offspring, to be made public not, as in 1422, when a noble's son sought to take his place among the male adults in the Great Council, but at birth. Approved marriage, producing bilaterally qualified sons, was now proclaimed the medium not only of noble heredity and the patriciate's reputation, but of the peace and unity of the regime; and the enforcement of proper marriage was now assigned to the oversight and record-keeping of a government magistracy. The act also declared that henceforth entries in the birth registers of the *avogadori di comun* would be the only valid documentation of the credentials of candidates for membership in the Great Council or for government office.[60] The identities of wives and mothers, officially noted at every stage of a noble's political career, were more than ever the measure of a family's conformity to the standards of patrician culture.

Their importance was affirmed even more strongly two decades later. In April 1526 the Council of Ten moved the locus of enforcement from the birth of sons to marriage itself, enacting a requirement that all noble marriages must henceforth be registered with the *avogadori di comun* within one month of the nuptials.[61] As in 1506, at stake was nothing less than 'the honour, peace, and preservation of our state', which rested on the 'immaculacy and purity' of the 'status and order of nobility'.[62] Reporting the Ten's deliberations, Marino Sanuto explained that 'many bastards have been accorded noble status' and 'the doge and the ducal council are incensed'.[63] Although aimed at bastard interlopers, the law's broader effect was to institute a civil marriage procedure for the ruling class. It was an elaborate procedure, requiring the presence of two of the groom's near kin and two of the bride's, all of whom were to swear to the legitimate marriage of the spouses and to 'declare the quality of the bride's father and her status'[64] – requirements that were almost certainly a response to the marriage, ten days earlier, between Andrea Michiel and the prostitute Cornelia Grifo. The information thus provided was then to be entered into yet another specially designated register and signed by all three *avogadori di comun*. Henceforth, any young man seeking to establish his noble credentials had to be born of a marriage recorded in that register; lacking that documentation, he would not be recognized as noble.[65]

[60] ASVe, Dieci, Misti, reg. 31, fol. 110r.
[61] ASVe, Dieci, Comuni, reg. 2, fol. 15v (26 Apr. 1526).
[62] 'Tener al tuto emaculato et neto el grado et ordine de la Nobilita . . . et in cio consister et l'honor et la quiete et la conservacion del stato nostro': *ibid.*, fol. 14v (25 Apr. 1526), a law reaffirming the requirements of the *Libro d'Oro* legislation.
[63] Sanuto, *Diarii*, XLI, cols. 201–3.   [64] ASVe, Dieci, Comuni, reg. 2, fol. 15v.
[65] *Ibid*, fol. 17r (*sic*; fol. 16 is lacking).

The Ten represented these measures as appropriate to a well-instituted republic, which, thanks to God's grace, Venice was – a phrase canonized in Domenico Morosini's 'De bene instituta re publica'.[66] In this treatise, written between 1497 and 1509, the politically influential Morosini proposed to reform the government by strengthening the hegemony of an oligarchical elite, who would thus be able to deal with the worrisome problems of too many poor nobles dependent on government jobs, and too many young nobles disrupting Great Council sessions.[67] Morosini's emphasis on institutions was echoed, though more optimistically, in the most widely read treatise on Venice's government, the *De magistratibus et republica Venetorum* of Gasparo Contarini.[68] The vein of political reflection represented by these works, urging institutional adjustments to enhance the governing mission of the patriciate, provided the context of the Council of Ten's efforts to safeguard the integrity of the ruling class by documenting the identities of the mothers of newborn nobles.

In contrast with the legislation of the 1420s, the Cinquecento laws were framed within Venice's most hallowed traditions. The marriage registration requirement of 1526, like the *Libro d'Oro* law, was associated with precedents set by 'our wise and benign ancestors' in their efforts to safeguard the purity of the patriciate.[69] This clothing of governmental innovation in the garb of tradition, a trait described by Angelo Ventura as the 'paradox of the Venetian cultural experience', captures the ideological evolution that the patrician regime had undergone since the 1420s.[70] Then, the state's intrusion into marriage-making had been opposed by libertarians who based their opposition to dowry limits on what they declared to be the venerable tradition of fatherly autonomy in family matters. In the anxious years after 1500, however, it was the proponents of state regulation anchoring their proposals in the heritage of '*sapientissimi progenitores nostri*' who, like their descendants in the Council of Ten, were depicted as having always promoted the common good, the stability of the ruling class, and the Almighty's favour by means of resolute government action, now aimed at equalizing the reproductive possibilities of all patrician houses, rich and poor, ancient and recent.

However, the very laws that would subordinate differences of wealth

---

[66] See G. Cozzi, 'Domenico Morosini e il "De bene instituta re publica"', *Studi veneziani*, 12 (1970), pp. 408–13 and *passim*; A. Ventura, 'Scrittori politici e scritture di governo', in *Storia della cultura veneta* (6 vols., Vicenza, 1976–86), III, pp. 546–8.
[67] Cozzi, 'Domenico Morosini', pp. 421–7; Ventura, 'Scrittori politici', p. 547; Silvano, *La 'Republica de' Viniziani'*, p. 32.
[68] E. G. Gleason, *Gasparo Contarini: Venice, Rome and Reform* (Berkeley and Los Angeles, 1993), p. 114. See also Silvano, *La 'Republica de' Viniziani'*, pp. 90–109; Ventura, 'Scrittori politici', p. 551–3.
[69] 'li savi et pieni di bonta mazori nostri': Dieci, Comuni, reg. 2, fol. 14v.
[70] Ventura, 'Scrittori politici', p. 561.

and antiquity to the government's levelling procedures had the effect of sharpening another distinction, that between nobles who married and those who did not. Though designed chiefly to scrutinize the wives and sons of nobles, the registration requirements decreed for marriages and births also certified the passages of noble men into marriage and father-hood. It was their marriages to respectable women and the births of their sons, both now ratified by official documentation, that secured the purity of the ruling class and its unbroken continuity from revered ancestors to unblemished successors. By thus reinforcing the generative exclusiveness which distinguished nobles from other Venetians, the new requirements enhanced the dignity of domestic patriarchy at the same time as they laid down rules for its exercise. In the process they consigned the growing percentage of permanent bachelors to a second-class patrician status, forever excluded from the ritual experience of registering their marriage and fatherhood, the means by which the sacred mission of the ruling class was to be perpetuated. Further stigmatizing such men, the extra-marital heterosexual options available to them, the women with whom they consorted, and the illegitimate offspring of their unions, were officially represented as polluting threats to the nobility's most sacred traditions.[71]

As in the early Quattrocento, the initiatives of 1506 and 1526 were coupled with new efforts to restrain dowries. In the aftermath of the dowry law of 1420, the official ceiling of 1,600 ducats became the standard patrician dowry, as many fathers saw conformity with an official norm of noble behaviour as a way of affirming their families' status; but it failed utterly to keep men of ambition and means from providing much larger portions. Nearly one-half of a group of 122 mid-century dowries recovered by widows or their heirs were larger than the official maximum of $1,066\frac{2}{3}$ ducats (that is, the two-thirds portion of the 1,600-ducat limit designated for dowry as distinct from *corredo*), and many doubled or even tripled it.[72] By the late 1490s, Sanuto reported, 'conspicuous private wealth produced many marriages with sizeable dowries, because it is now the prevailing practice to give large dowries, almost all greater than 3,000 ducats and some reaching 10,000 and more'.[73] In the face of this relent-less surge, the Senate in 1505 passed a second dowry-limitation measure, raising the maximum to 3,000 ducats, 'including all furnishings, personal effects, gifts, *corredo* and all other items'.[74] The near-doubling of the limit,

---

[71] Echoing references to sodomy: P. H. Labalme, 'Sodomy and Venetian justice in the Renaissance', *Legal History Review*, 52 (1984), esp. pp. 222–3, 232–4; Ruggiero, *Bound-aries of Eros*, pp. 127–34.
[72] ASVe, Giudici del proprio, De giudicatu, regs. 1 and 2; Chojnacki, 'Social identity', pp. 354–6.
[73] *Diarii*, I, col. 885.
[74] 'Computati tuti fornimenti, robe, doni, corriedi et cadauna altra cosa': ASVe, Senato, Terra, reg. 15, fols. 93v–4v (4 Nov. 1505).

during a period when the salaries of domestic servants and galley oarsmen remained stable, indicates how powerful the upward pressures on settlements had been since 1420.[75] But the differences between the two laws involved more than concession to irresistible family urges. In 1505, the Senate's determination to restrain dowries began the process that would make marriage a civil act in 1526, and led it to revise women's traditional inheritance rights.

The new law gave the state pre-emptive control of marriage. Whereas in 1420 penalties had been aimed at families discovered after the fact to have violated the dowry limits, now the parties were required to register contracts before the nuptials. A written copy of every marriage contract, containing the exact language used (*la forma de le parolle usate*), had henceforth to be registered before the *avogadori di comun* within eight days of its signing. Once the *avogadori* had verified its conformity with the new limit, they were to have it recorded verbatim in a parchment register designated for that purpose and 'kept under lock and key in the *avogadori*'s possession'.[76] The state thus introduced a documented civil procedure as a required part of the nuptial process, which until 1505 had been conducted away from government oversight: contracts were normally not drawn up by notaries; and even the dowry receipts that husbands gave their wives, though usually notarized, had not come under official scrutiny until passage of the 1449 law, noted above.[77] Now, however, betrothals were not only to be public events but would require official approval to proceed beyond the signing of the contract.

The requirement was given teeth. Failure to comply would result in a 100-ducat fine for the broker of the marriage, and a 500-ducat fine for the fathers of the two spouses, and forfeiture and fines for the husband, all of whom must appear in person before the *avogadori* to swear to the accuracy of the copy registered.[78] But a far tougher sanction targeted the marrying women. Henceforth, no widow would be allowed to reclaim her dowry unless it was recorded in the *avogadori*'s register. This was a radical departure from past practice and from the deeply engrained legal principle that the dowry, as a woman's inheritance, was ultimately her property.[79] By holding it hostage to her family's conformity with official norms, the government forced families to choose between matrimonial ambition and desire to provide for daughters. That the target of the sanction was the former rather than the latter emerges from another

---

[75] D. Romano, *Housecraft and Statecraft: Domestic Service in Renaissance Venice, 1400–1600* (Baltimore, 1996), pp. 139–43.
[76] ASVe, Senato, Terra, reg. 15, fols. 93v–4v.
[77] ASVe, Maggior Consiglio, Deliberazioni, reg. 22, Ursa, fol. 176r–v.
[78] ASVe, Senato, Terra, reg. 15, fol. 93v.
[79] Kuehn, 'Some ambiguities of female inheritance ideology', pp. 238–41; Klapisch-Zuber, 'The "cruel mother"', pp. 121–2.

provision of the law, which echoed the act of August 1420 exempting a woman's non-dowry inheritance from the limits on marriage settlements: as long as the surplus over 3,000 ducats was considered a legacy rather than an addition to the dowry, 'it should be freely hers, as is honest'.[80]

The Senate was reaffirming an important distinction. Parents were free to bequeath as much as they liked to their daughters; it was their lavish pursuit of desirable sons-in-law that must be restrained. Yet, the son-in-law would be the beneficiary of the sanctions for non-compliance with the law. Not only would he or his estate be exonerated from restitution of a deceased wife's or widow's dowry, but he would benefit doubly from his father-in-law's illegal extravagance, by gaining an exceptionally large dowry in the first place, then getting to keep it. The casualties of the transaction would be his widow, losing her inheritance, and her natal family, forfeiting the beneficence they could normally expect in the will of a married daughter. By expressly permitting non-dowry bequests to women while threatening their traditional rights to their dowries, the Senate was exploiting fathers' concern for their daughters as a way of discouraging dowry excess, and in the process distinguishing between women as daughters of generously affectionate parents and women as instruments of their families' matrimonial ambitions.

The state was dictating inheritance practice, with precisely calibrated sanctions. Its immediate goal was to force patrician fathers to discharge their responsibility for the transgenerational integrity of their family and its property, instead of alienating it in the quest for costly marriage alliances in the present. But, as in 1420, the deeper objective was to protect the interests of the noble rank and file by restraining a rich minority from further concentrating wealth and influence among themselves by bidding up, beyond the reach of less well-to-do nobles, the dowries commanded by the most attractive marriage partners.[81] The dangers of such concentration were clearly recognized in legislative debates of the time. 'In a well-ordered Republic', said an opponent of a 1511 proposal to give rich patricians special office-holding advantages, 'equality should always be maintained so that all can share in the benefits and advantages it brings';[82] and the diarist Girolamo Priuli commented that 'those who wish to preserve and maintain a good republic must above all preserve and maintain equality'.[83]

For the proponents of dowry limitation, good government in a well-

---

[80] 'la qual sia liberamente de la dona come e honesto': Senato, Terra, reg. 15, fol. 93v.
[81] For such tensions, see G. Cozzi, 'Authority and the law in Renaissance Venice', pp. 296–301, and F. Gilbert, 'Venice in the crisis of the League of Cambrai', pp, 286, 290, both in *Renaissance Venice*, ed. Hale; Finlay, *Politics in Renaissance Venice*, pp. 59–81; Gleason, *Gasparo Contarini*, pp. 125–8. Sanuto reports spirited debate in the Senate on the 1505 law: *Diarii*, VI, col. 253.
[82] Cozzi, 'Authority and the law', p. 314.   [83] Finlay, *Politics in Renaissance Venice*, p. 74.

instituted republic meant equality not just in the distribution of remunerative offices but in marriage possibilities as well. Citing the constant vigilance of 'our forefathers' against all things that offended 'our exalted Creator', they declared that excessive dowries not only impoverished noble families, but also gave rise to 'inconveniences of which every prudent person is aware', and which we may understand as the patrician majority's resentful frustration over the unreachable dowry levels of the rich. It was therefore 'the responsibility of our well-instituted republic to enact a remedy for that immoderate and pernicious custom, out of reverence for God and for the benefit of our city'.[84] Here was displayed the ideology of the early Cinquecento: the ruling class's fulfilment of its divinely ordained and historically proven mission of ensuring civil concord depended on political and social equality among its members. That required usurping the authority of *patresfamilias* over inheritance and marriage, of volatile potential owing to the inherent economic rivalry between the sons, who continued the family over time, and the daughters, who projected it outwards in the present. In contrast to the struggle between libertarian and statist interests over the 1420 dowry law, the new measure swept the Senate, passing with 116 favourable votes, three opposed, and one abstention.

Like their Quattrocento forebears, many fathers after 1505 embraced the official norm, demonstrating their nobility by obedience to the law and by meeting the dowry level deemed appropriate to patricians. In the first two years after the law's passage, forty-six – nearly two-thirds – of the seventy-two nobles who duly registered their daughters' marriage contracts acknowledged dowries of exactly 3,000 ducats, affirming 'by their oaths that this is a true contract conforming in all respects to the law',[85] and a further sixteen acknowledged dowries between 2,000 and 2,870 ducats.[86] Yet other fathers blithely ignored the new limit, giving their daughters dowries that were two or three times the new maximum, reaching 8,000 and even 10,000 ducats, which the diarist Sanuto reported as if they were common knowledge.[87] So in April 1535 the Senate responded with still more legislation, reaffirming its determination to restrain dowries but once again raising the ceiling, now to 4,000 ducats. In the process it gave dowry limitation a powerful, new, symbolic dignity, tying it to ideals of noble behaviour, public and private, individual and familial, rooted in Venice's most cherished traditions.[88]

---

[84] 'nascono etiam molti inconvenienti ben noti a la prudentia de cadauno. Per il che essendo officio de la nostra ben instituta republica asserir opportuno rimedio a tal immoderata et pernitiosa consuetudine, sì per reverentia del summo dio, come per beneficio de la cita nostra': Senato, Terra, reg. 15, fol. 93v.

[85] ASVe, Avogaria di comun, Contratti di nozze, reg. 140/1, fol. 5r.

[86] *Ibid.*, fols. 1r–66v.

[87] Sanuto, *Diarii*, XVIII, col. 330 (1514); *ibid*, LVII, cols. 478, 526 (1533).

[88] ASVe, Senato, Terra, reg. 28, fols. 151r–152r (29 Apr. 1535).

The senators blamed three categories of patricians for flouting the 1505 law. First were fathers who, 'heedless of their responsibilities', persisted in amassing money in order to give their daughters 'immoderate dowries'. Then came young men, so 'content to live off their wives' dowries', that they disdained 'business in the city, in overseas commerce or in any other worthy industry'. Finally, even the officials entrusted with enforcing the law had fallen short of their duty.[89] Women's dowries thus led men to forsake their proper roles as nobles in the domestic realm, in economic life and in the government itself. The Senate's response was to prescribe more precise rules for male conduct, with more carefully calibrated enforcement mechanisms, reinforced by the participation of the most exalted symbolic authority of the state – all centred on the movement and the property of women.

Young men's abandonment of the patriciate's mercantile traditions was particularly distressing. Like other commentators of the time, the senators looked back with nostalgia to the robust adventurousness of bygone days, contrasting it with the languid luxury now spreading through the patriciate, which many blamed for the crisis that had gripped Venice during the traumatic War of the League of Cambrai.[90] Especially galling was the economic effeminization displayed in men's dependence upon the wealth of their wives. This inversion of proper gender relations, negating domestic patriarchy, reinforced the current complaint that youths were losing their distinctive maleness, even to the extent of dressing like women, prompting sumptuary prohibitions of the fashion excesses of men as well as women.[91] To forestall further deviation from proper masculinity, the senators turned again to the *corredo*, the husband's proprietary share of the marriage portion. Ever since the law of 1420 had limited the *corredo* to one-third of the total settlement, that proportion had been the norm in marriage contracts, including those registered in keeping with the law of 1505.[92] Now in 1535 it changed. Although the maximum marital conveyance was increased to 4,000 ducats, the bride's

---

[89] 'dalle immoderate dote, et prohibite dalle leze nostre, ne advene, che li patri, et altri che hanno cura de maritar figliole . . . si dano ad accumular danari, per poter dar le dote excessive, et la gioventu nostra non si da piu al negociar in la cita, ne alla navigatione, ne ad altra laudevol industria, ponendo ogni loro speranza in ditte excessive dote, Et quando [i.e., se] la solenne et sancta parte . . . circa le Dote fusse sta dalli Magistrati nostre ben intesa, et ben eseguita, non havessamo visto tanti perniciosi effetti': *ibid.*

[90] Tenenti, 'Sense of space and time', pp. 20–4; U. Tucci, 'The psychology of the Venetian merchant in the sixteenth century', in *Renaissance Venice*, ed. Hale, pp. 352–9; Gilbert, 'Venice in the crisis', pp. 274–5.

[91] *Ibid*; G. Cozzi, 'La donna, l'amore e Tiziano', in *Tiziano e Venezia, convegno internazionale di studi, Venezia 1976* (Vicenza, 1980), pp. 53–4.

[92] E.g., 'segundo consueto de la terra': ASVe, Avogaria di comun, Contratti di nozze, reg. 140/1, fol. 4v (Piero Badoer and Cateruzza di Francesco Giustinian, 9 Feb. 1505/6).

family was not to 'sink more than 1,000 ducats in the form of the husband's third'. The *corredo* third was reduced to a quarter. In addition, the husband was to be fined the equivalent of one-half of any excess over 4,000 ducats. The Senate was here taking aim at bridegrooms who, living off their wives' dowries, spurned a patrician masculine ideal which blended Venice's commercial traditions with the economic mastery of the domestic patriarch. Ironically, however, its action had the effect of further transferring wealth to women. Whereas a wife dowered in accordance with the 1505 law could expect a dotal inheritance of 2,000 ducats, after deduction of her husband's 1,000-ducat *corredo*, her counterpart after 1535 would receive 3,000 ducats, while the husband's share remained stable.

Over-eager fathers also would pay a fine equal to one-half of any amount over the limit, but a new sanction menaced their immovable property as well. Evidently, many men had been including in their daughters' dowries real estate which they deliberately undervalued, to feign compliance with the 1505 law. To discourage this fraud, the senators now gave the fathers' kin the right to buy such properties at 15 per cent, neighbours at 25 per cent, over the value stated in the marriage contract. Even with the surcharges, such purchases would presumably entail the loss of the father's property for a price below its real value, a loss he could avoid by having real estate in dowries officially appraised under the supervision of the *avogadori di comun*. This feature was a clever ploy to discourage dowry cheating; it also marked a further incursion by the government into the management of private property, a further appropriation of the prerogatives of domestic patriarchs.

Two weeks later, on 12 May, the Senate took action to tighten supervision of the officials entrusted with enforcement of its dowry laws. In the process it raised the state's regulation of marriage to a new level of solemnity by instituting a ritual involving the most exalted authority in the Venetian state. A new law instructed the *avogadori di comun*, on pain of a 500-ducat fine, to have every contract read aloud on the Sunday morning following its registration, at a special session of the doge and the ducal council. After the reading, the doge and at least four of the six councillors were to countersign the contract. The senators underscored the importance of this procedure: 'because the graciousness of the most serene prince will certainly lead him to want that morning dedicated to this [reading], his councillors are obliged, on their oath of office, not to take up any other matters that morning until they have expedited the *avogadori*'s business'.[93]

[93] ASVe, Senato, Terra, reg. 28, fol. 154v (12 May 1535).

The Senate could reach no higher in displaying the importance of marriage contracts in the state's business. With this action it completed the decades-long transformation of noble marriage from a private transaction to a matter of supreme governmental concern, endowed with the ritual dignity essential to the multiform programme of *renovatio urbis* then being carried on under the reigning doge, Andrea Gritti (1523–38).[94] Manfredo Tafuri describes Gritti's programme as a 'radical renewal' of city and polity, pursued according to a 'unitary design, an organic policy implemented in a variety of areas, representing a peaceful rebirth' for Venice, the 'recovery of identity and internal prestige' lost in the War of the League of Cambrai a quarter-century earlier.[95] In this context, the involvement of the charismatic Doge Gritti in the campaign to restrain dowries put the state's regulation of noble marriage on a new plane. No longer just an effort to protect family fortunes and to promote the marriage possibilities of all noble families, it was now part of Venice's recovery of its shattered glory. The 'recovery of identity and internal prestige' was premised on a renewal of ruling-class *virtù*, as manifested in its domestic conduct, productive economic activity and discharge of governmental duties. The surest guide to *virtù* in all these areas was Venice's traditions, which all came together in patrician marriage. It was therefore incumbent upon the doge, his council and the *avogadori di comun* to ensure, by means of rigorously enforced procedures and solemn state ritual, that every patrician marriage conform to the principles laid down by 'i nostri maggiori'.

Hence it is not surprising that one of the authors of the dowry act was the eminent Gasparo Contarini, at the time himself a ducal councillor,[96] whose treatise *De magistratibus et republica Venetorum*, completed two or three years earlier, underscored the crucial importance of the doge's authority in enforcing the proper behaviour, public and private, of the nobles, on which the common good depended and for which 'our forefathers' in their wisdom and goodness, provided institutional guidance.[97] It was this same conviction that wrote into the 1535 dowry law procedure, presided over by the doge, to redirect patricians toward those traditional governmental, paternal and mercantile habits that had contributed to the ancient greatness of Venice and its ruling class.

---

[94] E. Muir, 'Images of power: art and pageantry in Renaissance Venice', *American Historical Review*, 84 (1978), pp. 34–6.
[95] M. Tafuri, *Venezia e il Rinascimento: Religione, scienza, architettura* (Turin, 1985), pp. 162–3.
[96] Gleason, *Gasparo Contarini*, pp. 110, 129. Contarini's co-author, Alvise Mocenigo, was also an important figure: Finlay, *Politics in Renaissance Venice*, pp. 253–4.
[97] Contarini, *La Republica e i magistrati di Vinegia* (Venice, 1544), p. IXr; Silvano, *La 'Republica de' Viniziani'*, p. 95.

Contarini brought to culmination, in ideological theory and legislative practice, a process begun in 1420. The *De magistratibus* and the dowry law of 1535 marked the convergence of three developments that had been coming together for a century: the state's growing direction of individual and familial activity in the domestic environment, in social relations and in public life; the refinement of the composition, relationships and ideology of a pluralistic ruling class; and the growing role of women as the symbol and medium of an articulated patrician culture. Marriage – who married, whom they married and the terms and fruits of their marriages – was the terrain on which the government asserted its authority to regulate the delicate interactions of noble families, generations and genders. The structure of patrician marriage fashioned by legislation between 1420 and 1535 was the rare fruit of shared interests between, on one hand, a majority increasingly hard-pressed to meet standards of noble social conduct set by a wealthy minority and therefore eager to conform to an attainable standard validated by the government, and, on the other, men of political weight concerned about the disruptive potential of the growing gap between the two.[98] According to Sanuto, Doge Gritti himself declared shortly after his election that 'in this state [*terra*] there are rich, middling and poor, and it is very fitting that the rich aid the middling and the middling the poor'; and there are indications that the Senate, the organ of dowry limitation, was regarded as the body representing the 'middling', seeking to maintain a balance between the truly impoverished nobles and the wealthy elite, which dominated the increasingly powerful Council of Ten.[99] This is not the place to sort through the complicated, and debated, politics of the early Cinquecento. But it is important to attend to the persistence of marriage legislation as a responsive and formative element in that socio-political environment, and in the long-term intersection of nobility, women and the state in Renaissance Venice.

[98] On such tensions, see Cozzi, 'Authority and the law', pp. 298–301, and *passim*; Finlay, *Politics in Renaissance Venice*, pp. 71–81.

[99] See Ventura, 'Scrittori politici e scritture di governo', pp. 549–52. Cf. Finlay, *Politics*, pp. 80–1.

Part III

Patterns of intermarriage

8 Marriage, faction and conflict in sixteenth-century Italy: an example and a few questions

Gérard Delille

This is the history of a single marriage, celebrated not long before April 1568, that of Giovan Prudentio Corcoli and Portia Filo, members of two noble families from Altamura, a large town in Apulia. It was a marriage like so many others and would have been paid only a fleeting glance were it not for the extraordinary narrative and genealogical documentation which accompanied it and which both illuminates the story in exceptional clarity and allows an understanding of a whole host of more general social mechanisms.

The Farnese, princes of Altamura since 1542, delegated the exercise of the extensive jurisdictional powers which they held over the fief to a governor and a captain nominated by them. These administrators wrote regularly to the prince who lived in Parma, to keep him up to date with important local events. Numerous representatives of the ruling class of Altamura also frequently took up their pens to write to the prince asking for offices, favours and advice, and in addition to denounce 'embezzlement' by their political opponents. For certain periods, and in particular for the middle of the sixteenth century which is the focus of concern here, the letters follow one another in a very rapid rhythm, sometimes at the rate of one or two a week, and allow the development of local political struggles and the behaviour of the principal actors involved in them to be followed in a detailed manner. In the years 1565–70, the Corcoli–Filo marriage was at the heart of heated debates in this abundant correspondence.[1]

These records were amply used by Giovanni Masi in his book *Altamura Farnesiana* (Bari, 1959), a work which is largely unknown and almost impossible to find today, but which in my opinion is one of the most interesting works of political history on Southern Italy in the modern

---

[1] This correspondence is preserved in Naples, Archivio di Stato (ASN), Archivio Farnesiano Altamura 2008–28. To these letters should be added a certain number in Parma in the Fondo esteri (Naples).

period. The author underlined the role of violent conflict in the power and continuity of the system of factions throughout the sixteenth and seventeenth centuries. But his gaze remained that of a man of the Enlightenment, who saw in factional conflicts only a degeneration of community order by an ignorant local ruling class impervious to notions of 'good government' conducted in the interests of the people (notions upheld at times by some of the Farnese administrators). Such an assessment of things, however, succeeded in reversing the order of priorities and impeded Masi from considering factions as a phenomenon in themselves, an expression of profound social mechanisms – and this is what the renewed study of Renaissance and early modern factions as a political phenomenon has achieved.[2]

To understand the Corcoli–Filo marriage and its significance better, it is necessary to go back to the 1540s when the Farnese took over as feudal overlords. Local conflict then seemed limited to relatively peaceable confrontations. A report of 1542 emphasized that the inhabitants 'are very obedient to justice' and 'loved and respected their patrons'.[3] It stated that the leader of the faction of the 'rich' or 'gentlemen' was a notary called Pompeo Corcoli, while the leader of the *popolo* (also known as *massari*) was a notary called Paduano de Rotis or de Rota (he had been mayor of Altamura in 1540–1 and led, against the advice of the nobles, the delegation entrusted with signing the act selling the fief to the Farnese).[4] The first group, 'frightened of losing their pre-eminence, hate the *Signoria* [the Farnese]';[5] the second, on the contrary, seemed more favourably dis-

---

[2] Among the most interesting works are O. Raggio, *Faide e parentele. Lo stato genovese visto dalla Fontanabuona* (Turin, 1990), E. Grendi, *Il Cervo e la repubblica. Il modello ligure di antico regime* (Turin, 1993), C. Povolo, 'La conflittualità nobiliare in Italia nella seconda metà del Cinquecento. Il caso della repubblica di Venezia. Alcune ipotesi e possibili interpretazioni', *Atti dell'Istituto veneto di scienze, lettere ed arti*, 151 (1992–3), C. Casanova, 'Potere delle grandi famiglie e forme di governo', in *Storia di Ravenna*, IV: *Dalla dominazione veneziana alla conquista francese* (Venice, 1992), A. Torre, 'Faide, fazioni e partiti, ovvero la ridefinizione della politica nei feudi imperiali della Langhe tra Sei e Settecento', *Quaderni storici*, 63 (1986), Torre, *Il consumo di devozioni. Religione e comunità nelle campagne dell'ancien régime* (Venice, 1995) (in particular the third part 'Devozione e parentela'), E. Muir, *Mad Blood Stirring. Vendetta and Factions in Friuli during the Renaissance* (Baltimore and London, 1993). Two older studies remain fundamental: O. Brunner, *Terra e potere* (Italian translation, Milan, 1983) and G. Maugain, *Moeurs italiennes de la Renaissance. La vengeance* (Paris, 1935).
[3] 'Sono ubidientissimi della giustizia' and 'amano et osservano li patroni': ASN, Archivio Farnesiano 2008.
[4] Masi, *Altamura*, p. 18. The legal division of the ruling class into two *ceti* (*nobili* and *popolari*) perpetuated the old medieval distinction between nobles and plebs and remained in force, with a few eighteenth-century modifications, until the Napoleonic reforms of 1806: see G. Delille, 'Storia politica e antropologia: gruppi di potere locale nel Mediterraneo occidentale dal XV al XVII secolo', *L'Uomo, società, tradizione, sviluppo*, 7 (1994).
[5] 'Per paura di perdere la loro preeminenza, odiano la Signoria': ASN, Archivio Farnesiano 2008.

posed towards them. But the political expression of this opposition between 'rich' and *popolo* was not straightforward, and the rivalry between
the orders (*ceti*) of nobles and *popolari* resulted in a conflict between two
factions each led by a notary and each including in reality members of
both orders. The factions appeared – and were to seem during the whole
of the sixteenth century and at the beginning of the seventeenth – as
transverse political constructions. The texts also underline their continual
ties to powers outside the community. A 'party' of the duchess of Gravina
(a neighbouring fief and traditional rival of Altamura) maintained itself
for years, and even in 1564 the leaders of the faction of Giovan Lorenzo de
Notariis condemned 'the disturbances caused by the duchess of
Gravina's followers'.[6] On the whole, the partisan participation of the
representatives of the feudal overlord or of the central power always
proved to be decisive to the progress or the victory of one faction or the
other.

From the 1550s the situation deteriorated. On 26 September 1550, the
count of Rumo warned the duke of Parma against the machinations of a
group that included 'Notar Nicola di Notar Gasparre, M. Giovan
Lorenzo de Notariis, Iacomo de Morello, Battista Perillo, Pompeo and
Giulio Spinnato and Notar Angelo Mondelli'.[7] The *erario* of the duke (the
administrator of his feudal possessions), Angelo Maggiore, added besides
that 'the notary Nicola di Notaro Gasparro and Battista Perillo and the
notary Angelo Mondelli, the leaders and founders of the contrary faction
in this city, having risen up against Your Excellency and his officials', had
been thrown in prison.[8] The episode reveals that a strong political group,
that of the de Notariis, led essentially by the notaries, was already formed:
the notary Nicola son of the notary Gasparro was none other than Nicola
de Notariis, son of Gasparro and father of Giovan Lorenzo, of whom
more later.[9] Nothing is known of the genealogies of Battista Perillo or of
the notary Angelo Mondelli, but the Spinnato, a 'noble' family, were
connected by marriage to the de Notariis: Pompeo was the husband of
Lucretia de Notariis, the daughter of Nicola and sister of Giovan
Lorenzo.

The texts remain very ambiguous about the political and power relationships between the de Notariis group and that led by the Filo/Rota.

---

[6] 'I tumulti provocati dagli adherenti della Duchessa di Gravina': *ibid*.
[7] *Ibid*.
[8] 'Notar Nicola di Notar Gasparro e Battista Perillo e anche Notar Angelo Mondelli capi ed
origine dell'inimica setta di questa città insorti contro V. E. e suoi ufficiali': *ibid*.
[9] Altamura, Archivio, Biblioteca, Museo comunale (ABMC), 166: 'Stemmi e famiglie
nobili d'Altamura'; Giuseppe Campanile (uncertain attribution), *Alberi delle famiglie nobili
d'Altamura* (beginning of the seventeenth century); V. Frizzale, *Alberi genealogi delle
famiglie nobili di Altamura* (1755).

This latter faction, profiting from the confiscation of the Farnese fiefs by the Spanish crown in 1551, recovered supremacy at the local level and manoeuvred 'to dominate the poor'.[10] At the beginning of 1556, the fief was sold to the duchess of Gravina (an Orsini), but this solution apparently united everyone against her and before the end of 1556 the fief was restored to the Farnese. The report sent by Domenico Guardini to the duke of Parma on this occasion is important for its choice of vocabulary and expressions. It emphasized in a lucid fashion the tensions which prevailed in the management of the commune (*università*) and which led to the confrontations of 1560–70.[11] Guardini condemned the method of election and government which allowed the successful candidates (*eletti*) to operate without any control and to exercise real civil tyranny (*tirannide civile*). He did not confine himself to general political assessments, but also reported precise and concrete facts which are very precious: 'This city, Excellent Signor, is divided into two camps, one called *massari* or plebs or people, the other the well-educated or gentlemen, that is the rich or black coats. The leaders of these two camps are, of the rich or gentlemen M. Pompeo [Corcoli], of the people or *massari* the notary Paduano [de Rota]'.[12]

At this point, our earlier depiction of the situation seems to come into question, for the names advanced by Guardini do not correspond to those of the preceding texts. At first sight, we might conclude that we have here constantly changing factional struggles, as in the case of Liguria studied by Osvaldo Raggio.[13] But this would be superficial and would lead to an erroneous interpretation of the facts. A precise study of the genealogies of these new protagonists allows clarification. Pompeo Corcoli is none other than the husband of Maria de Notariis, sister of Giovan Vincenzo: here is confirmation of the existence of the de Notariis/Corcoli faction which will later be seen in action. The wife of Paduano de Rota is unknown but his son Giovan Felice is married to a Filo, an alliance that was to be repeated later, since Marcello Filo, nephew of Gratiano Filo, leader in the 1560s and 1570s of the faction opposing the de Notariis/Corcoli, also married a Rota woman.[14] On the other hand, it was probably the marriage of Pompeo Corcoli with Maria de Notariis which welded together the

---

[10] 'Soperchiar li poverelli': Masi, *Altamura*, p. 26.
[11] Guardini's report of 9 Dec. 1556 (ASN, Archivio Farnesiano 2008) was analysed at length by Masi.
[12] 'Questa città, Ecc.mo Sigr. è divisa in doi volontà, l'una si chiama massari, plebe, popolo, l'altra litterati o gentilhuomini cioè facultosi o dalle cappe negre. Capi di queste due volontà i ricchi o gentilhuomini se ne è fatto M. Pompeo del popolo o massari Notar Paduano': ASN, Archivio Farnesiano 2008.
[13] Raggio, *Faide e parentele*.
[14] All this information is taken from the Campanile genealogies in ABMC.

faction, and accentuated its newly 'noble' social character, as the 'old nobility' were represented by the Filo. What Guardini's text reveals is rather the reinforcement of social representation expressed by the factions: the Filo allied to the Rota moved in the direction of the *popolo*, while the de Notariis/Corcoli gradually shifted towards the nobles and the 'rich'. The vital link with the events of the 1550s is thus restored and the whole framework, within which the confrontations examined here unfolded, appears to be securely in place.

In February 1556, while the fief was under the control of the duchess of Gravina, an order to imprison Antonio Petronelli was sent out.[15] The Petronelli affair dragged on for years. A letter from the mayor and the *eletti* of 20 August 1562 stated that 'the magnificent Antonio Petronelli is persecuted by the inquisition on account of evidence given by his greatest enemies',[16] and asked the duke to intervene on his behalf. The name of Antonio Petronelli crops up frequently in the correspondence of the following years, until the beginning of the 1570s, as one of the main members of the faction of Gratiano Filo.

From then on, events moved quickly and took on a violent character. On 18 March 1564, the *auditore* of the Farnese in Naples, Giovan Ferrante Zuniga, wrote to Cardinal Farnese asking him to reprieve Giovan Vincenzo de Vito and Adorno de Festina, condemned respectively to two and five years of exile. The first belonged to the faction of Gratiano Filo, the second, who was guilty of murder, to that of the de Notariis/Corcoli. Zuniga's comment on these events was terrifying: 'Altamura is a place of factions and enemies who will eat each other's hearts out.'[17] Three months later, on 17 June 1564, the whole town asked the feudal overlord to intervene in order to avoid disturbances 'as certain tempers are current in one faction of our powerful citizens, out of which some irreparable disorder could arise if Your Excellency does not deign to intervene in time ... and send a captain who should also be a doctor [of laws] and an expert in government, and most importantly, he should be strong and assertive so that everyone stays in their place'.[18]

---

[15] ASN, Collaterale curiae 17, fol. 7r.
[16] 'Lo Mag.co M. Antonio Petronelli sia travagliato nella Santa Inquisitione per testimonianze di nemici suoi capitali': ASN, Archivio Farnesiano 2008. The intervention of the inquisition and its manipulation by local political factions is similar to that encountered in Murcia at around the same date: see J. Contreras, *Sotos contra Riquelmes: Regidores, inquisidores y criptojudios* (Madrid, 1992).
[17] 'Altamura è terra di parte et di innimicitie che si magnariano il core l'un l'altro': ASN, Archivio Farnesiano 2008.
[18] 'Correndo alcuni humori fra una parte dei nostri citadini potenti onde poria nascer alcuno irreparabile disordine quando non si obiasse a tempo che V. S. Ecc. si degni interponer... che ne mandi il capitano et quello sia doctore et esperto nel governo et quel che più importa vigoroso et virile acciò ciascun sia nel suo grado': *ibid.*

In reality, the confrontation between the two factions quickened. On 18 June 1564 Giovan Lorenzo de Notariis, Giovan Fulgentio Corcoli, Antonio de Vito and Angelo Laura, that is the main leaders of the de Notariis faction, denounced their opponents Giovan Vincenzo di Vito, Pietro Aurelio Filo 'and other relatives' ('e altri loro parenti') as trouble-makers and partisans of the duchess of Gravina. On the same day, Giovan Francesco Barbentano, an adherent of Gratiano del Filo, sent the duke of Parma a long Latin poem and took the opportunity to denounce the climate of violence which reigned in the town – 'what can I say about the manner in which dissolute men go about armed at night; carrying a sword is not enough but they must have pistols, pikes and muskets' – and more precisely the aggression of which he had been a victim ('the doctor Giovan Lorenzo [de Notariis] and Angelo Laura and Giovan Antonio di Vito assaulted me with insulting words without my having offended them').[19] Without lingering over the people who made up the different factions, it should be noted that the Viti appear to have been divided, since Antonio, who was married to a Corcoli, was on the side of the de Notariis, while his nephew Giovan Vincenzo was on the side of the Filo. These last appeared still to be firmly in the faction led by Gratiano Filo.

Even so, the conflict was still hidden at this stage, and all the balances were not yet upset. In the town council of 1566–7 whose composition is known through a letter of 9 September 1567, the presence of Giovan Angelo Laura and of Giovan Fulgentio Corcoli, respectively mayor and elected representative of the nobles, belonging to the de Notariis faction, was offset by that of Vincenzo Castelli and Giulio Filo, elected noble representatives of the Gratiano Filo faction. What is more, the two main protagonists were present, but in the background: Giovan Lorenzo de Notariis was *advocato maggiore* of the commune and Gratiano Filo was its treasurer (an office traditionally reserved for a member of the *popolo*, which confirms the social shift of this faction). This did not stop the Filo faction from denouncing, in a letter of 10 August 1567, the take-over of the commune by the de Notariis: 'the government is always found to be in their power'. Was this a fact or a political denunciation put forward on the eve of the town council elections? It does not matter much. What is important about this letter is that it was accompanied by an exhaustive list of twenty-nine signatures of the constituent members of the Filo faction.[20] The presence should

[19] 'Che dirò del modo che vanno la nocte armati gli homini licentiosi et non basta portar spada, ma scoppetti, ronche et scoppettuoli', 'Giovan Lorenzo doctor et Angelo de Laura et Giovan Antonio di Vito me assaltarono con parole ingiuriose senza haverli offesi': *ibid.*
[20] ASN, Archivio Farnesiano 2009. The twenty-nine names included Antonio Petronelli, Giovan Jacopo Melodia, Giovanni Castello, Ottavio Castello, Giulio Filo, Antonello de Viti, Pietro Aurelio Filo, Felice Castello, Gratiano Filo, Giovan Vincenzo Viti, Scipione

be noted of a consistent number of the Filo family (who once again appear politically solid), of members of the Viti family, of an important person such as Giovan Jacopo Melodia and of a member of the cadet branch of the de Angelis (Manilo Angeli), already remote (second or third degree) from the senior branch of Theodosio who for the moment seemed to maintain political neutrality.

The election of the new council was stormy. Debate centred on the concrete problems of the election of representatives within the council. Giulio Filo in a letter of 9 September 1567 condemned the manoeuvres of the de Notariis faction which had 'lost' the written text of the town statutes. Giovan Jacopo Melodia followed his lead: 'almost the whole the town is always in the power of the same parties'.[21] On 15 November 1567 the captain Ilario Ventura sent the duke of Parma a letter which was pessimistic in both tone and substance:

The government of Altamura is in the hands of a few people who alone and tyrannically keep power by transferring the management of public affairs amongst themselves in turn, amid great cries and lamentations from all the others and universal resentment from the rest of the city, because they tend in the exercise of their offices to take their revenge, when the occasion presents itself, and to weigh down with burdens those who do not want to belong to their party, and out of this grow many other disorders . . . These nobles are divided into two opposed, enemy factions, though there are a few among them whom I would consider to be neutral . . . Between the factions hate and rancour reign, with continual badmouthing accompanied occasionally by deeds of hand.[22]

Ilario Ventura did not cite names but the accusation is clear and echoes in part the main themes already developed by Domenico Guardini in 1556. The governor, Giovan Marco Biondi, who was also nominated by the feudal overlord, for that matter acknowledged the facts but minimized them; the argument that he used for this is important: 'because there is a bit of hate between the leaders, none of them ever wishes that an opponent be elected, and for this reason they hold a few secret meetings . . . but in the end because they are all related to each other . . . without other danger of scandal they quieten down after a few unimport-

Filo, Marcello Filo, Giovan Francesco Viti and Manilio de Angelis, who will all appear in the text.
[21] 'E quasi la Università sempre si ritrova in poter de li medesimi parti': *ibid.*
[22] 'Si trova posto in mano di alcuni pochi che vanno tirannicamente mantenendo solo, col trasferirse a vicenda il maneggio delle cose pubbliche e grandi lamenti et esclamationi di tutti gl'altri et risentimento universale de tutto lo resto della città perchè sogliono poi nelle loro administrationi vendicarsi dove se gl'appresenta l'occasione et fare molti aggravii a quelli che non vogliono seguire la parte loro et ne nascono molti altri disordini . . . questi nobili si trovano divisi in due fattioni nimice e contrarie benchè ce ne siano alcuni pochi ch'io domanderei neutrali . . . tra questi sempre regnano odii, rancori et uno continuo dire male congiunto alle volte con fatti di mani': *ibid.*

ant or irrelevant words, exactly as happened this year, when many people claimed that someone had been elected in contravention of the town statutes'.[23]

The problem of the role and political deployment of marriages arises between these two apparently contradictory statements. The first emphasizes the profundity of the division into two factions – in Italy at the end of the fifteenth century and during the sixteenth there were always and everywhere only two opposing factions – while the second, on the contrary, stresses ties of kinship and alliance as factors of stability and peace. As will be shown, Ilario Ventura and Giovan Marco Biondi were alternately right and wrong. Marriage and alliance strategies did not prevent political division into factions. On the contrary, they were necessary to make the system work; as we shall see, they defined and made concrete the political classification of the different family lines, and they stopped political conflicts from degenerating into violence.

Two episodes should help to define and understand this problem better. The first episode is reported once again in a letter, sent at the beginning of 1569 by a certain number of adherents to the Gratiano Filo faction. They condemned with renewed vigour the take-over of the commune by the de Notariis faction, and proceeded, through a detailed exposition of the relations of kinship and alliance which connected the administrators, to an analysis of the mechanisms which prevailed during the seizure of power. First, they underlined that 'there are statutes which make clear that in the council of the commune relatives in the first and second degree of consanguinity or affinity such as two brothers, two first cousins, a father-in-law and a son-in-law, an uncle and a nephew are not allowed to enter [at the same time] . . . nor those who have relatives in the first and second degree of consanguinity or affinity'.[24] Then they emphasized that these statutes had been regularly violated by 'those who wanted to hold on to control of the town council, as for many years have M. Giovan Lorenzo de Notariis, his nephew M. Fulgentio Corcoli and other relatives, who finding themselves on the council ran the town and the government in their own way through ties of kinship and friendship

[23] 'Perchè essendo qualche puoco d'odio tra li principali niun d'essi vorria mai che s'elegesse il suo contrario e per tal causa si vano facendo qualche pratiche secrete . . . ma all'ultimo per essere poi tutti congiunti di parentado . . . e così senza altro pericolo di scandalo s'acquetano doppo qualche parole puoco o niente relevanti com'è intravenuto punto quest'anno pretendendosi per molti che alcuno fosse stato eletto contra la disposi-tione delli capitoli': *ibid.*
[24] 'Vi erano anco capituli che in detta università non vi entrassero parenti in primo e secundo grado di consanguinità o affinità come son dui fratelli carnali, consubrini carnali, dui confrati socro o genero zio o nipote . . . nè chi havessero parenti in primo o secondo grado di consanguinità o affinità': *ibid.*

with those who were elected'.[25] The denunciation then became more precise:

two years ago M. Giovan Lorenzo . . . finding himself elected and *avocato* and able to arrange the council according to his will, caused . . . the following year his father-in-law M. Thomaso del Lauro to be elected mayor, and his own first cousins Colantonio di Ciaccia and Antonio de Cornacchia, his nephew Geronimo Festina, his brother-in-law Pompeo Spinato, his cousin Pascarello de La Terza, his wife's first cousin Giovan Giacomo Melodia, and the father-in-law, M. Raimondo Cinnamo, of his nephew Giovan Francesco Corcoli, all to be elected to places on the council. M. Giovanni Antonio di Vito, the husband of one of his nieces and the son-in-law of M. Fulgentio was made treasurer, Mazentio Festina, his nephew, was made vice-treasurer, another nephew Horatio Perillo was made judge of the *Bagliva* . . . control lay entirely in the hands of relatives of the said Giovan Lorenzo and M. Fulgentio.[26]

This text is important because it shows clearly the continuing prominence of the role of kinship ties in the organization of political structures, and in particular of town councils, in this sixteenth-century milieu. The example of Altamura is not at all exceptional in this period from this point of view; it confirms what has already been demonstrated for the large town of Manduria during the same period.[27] But if 'control lay entirely in the hands of relatives of the said Giovan Lorenzo and M. Fulgentio', it should be noted that none of the people on the council were called de Notariis or Corcoli. As a consequence, political structures at all levels were built through women, and were entirely worked out on the basis of marriage alliance (and not through the male blood line of descent). In order to perform this political role properly, the alliance also

[25] 'Chi haveva intentione di tener il regimento in mano cussì come da molti anni in qua ha tenuto M. Giovan Lorenzo de Notariis, M. Fulgentio Corcoli suo nepote et altri parenti, li quali ritrovandosi nel conseglio hanno fatto la università et regimiento in modo loro, havendo avuto la parentela et amicitia con li eletti': *ibid.*

[26] 'Due anni sono, M. Giovan Lorenzo . . . trovandese eletto et advocato et disponendo del consiglio a suo modo procurò . . . che nel'anno prossimo passato fusse eletto M. Thomaso del Lauro suo socro per sindico, Colantonio di Ciaccia suo fratello consonbrino per eletto, M. Antonio de Cornacchia suo fratello consonbrino per eletto, Geronimo Festina suo nepote per eletto, Pompeo Spinato suo cognato per eletto, Pascarello de La Terza suo cogino per eletto, M. Giovan Giacomo Melodia consobrino della moglie per eletto, M. Raimondo Cinnamo socro di Giovan Francesco Corcoli suo nepote, per eletto, M. Giovanni Antonio di Vito, marito d'una sua nepote, cognato di M. Fulgentio, camberlingho, Mazentio Festina suo nepote per vice camberlengo, Horatio Perillo suo nepote per giudice della Bagliva . . . il regimento era tutto nel parentado del detto Giovan Lorenzo et M. Fulgentio': *ibid.*

[27] G. Delille, 'Le projet Manduria. Notes pour une étude du pouvoir local aux XVIe et XVIIe siècles', in *Società, congiunture demografiche e religiosità in Terra d'Otranto nel XVII secolo* (Galatina, 1990), and Delille, 'La paix par les femmes', in *'Alla Signorina'. Mélanges en l'honneur de Noëlle de la Blanchardière* (Rome, 1995; Ecole Française de Rome).

had to involve families from the other *ceto*, noble or popular. To take the relatives and allies of Giovan Lorenzo de Notariis on the Altamura council in 1568, Tomaso Laura, Colantonio Ciaccia or Geronimo Festina were like him nobles, while M. Antonio de Cornacchia, Pascarello La Terza or Cataldo Lattaruolo[28] were, on the other hand, *popolari*. This means that at some point there had been marriages between members of these two *ceti*. If the factions were always transverse political constructions which cut across social groups and linked the nobles and the *popolari*, they were based on cross-group marriages which thereby constituted one of the fundamental elements of social mobility between the *ceti*. Wherever it is possible to carry out an analysis of this sort, either on the basis of narrative documentation or using lists of the members of the town council and genealogical information which allows kinship and alliance ties to be checked (which is very rare in the sixteenth century),[29] at bottom there is the same reality: marriage is the cornerstone of all alliances and all political constructions. But this being so, it is also a fundamental element of disaggregation and 'segmentation' (in a general sense) in large families, and in particular in the large lineages which still often dominated the local political scenes. It is here that the second episode, the marriage between Giovan Prudentio Corcoli and Portia Filo becomes relevant.

In the game of local struggles, governor Biondi in reality had already secretly sided with the de Notariis faction and it was he who effectively plotted for the realization of the marriage which is the major event of this whole history. In a triumphant letter written on 3 April 1568 to the duke of Parma, Biondi exclaimed: 'my plan has succeeded so well that a brother of Giovan Fulgentio Corcoli has married a daughter of Giulio Filo, and because of this relationship all hate has ceased, all rancour has been put aside and all envy has been extinguished, not only between these two principal families, but also among their relations, friends and

[28] Cataldo de Lattarulo, elected in the same council and nephew of Giovan Lorenzo de Notariis, is curiously not mentioned in the letter cited above. It should be underlined that all these kinship ties with *popolari* families are not mentioned by the Campanile genealogies compiled at the beginning of the seventeenth century which also serve as *a posteriori* justification of the closing of the noble *ceto*; all the marriage alliances with noble families are, on the contrary, indicated with precision and are accurate.

[29] As far as Puglia is concerned, studies of this sort are possible for Manduria (using the 'Libro magno delle famiglie di Manduria' in the municipal library there) and for Lecce (using lists and genealogies in P. Palumbo, *Storia di Lecce* (Galatina, 1981), F. Gaudioso, *Lecce in età moderna. Società, amministrazione e potere locale* (Galatina, 1996) and A. Foscarini, *Armerista e notiziario delle famiglie nobili, notabili e feudatarie di Terra d'Otranto (oggi provincie di Lecce, Brindisi e di Taranto) estinte e viventi, con tavole genealogiche* (Lecce, 1903 and 1927; repr. Bologna, 1971)).

followers'.[30] He reiterated these sentiments a few months later 'at the time when there existed hate and particular enmity between them which now, thank God, have been completely extinguished'.[31] Peace was achieved through women, through marriage. But what governor Biondi did not say or did not want to say is that this 'peace', brought about by the Filo/Corcoli marriage, was based on the break-up of the political unity of the Corcoli, a rupture which permitted an enduring reversal of alliances and the momentary victory of the de Notariis faction. All these things would condition local political life until the end of the sixteenth century and the first years of the seventeenth.

From October 1568 onwards, the Gratiano Filo faction reacted forcefully and condemned the factional scheming of Biondi. The *auditore* Zuniga wrote to the duke from Naples: 'Gratiano del Filo of Altamura has come here to Naples complaining of certain wrongs which he claims Signor Biondi has had done to him'.[32] On 1 October, a letter signed by only eight people (as opposed to the twenty-nine of 10 August 1567) arrived in the form of a detailed denunciation: '[Biondi], having made there many friends and accomplices, did not now want to relinquish this office, in contravention of the privileges of this city and the laws of this kingdom'.[33] The governor was probably not without blame because several years later, in 1570, a trial was opened by the royal fisc accusing him of horse smuggling.[34] But the *auditore* Zuniga ended by coming to the defence of the governor (who had also been appointed captain) 'for having calmed down all these enmities' and he depicted Gratiano Filo as 'a very insolent man . . . who always quarrelled with the captains and governors'.[35] The die was cast: with the support of the feudal administrators, the de Notariis faction triumphed and from the end of 1568 lashed out at its enemies. Reports of acts of violence, fiscal victimization and

[30] 'M'è talmente riuscito il disegno che un fratello di M. Giovan Fulgentio Corcoli ha pigliato per moglie una figlia di M. Giulio Filo, per il quale parentado è cessato ogni odio, deposto ogni rancor e spenta ogn'invidia non solo tra queste due famiglie principali, ma ancora tra li lor parenti, amici et adherenti': ASN, Archivio Farnesiano 2009.

[31] 'In tempo anco che tra di loro erano odii e particolar inimicitie le quali hora per gratia di N. S. Iddio del tutto son estinte': *ibid.*

[32] 'Gratiano del Filo d'Altamura è venuto qui in Napoli a dolersi et aggravarsi d'alcuni aggravi che pretende li habbia fatto il Sr. Biondi': *ibid.*

[33] 'Havendo ivi contrattato molte amicitie et compari non gli pare hora di deponere detto offitio contra la forma degli privilegi di detta città e legge di questo regno': *ibid.* Giovan Vincenzo Viti, Giulio Petronelli, Gratiano Filo and Giovan Francesco Filo were among the signatories.

[34] ASN, Contestazioni giudiziarie, ex Pandetta Marullo 156: Atti del regio fisco contro Gio. Marco Biondi, ex capitano di Altamura per contrabando di cavalli.

[35] 'Per havere quietato tutti l'inimicitie' and 'un uomo insolentissimo . . . voler sempre pigliarsela co' capitani o governatori': ASN, Archivio Farnesiano 2009.

usurpation of the land of members of the Gratiano Filo faction recur constantly in the letters of 1569–70. But it was above all through a partisan use of justice that enemies were struck: the de Notariis faction put pressure on the feudal overlord (usually with success) to obtain pardon for its members who were sentenced or prosecuted, and went all out against the adherents of the Gratiano Filo faction to obtain trials which led to heavy penalties, such as banishment, confiscation of possessions, imprisonment and even the death penalty.

If the names of October 1568 were reduced to eight, they nevertheless had all been part of the Filo faction in August 1567. At the beginning of 1569 and up to the early years of the 1570s, the core of the faction which remained opposed to that of the de Notariis was always constituted by the Filo. Here it is important to clarify how the political break-up of the Filo family came about. It was not the result of pure chance or the choice of one or other individual, as a rapid reading of the texts and names might suggest, but it followed the fault lines of the main branches. This is obvious if all the Filo protagonists in this history are put back into their genealogy. Before the marriage of Portia Filo and Giovan Prudentio Corcoli, the lineage consisted of four principal branches (a fifth, represented only by Jacopo, a priest, was about to become extinct). Each branch was represented in the faction of Gratiano by one of the heads of the family: apart from Gratiano, who was probably the oldest member of the senior branch (A), there was Marcello for branch B, Giulio for branch C and Pietro Aurelio for branch D (see figure 1). In terms of genealogical proximity, A is closer to B (brother and nephew) than to C and D (first cousins and third cousins). After the Filo/Corcoli marriage, Giulio Filo transferred to the de Notariis faction. Gratiano remained head of his faction, but his nephews Jacopo and Marcello, instead of following him, followed their distant, third-degree cousin, Giulio. In the same fashion, Giovan Francesco did not follow his nearest cousin, Giulio, but his most distant cousin, Gratiano (see figure 2). The *political* segmentation did not take place according to the rule of 'the closer the better' (A ought to ally with B against C and D) but on the contrary followed the rule of the greatest distance, or in simpler terms, the closest branches became integrated into opposing factions. All this seems to contradict completely the classic schemata of segmentation which fundamentally observe the rule of proximity. But perhaps the contradiction is merely apparent and poses an essential problem about the interpretation of segmentary mechanisms: this is *political* segmentation, a game of political alliances.

Here is not the place to rehearse the classic theory of segmentation as elaborated by Evans-Pritchard and Fortes, a theory much criticized by

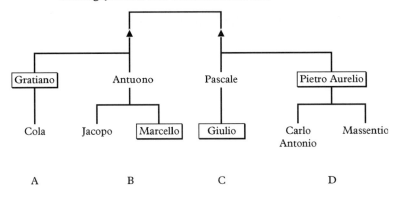

Fig. 1 The Filo lineage and adherents to the faction of Gratiano Filo on 10 August 1567 (in boxes)

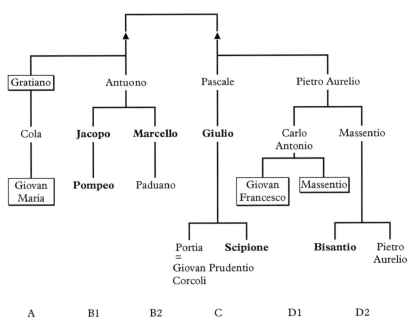

Fig. 2 Names in **bold**: adherents of the Giulio Filo/de Notariis faction. Adherents to the Gratiano Filo/Claudio de Angelis faction (in boxes)

Holy and many other authors after him.[36] In the political confrontations described, the problem is to understand the relative weight, on the one hand, of friendships between leaders, of constructions of networks, of political alliances, of 'the balance of the entities in question',[37] in a word, of the political game itself; and the weight, on the contrary, of 'balances between segments', that is the possible structural rules which govern the division into segments. We here want simply to suggest some questions and analytical methods for a more general study of the 'dynamics of conflict' which allows a clarification of the issue. The thesis which we propose to expand is that of the existence of a strong opposition between 'private' segmentation, which follows the rule of proximity, and 'political' segmentation, which on the contrary tends to contradict it. The political history of Renaissance Italy is full of examples of large families whose different branches belong to opposing parties (one example is the Acquaviva in Southern Italy); this tactic was often discovered to be an excellent guarantee of survival for the family, as the 'winner' generally incorporated the possessions of the 'loser'. This presupposes a radical distinction between the private and political spheres which does not exist (or only in a small degree) in the 'segmentary' societies studied by anthropologists.

These alliances were effective at the level of political struggle but this does not mean that they remained effective at all levels of the dynamics of conflict. On 1 July 1580 a serious incident took place on the steps of the cathedral: Gratiano Filo, in conversation with others, met and attacked one of his enemies, Epifanio Corrado, cousin of Giosuè Corrado, once an adherent of the Gratiano faction. The situation deteriorated and blood ran: Epifanio and Gratiano both died from their wounds. Those involved, either in the incident or in the subsequent trial, were very numerous: members of the Petronelli, Viti and Castelli families, who belonged to the Gratiano faction, or their brothers or sons. Above all there were many of the Filo: Pietro Aurelio and his son, the cleric Flaminio, Carlo Antonio – that is, all the Filo who remained close to Gratiano. The incident was political, and action was dictated by adherence to faction.

It was completely otherwise in a series of trials held between 1598 and 1603 which set Giuseppe and Orazio Campanile, first cousins, against Giovan Vincenzo Carello, a cousin of Orazio but through the female line.

---

[36] E. Evans-Pritchard, *The Nuer* (London, 1940), Evans-Pritchard, *Kinship and Marriage among the Nuer* (Oxford, 1951); M. Fortes, *The Dynamics of Clanship among the Tallensi* (London, 1945); L. Holy, '"Nuer politics". Segmentary lineage systems reconsidered', *The Queen's University Papers in Social Anthropology*, 4 (1979). For the state of the debate, see M. Verdon, *Contre la culture. Fondement d'une anthropologie sociale opérationnelle* (Paris, 1991).

[37] 'les équilibres dans les masses en présence': Verdon, *Contre la culture*, p. 255.

The incident this time was strictly private. Giovan Vincenzo was accused of having held Caterina Manerba, the wife of Orazio, at his house (he had probably abused her). Giovan Vincenzo would end by being assassinated by Caterina's nephew, Belisario Manerba. In this affair, all the protagon-ists lined up in one camp or the other following a very strict rule of kinship proximity which ignored all political membership of either faction.[38]

We are faced by apparently contradictory behaviour. On one side, there is a political construction, the faction, which involves vertical relation-ships and networks, linking the leader to the troops. These relationships, mainly constructed and then consolidated through marriage alliances, tend to break down horizontal solidarities within family lineages. On the other side, there are private or social conflicts which tend, instead, to reactivate these horizontal solidarities and networks, according to the fundamental rule of kinship proximity: 'me against my brother, me and my brother against my cousins, me, my brother and my cousins against the world' (Berber proverb).

How can such contradictory behaviour exist? What is needed is a study of the internal dynamics of conflict, a sensitive study devoted less to the nature of conflicts, to offences and their possible statistical measurement (assaults, murders, thefts), to the functioning of the judicial apparatus or to the cultural confrontations that a trial could activate,[39] than to the body of relational mechanisms established according to the genealogical, social and political positions of the people initially involved. As the examples cited above (and the Berber proverb) suggest, the opposition between ego and his brother does not activate the same type of link as an opposition between ego and distant cousins or non-relatives. Nor does anything stop individuals, who are defined as mortal enemies in their clashes over internal political problems of the commune, from ending up as friends and allies in larger conflicts of, for example, commune versus feudal overlord, or in private conflicts between one of their common relatives and a stranger. What one must try to understand is why in such a situation one type of network is activated rather than another; and where the limit is between the 'political' which seems to activate vertical solidarities and the 'private' which seems to activate horizontal solidarities.

One of the essential qualities of a leader of a faction, of a political man, is without doubt knowing how to avoid political conflicts being trans-formed into or superimposed onto private conflicts. One understands

---

[38] These trials are in the Processi criminali in the Archivio capitolare of Altamura. Copies are in ABMC 130 (Orazio Campanile) and 157 (Gratiano Filo).

[39] On which see C. Ginzburg, *I benandanti: stregoneria e culti agrari tra Cinquecento e Seicento*, third edn (Turin, 1979); Ginzburg, *Il formaggio e i vermi: il cosmo di un mugnaio del '500*, fifth edn (Turin, 1976).

better, thus, the role of leadership of the de Notariis/Corcoli in the 1560s and 1570s: these two families were not lineages like the Filo, but simple, isolated groups of brothers; Giovan Lorenzo and Fulgentio had brothers but not cousins. Their alliance networks were less extensive but more coherent than those of the Filo, and they were not threatened by possible internal segmentation.

It should be underlined that the mechanisms of segmentation that have been analysed in the example of the Filo appear in all the other lineages. It has been seen that the Viti were already, before 1568, divided between Giovan Antonio, husband of Fidelia Corcoli, and a partisan of the Corcoli faction, and his nephew Giovan Vincenzo, husband of Giulia di Renzo and an adherent of Gratiano Filo. Between 1598 and 1603, a period in which struggle between the factions of Scipione Filo (an ex-member of the de Notariis faction) and Claudio de Angelis (an ex-member of the Filo faction) took a violent turn, and when the adherence to one or the other was particularly well defined, all the big lineages appeared divided and all these divisions were sanctioned by marriage: Giovan Fidelio Cinnamo, husband of Lorita de Notariis, belonged to the Filo/de Notariis/Corcoli faction, but his cousin Giulio, husband of Pompea Giannellis, belonged to that of the de Angelis; Mauritio Melodia, husband of Adelia Castelli, belonged to the de Angelis, but his cousin, Franchino Melodia, husband of Vincenza Filo, belonged to Scipione Filo's faction. The most spectacular segmentation was that of the de Angelis themselves: Claudio was the leader of the 'popular' faction opposed to that of Scipione Filo, but his cousin in the third degree, Manilio, belonged himself to the faction of Scipione Filo. It is also interesting to note that the reversal of alliances brought about by the Corcoli/ Filo marriage in 1568 seems to have provoked a general rearrangement of a whole chain of alliances and segmentations in other families. In August 1569 one of the leaders of the de Notariis/Corcoli faction actually joined the opposite camp: 'M. Angelo di Lauro, as soon as he arrived in Altamura, broke unpleasantly with Gio. Fulgentio [Corcoli] and moved from being in the same faction to joining that of the good Gratiano del Filo, Giovan Vincenzo de Vito, Antonio Petronelli, Giosuè Corradi'.[40] Note that when this event took place, Angelo was the husband of a daughter of Carello di Notar Carello, one of the most eminent of the Gratiano Filo faction, that Angelo's brother Giovan Geronimo Laura also joined the Filo faction,[41] but that another Tomaso Laura, whose exact

---

[40] 'M. Angelo di Lauro subito gionti in Altamura, con Gio. Fulgentio si sono di mal modo rotto insieme et M. Angelo che della fattione istessa era, hora s'è ritirato all'altra fattione che è quella di quel buon Gratiano del Filo, di Giovan Vincenzo de Vito, di Antonio Petronelli, di Giosuè Corradi': ASN, Archivio Farnesiano 2009, letter of 13 Aug. 1569.

relation to the others is not known (he was not a brother), continued to be described as an 'associate (*socio*) of Giovan Lorenzo de Notariis'. The segmentation led, as has been seen, to astonishing criss-crossing in the leadership of the factions: the de Notariis/Corcoli faction became the Filo faction at the end of the sixteenth century, while the Filo faction became the de Angelis faction. If the Campanile genealogies are to be believed, the de Angelis were in reality a branch of cousins of the de Notariis; 'giodice Angelo', an ancestor of the de Angelis, was the brother of 'notare Gualtiero', an ancestor of the de Notariis, at the end of the fifteenth century. All this naturally poses an important methodological problem: too often not only the texts of the period (accounts of political struggles, chronicles) but also contemporary historians conclude on the basis of continuity of names that there was a continuity of factions, or conversely on the basis of changes of name that there was a remodelling of factions. It has been demonstrated here that this is completely false.

Before putting forward a final consideration concerning the role and function of marriage alliances, the narrative of this history must be concluded. On 13 January 1571, Giovan Prudentio Corcoli, who by his marriage had assured the triumph of his faction, was assassinated and the store-house (*massaria*) of the Corcoli was burnt down. A notary, Pier Jacomo Pepe, was accused of murder and imprisoned.[42] The complicity of the Farnese agents, perhaps concerned at the overweening power of the de Notariis faction, was probable even if it could not be proven: Giovan Francesco Corcoli accused by name the governor Bombasi and the notary Giovanni Federico Maggiore, who would be appointed *erario* of Altamura by the prince in December 1572, of being responsible for the murder.[43] A parable ended in a ritual of violence foretold.

But the reversal of alliance sealed by the marriage of Giovan Prudentio and Portia was longlasting, as has already been underlined. It was anyway 'completed' on Giulio Filo's part, by the marriage of two other daughters, Sulpitia and Fidelia, to prominent members of the de Notariis/Corcoli faction, as it happened Troiano de Notariis, son of Giovan Lorenzo, and Giovan Jacopo Rossi. In the last years of the sixteenth century, after a long period of calm and domination by the de Notariis/Corcoli/Filo, the struggles started again. In this context, the relations between the allies were not always easy and they had to be regularly strengthened by new

[41] On 22 Aug. 1569, he signed, with Giovan Vincenzo de Vito, his brother Angelo Laura, his brother-in-law Giovan Mattia Carello, Gregorio Continisio the brother-in-law of Giovan Mattia, and Agostino Veglione a cousin of Gregorio, a virulent letter against the de Notariis/Corcoli faction.

[42] ASN, Archivio Farnesiano 2008, letter of Theodosio de Angelis to the duke of Parma, 27 Sept. 1571.

[43] Masi, *Altamura*, p. 60. Cf. Parma, Archivio di Stato, Esteri 266, letter of 30 Nov. 1571.

marriages. A letter of 25 August 1596 stated that Scipione Filo was 'feuding with Cola de Notariis, and at the last Carnival they were reconciled, with a new marriage (*parentela*) taking place'.[44] This new marriage was that of Giulio Filo, son of Scipione, to Tuccia de Notariis, daughter of Cola. This was a very political marriage, caused, it seems, by the needs of the moment to invigorate a failing alliance, but which when placed in the chain of marriages and descents during the three generations under scrutiny here, completes a very 'classic' schema in anthropological terms, that of the finishing-off of alliances in collaterality ('bouclage d'alliance dans la collatéralité') (see figure 3).

The narrative texts describe the marriages of Giovan Prudentio Corcoli/Portia Filo and Giulio Filo/Tuccia de Notariis in terms of immediate and apparently very 'fluid' political relations: the reversal of alliances at the instigation of the governor in the former case, and the necessity of buttressing difficult relations in the latter. Conversely, the reinsertion of these alliances in the larger genealogical whole, over several generations and several families, makes them appear as simple elements of defined structural organization which again suggest certain schemata and fundamental concepts from social anthropology. Which explanation is the correct one? The first, without doubt the simplest, could come from a straightforward reading of what the texts tell us. This political explanation, focused on the short term and on the constant flux of events, leads to a denial of all constructs, such as mechanisms of reciprocity and lineage segmentation, regarding them as the chance result of a general group endogamy and as concepts foreign to the social actors themselves.[45] A second explanation, more complex, would insist that the texts do not tell us everything, and are incapable of describing how phenomena are stratified over time. This structural explanation is focused on the *longue durée*, and underlines the frequency of the proposed schematic interpretations. The schemata of alliance and reciprocity are not casual. The genealogies of noble lineages in Altamura or families in Manduria offer dozens of similar examples for the same period of finishing off in collaterality. The marriages of two other sisters of Portia Filo, Fidelia and Sulpitia, resolved themselves equally in terms of even simpler exchanges between collateral relatives (see figure 4).[46]

Are these two explanations necessarily incompatible, and do we have to choose one or the other? All the historiographical debate of the last twenty years has tended progressively to tip the balance away from the 'struc-

[44] ASN, Archivio Farnesiano 2009.
[45] This is the position of D. Scheinder, *A Critique of the Study of Kinship* (Ann Arbor, 1984).
[46] A great number of similar examples for the sixteenth century are provided by the 'Libro magno delle famiglie di Manduria'.

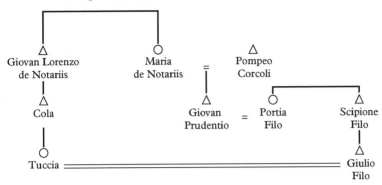

Fig 3   Marriage among the de Notariis/Corcoli/Filo (mid to end of the sixteenth century)

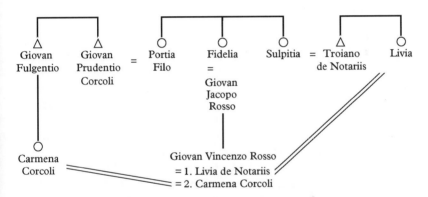

Fig 4   Political alliances and matrimonial exchanges (mid-sixteenth century)

tural' explanation towards the 'political' explanation. But at this level these adjustments run the risk of becoming meaningless. The real problem is rather to understand how one passes from the political to the structural and vice versa. For that, one needs to understand how action itself is constructed, according to which rules and within which margins of freedom. A study of the dynamics of conflict, which has been suggested in the course of this article, can allow an understanding of this important problem.

9 Marriage in the mountains: the Florentine territorial state, 1348–1500

Samuel Kline Cohn, Jr

Recent studies of marriage in late medieval and early modern Italy have challenged generalizations about kinship drawn from the anthropological study of primitive societies. By the late Middle Ages kinship exchanges were complex and their rules largely indecipherable within the time-frame of a single or even several generations. In unravelling the intricacies of dowry reciprocity and the micro-political exchanges between lineages, historians Anthony Molho and Gérard Delille[1] have shown the importance of historical analyses that extend beyond the anthropologist's limited time-frame of a generation. Instead, the balancing of exchanges in daughters and dowries could stretch over generations. Nor were these systems of exchange ever perfectly reciprocal as some families declined and others rose. But, despite pointing to such accidents, these historical studies have stressed the regularities, seeking to understand the underlying rules of endogamy in terms of class and kinship.[2]

By contrast, this essay will use marriage contracts to examine geographical exogamy – the extent to which families sought new relations that went beyond the boundaries of the parish, neighbourhood and larger regional and political districts. As part of a larger study of the Apennine mountains north and east of Florence and their incorporation into the Florentine territorial state after the Black Death of 1348, this article will

---

[1] G. Delille, 'Classi sociali e scambi matrimoniali nel Salernitano', *Quaderni storici*, 33 (1976); Delille, *Famille et propriété dans le royaume de Naples (XVe–XIXe siècle)* (Rome, 1985); A. Molho, *Marriage Alliance in Late Medieval Florence* (Cambridge, Mass., 1994).

[2] In addition to the works of Delille and Molho, see C. Klapisch-Zuber, *Women, Family and Ritual in Renaissance Italy* (Chicago, 1985); R. Merzario, *'Il paese stretto' – strategie matrimoniali nella diocesi di Como, secoli XVI–XVIII* (Turin, 1981); and O. Raggio, *Faide e parentele. Lo stato genovese visto dalla Fontanabuona* (Turin, 1990), esp. pp. 113–24. For investigations of the rules of endogamy, see J. Goody, *The Development of the Family and Kinship in Europe* (Cambridge, 1983) and the criticisms levelled by D. Herlihy, *Medieval Households* (Cambridge, Mass., 1987), pp. 16–17. In *Famille et propriété*, Delille does consider briefly exogamous marriages in the countryside of early modern Naples (pp. 197–202), but principally as a means for uncovering patterns of migration.

compare the lowlands just outside the city walls of Florence with the highlands. Do the social and kin networks structured by marriage underscore the generalizations of Fernand Braudel for the early modern Mediterranean world and Giovanni Cherubini for the Tuscan Apennines of the late Middle Ages? In contrast with the lowlands, were these communities characterized by an 'egalitarian poverty'? Were they culturally and even genetically isolated? Was the principal escape from these harsh lands migration downward, either to the lower plains or to cities?

In an attempt to answer these questions, I have sampled marriage acts from the vast Florentine notarial archives of the fourteenth and fifteenth centuries. While marriage acts and other notarial business can be gathered relatively easily and in large numbers for peasants residing in the valleys and hills surrounding Florence, the historian must search hard to compile such samples for the mountain hamlets along the northern and eastern perimeter of the Florentine territorial state. Such difficulties arise in part from the absence in the Archivio di Stato in Florence of an adequate topographical index for its vast notarial archive (the *notarile antecosimiano*) of over 18,000 volumes.[3]

But the problem stems more from the accidents of survival than from the absence of adequate analytical inventories. Perhaps because of war, peasant insurrections, the difficulties of preserving notarial protocols in local archives or transporting copies of them to the communal archives of Florence (as required by law),[4] notarial records for those communities on the outer fringes of the Florentine territorial state have had much lower rates of survival than those nearer the city, especially before 1400. On the other hand, it should not be assumed that the notarization of marriages and other business simply occurred less frequently in these mountainous and more distant regions from the city centre. When notarial protocols do survive, they are filled with an abundance of small transactions, numerous marriage and dowry contracts among local peasants, and *pax* or *laudum* contracts, which settled disputes between peasants over matters with little at stake, at least in monetary terms.

The one surviving protocol of the notary Ser Antonio di Giusto da Bruscoli (1428–35) is a case in point. Centred on the communes and parishes within the Alpi fiorentine, his business records hundreds of acts within these seven years. They comprised the meeting of parishioners to select their syndics, settlements of disputes between mountain peasants,

---

[3] I wish to thank Franek Sznura for sharing with me his immense knowledge of the Florentine notarial archives. I expanded my list of mountain notaries taken from the nineteenth-century topographical index of notaries by searching through the notarized conveyances found in the margins of the *catasto* of 1458–60 – the earliest *catasto* to calculate property values from earlier notarized transactions.

[4] *Statuta populi et comunis Florentie (1415)* (3 vols., 'Freiburg', 1778–83), III, pp. 140–1.

sales of small strips of land and houses for as little as $4\frac{1}{2}$ *lire*.[5] In these seven years, he drafted seventy-two separate marriage contracts, several of which conveyed sums of as low as 50 *lire*. Moreover, in his and other notaries' protocols, as well as in the *catasti* of 1458–60 and 1487, the names of numerous other notaries who worked the northern hills and mountains of the Mugello appear, but no longer survive in the present-day inventories of the Archivio notarile antecosimiano.

With these difficulties in mind, I have been able to compile a sample of 506 marriage acts for the Trecento and Quattrocento. From these I have carved out three zones for comparison: one for the plains and another two for the mountains. The sample for the plains comprises the suburban parishes of Santa Maria Novella that touched the city walls and extended down the alluvial plain of the Valdarno inferiore to the borders of the former *contado* of Prato; they include the *pievi* of San Giovanni, Santo Stefano in Pane, Sesto and Campi and correspond largely with a sample of villages I previously collected from the *estimi* (tax surveys) and *catasti* of the fourteenth and fifteenth centuries. Throughout this essay, I call this sample 'the plains'.

The first of the mountain districts comprises large tracts of the northern Mugello, north of Scarperia, passing over the Giogo Pass, running through Firenzuola and its vicariate of the Alpi fiorentine to the borders of the Bolognese state. The notaries in this sample worked as far west as the Calvana mountains of the former *contado* of Prato and touched the borders of Pistoia. To the north-east, the sample stretched through the Podere fiorentino to the borders of Romagna. Included in this sample were districts known in the tax records and other official documents as the Lega di Scarperia, the *prope Alpes* near the Futa Pass, the Alpi Fiorentine centred around the new town of Firenzuola, and the Podere Fiorentino bordering the Romagna. Similar to the sample from these plains, these marriages cluster in villages that I previously selected from the tax registers. I call these mountain villages the 'upper Mugello'.

The third zone comprised the Aretine Casentino, which extended from the borders with Romagna and swept south through the 'Montagna fiorentina', along the spine of the Pratomagno mountains and west into the former Aretine *contado* that in the early fifteenth century became incorporated into the vicariate of the Valdarno inferiore.[6] In addition, this sample includes the mountainous zones of the vicariate of Anghiari on the

---

[5] Florence, Archivio di Stato, Notarile antecosimiano (hereafter Not. antecos.), 792, fol. 151v. All further archival references are to this archive.

[6] On the formation of this new vicariate, see *Le consulte e pratiche della repubblica fiorentina (1404)*, ed. R. Ninci (Rome, 1991), pp. 18, 25–7, 29; and my 'Sex and violence on the periphery: the territorial state in early Renaissance Florence', in *Women in the Streets: Essays on Sex and Power in the Italian Renaissance* (Baltimore, 1996).

western-most borders of the former territory of Arezzo. These do not correspond to the villages I have previously examined through tax records, but were chosen because of the relatively rich survival of notarial records for this mountainous area during the fifteenth century. I call this sample the Aretine mountains.

The marriage acts found in these samples were celebrated by forty-two different notaries. They are not, however, spread equally among these zones nor across time. Instead, nearly two-thirds of them included at least one spouse from the plains outside of Florence (and indeed because of the survival of notaries who resided in or near the city of Florence, the numbers of marriages found in this sample could have been multiplied several times). Second in number come the mountain zones of the upper Mugello and then the Aretine mountains. The preponderance of these acts (96 per cent) were redacted after the Black Death, and almost two-thirds of them were drafted during the Quattrocento. For the mountains, the samples are skewed even more towards the fifteenth century. For the fourteenth century, I was able to find only eighteen marriage or dowry contracts for the upper Mugello (15 per cent of this region's sample) and all of them were redacted after the Black Death of 1348. I discovered no notarial protocols antedating the fifteenth century for the Aretine mountains.[7]

In almost half of these contracts (233) both the marriage and dowry were redacted by the same notary either on the same day or separated by only a few days. Another third of these documents (176) were 'confessions' of dowry payments without the marriage contract and 15 per cent (76) were marriage contracts without any mention of the dowry. The remaining 4 per cent comprise an assortment of different acts such as promises of dowries or engagements (*sponsalatii*), *finis dotis*, or recognition that the dowry had been paid, and dowry credits or portions of dowries paid sometimes years after the marriage had been consummated. When the marriage and dowries were celebrated in separate notarial acts, the marriage was usually celebrated in the bride's parish and the dowry transaction took place in the groom's.

One should not assume that marriages without accompanying notarized dowries meant that these spouses married without notarized dowries. Indeed, as with those from the city of Florence,[8] spouses in the Florentine *contado* who celebrated their marriages and dowries with

---

[7] Fourteenth-century marriage acts for the Aretine mountains may exist in the archives of Arezzo. However, I doubt it, since the numbers of the notarial acts housed there are few (fourteen fragmentary volumes) and pertain mostly to the city of Arezzo. See *Guida generale degli Archivi di Stato italiani* (4 vols., Rome, 1981–94), I, p. 379.

[8] S. Cohn, Jr, *The Laboring Classes in Renaissance Florence* (New York, 1980), pp. 23–4.

different notaries were on average wealthier than those who celebrated both acts with the same notary and usually on the same day. For instance, on 21 February 1367, Biagio the son of Lapo di fu Feo di Beze from San Martino a Sesto married Francesca the daughter of Stefano di Andrea di Ture from the same village.[9] No dowry followed the marriage act or can be found in the subsequent business of the notary, Ser Piero di Mazzetto di Talento of Sesto. But the families of both partners can be traced in the tax survey or *estimo* of 1371 and both were among the propertied households of Sesto, indeed among the wealthiest in this large parish.[10] The household of the bride possessed property valued at 25 florins, more than double the median village household value. More impressively, at 75 florins of taxable property, the father of the groom, Lapo, who by 1371 headed a household with two married sons and their families including Biagio, Francesca and their one-year old son, shared with two other villagers the highest property values in the entire *pieve* of Sesto.[11]

A comparison of marriages between the mountains and plains within the early territorial state of Florence suggests several tendencies which go against the grain of what historians have assumed about mountain society in late medieval and early modern Europe. First, they have concluded that mountain hamlets were characterized by an egalitarian poverty. Accordingly, mountaineers were poorer on average than those further down the slopes, but at the same time their communities had not suffered from the effects of commercial agriculture, urban investment in the land market, and, in Tuscany, the spread of the *mezzadria* system. To use Giovanni Cherubini's word, the mountains had not yet been 'proletarianized'.[12]

In a study of the late fourteenth- and fifteenth-century Florentine *estimi* and *catasti*, I have challenged these conclusions by comparing the distribution of wealth in the plains near Florence with the mountain communes of the Alpi fiorentine. Instead of 'mountain egalitarianism', I found that the contrasts in taxable household wealth were often more extreme in the highlands than in the plains and that the wealthiest peasants found within the Florentine *contado* (at least for the quarter of Santa Maria Novella) hailed from alpine villages such as Montecarelli and Montecuccoli.[13]

---

[9] Not. antecos., 13533, n.p., 21 Feb. 1366.
[10] Unfortunately, only a fragment of the *estimo* of 1364 survives for the village of San Martino.
[11] Estimo, 215, fols. 86v, 88r, respectively.
[12] 'La società dell'Appennino settentrionale (secoli XIII–XV)', in G. Cherubini, *Signori, contadini, borghesi: Ricerche sulla società italiana del basso medioevo* (Florence, 1974), pp. 130–1.
[13] 'Inventing Braudel's mountains: the Florentine Alps after the Black Death', in *Portraits of Medieval and Renaissance Living*, ed. S. Cohn and S. Epstein (Ann Arbor, 1996).

To be sure, tax records as an estimate of wealth both past and present are fraught with uncertainties. As in most societies the rich could better conceal their wealth than the poor. Similarly, mountaineers, whose lands were more distant from city centres and thus further removed from the surveillance of urban tax officials, may have been better positioned to conceal their wealth. In addition, a greater proportion of mountain wealth was tied up in animals and other movables easier to hide than land or houses. But such biases would suggest that the mountaineers would have been even more wealthy *vis-à-vis* the plains than their tax records reveal.

Dowry prices[14] give us another angle for viewing the differences in the levels of wealth and its distribution within mountain and lowland communities. In isolation, it might be argued that they provide a less reliable index for comparing wealth than the figures from the tax records. As historians have recently argued, the dowry was not strictly speaking an economic good but conveyed a sense of honour and had determinants other than simply supply and demand.[15]

Moreover, historians have assumed that the notary served only those who could pay his fees[16] and thus recorded the acts only of the propertied classes in the city and countryside. According to these assumptions, workers, propertyless artisans and the run-of-the-mill peasant must have had to rely on other unofficial arrangements,[17] and hence their marriages would have resembled the common-law marriages found among the labouring classes of early industrial England.[18]

---

[14] Two-thirds of the dowries (283) were evaluated in *lire* and slightly less than one-third in florins (132 or 31 per cent). For the remainder, one was given in *scudi*, another in ducats and seven in Bolognese *lire*. To standardize currencies over time I followed R. Goldthwaite's tables in 'I prezzi del grano a Firenze dal XIV al XVI secolo,' *Quaderni storici*, 28 (1975); and P. Spufford, *Handbook of Medieval Exchange* (London, 1986), pp. 1–30, 72–80.

[15] See my *Laboring Classes*, pp. 49ff.; Molho and J. Kirshner, 'The Dowry Fund and the marriage market in early Quattrocento Florence', *Journal of Modern History*, 50 (1978), pp. 403–6; and Molho, *Marriage Alliance*, pp. 11–18.

[16] I have not been able to find a list of notarial fees for fifteenth-century Florence; they are not listed in the section 'De arte iudicum et notariorum' of the 1415 statutes. But, according to the Sienese statutes of 1545 (*L'ultimo statuto della Republica di Siena (1545)*, ed. M. Ascheri (Siena, 1993), p. 445), the notarial fee for a marriage contract was 10s in the city, 20s within a one-mile radius of Siena and 25s for further afield. Thus, by this price list, a notarial fee for a 50-*lire* dowry would have constituted 0.25 per cent of the dowry. From the mid-fifteenth to the mid-sixteenth century, dowry prices had increased exponentially: see S. Cohn and O. Di Simplicio, 'Alcuni aspetti della politica matrimoniale della nobiltà senese, 1560–1700 circa', in *Forme e tecniche del potere nella città (secoli XIV–XVII)*, ed. S. Bertelli (Perugia, 1979–80).

[17] For instance, A. Stella, *La révolte des ciompi: les hommes, les lieux, le travail* (Paris, 1993), p. 260, assumes that not even skilled artisans in the wool industry had access to notaries or made notarized marriages.

[18] J. Gillis, *For Better, For Worse: British Marriages, 1600 to the Present* (New York, 1985), ch. 7.

By this reckoning, the poor of fourteenth- and fifteenth-century Florence would have escaped the notary and thus must remain largely hidden from documentary society. The only glimpses of them would be afforded by the occasional listing in a tax register or in registers of charitable causes. Thus, if these historians are to be believed, notarized acts of marriage and dowries would represent only the elite of peasant society. But, to my knowledge no-one has bothered to trace the peasants or urban workers who appear in notarial contracts to see what their economic status may have been in contemporary tax lists – the *estimi*, the *lire* and the later *catasti*. What proportion of the peasants married and gave dowries (at least notarized dowries)? Did those without any taxable property, the *nullatenenti*, or even the very poorest, the *miserabili*, appear at all in notarized contracts exchanging dowries?

At the same time, other historians have followed contemporary wisdom claiming that, without a dowry, there was no marriage in late medieval Italy, even 'no social relations' without the dowry.[19] But the tax records clearly show many without taxable property living in nuclear or even in complex joint families in the city and especially in the countryside of Florence. Did this mean that such families had been bonded without the sanction of an official notarial act, or even that these were families whose marriages had been clandestine or celebrated by 'unofficial' ceremonies at the village level now lost from the historian's documentary evidence? Indeed, glimpses of such arrangements do filter through the documents, such as nominal dowries of pennies cited by Cesare Paoli, token dowries such as a garland of flowers, and legal battles over marriages based on a man's or a woman's word and the exchange of rings.[20] Nor were such unions without a notarial presence necessarily against the law: as late as the mid-sixteenth century, Tuscan statutes recognized that marriages could be proven without notarized marriage or dowry contracts.[21]

Given the uneven survival of notarial records before the sixteenth century, the extent to which peasants lived in marriages without notarized contracts can never be known for certain.[22] But the linking of even a small

[19] Molho, *Marriage Alliance*, p. 18.
[20] Paoli, *Mercato, scritta e denaro di Dio* (Florence, 1895); Molho, *Marriage Alliance*; G. Brucker, *Giovanni and Lusanna: Love and Marriage in Renaissance Florence* (Berkeley, 1986). In addition, see *Statuta (1415)*, III, pp. 114–15. This law required even those who received dowries without a notarial instrument to pay the *gabella dei contratti*.
[21] See *L'ultimo statuto della Republica di Siena*, p. 193.
[22] For the Sienese notarial records, I once calculated that less than 2 per cent of notarial protocols survive before 1400. This calculation was based on a comparison of the number of notaries listed in the *gabella dei contratti* and the surviving notarial inventories. Because of the nineteenth-century archivists' decision to destroy the *gabella dei contratti* records in Florence, no such comparison can be made for Florence and northern Tuscany.

sample of notarized marriages to the extant tax registers might reveal whether those without landed property or other taxable wealth ever had recourse to notaries, paid their fees[23] and gave monetary sums as dowries. For the purposes of this essay, I have examined the smallest dowries found in these samples – dowries of 50 *lire* or less, which represent the lowest 10 percentile of dowries found in the samples for the years 1364 to 1428.[24] Such a dowry was less than a third of the median dowry given by those I defined in my *Laboring Classes* as the poor during the second half of the Trecento.[25] As bad as conditions may have been for these urban workers of late Trecento Florence, they appear far better off (at least in terms of their dowries) than their relatives left behind in the Florentine *contado*.

I have considered the years 1364 to 1428 because of the survival of Florentine tax surveys for the countryside. The year 1364 was the first of the *Capi di famiglia estimi*, which, in addition to specifying the household tax assessment, supplied figures for the estimated values of peasant property.[26] These surveys redacted by village syndics in the rural parishes (*popoli*) and communes were then submitted to the tax officials in Florence, where the final tax assessment or tax base was established. This figure then became the base rate for a variety of taxes (the ordinary, the extraordinary and the salt tax) which would endure roughly over the next ten years. The end point, 1427–8, marked the arrival of the *catasto*, one of the most thorough-going tax surveys for any community or city-state in Europe before the formation of the modern bureaucracies in the nineteenth century.[27] Between these two dates, the Florentines made five other surveys: in 1371/2, 1383/4, 1393/4, 1401/2 and 1412/14.

Out of my 506 sample marriages, forty-seven fathers, brothers or the brides themselves offered dowries of 50 *lire* or less; between 1364 and 1428, seventeen such dowries appear. Of these, eleven forged relationships in which at least one of the partners or their guardians resided in one of the twenty-nine villages I had previously sampled from the tax registers of the rural quarter of Santa Maria Novella, Florence. Of these, much to

[23] In addition to the notarial fee, the husband was obliged to pay a tax on his dowry (the *gabella dei contratti*), which amounted to 6d per *lira* or 2.5 per cent of the dowry (*Statuta (1415)*, III, p. 95). Although theoretically he had to pay this fee whether or not the dowry was notarized (*ibid.*, pp. 114–15), it would have certainly been unlikely that the commune would have collected it if the marriage agreement had been informal and undocumented.
[24] For these years the median dowry was 110 *lire* and the average 130 *lire*. For the entire database, it was 128 and 165 *lire*, respectively.
[25] Cohn, *The Laboring Classes*, pp. 71–7.
[26] The first tax listed in the *Capi di famiglia* series was an estimate of 1356, but it was no different from earlier hearth taxes.
[27] D. Herlihy and C. Klapisch-Zuber, *Les Toscans et leurs familles: une étude du catasto florentin de 1427* (Paris, 1978).

my surprise, I have been able to trace all but one marriage partner who resided in one of my sample villages back to the extant *estimi* or *lire* rolls. These examples are suggestive and give us insight into a world often assumed to be beyond the documentary pale. Of these ten marriages, not a single father, husband or bride possessed taxable property in the *estimi* drafted just before or after these marriages. Instead, each partner and their families were *nullatenenti*, that is, they possessed no landed wealth or even animals or other movables that the local syndics or the Florentine officials deemed worthy of mention or of evaluation. Moreover, their final tax assessments listed in the registers of the *libbre* or *lire*, list these spouses and their families with some of the lowest assessments found in their villages, with tax bases as low as 6s (*soldi*). Only the physically impaired and aged widows living alone were assessed at lower rates.

Just who were these individuals? In 1364, Dino di Guardo from the village of San Martino a Sesto in the Arno plain six miles to the west of Florence gave a dowry of 50 *lire* for his daughter Giovanna to marry a man from the *pieve* of Casaglia north of Calenzano (and not among my sample villages).[28] Unfortunately, only a fragment for the village of Sesto survives for the survey (*estimo*) of 1364. But in the city's final assessments of the following year, the *lira* registers, Dino was assessed at 6s, revealing this man to be among the poorest in the village, a *nullatenente* or even a *miserabile*.[29] Indeed, the assessments of those without property, especially if they possessed large families with able-bodied young men, might climb as high as two *lire*. On the other hand, in all the villages I have surveyed from 1364 to 1427 no-one with an assessment as low as 6s possessed any taxable wealth. By 1371, when the local syndics surveyed their parishioners again, Dino had either died or moved on from Sesto.[30]

On 27 October 1364, Lotto, son of the former Martino di Lotto di Maffeo from Sesto, married Francesca from his village, the daughter of Bartolo, son of the former Ture. On the same day he received the small dowry of 45 *lire*.[31] Both the husband and the father of the bride were listed in the *lire* assessments of 1365, and both were assessed at 7s, an amount indicative of those whose only taxable assets consisted in their labour power.[32] By the survey of 1371 – the first to list all family members and to give ages – Lotto, then thirty-five, was the head of a family of four. His wife Francesca was only twenty (meaning that she may have married at

---

[28] Not. antecos., 13533, n.p., 30 Mar. 1365.
[29] Estimo, 283, fol. 17r. Indeed, the local village syndics in some villages divided those without property from the propertied peasants, labelling the former as those 'qui sunt pauperes et miserabiles et qui nichil habunt in bonis'. See, for instance, the village survey for the alpine commune of Montecarelli in 1394, Estimo, 219, fols. 449r–50r.
[30] Estimo, 215, fols. 83r–89v.   [31] Not. antecos., 13533, n.p.
[32] Estimo, 283, fols. 17r–19v.

the tender age of thirteen, but because of age rounding it is difficult to know for certain) and she had given birth to at least one daughter of four and a boy of two. In the intervening six years between the *lire* of 1365 and 1373, Lotto's tax assessment had declined from its miserable level of 7s to 6s 6d,[33] and in 1371 he was listed as without any taxable wealth.[34] At fifty-five, Bartolo, the father of the bride, continued to reside in Sesto in 1371 and in 1373 as the head of a nuclear family of five. He too was assessed at 6s 6d and possessed no taxable wealth.[35]

On 19 February 1365 (1364 Florentine style), Tedalino (or Tedaldo or Tedaldino), the son of the former Bernardo, received a dowry of only 30 *lire* from Schelmo di Lapo to marry Margarita.[36] This dowry constituted the fourth lowest sum found in these marriage samples. Again, both families came from the village of Sesto and were assessed at tax rates levied on those without property – the base rate of 7s.[37] By the next survey of 1371 Tedaldo was assessed at 8s based solely on his and his sons' labour power; the household was listed without taxable property. Unfortunately, by 1371, Schelmo was no longer assessed as a resident of Sesto.[38] While it was presumably Margarita's first marriage (notaries customarily record women with deceased husbands as widows), it becomes clear from the tax survey of 1371 that it had been the second marriage for Tedaldo.

This unusually small dowry sum, low even by the standards of those without real holdings or other taxable goods, might be explained by the ages of the spouses and of Margarita in particular. In 1371, Tedaldo gave his age as fifty and Margarita's as forty-five; thus at the time of marriage Tedaldo may have been around forty-three and Margarita about thirty-eight. But despite her age, she was fecund, bearing for Tedaldo in seven years of marriage two boys who survived infancy (one was seven; the other five), suggesting that Margarita may have been pregnant at the time of her marriage (which may again help to explain the low dowry).[39] This household contained yet a third son, Maso, aged twelve, born from a previous marriage.

In 1367, Dino the son of the former Filippo of San Quirico Capalle within the *pieve* of Sesto (but not among my previously sampled villages) married Domenica the daughter of Matteo di Tano from the parish of Santa Maria Padule also in the *pieve* of Sesto and received the modest dowry of 45 *lire*.[40] In 1365, Matteo was assessed higher than anyone else in his parish at 1 *lira* 14s. Further, in 1373, he appears with an assessment of 1

---

[33] Estimo, 284, fols. 20r–23r.   [34] Estimo, 215, fol. 84v.   [35] *Ibid.*, fol. 88r.
[36] Not. antecos., 13533, n.p.   [37] Estimo, 283, fols. 17r–19v.
[38] He appears neither in the *estimo* survey of 1371 nor in the *lira* of 1373.
[39] On such accidents and their effect on dowry prices, see Molho, *Marriage Alliance*, pp. 244–8.
[40] Not. antecos., 13533, n.p., 25 Apr. 1367.

lira 12s.[41] – still among the highest in Padule. But Santa Maria Padule was a small and impoverished village in the marshlands or swamp in the Valdarno inferiore south of Sesto,[42] and Matteo's relatively high assessment was not connected with any landed property but determined solely by his household's labour power. In 1365 he was assessed as a joint family with his son, but possessed no landed or other taxable wealth. Nor had his condition changed dramatically by the next more detailed survey of 1371; he was without lands, animals or other taxable wealth but continued to live with his wife, a married son now twenty-two years old, another adult son of eighteen and a second nubile daughter of fifteen.[43]

On 30 May 1367 the notary Ser Piero di Mazzetto di Talento of Sesto transacted an unusual double marriage – the only double marriage in my marriage sample.[44] It coupled the widower Vinta or Binta[45] son of the former Pasquino from Sesto with the widow Nicolosa, daughter of the former Paolo di Benzo, formerly of Sesto, and at the time of marriage residing in Santa Maria a Quarto, and Pasquino the son of Vinta with Francesca the daughter of Nicolosa.[46] For the two marriages, Nicolosa gave a single dowry of 40 *lire* – a package deal. In the 1365 *lira*, Vinta was assessed at the low level of 7s common for those without property.[47] In the next survey of 1371 the two couples – father and son and their new brides – were taxed as a single household and remained without taxable property. In 1373 they were assessed at a tax base of 10s.[48]

In 1394, to marry Caterina the daughter of the deceased Giovanni di Chinale, the widower Bartolo called Veloncino, the son of the former Andrea from Sesto, received a dowry of 25 *lire* from Domenico di Renzi from the urban parish of Santa Maria Maggiore.[49] Perhaps Domenico presented Caterina's dowry because she had been his domestic servant. As Christiane Klapisch-Zuber has shown from patrician diaries (*ricordanze*), servants from the countryside often worked as domestics in order to accumulate a dowry.[50] In real terms this sum may represent the lowest

---

[41] Estimo, 283, fol. 26r.

[42] In my survey of twenty-nine villages in the late Trecento and early Quattrocento *estimi* from the quarter of Santa Maria Novella, Santa Maria Padule was either the poorest or the next poorest village, 1371–1412. In the estimo of 1371, only one household out of the eight possessed any taxable wealth.

[43] Estimo, 215.

[44] These marriages contrast markedly with the sample of peasant marriages studied by Delille, 'Classi sociali e scambi matrimoniali', for southern Italy, where double marriages, in which two families exchanged their sons and daughters, were common.

[45] In the *lira* and the notarized marriage act, he is listed as Vinta, but in the *estimo* of 1371 (215), his name is given as Binta.

[46] Not. antecos., 13533, n.p.   [47] Estimo, 283, fols. 17r–19v.   [48] Estimo, 215, fol. 83v.

[49] Not. antecos., 13521, fol. 216v, 2 Sept. 1394.

[50] Klapisch-Zuber, 'Women servants in Florence during the fourteenth and fifteenth centuries', in *Women and Work in Preindustrial Europe*, ed. B. A. Hanawalt (Bloomington, 1986).

dowry found in these documents. Similar amounts appear in these samples only before the violent surges in grain prices that ensued after the Black Death and during the early 1350s. In 1394, at age forty and now the head of a family of six, Bartolo was registered at Sesto without any taxable wealth[51] and assessed at 7s.[52]

Finally, in 1397, Giovanni along with his brother Corso, the sons of the former Jacopo from the parish of Santa Maria a Quarto in the *pieve* of Santo Stefano in Pane, received a dowry of 50 *lire* from Nicolosa, the widow of Lotto di Guccio from the parish of Santo Stefano in Pane, and then residing in San Lorenzo outside the walls of Florence, for her own marriage to Giovanni.[53] The *estimo* of 1394 lists the family of Jacopo di Naddo as recent immigrants to Quarto from the parish of San Michele a Castello less than a mile to the west. They arrived with no taxable wealth and were assessed at the surprisingly low figure of 4s, a sum usually reserved for the most destitute, aged widows living alone. It was especially low given that the family possessed two seemingly able-bodied young men, the brothers Corso and Giovanni.[54]

Thus, of these low but notarized dowries, not a single individual spouse or parent of the betrothed possessed any taxable wealth. Instead, they were variously categorized in these records as *nullatenenti*, *pauperes* and *miserabili*. Notarized business and documentary culture in the region of Florence for the late Trecento and Quattrocento penetrated the social scale lower down than historians have recently been willing to accept; indeed it encompassed the lowest groups found in the tax records. What would have constituted a respectable dowry for a propertied peasant during the latter half of the fourteenth century? Although more research is needed on this, it is clear that peasants of modest means and subject to violent changes of fortune did receive dowries even of 50 florins or more, three times or more the dowries surveyed above, and around the average dowry exchanged by disenfranchized Florentine artisans during the late Trecento. For instance, in 1383 Giovanni in some records, Nanni in others, and called Nannino, the son of the deceased Giovanni from the parish of San Romolo Colinata in the *pieve* of Sesto, received a 50-florin dowry for his betrothal to Andrea the daughter of Bondo di Totto from the parish of San Martino a Sesto.[55] In the *lira* register of 1384, her father, Bondo, was assessed at a tax base of 17s 6d,[56] and in 1383 his property was valued by the local officials at only 50 *lire*.[57] Unfortunately, the tax officials did not begin to itemize and describe the possessions in these tax surveys until the *estimo* of 1401/2, but in the late fourteenth century this sum

---

[51] Estimo, 286.   [52] Estimo, 219, fol. 435v.
[53] Not. antecos., 13521, n.p., 26 Dec. 1397.   [54] Estimo, 215, fol. 545r; estimo, 286.
[55] Not. antecos., 13521, fol. 116v.   [56] Estimo, 285.   [57] Estimo, 217, fol. 883.

would not have been enough to purchase even a small farm (*podere*); its value was the equivalent of a few scattered strips of land and perhaps a number of small farm animals or a mule. In the *Capi di famiglia* survey of 1393, Bondo was listed among the *morti*, having died two years earlier. After his name, the village scribe added the cryptic remark: 'del suo è rimasto allo spedale di San Gallo'.[58] It is not clear whether the 'del suo' referred to his belongings or to the surviving members of his household. But for other listings the 'rimasti' clearly referred to surviving family members and not to property. Thus, even those who gave substantial dowries, at least by peasant standards of the late Trecento, and who possessed taxable property might be only one step ahead of the clutches of poverty or among those seeking entry into the charitable institutions of the city.

In 1370 Bartolomeo di Jacopo di Vanni from the commune of Mangona was one of the few from the mountains to marry into the city, taking as his bride Antonia di fu Gialdo di Gano from Florence's cathedral parish of Santa Reparata with a respectable dowry of 310 *lire* paid by her brother.[59] His marriage, however, was not an attempt to escape the mountains for an urban way of life and its opportunities. Instead, he brought his urban bride back to the mountains; in the following year they were both registered as a part of the household of Bartolomeo's father (Jacopo) in Mangona. Assessed at 8 *lire* 12s and with landed property and movables valued at 300 *lire* in the tax survey of 1364, Jacopo was the second wealthiest in this large mountain commune. Yet, with war, plague and other natural calamities during the 1360s and 70s, fortunes in the countryside and especially in the mountains of the upper Mugello were fickle. These problems were compounded by Florentine taxation, which with the wars against the local ruling Ubaldini lords, and later against invading troops from Milan, weighed heaviest on mountain communes such as Mangona.[60] The fate of Jacopo and his son, Bartolomeo, lends biographical detail to this crisis in the upper Mugello. By the assessment of 1371 they had lost their fortunes; the value of their property had shrunk to a slim 10 *lire*, the price of a draught animal, and their assessment was reduced to 16s – an amount often charged to those without property.[61]

Thus, even the relatively wealthy in these early Renaissance villages were never far from poverty. These cases demonstrate that the poor, like the rich, relied on notaries and, even if for only a single moment in careers punctuated by calamity and want, they could save enough to produce a

[58] Estimo, 219, fol. 444r.   [59] Not. antecos., 922, fol. 13r, 27 Apr. 1370.
[60] See S. Cohn, 'Insurrezioni contadine e demografia: il mito della povertà nelle montagne toscane (1348–1460)', *Studi storici*, 36 (1995).
[61] Estimo, 215.

dowry for their daughters or their sisters. Moreover, as far as our record linkages allow, no matter how far from the city or how poor, these peasants sought out the local notary to confirm their marriages and dowry exchanges, even though they were not required to do so by communal statute.

While notarized dowries may well have extended through village hierarchies, it still might be argued that the dowry remains dubious as a benchmark of wealth or even status in the early Renaissance. Yet the dowry prices found in these documents largely corroborate patterns of wealth derived from the tax registers.[62] Like the tax surveys, they do not show peasants in the plains and near the city to have been substantially richer than those from the mountain hamlets on the Florentine periphery. Indeed, when all the dowries are considered, those of the upper Mugello emerge as the wealthiest among these sample marriages. On average their dowries (ninety-four in number) were about 200 *lire*, and if only those from the Santa Maria Novella side of the Mugello are considered, their average dowry increases further to 220 *lire*.[63] These highlanders were followed by those from the Aretine mountains, who on average gave dowries of 187 *lire*.[64] By contrast, fathers, brothers or the brides themselves in the plains spent only 147 *lire* to marry.[65]

The median values, however, give a different ranking: the Aretine mountains led with 150 *lire*, followed by the plains (130 *lire*) and, in last place, the upper Mugello with 100 *lire*. These discrepancies raise questions about another generalization – that wealth in the mountains was more evenly distributed than in the 'proletarianized' plains, supposedly characterized by large gulfs between rich and poor. Instead, the standard deviations of the distribution of these dowries mark the Mugello highlanders with the greatest inequalities in dowries, followed by the Aretine mountain valleys. It was in the lowlands that dowries reflected the most egalitarian distribution of wealth in these three regions.[66]

These results, however, need to be qualified for differences in the chronological make-up of our samples. Whereas all the dowry prices for the Aretine mountains and almost 90 per cent of those from the upper Mugello come from the fifteenth century, two-thirds of the lowland

---

[62] See Cohn, 'Inventing Braudel's mountains'.
[63] These results corroborate Cherubini's findings from the *catasto* of 1427: the well-being of the Apennine highlanders increased from east to west. See 'La società dell'Appennino'.
[64] Based on sixty-three dowries.
[65] Based on 220 dowries. The average dowry of a residual group of forty-seven dowries comprising various places across the Florentine *contado* but concentrated in the hills south and east of Scarperia was 155 *lire*.
[66] The standard deviations were 319.95 for the Mugello highlands, 254.27 for the Aretine mountains and 111.75 for the plains of the Valdarno inferiore just beyond the city walls of Florence.

dowries were drawn from Trecento marriage contracts. Although the late Trecento through the 1470s may have been a deflationary period in Tuscany as far as grain prices and perhaps other foodstuffs were concerned,[67] the same cannot be said for peasant dowries.

Average dowries doubled after the Black Death (see table 1) and then doubled again by the first quarter of the fifteenth century, reaching 265 *lire*. In the last quarter of the fifteenth century they began to decline, that is, just at the moment when grain and other foodstuffs began to rise.[68] The median values show a more steady trend and probably provide a more reliable index of dowry prices. Similar to the means, they more than doubled after the Black Death but continued their upward spiral until 1475, when they peaked at 172 *lire*. Afterwards, they declined through the early years of the sixteenth century, when dowry prices (based on a small sample of twenty-two marriages) had fallen drastically to 100 *lire* or about where they stood just after the Black Death. In real terms, however, these dowries reflect a much more impoverished peasantry. This decline corroborates a similar pattern traced through the *estimi* and *catasti* of the fourteenth and fifteenth centuries. While peasant fortunes in both the mountains and the plains had increased steadily from the first decades of the fifteenth century to 1460, by the *catasto* of 1487, the Florentine peasants (at least from my sample in the quarter of Santa Maria Novella) had ceased to prosper.[69]

Thus, a comparison of dowries divided by period would make a more reasonable comparison of these regions. For the Trecento, only the plainsmen and Mugello highlanders can be compared; moreover, such a comparison can only be suggestive given the small number of notarized marriages that survive from these highland communities. Nevertheless, the average dowry of these mountaineers exceeded those from the plains (125 *lire* to 110).[70]

On the other hand, more reliable comparisons can be drawn from the Quattrocento marriage samples. These show a shift in the rankings: the plainsmen appear with the highest average dowries of 216 *lire*, followed by the Mugello highlanders (209) and then those from the Aretine mountains (187). However, dowry inflation in the plains may have been given an extra boost by Florence's *Monte delle doti* (Dowry Fund) founded in

---

[67] Goldthwaite, 'I prezzi del grano'.
[68] For Tuscany, see *ibid.*; for other areas of Europe, see E. Le Roy Ladurie, *Les paysans de Languedoc* (Paris, 1966), and W. Abel, *Agrarkrisen und Agrarkonjunktur in Mitteleuropa vom 13. bis 19. Jahrhundert* (Berlin, 1935).
[69] Cohn, 'Insurrezioni contadine'.
[70] There are only eleven dowries for the Mugello and 143 for the plains. If we consider only marriages after 1350, the differences narrow, but only slightly, from 125.27 (11 marriages) to 134.51 *lire* (134 marriages).

Table 1. *Average dowries*

Period	Frequency	Mean	Median
Before 1351	11	58.27	40.00
1351–1375	108	110.56	98.75
1376–1400	43	121.04	115.00
1401–1425	11	264.91	134.00
1426–1450	108	179.12	122.50
1451–1475	97	217.39	172.16
1475–1510	46	198.16	146.95
Total	424	165.68	128.00

1425 and which can be seen in our samples by the last quarter of the fifteenth century. In several cases, the notarized dowries reveal lowlanders able to cash in their *Monte* investments, which added as much as 100 florins to their dowries.[71] By contrast, none from the mountains found in these samples were assisted by the Florentine *Monte*. As Anthony Molho has found more generally, distance from the city, whether with the rich or the poor, made the critical difference in whether a father from the *contado* or the territory of Florence would have been able to invest in the *Monte delle doti* and thus would have benefited from what he has shown to have been very handsome rates of return.[72]

But, despite such shifts in the Quattrocento, the differences in amounts still do not reflect the Braudelian contrasts between lowland wealth and mountain poverty. Indeed, the differences between the plains and the Mugello mountains were insignificant, and if the highlanders from the Alpi fiorentine are figured without their poorer countrymen further east from the drier mountains of the Podere Fiorentino, then these mountain peasants still exchanged the highest dowries in these samples – on average 228 *lire*.[73] On the other hand, the distribution of dowry prices during the Quattrocento does not differ substantially from the picture previously presented by the sample as a whole: again, instead of mountain equality, extremes in wealth were more accentuated at the higher altitudes. Equity reigned in the plains, not in the mountains.[74]

[71] For example, in a marriage of 1462 between spouses from Campi, 59 florins of a 87-florin dowry (370 *lire*) were paid by the *Ufficiali di Monte*: Not. antecos., 13534, fol. 518v; and *ibid.*, fols. 70r–v, 178r, 318v for further examples.

[72] On *Monte delle doti* investments within the territory of Florence, see Molho, *Marriage Alliance*, pp. 111–23; on the *Monte* schemes and their profitability, see ch. 4.

[73] This average is based on sixty-three dowries from villagers in the *prope Alpes* and the Alpi fiorentine. Significance is tested by a *t*-test: $t = 0.16$ with 158 degrees of freedom.

[74] The standard deviations in dowry prices were lowest in the plains (146.69), followed by the Aretine highlands (254.27), and then by the Mugello highlands, where the standard deviation more than doubled that of the plains (338.00).

In addition to indications of wealth, the marriage records allow the historian to reconstruct social networks. However, occupational ties remain mostly opaque in these documents. As might be expected, the great mass of these rural inhabitants were peasants and when the notaries did identify them by occupation (a rare occurrence in comparison to notarial identification of city-dwellers), *laborator terre* was the most common label. Of the 1,012 marriage partners in these samples, only eighteen husbands and nine fathers of the brides bore a profession other than that of farm labourer. These included a notary, a dealer in linen (*linaiolo*), a butcher, a barber, a porter, two masons, two innkeepers, two cobblers, three ironmongers, a sand digger or dealer in sand (*renaiolo*), an unspecified shopkeeper (*botteganus*) and, most predominantly, twelve millers. The paucity of such professions, nonetheless, corroborates trends found for individual professions in late medieval Florence, studied by Plesner, Martines and Park. By the period of the Black Death or shortly thereafter, Florence ceased to be able to draw its reserves of lawyers,[75] notaries,[76] and doctors,[77] from its surrounding countryside; the Florentine *contado* had been drained of its native professional talent.

Yet the families of spouses who possessed occupational identities remained among the wealthiest in their villages. On average their dowries doubled those identified as peasants or without occupations (317 *lire* as opposed to 161). Moreover, this elite of rural artisans may well have possessed a certain sense of community separate from the mass of rural toilers of the land. Of the nine brides whose fathers were identified by a profession, six married other artisans. Of those artisans who intermarried, their average dowry was 567 *lire* or three and a half times the average rural dowry.

Florentine notaries identified the residences of the spouses in these marriage acts far more often than their occupations. Remarkably, only eight of these 506 marriage contracts failed to identify the parish or village of both spouses and their families.

Despite the notaries' consistency in identifying spouses by place, interpretation is nonetheless limited by the differences in the units of territory used by notaries and other officials of the Florentine state to identify villagers. First, in the plains near the city of Florence, notaries used the parochial divisions between parishes and the larger groupings of the *pievi* established during the central Middle Ages.[78] In the upper Mugello parish

---

[75] L. Martines, *Lawyers and Statecraft in Renaissance Florence* (Princeton, 1968), pp. 149ff.

[76] J. Plesner, *L'émigration de la campagne à la ville libre de Florence au XIIIᵉ siècle*, trans. F. Gleizal (Copenhagen, 1934).

[77] K. Park, *Doctors and Medicine in Early Renaissance Florence* (Princeton, 1985), pp. 76–84.

[78] On these divisions, see C. Boyd, *Tithes and Parishes in Medieval Italy: The Historical Roots of a Modern Problem* (Ithaca, 1952); *Le istituzioni ecclesiastiche della 'societas christiana' dei*

jurisdictions were meshed with new and considerably larger secular boundaries. This was especially true for the second rung of geographical identification: after 1373 the *pievi* of S. Maria Bordignano, San Gavino Adimari and others were cited less often and were instead subsumed into larger, new secular nomenclatures. The secular districts of the Alpi fiorentine and the Podere Fiorentino came more into play in notarial protocols and especially in the Florentine tax registers. Finally, the villages of the Aretino did not rely on the older ecclesiastical parish structure at all, but were divided according to secular divisions – villages (*ville*), *curie*, *podesterie* and vicariates. In addition, parish structure was not absolutely stable throughout this period; smaller parishes were joined with larger ones, especially after the devastations of the Black Death.

Despite these problems, I have tried to assure consistency in comparing the spatial patterns of marriage over time by relying on the divisions of parishes into *pievi* and *ville* into vicariates as listed by the tax officials in the *catasto* of 1427. I have then created four categories of geographic intermarriage: (1) within the parish or village – the smallest unit supplied by either the tax officials or the notaries; (2) within the *pieve* (or the vicariate for the Aretine mountains and the Upper Mugello); (3) between contiguous *pievi* or vicariates; and (4) across *pievi* or vicariates, which often meant across large divides in physical as well as political geography – mountain valleys, quarters of the *contado* and even boundaries of the Florentine city-state.

Unfortunately, these divisions were not consistent in territorial size or population. Parishes could vary greatly in population. For instance, within the *pieve* of Sesto (from which the preponderance of the marriages within the plains were drawn), the parish of San Martino a Sesto counted 117 households and 509 individuals in 1427, while the neighbouring parish of Santa Maria in Padule within the same *pieve* possessed only 15 households and a population of 71.[79] Similar discrepancies characterized the communities in the mountains.

Nor was the second rung of topographical identification – the *pievi* of the plains, such as Santo Stefano in Pane, Campi or Sesto, or the regions such as the Alpi fiorentine or the vicariates such as Anghiari – of uniform size, either in territory or population. But, unlike the differences in the first rung of analysis – the parish or village – which mixed large and small

secoli XI–XII, diocesi, pievi e parrocchie: atti della sesta settimana internazionale di studio (Milan, 1977); Istituzioni ecclesiastiche della Toscana medievale, ed. C. Wickham, M. Ronzani, Y. Milo and A. Spicciani (Galatina, 1980); Pievi e parrocchie in Italia nel basso medioevo (secoli XIII–XV), atti del VI Convegno di storia della Chiesa in Italia (2 vols., Florence, 1981).

[79] These figures are derived from the computer tape prepared by Herlihy and Klapisch-Zuber on deposit at the Data Library, University of Wisconsin (Madison).

villages within all three regions in our analysis, the sizes of these larger secondary units introduce a considerable bias to our analysis. The earlier *pieve* divisions for the plains were much smaller, especially in surface area, than the new secular units created by the Florentine state at the end of the fourteenth century. Further, these new regions encompassed more diverse geographies than the older, smaller *pievi*; the new secular zones were divided by mountains and the distances between villages within these new jurisdictions would have taken considerably more effort and time to traverse than a casual glance at a modern map might at first suggest.

With these difficulties and biases in mind, table 2, nonetheless, shows the very opposite picture of mountain communities taken anachronistically from mountain communities in the modern period[80] or from Braudel's magisterial survey of the Mediterranean in the age of Philip II. The marriage records for the mountains of the early Renaissance in the territory of Florence do not highlight isolated communities, hollows of cultural and biological endogamy. Rather, it was in the plains near the city that one-third of those sampled married within their own parish. Nor was intermarriage common only within the larger parishes of San Martino a Sesto or Santo Stefano in Pane. Even in the tiny parish of Santa Maria in Padule with only fifteen households in 1427 and with as few as six in the late Trecento and early Quattrocento *estimi*, the rate of endogamy was not substantially less than the average for the plains.[81]

By contrast, less than 17 per cent married within their parishes in the mountain villages of the upper Mugello, that is, about half as many as in the plains. In the poorer Aretine mountains, the rate was lower still: a negligible 8 per cent or one-quarter of that found in the lowlands just beyond the city walls of Florence. When the second geographical rung is considered – that of the *pieve* or the newer secular districts – little difference appears between these three regions. But a glance at a map shows that such intermarriages in the mountains could cover considerably more distance than in the smaller *pievi* of the plains surrounding the city of Florence. For instance, from Sesto to the city of Florence was about six miles, but such a marriage journey would cross four *pievi* – Sesto, Santo Stefano in Pane, S. Giovanni fuori le mura and into the city – and would be classified as a fourth-category marriage. In contrast, spouses residing in Piancaldoli and Castro, both within the commune of the Alpi fiorentine, were separated by 20 kilometres as the crow flies and much more after the mountain passes of the Futa and the Raticosa had

[80] See J. R. McNeill, *The Mountains of the Mediterranean World: An Environmental History* (Cambridge, 1992).
[81] Of seven marriages, two took place within the confines of this tiny parish and three others within its *pieve* of Sesto.

Table 2. *Marital endogamy by region*

Region	Marriage within parish (1)	Marriage within *pieve* (2)	Marriage between contiguous *pievi* (3)	Cross-boundary marriages (4)	Total
Plains	82	59	78	36	255
	32.16%	23.14%	30.59%	14.12%	100%
Upper Mugello	20	27	29	43	119
	16.81%	22.69%	24.37%	36.13%	100%
Aretine mountains	5	18	17	22	62
	8.06%	29.03%	27.42%	35.48%	100%
Total	107	104	124	101	436
	24.54%	23.85%	28.44%	23.17%	100%

been negotiated. Yet such a marriage would have been endogamous to the second rung of territory and thus classified as a second-category marriage.

Finally, for the fourth geographical rung – that which crossed not only *pievi* but major lines of jurisdiction such as the border between Bologna and Florence or skipped over contiguous *pievi* and other districts – the mountains again show a more cosmopolitan world than that of the enclosed lowland communities outside the city. While only 14 per cent of lowlanders contracted these longer distance relationships, those in the mountains more than doubled this rate. For both the Aretine mountains and the upper Mugello, over a third of the marriage partners travelled across neighbouring districts and often into other city-states to find their spouses. For the plains even these fourth-category marriages did not often traverse great distances. Two-thirds (23) of them were marriages in which one spouse resided in the city of Florence and thus may have required a journey of no more than two to three kilometres, far less than an inter-regional marriage in the Alpi fiorentine.

In addition, instead of moving up and down mountain valleys along the major trade routes that linked Florence with cities to the north and east, a number of these fourth-category marriages in the Mugello highlands cut laterally east and west over the mountain ridges across the valleys of the val Marina, the Calvana and the Bisenzio north of Prato and into the *contado* of Pistoia. Again, contrary to the generalizations of Braudel and others, it was not the lure of the lowlands or the city that drove mountaineers across large territories in search of their future wives and husbands. Of 121 marriages from the upper Mugello, only three took their partners from the city of Florence and none married into the alluvial plains of the

Valdarno. In this regard, the marriage arrangements of the Aretine mountains were little different; only one out of a sample of sixty-four marriages married a city spouse (a Florentine), and in this case it was the only noble marriage found in my samples.[82] Curiously, not a single spouse from the Aretine mountains married into the city of Arezzo.

For some, such as those around Firenzuola and further north, the Giogo Pass, its terrain and its bandits[83] may have hindered mountaineers from moving southward and thus marrying into the plains of the lower Mugello, the Valdarno, or into the city of Florence. But east–west travel was even more steep and treacherous. Although the new twelfth-century roads[84] that ran through the river valleys may have allowed pilgrims and urban commerce to travel more directly and more easily between urban centres, the steep east–west meandering animal paths and tracks across the mountain ranges north of Florence had by no means disappeared or been displaced. From these marriage contracts, they appear to have persisted through the fifteenth century and on as the major arteries for local populations who pastured their animals on the high plateaux of the Mugello. It was along these routes, more than along the new arteries of long-distance merchant trade, that the men and women of the Mugello highlands appear to have met, traded, arranged marriages and established new bonds of kinship.

How then do we explain this reverse image of Braudel's mountains? Why were peasants in the plains, who were closer and more involved in urban culture and commerce, more insular in their movements than those residing in the more difficult terrains of the mountains far removed from urban life?[85] The answer may simply lie in the differences in work and land tenure. The plains surrounding Florence were dominated by short-term leases and the *mezzadria* system. These required peasants to renew their contracts and to move every two to five years but within tiny orbits, often from one farm to the next even within the same village, as is well illustrated by the hundreds of leases and *mezzadria* contracts drafted by the Mazzetti family of notaries, who worked for at least three generations within the communities of Campi, Sesto and S. Stefano in

---

[82] Not. antecos., 16091, fol. 94r–v, 23 Dec. 1460.
[83] For instance, Provvisoni, registri no. 88, fols. 86r–7r, 17 Apr. 1399, 'Pro hedifitiis supra Jugo Alpium Florentinorum', which describes the Giogo Pass as a place of murder and robbery, swarming with bandits and men of evil ways.
[84] On the road revolution, see J. Plesner, *Una rivoluzione stradale del dugento* (Copenhagen, 1938). For later studies on roads and long-distance travel, see J. Larner, 'Crossing the Romagnol Appennines in the Renaissance', in *City and Countryside in Late Medieval and Renaissance Italy: Essays presented to Philip Jones*, ed. T. Dean and C. Wickham (London, 1990); and T. Szabó, *Comuni e politica stradale in Toscana e in Italia nel Medioevo* (Bologna, 1992).
[85] Cf. *Viaggio in Italia di Michel de Montaigne (1580–1581)* (Milan, 1942), p. 149.

Pane.[86] In contrast, those from the mountains travelled great distances, especially if they possessed flocks of sheep or other animals. But, even if they did not, because of war and disastrous taxation (at least until the *catasto* of 1427), mountaineers were forced to migrate over long distances as can be seen in the records of the late Trecento and early Quattrocento tax surveys, the *Capi di famiglia*.[87] In both cases, marriage patterns appear to have followed patterns of migration.

In conclusion, marriage records from the territory of early Renaissance Florence have enabled us to peer into the communities of peasants, and in particular into the lives of the less often studied mountaineers, previously viewed largely through the writings of prejudiced contemporaries from the cities.[88] Dowry prices and the notaries' consistent identification of spouses and their families by place names has allowed us to question older generalizations about mountain communities in the late medieval and early modern periods. First, a comparison of the dowries of mountaineers and lowlanders who lived near the city of Florence do not reflect a mountain egalitarianism founded on poverty. Instead, dowry prices were no more substantial in the plains than in the mountains and in some districts such as the Alpi fiorentine they exceeded those in the plains for both the Trecento and Quattrocento, even though these more distant peasants had no access to the city's advantageous investment scheme, the *Monte delle doti*. Moreover, the distribution of dowry prices in the mountains was more skewed than in the plains, reflecting the opposite of what historians have heretofore assumed; society was less egalitarian in the mountains than in the plains.

Second, the residences of spouses show the plains near the city, not the mountains, as the insular communities in which a third of the spouses married within their own villages, no matter whether they were large or small parishes. On the other hand, mountaineers, perhaps because of their migratory patterns with their animals, together with more permanent moves across mountain valleys and even across regional boundaries, were the cosmopolitan peasants of the Florentine territory, a third of whom married over long distances across mountain valleys, the internal

---

[86] Not. antecos., 13521–13532; their records survive from 1348 to 1426 with only a few lacunae.

[87] For the differences in rates of migration and the places of migration between the mountains and the plains in the quarter of Santa Maria Novella, see my 'Inventing Braudel's mountains'.

[88] In addition to the work of Braudel, see C. Bec, 'La paysan dans la nouvelle toscane (1350–1530)', in *Civiltà ed economia agricola in Toscana nei secc. XIII–XV: Problemi della vita delle campagne nel tardo medioevo* (Pistoia, 1981); and the articles of G. Cherubini collected in *Signori, contadini, borghesi, Scritti toscani, l'urbanesimo medievale e la mezzadria* (Florence, 1991) and *Fra Tevere, Arno e Appennino: valli, comunità, signori* (Florence, 1992).

divisions of the Florentine *contado* and further into the territories of foreign city-states.

Finally, this study sheds new light on late medieval and early Renaissance marriage itself. The successful linkage of the lowest of notarized dowries to the tax records has shown that the roots of notarial and documentary culture sank deeper into the social bedrock of early Renaissance Florence than historians have believed. Even the most impoverished of rural Florentine families sought out the official sanctions of notaries and paid their fees to formalize their marital ties in writing. Such insistence on notarized and thus publicized marriages was widespread in the territory of Florence long before the reforms of the Council of Trent and the church's new levels of surveillance into the private acts of peasants and urban artisans alike. In early Renaissance Florence, it may not have been so much the church as the state backing parental control that demanded officially recognized marriages. As far as these records reveal, in every case in which a spouse had a living father, the father was present in the dowry exchange. Fathers, moreover, appeared not only with their daughters in bestowing the dowry but also alongside their sons receiving the dowry. Indeed, such control and cooperation went beyond fathers; it is not uncommon in these notarial acts to see mothers, brothers and uncles accompanying the groom as the party that received the dowry.

Those without taxable property did have recourse to notaries and at least for one moment in their lives saved what they could from their daily toil to provide a dowry for their daughters or sisters. Thus, the dictum 'no dowry, no marriage' rings true not only for the urban elites, but even for the propertyless households of the Florentine countryside. To that rule might now be added another – 'no notary, no marriage'. Not only the dowry but the notarized 'public' act was crucial to the late medieval and early Renaissance marriage in the eyes of peasant families and their village communities, even though communal law did not require it. While clandestine, unofficial and non-notarized marriages and dowries surely must have existed, the record linkages between notarial and tax records allow us to confirm that such marriages were not the norm. No matter how poor the family, nor how distant from Florence, peasant communities saw the public notary as an essential participant in the late medieval and Renaissance marriage celebration.

10 Marriage and politics at the papal court in the sixteenth and seventeenth centuries

Irene Fosi and Maria Antonietta Visceglia

By its very nature, the papal court was unique. Because of his office, the pope was permanently surrounded by an aura of veneration accorded to no other monarch in Western Europe. This in itself would be sufficient to distinguish the papal court from all others. But there were other distinctive features; it was, for instance, the only court in Europe which was entirely male-dominated. Save in the most exceptional times, women played no part in the life of an institution whose dominant ethos involved devotion to the principle of celibacy.[1]

While Italian historiography has responded with ever-increasing interest to current concerns with family, family relationships and marriage, first under the influence of historical demography, then within the context of social history, the study of marriage strategies in Rome, whether in the city as a whole or within the narrower confines of the court, seems to have been strangely neglected. Certainly, the progressive establishment there during the sixteenth century of a curial machinery of government based on ecclesiastical celibacy, and the extension of bureaucratic structures from which laymen were for the most part excluded, brought about a peculiar system of family interrelationships whose workings are still largely to be clarified and studied. The period saw a profound transformation of the social physiognomy of the city when the process of establishing mechanisms of government for court and curia was so sustained and decisive as to modify substantially the features of the city elite. What role did marriage play in this during the fifteenth and sixteenth centuries? Let us take contemporary witnesses as a starting point.

Marco Antonio Altieri was the product of a humanist education and a member of the civic nobility moulded by their exercise of civic office and jealous guardians of their own privileges; between 1506 and 1520 he wrote the long dialogue *Li nuptiali*.[2] The interlocutors were Roman

---

[1] J. Hook, 'Urban VIII. The paradox of a spiritual monarchy', in *The Courts of Europe. Politics, Patronage and Royalty, 1400–1800*, ed. A. G. Dickens (London, 1977), p. 214.

[2] Marco Antonio Altieri, *Li nuptiali*, ed. E. Narducci (Rome, 1973).

noblemen. In reconstructing the symbols and patterns of traditional marriage ritual and in seeking to reconcile the city and the curia, Altieri 'laid the foundations of an ethnology of marriage'.[3] However, the value of *Li nuptiali* is not only anthropological. 'Written in a language combining the cadences of Latin and of Roman dialect'[4] and to celebrate the marriage of Gabriello Cesarini and Giulia Colonna, the dialogue also contains a defence of a moral view of marriage, 'which perpetuates the family name and exalts the family group with special advantage to their place of origin'.[5] Central to the text is the heartfelt lament that in the most recent times the civic nobility had become distanced from this way of thinking. Young men delayed marriage in the expectation of a large dowry, used up their inheritance and showed little respect for the sacrament of marriage. In moralistic tones, Altieri extolled the war-like qualities of Roman nobles and their prowess in 'manly arts', and recalled the ancient marriage rites and the high incidence of marriage in the past.[6]

In *Li nuptiali*, Altieri pointed to a link between the increase in dowries, the decline of marriage and the consequent increase in celibacy, and the disappearance of entire lineages. He enumerated at length the 'magnificent' families 'glorious in their wealth, their numbers and their antiquity',[7] who were extinct or weakened in a city by now 'denuded' of its ancient nobility, and he attributed this to the increase in dowries, the adoption of a more ostentatious, less austere life-style and the increase in exogamous alliance at the expense of social endogamy, all as a result of the new role of the court and the curia. In *Li nuptiali*, endogamy is the rule and the norm, the only mode of behaviour that can guarantee a modicum of cohesion within the patriciate, whose unity was certainly threatened. However, Altieri's political philosophy is one of conciliation: the patriciate, in order to strengthen itself, could also take advantage of the possibilities offered to the city by the curia.[8] The example of the Cesarini, to whom the work is dedicated, allowed Altieri to extol simultaneously illustrious alliances and careers in the curia, citing Cesarini marriages with the Brancaleoni, the Colonna and the Sforza, and the careers in the curia of Giorgio, an apostolic protonotary, Giovanni, an auditor of the chamber, and, above all, Cardinal Giuliano.[9]

Written at the beginning of the early modern period, *Li nuptiali* would seem to reconcile two apparently contradictory elements: civic rhetoric

[3] C. Klapisch-Zuber, 'Une ethnologie du mariage au temps de l'humanisme', *Annales*, 36 (1981), p. 1016.
[4] V. De Caprio, 'La letteratura delle città-stato. Roma', in *Letteratura italiana. Storia e geografia*, II: *L'età moderna* (Turin, 1988), p. 451.
[5] Altieri, *Li nuptiali*, p. 4.   [6] *Ibid.*, pp. 26–8.   [7] *Ibid.*, p. 15.
[8] S. Kolsky, 'Culture and politics in Renaissance Rome: Marco Antonio Altieri's Roman weddings', *Renaissance Quarterly*, 40 (1987).   [9] Altieri, *Li nuptiali*, p. 10.

and the awareness of the central position of the papal court in the staking out of new cultural and social possibilities. Exploiting rather than rejecting their own roots, the Roman nobility could strengthen their chances of survival and defend themselves against attack by other families from outside – by the Florentines, for example. Increased dowries, marriages below the social status of the families, resort to celibacy, friction between urban and courtly life-styles were all elements in a complex process of social transformation which characterized urban Italy at the turn of the fifteenth century, but which assumed specific features in different places.[10]

What attitude was adopted in Rome by the city and papal authorities in the face of the phenomenon of dowry increase? In the course of the fifteenth century, from Martin V (1425) to Innocent VIII (1487), there was a steady flow of legislation governing intermarriage and the amounts of dowries.[11] In particular, the statutes of 1471 put a ceiling of 800 florins on dowries and of 600 florins on weddings and trousseaux. However, Paul II exempted foreigners from the restrictions, and Innocent VIII introduced a two-tier system, with the dowry pegged at a maximum of 1,000 florins for Roman citizens but without limit for 'foreign barons, magnates and courtiers'.[12] At the end of the fifteenth and the beginning of the sixteenth centuries, the Roman patriciate was particularly attracted to exogamous alliances within curial circles, a process encouraged by the papacy. The causes of this were the presence of the court, the growing internationalization of Rome and the lessening of differences in economic behaviour among the Roman nobility.[13]

In 1532, the 'Bando et reformatione delle donne romane' raised the dowry maximum to 2,000 ducats but still exempted foreigners.[14] It was not until the second half of the century that a single rule applied to both Romans and foreigners. The dowry reform introduced by Pius V in 1567 raised the ceiling of dowries to 4,500 ducats for everybody.[15] Finally, in

---

[10] See, on Venice, S. Chojnacki, 'Dowries and kinsmen in early Renaissance Venice', *Journal of Interdisciplinary History*, 5 (1975); on Florence, A. Molho, *Marriage Alliance in Late Medieval Florence* (Cambridge, Mass., and London, 1994); and on Naples, G. Vitale, 'La "sagax matrona" napoletana del '400 tra modello culturale e pratica quotidiana', *Prospettive settanta*, 8 (1986).

[11] A. Esposito, 'Matrimoni "in regola" nella Roma del tardo Quattrocento: tra leggi suntuarie e pratica dotale', *Archivi e cultura*, 25–6 (1992–3).

[12] On this legislation, see A. Esposito, '"Li nobili huomini di Roma". Strategie familiari tra città, curia e municipio', in *Roma Capitale (1447–1527)*, ed. S. Gensini (Pisa, 1994).

[13] A. Modigliani, '"Li nobili huomini di Roma": comportamenti economici e scelte professionali', *ibid.*

[14] *Libri statutorum almae urbis Romae* (Rome, 1567).

[15] *Statuto et ordine del pubblico conseglio del popolo romano sopra la riforma della dote confirmato da N.S. Papa Pio quinto* (Rome, 1567).

1586, Sixtus V confirmed the legislative measures of Pius V, raising the ceiling to 5,000 *scudi*.

These legislative developments can be supported by documents in the series 'Famiglie romane' in the state archives in Rome, a collection of notarial records pertaining to noble families in the sixteenth century, which allows detailed study of long-term family and matrimonial dynamics. We have worked on a sample of 500 legal documents (1500–1600) from this series relating to marriage,[16] which show the prevalence of dowries paid in money rather than property, although the precise amount is not always indicated. In the first decades of the century (1500–27), the average dowry (148 cases) was around 2,000 ducats. This increased to 3,460 ducats (158 cases) between 1528 and 1550. In the second half of the century (for which many registers are missing), the average dowry was 4,400 *scudi* (101 cases) between 1551 and 1574, and 7,800 *scudi* (69 cases) between 1575 and 1600.[17] The rate at which dowries increased was considerable throughout the sixteenth century, growing more marked in the closing decades and reflecting the general economic trend and rate of monetary inflation. The largest dowries – from which we have, moreover, omitted the figures for dowries of papal families because their exceptionally high level would have falsified the average – consistently exceeded the limits fixed by statutory legislation.

The notarial records also furnish evidence of the phenomenon of indebtedness incurred through dowry provision. Throughout the century there are traces in the documents of cases brought by families for unpaid dowries, with the consequent sale of property in city and country, in order to meet the obligation undertaken. Behind these enforced sales to meet dowry obligations can be identified a phenomenon that affected even the greatest families. Some were not able to pay the entire dowry agreed: thus, Alessandro Colonna, whose daughter had married the Neapolitan nobleman Marco Antonio Gambacorta and who had paid only 1,900 *scudi* of the promised 10,000, undertook to pay the rest to his niece Virginia when she reached twelve years of age.[18] Others tried to limit the sum involved: in 1557, Cardinal Nicolò Caetani wrote to his brother Bonifacio suggesting a marriage between one of his young daughters and Giuliano Cesarini; the latter was in prison and, because of his position

---

[16] For types of marriage documentation in Rome, see A. Esposito, 'Strategie matrimoniali e livelli di ricchezza', in *Alle origini della nuova Roma. Martino V (1417–1431)*, ed. M. Chiabò, G. D'Alessandro, P. Piacentini and C. Ranieri (Rome, 1992), pp. 371–5.

[17] For a statement of the value of monetary units given in the *Statuti di Roma del 1580*, see G. Garampi, *Saggi di osservazione sul valore delle antiche monete pontificie* (Rome, 1766) and J. Delumeau, *Vie économique et sociale de Rome dans la seconde moitié du XVIe siècle* (2 vols., Paris, 1957–9), ii, pp. 653–88.

[18] Rome, Archivio di Stato (ASR), Famiglie romane 4, fol. 84.

and because he was very indebted to the cardinal, was willing to agree to a dowry of only 15–16,000 *scudi*.[19] For the lesser nobility this phenomenon assumed the more dramatic proportions of a real landslide of wealth towards social groups connected with the curia.

It is worth asking what barriers dowries erected between social groups and how it was possible to overcome them. Sandro Carocci has studied the emergence of a terminology regarding the Roman nobility at the end of the Middle Ages which distinguished between *nobiles*, a title generally accorded those who enjoyed a certain level of wealth from their landed estates and who at times occupied positions in local government, and *magnifici viri*, a description which 'sought to set apart the lineages of the most eminent families from the rest of the aristocracy'.[20] The notarial documents of the early sixteenth century use various modes of address: 'nobile signore' and 'patrizio romano' for the civic nobility; 'illustrissimo signore' for the baronage; 'magnifico, potente ed illustrissimo signore' for members of the most eminent families. Parallel to this specific and varied use of honorific titles, an analysis of dowries shows a clear bipolarization between the great feudal nobility and the civic nobility.

At the beginning of the century, the dowries of the feudal nobility were far removed from the rest of the nobility. There were, however, variations within the group, with dowries ranging from the 15,000 ducats given by the Colonna in 1506 and in 1515, to the 10,000 ducats paid by the Caetani and the 6,000 ducats paid by the Savelli in 1524 and by the Anguillara in 1505.[21] In mid-century, when a good patrician dowry was around 5,000 *scudi*, Agnesina Colonna was married to Orazio Caetani with a dowry of 30,000 *scudi*. By the end of the century, only a few families of the civic nobility were able to pay dowries on the level of the feudal nobility, while the dowries of the highest nobility continued to mount, reaching, in some cases, the level of dowry payment made by papal families.

Dowry payments thus play a part in defining the identity of the various components of the nobility and in mapping the hierarchy within the group. Moreover, the monetary value of the dowries of the city nobility seems to be variable, although bounded by precise limits that marked them off from those of the great nobility, and was also differentiated within a single family. Thus, for example, in 1530, the nobleman Ciriaco Mattei, who was a conservator (*conservatore*) several times in the first half of the century, gave his daughters Orazia and Alsilia in marriage to

[19] Rome, Fondazione Caetani, Archivio Caetani 13152.
[20] S. Carocci, 'Una nobiltà bipartita. Rappresentazioni sociali e lignaggi preminenti a Roma nel Duecento e nella prima metà del Trecento', *Bullettino dell'Istituto storico italiano per il Medio Evo*, 95 (1989), p. 11.
[21] The same phenomenon, based on evidence from notarial documents, is noted for the early fifteenth century by A. Esposito, 'Strategie matrimoniali e livelli di ricchezza', p. 583.

Pamfilio Pamfili and Angelo Massimi respectively, each with a dowry of 3,500 ducats. A third daughter, Ortensia, married in 1538 to the 'noble youth' Giacomo Santacroce, with 1,500 ducats assigned on her marriage, received an additional sum from a property sale. In the 1540s, Ciriaco Mattei negotiated marriages with the Margani, setting up a double alliance between Sabba Mattei and Flaminia Margani in 1540 and between Sabba's sister and Giacomo Margani in 1542. In both cases, the dowry was to be 5,000 ducats. In a relatively short period of time, just over a decade, the dowry paid, within a single family, had tripled. In addition to the amounts of dowry payment, other important distinctions between titled lords and civic nobility emerge from an analysis of sixteenth-century dowry contracts. The *magnifici viri*, the smallest group of the feudal nobility, practised a narrow social endogamy, at times, however, extending their circle of alliances to families of the same sphere outside the papal states. Just how restricted the range of choice was for a great nobleman is shown by the reflections of Cardinal Bonifacio Caetani in 1615, reviewing the few possibilities for Duke Francesco. 'Negotiations [*la piazza*] are becoming ever tighter. The constable [*conestabile*] has only two daughters, one aged ten and the other aged four, but he does not wish to marry them, holding them back for some future pope. Prince Doria has four rich daughters, but they may marry only a Spanish grandee.'[22]

The choice between endogamy and exogamy was not so clear-cut for the civic nobility. Undoubtedly, those families defined as 'patricians' in the notarial language of the sixteenth century – the Altieri, Albertone, Astalli, Caffarelli, Capranica, Cavalieri, Cenci, del Bufalo, Gottifredi, Maffei, Mattei, Muti – tended to reinforce the characteristics of their group by repeated intermarriage, thus following endogamous practices.[23] However, we also find patterns of alliance between the civic nobility and foreign brides whose fathers were connected with the court and who regularly brought with them higher dowries than girls from the social background of their future husbands. Most frequent were alliances between members of the curial bureaucracy (apostolic scriptors, procurators of the penitentiary, abbreviators and, above all, consistorial advocates) who were not part of the circle of known Roman families,[24] and daughters of the civic nobility.

[22] Rome, Fondazione Caetani, Archivio Caetani 17421.
[23] On the relationship between social and territorial endogamy among urban groupings in Rome, see H. Broise and J. C. Maire Vigueur, 'Strutture famigliari, spazio domestico e architettura civile a Roma alla fine del medioevo', in *Momenti di architettura*, in *Storia dell'arte italiana*, part III: *Situazioni, momenti, indagini*, ed. F. Zeri (Turin, 1983), V, pp. 140ff.
[24] On the importance of having a consistorial advocate in the family, see A. Esposito, '"Li nobili huomini di Roma"', p. 380.

If, at the beginning of the sixteenth century, the division between court and city, which was the central theme of Altieri's writings, was still marked, in the first half of the century women can be seen as the fundamental element in a process of integration. The case of the Pamfili, who emigrated from Gubbio and worked in the legal profession in Rome at the end of the fifteenth century, is instructive. Angelo Benedetto Pamfili, who died in 1501, twice married into the Roman nobility (Emilia Mellini and Porzia Porcari), into families connected with both the curia and the municipality.[25] In 1531 Pamfilio, Porzia's son, was made corrector of apostolic letters and married Orazia Mattei, daughter of the Ciriaco mentioned above. The Pamfili were now connected to the curial bureaucracy and it was through the curia that they further strengthened the ties contracted through marriage. In the succeeding generation, Camillo Pamfili, an abbreviator and a conservator, married Flaminia del Bufalo, whose mother was a Serlupi. In the marriage contract, Camillo was described as a nobleman.[26] His sister Flavia reinforced the alliance with the Porcari by marrying Francesco Porcari, while his brother Girolamo followed an ecclesiastical career, becoming a cardinal in 1604. His maternal cousin, Gerolamo Mattei, was already one, and Innocenzo del Bufalo was also promoted to the cardinalate in the same year.[27]

Thus, within the sacred college, different surnames concealed very close family ties which had been achieved through women. Marriage alliances and careers in the curia among related families went hand in hand. The character of an open society that contemporaries recognized in Rome,[28] and the ability of the court to act as an integrating and amalgamating force which increased the drive towards exogamous alliances, coexisted with another characteristic of the city. Sixteenth-century Rome was a mosaic of professional and national groups. Each group tended to function as a microcosm, while forming in turn relations of dependence with the family of the reigning pope. The marriage market in Rome was accordingly complex in character. The strong groups, as we shall see with the Florentines, while adopting all the strategies of social integration, tended, at least until the mid-seventeenth century, to pursue a policy of endogamous marriage in defence of their economic pre-eminence and their cultural identity.

[25] I. Jones, 'Le lettere di Pamphilio Pamphili sul sacco di Roma', in *Blosio Palladio di Collevecchio in Sabina nella Roma tra Giulio II e Giulio III*, ed. E. Bentivoglio (Collevecchio in Sabina, 1990).
[26] ASR, Famiglie romane I, fol. 143v.
[27] B. Borello, 'Du patriciat urbain à la chaire de Saint Pierre: les Pamphili du XVe au XVIIe siècle' (dissertation, Ecole des Hautes Etudes en Sciences Sociales, Paris, 1993–4).
[28] For example, G. F. Commendone, *Discorso sopra la corte di Roma*, ed. C. Mozzarelli (Rome, 1996).

Let us now consider the character of marriage policy within a homogeneous social group such as the Florentine merchants and bankers who, after the return of the popes from Avignon, constituted the most numerous and powerful Italian community in Rome.[29] The fact that many families of this community settled permanently in the city shows how Rome and the court were seen to offer new and prestigious opportunities which would have been difficult to realize in their place of origin. The financial means available to the Florentine and Genoese merchants and bankers made it possible to meet the pressing needs of the apostolic chamber and of the papal family itself, and thus to establish a close relation of dependence, clientage and protection with them. Marriage policy had to take account of this progressive shift in the centre of gravity towards the Roman curia; and in this circumstance it was opportune to preserve and strengthen identity of origin and economic power. Individual and group strategies, including matrimonial ones, have to be understood in relation both to the immediate milieu – the Florentine community and in particular its financial oligarchy – and to the structural changes within the court and the Roman curia in the course of the sixteenth century.

Contracting an advantageous marriage with members of the papal family was a common ambition, also, for the Florentine financial elite. From the end of the fifteenth century, the political *rapprochement* between Rome and Florence and the election of Medici popes meant that such an ambitious project became realizable for a small group of the mercantile elite whose prestige and wealth already set them apart. Very telling here are the marriages of Antonio Altoviti who, after his first, strictly endogamous, marriage to Dianora, daughter of Stoldo Altoviti, contracted a second marriage with Clarenza Cybo, sister of Innocent VIII.[30] Thanks to this valuable connection, Altoviti, already well established as a banker, was able to expand further his flourishing commercial and financial activities in Rome, setting in motion a close personal relationship with the curia, destined to be inherited by his son Bindo, one of the most powerful bankers of his generation. Together with Filippo Strozzi, Bindo very soon became the leading spirit behind the pro-French, anti-Medicean opposition; and his family's marriages were an explicit expression of his political position. In 1511, he married Fiammetta Soderini, niece of Cardinal

[29] A. Esch, 'Florentiner in Roma um Quattrocento. Namenverzeichnis der erstern Quattrocento-Generation', *Quellen und Forschungen aus italienischen Archiven und Bibliotheken*, 52 (1972); M. Bullard, '"Mercatores Florentini Romanam curiam sequentes" in the early sixteenth century', *Journal of Medieval and Renaissance Studies*, 6 (1972).

[30] L. Passerini, *Genealogia e storia della famiglia Altoviti* (Florence, 1871), pp. 71–88 (tav. IV); A. Stella, 'Altoviti, Bindo', in *Dizionario biografico degli italiani* (Rome, 1960), I, pp. 574–6.

Francesco and of Piero, the *gonfaloniere* of the Florentine republic; by her he had a son, Giovanni Battista, who chose an endogamous option with political overtones by marrying Clarice, daughter of Lorenzo Ridolfi and Maria Strozzi, herself the daughter of Filippo. Strict endogamous practice remained characteristic of the Altoviti family over a long period, also in the lateral lines. Their withdrawal from mercantile activities after the closure of the Roman bank in 1590 did not deflect their tendency to intermarry with co-nationals in order to satisfy shared economic interests.

The marriage policy of the Altoviti, characterized by a powerful combination of economic and political motives, allows some general observations. Endogamous choices, though prevalent within the Florentine colony, were not the only possible ones. Different motivations depended on circumstances, on the political relationship between Florence and the papacy, on the individual and collective economic interests involved and on future opportunities and aspirations.

Within the first generation of Florentine families who emigrated to Rome, intermarriage within the milieu of origin clearly emerged as the predominant tendency. This endogamous pattern at times remained strong through successive generations, above all in families with continued involvement in mercantile and financial activities. However, marriage within the national grouping was not exclusively motivated by economic interest. It symbolized a deep and conscious defence of cultural identity, and of the political traditions of the family, and revealed an elitist sense of superiority, not simply economic, which had to be protected and consolidated within a multiform and segmented society such as Rome. Here in the sixteenth and seventeenth centuries is confirmed the endogamous tendency that Anthony Molho has identified in the matrimonial policies of the Florentine patriciate at the end of the fifteenth century.[31] The absence of specific studies of the Genoese community in Rome makes it impossible to define or compare individual or collective behaviour or to describe the marriage strategies within that mercantile group which, from the end of the fifteenth century to the mid-seventeenth century, competed with the Florentines for financial hegemony in Rome. There are, however, numerous indications of a strong tendency towards endogamous practice within the Genoese community.[32] If endogamy emerges as the mechanism most frequently used by the economically powerful Italian national groups in Rome to defend their strong sense of belonging and of superiority, within the Florentine community it did not

---

[31] Molho, *Marriage Alliance*, pp. 332–3.
[32] A case of strict endogamy is that of the Giustiniani: K. Hopf, *Les Giustiniani dynastes de Chios* (Paris, 1888); *Legati e governatori dello Stato Pontificio (1550–1809)*, ed. C. Weber (Rome, 1994), pp. 703–6.

exclude an openness towards, and involvement in, strategic intermarriage with the Roman nobility, in all its diverse and not always well-defined elements.

A case symbolic of the move towards precocious Romanization is that of the Salviati.[33] Jacopo had married Lucrezia, daughter of Lorenzo the Magnificent and sister of Giovanni, the future Leo X. Appointed salt commissioner, then treasurer of the salt works and of the province of Romagna, Jacopo became very wealthy thanks to the support of the pope. His arrival in Rome signalled a change in his matrimonial ambitions for his numerous descendants. The endogamous policy pursued in Florence until then was abandoned in a search for more prestigious alliances with the feudal or semi-feudal nobility, not only of the papal states, but also of other parts of Italy, and even of France. A significant illustration of this is the marriage contracted in 1514 between Lorenzo, the son of Jacopo and Lucrezia, and Costanza Conti. The Conti, together with the Orsini, Colonna and Savelli, were among the most ancient and prestigious families of the Roman baronage. The aim of such an alliance was to legitimize fully the entry of the 'merchant' Salviati into the world of the Roman nobility. This strategy of alliance with the nobility was expressly promoted and orchestrated by Leo X, and the marriage with the Conti took on, at that particular moment, a very precise political significance. One of the first acts of Leo X was that of reassigning powers, formally at least, to the Capitoline magistracies, which were a preserve of the civic nobility and of the most ancient feudal nobility, and whose powers Leo's predecessor, Julius II, had considerably limited and debased. It was, however, a political gesture that sought to reconcile the local nobility to papal authority, in order to make possible subsequent collaboration with the Capitoline magistracies, particularly in financial matters. The marriage of Lorenzo Salviati and Costanza Conti thus assumed the same symbolic significance of reconciliation as the festivities in September 1513 at the Campidoglio to celebrate the granting of Roman citizenship to Lorenzo and Giuliano de' Medici.[34] For the descendants of Lorenzo Salviati, this union marked the beginning of a transformation in status and way of thinking that became ever more removed from that of the Florentine mercantile patriciate.

If the direction taken by Lorenzo Salviati represents a precocious example of Romanization and the consequent ennoblement of a mercantile family, others, a few decades later, made similarly exogamous choices.

---

[33] P. Hurtubise, *Une famille-témoin: Les Salviati* (Rome, 1985), pp. 233ff.

[34] For the political importance of this celebration, see B. Mitchell, *Italian Civic Pageantry in the High Renaissance. A Descriptive Bibliography of Triumphal Entries and Selected Other Festivals for State Occasions* (Florence, 1979), pp. 119–24.

The Soderini, for example, did so in 1562, when Alfonso married Anto-
nina Mattei, who came from a family of urban nobility in clear ascent
during the sixteenth century.[35] On the female side, the Strozzi also
married into the Roman nobility when, in 1561, Maddalena contracted a
marriage with Flaminio dell'Anguillara.[36] It is not easy to identify the
motivation behind matrimonial choices. In general, the decision to marry
outside the national community is characteristic above all of the second
generation of 'mercatores romanam curiam seguentes'. Filippo, the son
of Bartolomeo Carducci, a Florentine merchant very active in the first
decades of the sixteenth century, had married his fellow Florentine Costanza, daughter of Raffaello Ubaldini. In 1542, he was granted Roman
citizenship, thanks to the favour Paul III showed the Florentine opponents of the Medici principate. His son, Annibale, was to marry Lavinia de'
Cavalieri, a Roman noblewoman. At a time when banking activities
began to show the signs of weakness that were to lead to the eventual
closure of credit operations, intermarriage with the Roman nobility was a
clear sign of a change of direction.[37] The examples are many: it is enough
here to consider some of the most significant cases as an expression of
group tendencies, in order to underline the dangers of oversimplification
that come from reducing marriage policy to a single type.

Bartolomeo Ruspoli, who arrived in Rome in 1529 and who, through
the protection of the Altoviti, became involved in their various and
flourishing activities, contracted an endogamous marriage carefully set
up to guarantee appropriate and effective papal protection. He married
Maria Ardinghelli, the niece of Cardinal Niccolò, an influential member
of the Farnese faction and an intimate associate of Paul III. The Ruspoli
were thus integrated into the mechanisms of the curia and the papal
court, and Bartolomeo's children, both sons and daughters, were all
married into families of the Roman nobility: Muti, Cavalieri and Floridi.
These were families no longer as economically successful as they had
once been, but who were able to add 'an ancient name' to the mercantile
wealth of the Ruspoli and offer a well-entrenched network of protection
in the urban world. Gradually, and certainly by the seventeenth century,
the Ruspoli had lost their identity as Florentine merchants, referring to
themselves exclusively as Roman nobles.[38]

For the majority of Florentine families in Rome, endogamous practice
ceased to be predominant only in the mid-seventeenth century. However,
a Roman marriage could exercise its attraction, as it had done for the

---

[35] ASR, Famiglie romane, t. 10, fol. 43.   [36] *Ibid.*, 5, fols. 17–22.
[37] *Ibid.*, 23, fols. 78r–81r.
[38] I. Fosi, 'Genealogie e storie di famiglie fiorentine nella Roma del Seicento', in *Istituzioni e
società in Toscana nell'età moderna* (2 vols., Florence, 1994), I.

Salviati and the Ruspoli, not only because of the honour that came from ennoblement and from acquisition of ancient lineage. Intermarriage with members of the baronage and the civic nobility implied an integral involvement in ownership of allodial and feudal properties and the assumption of considerable powers and privileges, especially in the legal sphere. It also meant acquiring greater power within the structures of urban government. Roman citizenship was obtained through marriage, as well as through privilege, through owning property in the city and residing there for at least ten years. It followed from this that, by the sixteenth century, the majority of Florentine merchants were also Roman citizens. Nonetheless, marriage was seen as the clearest sign of a wish to settle permanently and assimilate into the host society. It remains, however, true that the attainment of curial positions and honours, the amassing of substantial landed wealth, and the social transition from mercantile status to noble *rentier* were achieved by many Florentine families for the most part by measures other than marriage. The family trees of the Bandini, Acciaiuoli, Falconieri and Sacchetti, for example, display a steadfastly endogamous policy[39] which, while seeking to consolidate already existing economic ties, also fostered career-seeking ambitions in the curia, especially for those enjoying the protection of the Florentine papal families: the Medici at the beginning of the sixteenth century, the Aldobrandini and Barberini a century later.

The marriage policy practised by the Sacchetti family between the late sixteenth and the early seventeenth century can be seen as representative of the behaviour of the group in general.[40] It clearly maps out the stages of a social transformation played out over a century, beginning with success in mercantile and financial activities, but substantially conditioned by the relationship with the Barberini. In 1580, Matteo Sacchetti's son, Giovanni Battista, an anti-Medicean Florentine exile and enterprising merchant, married Francesca Altoviti, the daughter of Alessandro, himself a banker summoned to Rome by the heirless Giovanni Battista Altoviti, whose considerable fortune Alessandro was to inherit. Sacchetti's choice took place within the milieu of shared Florentine origin, a political ambience loyal to the anti-Medicean tradition which was already declining into a memory of an idealized republican past. The economic fortune of the Altoviti was in decline and in 1590 the bank was finally closed, but the marriage of Francesca and Giovanni Battista Sacchetti

---

[39] Marriage within the group of origin was a feature also for the Magalotti, Nerli and Rinuccini families. See C. Weber, 'Fünfzig genealogische Tafeln zur Geschichte der römischen Kurie in der frühen Neuzeit', *Quellen und Forschungen aus italienischen Archiven und Bibliotheken*, 73 (1993).

[40] For a more extensive analysis of the social transformation of this family, see I. Fosi, *All'ombra dei Barberini. Fedeltà e servizio nella Roma barocca* (Rome, 1997).

had the effect of transferring to the Sacchetti financial resources, property, profitable links with the curia and client relations already established by the Altoviti. These proved of fundamental importance for the ecclesiastical career of Giulio Sacchetti, as well as for the military career of Giovanni Francesco, for the financial success of Marcello, private treasurer and depositor of Urban VIII, and for ensuring the protection of the Farnese, the Aldobrandini and Cardinal Ottavio Bandini. Even more decisive was the protection and favour accorded by the Barberini, whom Giovanni Battista Sacchetti had helped financially when they first began to make their way in the curia, a process crowned by the election of Maffeo as pope in 1623. In this studied exchange of favours and protection, the intermarriage with the Altoviti marked the beginning of a time of economic growth and social prestige, which was also based on a wise choice of protectors within the papal court and which led in 1623 to the appointment of Marcello Sacchetti as depositor general and private treasurer. From then on, the Sacchetti's marriage policy had to subsume itself to the wishes of their 'masters' – as they themselves referred to the Barberini – and to the need to preserve intact the Barberini's protective benevolence towards the whole family.

The Sacchetti family tree displays a steadfastly endogamous pattern from the beginning of the sixteenth century to the end of the seventeenth in both male and female lines. Marriage was an essential opportunity for consolidating family alliances and boosting economic prosperity, as the marriages of the daughters of Giovanni Battista reveal. The marriage of Clarice Sacchetti and Luigi Altoviti, business partner of her father and brother, was strictly endogamous, consolidating a bond between the two families that was to continue throughout the seventeenth century. Ottavia's first marriage was to Piero Alberti, the son of Margherita, daughter of Neri Ardinghelli, who, as we have seen, had close relations with the Farnese faction. When Piero died in 1616, a second husband from within the Florentine community was chosen for Ottavia. The choice fell on Orazio Falconieri, the son of Maddalena Albizzi and Paolo Falconieri who, during the pontificate of Sixtus V, was consul of the Florentine community and had acquired a considerable fortune from the salt monopoly. The Falconieri, at the beginning of the seventeenth century, consolidated their own social and economic position thanks to the protection of the Aldobrandini and Borghese popes, and the marriage to Ottavia Sacchetti was certainly a positive step. Orazio was already a partner in many of his father-in-law, Giovanni Battista's, financial activities, as can be seen from the 'Quadernetto di ricordi',[41] but in this case it was the

⁴¹ Rome, Archivio Sacchetti 6, pos. 42.

position of the bride and her family that conferred an enhanced prestige which was social and economic in character, thanks to the close relations between the Sacchetti and the Barberini. The marriage to Orazio Falconieri was not, however, regarded by Ottavia's brothers as an enhancement, either economically or socially. Matteo Sacchetti's letters to his brothers[42] show a conscious superiority towards their brother-in-law, regarded as no more than a business partner, a mere 'creature' of theirs, whose opinion they were not called upon to consult when it came to important decisions on economic and family matters. From the point of view of the Falconieri, however, this marriage gave them access to the curial network of the Sacchetti and the valuable patronage of the Barberini. The ecclesiastical career of Lelio Falconieri was advanced through the protection of his brother-in-law, Cardinal Giulio Sacchetti, who in 1635 secured his appointment as nuncio to Flanders, the first step on the career ladder which concluded with his election as cardinal in 1643.[43] The Florentines in Rome, oscillating between a predominantly endogamous tendency directed at safeguarding their economic interests in Rome and Romanization through marriage into the nobility, came nonetheless to assume a curial character – as did the Sacchetti and the Falconieri – which assimilated their behaviour to that of other curial dynasties.

It is useful, before turning to the marriages of sons in the Sacchetti family, to investigate marriage strategy within cardinals' families. The prevailing type of family with curial connections which emerged in the course of the sixteenth century centred on the figure of the ecclesiastic. 'In the households of prelates and even more so in those of cardinals, it was the churchman who was the head of the family, not his married brother with children.'[44] Renata Ago has frequently stressed the distinctive configuration of these families, in which the recognized head was the prelate, who exercised his control through the more subtle instruments of persuasion rather than the more rigid ones of formality and authority, establishing within the group, on matters of education and the management of the young, a collaborative relationship with the women, and in particular with the first lady of the house, to the disadvantage of the married male brothers. In addition, very often, the prelate was also the firstborn, in accordance with the practice of assigning the eldest son to a career in the church which, initially widespread among non-noble urban families,[45] was by the end of the seventeenth century also a feature of

---

[42] *Ibid.*, Registro di lettere C.
[43] M. Sanfilippo, 'Falconieri, Lelio', in *Dizionario biografico degli italiani* (Rome, 1994), XLIV, pp. 382–5.
[44] R. Ago, *Carriere e clientele nella Roma barocca* (Rome, 1990), p. 68.
[45] G. Delille and A. Ciuffreda, 'Lo scambio dei ruoli: primogeniti e cadetti tra Quattrocento e Settecento nel Mezzogiorno d'Italia', *Quaderni storici*, 83 (1993).

high-ranking families. We can thus regard the model of the curial family as a variant of the feudal-seigneurial family model. The churchman, and even more the cardinal within a family, saw the marriage of his nephews and nieces as a delicate issue in which he alone had competence. Evidence for this phenomenon comes above all from the form of notarial documents: marriage contracts were drawn up for the bridegroom or the bride with the prelate in first place, sometimes with the father, but also alone. The phenomenon finds further confirmation, rich in significant detail, in family archives.

Let us consider the Spada family, which has been studied by Ago in a later period. The text of the promise of marriage made in Frascati on 27 October 1635 between Orazio Spada and Maria Veralli listed the individual guarantors of the decision to marry: the pope himself, the cardinal nephews of the pope, and in first place the Cardinals Spada and Rocci, uncles respectively of Orazio and Maria.[46] At the beginning of the seventeenth century, the Spada were still finding their place in Roman society. In 1631, Paolo, the grandfather of Orazio, had died. He was an ambiguous figure, a successful, unscrupulous speculator, treasurer of the Romagna and farmer of the salt tax of Cervia and Cesenatico, who had accumulated a fortune, through legal and illegal means, estimated by contemporaries at 3–400,000 *scudi*. The existence of fifteen children from two marriages to Francesca Ricciardelli of Rimini and Daria Albicini of Forlì risked blocking the expansion of the family's fortune and fragmenting their inheritance. While the family's financial portfolio, divided between land holdings situated mainly in the Romagna and income from investment, was shared between the firstborn sons of the first and second marriages (Giacomo Filippo and Francesco respectively), their father's ambition was concentrated on the career in the church of Bernardino. An expensive position as chamber clerk was acquired for him before he was appointed nuncio to France; and Urban VIII made him a cardinal in 1626.[47]

In their father's will, Bernardino, together with his brother Virgilio, a highly cultured Oratorian, with expert knowledge of mathematics and architecture, were made heirs jointly and severally of the Roman patrimony and declared responsible for the guidance and matrimonial choice of the numerous descendants, divided into several branches, in Rome and the Romagna. From the beginning of the 1630s, the cardinal became a skilful weaver of family relationships. The marriage of his nephew Orazio,

---

[46] ASR, Archivio Spada–Veralli 280.
[47] For Bernardino's career, see M. A. Visceglia, 'La giusta statera de' porporati. Sulla composizione e rappresentazione del sacro collegio nella prima metà del Seicento', *Roma moderna e contemporanea. Rivista interdisciplinare di storia*, 4 (1996).

the son of Francesco and Camilla Severoli, was an alliance patiently constructed by him. But why was Maria Veralli chosen as the bride of Orazio and as the heir of the cardinal? In accordance with what framework and what criteria?

Maria was a young woman, seventeen or eighteen years old, 'tall and well-built', 'with a fine complexion', 'without any personal defect, of a most noble appearance'. She had no brothers and just one sister, Giulia, twenty-two or twenty-three years old, a hunch-back 'of imperfect health'. Her weakly constitution seems to have reassured the Spada, who in their family papers remark that Giulia was inclined to celibacy 'as a consequence of her piety and physical disability'.[48] Maria came from a noble family who were closely related through the female line to the Cesi of Acquasparta and who had come into possession of the feudal title to Castel Viscardo through the marriage of Matteo Veralli, Maria's grandfather, to Giulia Monaldeschi della Cervara, of an ancient feudal family. At the time of the marriage negotiations, Maria's father was seventy-three years old and, 'of necessity', the family inheritance would be divided between the two sisters at his death. The Spada made careful calculation of the Veralli inheritance, estimating it at around 70,000 *scudi*.[49] Fifteen thousand *scudi* were tied up in dowry obligations, but Maria and her sister Giulia were also testamentary beneficiaries of Cardinal Fabrizio Veralli, their uncle. Maria had a modest dowry of 8,000 *scudi*, drawn from the cardinal's legacy. The Spada commented on this in their papers, even several years after the marriage, making such comparisons as seemed appropriate:

The Cardinal de Torres negotiated a Serlupi for his nephew with a dowry of 35,000 *scudi* before he himself was even promoted. Costaguti paid out a similar sum for his sister. That cripple Santacroce, son of Marchese Valerio, had, I think, at least 27,000 with the Orsini bride. The late Ottavio Ubaldini, that poor feeble knight, had 25,000 with his Accoramboni bride. A nephew of Cardinal Capponi who married an Orsini of Pitigliano, only sister and presumptive heiress of her only brother received a dowry of 30,000 *scudi* and also inherited the property of the family.[50]

Clearly Maria, in the absence of male heirs, was herself to inherit her father's feudal holding and this altered her financial position.

However, it was not economic calculation alone that made Maria an attractive match for many young Romans and, in particular, for the Spada. The Spada were not members of the nobility and Bernardino was

[48] ASR, Archivio Spada–Veralli 280.
[49] On Castel Viscardo, see M. D'Amelia, *Orgoglio baronale e giustizia. Castel Viscardo alla fine del '500* (Rome, 1996).
[50] ASR, Archivio Spada–Veralli 455.

their first cardinal at the curia. Maria belonged to the lesser feudal nobility, but most importantly of all she brought with her an unquantifiable patrimony that represented her real value: a dense family network of ecclesiastics over several generations with numerous connections within the curia. The Spada family archive contains a brief survey schematizing the network of relationships connecting Maria to families of the curia: from blood relationships with the Cardinals Girolamo and Fabrizio Veralli on the paternal side and with Cardinal Ciriaco Rocci on the maternal side, to the more distant relationship with the Cardinals Ariggoni, Carpegna, Mellini and Jacovacci, including the link through Maria Jacovacci, sister of her paternal great-grandmother, Giulia Jacovacci, with Pope Urban VII. Maria Veralli therefore was related within the fourth degree to a pope and eight cardinals. Behind the able Cardinal Spada's choice of a bride for his nephew Orazio we can see a shrewd, cold, genealogical appraisal, a patient reconstruction of Maria's descent, as if to calculate whether those names of cardinals to whom the girl was related would serve adequately to compensate for the brevity of Cardinal Bernardino's membership of the sacred college.

Precisely because the marriage of a member of a cardinal's family was always a concern of the curia, objections could always be made by the curia and by the papal family itself. The Spada–Veralli alliance did not meet with the initial agreement of the Barberini, who had thought of Maria as a bride for their maternal cousin, Lorenzo Machiavelli:

Cardinal Barberini and others in the family wanted Maria Veralli to marry their own Lorenzo Machiavelli and promoted their cause with some enthusiasm. Cardinal Rocci gave them the assurance they wanted and Cardinal Spada, although he at once offered to withdraw and give place to them, nevertheless fears that his 'masters' remain suspicious . . . Cardinal Rocci is now convinced that he is out of favour with his 'masters' and in particular that for this reason he was not given the archbishopric of Benevento and fears that in future he may suffer further disadvantages.[51]

We do not know how the initial opposition of the Barberini was overcome or how the negotiations continued. The clauses of the marriage contract were finally drawn up stipulating for Maria a dowry of 8,000 scudi, her half share in the future inheritance of Castel Viscardo and the palace on the Corso. For his part, Cardinal Spada promised to support the new family, at his own expense, with 'food, clothing, habitation, servants, horses, carriages and everything else they found necessary and appropriate to their status'.[52] Together the two cardinals, Spada and Rocci, further undertook to procure for the bridegroom the title of

[51] *Ibid.* 280.   [52] *Ibid.*

marquis. The feelings and wishes of Orazio have left little trace in the family papers apart from an expression of his gratification at the outcome of the negotiations.[53]

The historical debate regarding matrimonial behaviour in *ancien régime* society, in particular within the upper classes, centring on the question as to whether such behaviour was governed by individual choice or entirely by the mechanisms of family control and solidarity,[54] has little bearing on the unique situation in Rome. Here, the curia, an organism of 'nests of brothers or cousins' in Peter Partner's felicitous phrase,[55] seems to have entirely enveloped the individual members of its families.

Marriage negotiations, while requiring little active involvement on the part of the protagonists, were wide in scope and, in accordance with the functioning of the court, brought into play appointments, careers and the balance of factions within the curia. It is thus not by chance, perhaps, that at the very time the Cardinals Spada and Rocci were concluding their plans for the marriage of their nephew and niece respectively, their names appear several times in the papers of the council of state (*Consejo de estado*) in Madrid. Rocci was judged 'devoted' to the service of the king and trustworthy also on account of his prospering connections through marriage (especially the connection with Cardinal Arrigoni). Spada, who was trying to find favour with Spain and to place a nephew at the court in Madrid, was, however, mistrusted for his past connections with France. Thus the marriage was probably a means for Bernardino Spada to accelerate his process of alignment with the group of cardinals who, while 'creatures' of the Barberini, were not entrenched Francophiles, and were also prepared to play the Spanish card.[56]

The experiences of other families of the time show further aspects of this pattern of family relationships particular to the curia, in which the will of the cardinal uncle and the indispensable approval of the reigning pope were fundamental in the arrangements and decisions regarding alliances, dowries and entrance into religious life.

Let us turn again to the Sacchetti family. While the marriages of the daughters of Giovanni Battista Sacchetti and Francesca Altoviti all followed traditional endogamous practice, marriage strategy with regard to

[53] *Ibid.*
[54] See especially L. Stone, *The Family, Sex and Marriage in England, 1500–1800* (London, 1977); R. Trumbach, *The Rise of the Egalitarian Family* (London, 1978); R. B. Outhwaite, 'Problems and perspectives in the history of marriage', in *Marriage and Society. Studies in the Social History of Marriage*, ed. Outhwaite (London, 1981). A consideration of this issue within a Roman context, but for a later period, is in M. Pelaja, *Matrimonio e sessualità a Roma nell'Ottocento* (Bari, 1994), pp. 16ff.
[55] P. Partner, 'Ufficio, famiglia, stato: contrasti nella curia romana', in *Roma Capitale, 1447–1527*.
[56] Simancas, Archivo General, Estados Pequeños, legajo 3837 and legajo 3843.

the sons was more complex and had to take account of political constraints and, above all, secure the approval of the Barberini, their 'masters'. The choice of a bride for Giovanni Francesco, a younger son of the Sacchetti who, between 1624 and 1629, was commissioner general of the papal troops in the Valtellina and then at the siege of Casale, was viewed as a difficult diplomatic situation in which his brother, the cardinal, was the protagonist. The marriage was to bring the family added social prestige and greater wealth, and to open up new and profitable social relationships. The drafts of the letters sent by Matteo Sacchetti to his brother Giulio reveal apprehension and unease, different ideas on family strategy, on relations with their 'masters', with the Florentine community and with their relatives. Private correspondence also reveals ways in which the Barberini exercised direct control over the matrimonial choices of the cardinals in their circle, using the network of relations so created to build around themselves a wide political consensus. The churchman in the family, in this case Cardinal Giulio Sacchetti, became the prudent architect of strategies promoting the family which were guaranteed and protected by papal support. Between 1628 and 1630, the plans for a marriage with Beatrice Tassoni, a member of one of the most prestigious noble families of Ferrara,[57] seemed to be making good progress despite difficulties caused by war. Matteo reminded his brother that 'nothing was being done about the marriage in Florence or here, but Your Excellency should press forward [in Ferrara] and, God willing, may you succeed. It should not', he added, 'be allowed to lapse because of the imminent war since the pope has always wanted this marriage of Giovanni Francesco's even after the disturbances in Italy.' But he warned the cardinal, who was the real architect of family policy, to 'reflect on the fact that the girl was not a beauty', seeking also to consider Giovanni Francesco, who seems, from the correspondence, to have been almost a stranger to the negotiations that concerned him.

Cardinal Giulio Sacchetti persuaded dukes Cesare, then Francesco, d'Este to agree to the marriage, since 'it was not customary for princes to allow good dowries to leave the state'.[58] In order to conclude the match it would have been necessary for Giovanni Francesco Sacchetti, Florentine patrician, to acquire a feudal title in the dukedom of Modena, thus becoming the subject of another prince. The prospect did not please the cardinal, at the time papal legate in Ferrara and representative in the city of Urban VIII, to whom he owed the rapid growth of his career and the

[57] On the Tassoni, see V. Spreti, *Enciclopedia storico-nobiliare italiana* (6 vols., Milan, 1928–42), III, pp. 233–5.
[58] Rome, Archivio Sacchetti, Registro di lettere 7 ter, letters of Cardinal Giulio Sacchetti (unnumbered folios).

wealth of his family. The prudent churchman continued to express in his letters his dignified acceptance of subordination and respect for social hierarchy, which imposed clearly defined roles, with a consequent reflection of prestige and honour on the family and the figure of the celibate. From Rome, Matteo suggested breaking the family's endogamous tradition, displaying more concrete ideas on the marriage of his brother and the expectations for the whole family which depended on it. Cardinal Francesco Barberini's decided preference for a girl of the Bandini family in Florence did not prevent Matteo from reminding his brother, the cardinal, of other possible solutions. There was in Rome a young woman of the Mattei family whom 'it seems to me we could obtain through Marchese Bentivoglio if she gets used to the idea of not wanting a second carriage, being otherwise treated appropriately'. Moreover, her dowry was not to be overlooked, being in the region of 50,000 *scudi*. There was also a Corsini girl in Florence, but here difficulties arose 'because Cardinal Antonio did not trust Monsignor Corsini's word, and I told Barberini outright that the business should not go forward because Corsini does not get along with the Borghese, nor with the Savoy, and is the sort of person who acquires enemies'.[59] The marriage thus took on increasingly the characteristics of a large-scale negotiation which required keeping several fronts open because of difficulties and uncertainties caused by relations between the political groupings of the families, the Roman curia and the factions within the sacred college. All this involved the family of the bridegroom, its 'masters' and protectors, its friends and enemies, its Florentine relatives and the grand-duke himself.

The match with the Bandini enjoyed the favour of the grand-duke of Tuscany. This brought satisfaction to Matteo Sacchetti, who saw the lengthy and open loyalty of his family towards Florence recognized and rewarded. The precise political significance of the match was a sweetener between Rome and Florence, given the 'mistrust existing between our masters and them', particularly after the duchy of Urbino came under the direct control of Rome.[60] Florence had not welcomed the election of Maffeo Barberini as pope. Pro-French and at the same time anti-Medicean, he represented in these years a real threat to the equilibrium in central Italy because of his manoeuvres to secure the return of Urbino to the direct control of the holy see. A Florentine marriage with one of the families closest to the pope could prove a useful

---

[59] S. Andretta, 'Corsini, Ottaviano', in *Dizionario biografico degli italiani* (Rome, 1983), XXIX, pp. 664–8.
[60] On relations between the grand-duchy and Urban VIII, see L. Pastor, *Storia dei Papi* (16 vols., Rome, 1961), XIII, pp. 272–4 and F. Diaz, *Il granducato di Toscana. I Medici* (Turin, 1976), pp. 380–3.

means of strengthening a web of relations between the two states torn by political tensions.

Matteo forcefully urged his brother, the cardinal, to expedite the negotiations, all the more so as Giovanni Francesco himself was not pleased 'that his marriage was being made such an issue, and I have to tell your Excellency he is very ready to enter into negotiations for a non-Florentine bride and is even considering the fatal step of not marrying at all'.[61] Matteo did not hide his preference for the Roman match, but meanwhile, thanks to the joint labours of the cardinal brother and Antonio Barberini, the negotiations with the duke of Modena were also going well. The cardinal nephew, Francesco Barberini, together with the Constable Colonna, took it upon himself to bring an end to the matter and everything pointed to a rapid conclusion of the noble match in Ferrara.

From these marriage negotiations thus emerge the divergent positions of the brothers on the value and significance that the choice of a bride assumed for the whole family. We are dealing with symbolic stances which would influence the future of the family and its individual members. On one side, there is the cardinal, the figure of the greatest prestige, who had to lead the negotiations and embody the honour and social status of the family; he showed himself tied to the Florentine tradition of the lineage and its enhancement. On the other side, his brother Matteo had become convinced that the family should seek honour and social prestige at court, and exerted himself to find a good match for Giovanni Francesco beyond the bounds of traditional, national endogamy more in line, in his view, with the mercantile past than with the present, still less with a future by now linked to aspirations of nobility and careers in the curia. 'I want to see *Signor* Giovanni Francesco married so that the world will not judge us weak ... because I do not think it so parlous, although we do need a little time to let grow what has been sown, nor do our aspirations exceed our position'.[62] A good marriage signified family reputation, a growth of prestige and the papering over of internal and external tensions and difficulties which could reduce or ruin the public image of the family.

The choice of a bride from the most ancient Este nobility was, moreover, an extraordinary opportunity for the family of Cardinal Giulio Sacchetti, papal legate in Ferrara, to forge a lasting link with the local nobility and to gain further prestige and substantial property. But for the cardinal the conclusion of this match also represented a triumph, not only in terms of personal prestige, but as a symbolic strengthening of the power of Rome in Ferrara, since the legate became a privileged

[61] Rome, Archivio Sacchetti, Registro di lettere 7 ter.   [62] *Ibid.*

interlocutor and powerful dispenser of patronage for the local citizens and elite.

The few examples we have presented are illustrative of behaviour that was characteristic of cardinals' families in Rome in the early modern period. Within them, marriage strategy was developed by the cardinals, taking account of family traditions, intermarriages contracted in the past and economic interests in the present, but also having an eye to the alliances and factions within the curia. Networks of families moulded the structure and composition of the sacred college which in turn conditioned them.

But there was, finally, a further and closer interdependence between the figure of the cardinal and the phenomenon of marriage, which operated through the mechanisms by which cardinals were nominated. Recently, Christoph Weber has reconstructed some constant features in the conferring of the rank of cardinal between the sixteenth and the nineteenth centuries: promotion as a reward for support in the conclave; nomination at the behest of monarchs; elevation after a career in the curia and in conjunction with the purchase of a very expensive venal office; and the cardinalate as a marriage gift ('Kardinalshüte als Hochzeitgeschenk').[63]

The principle was simple: the marriage of a member of a papal family or a family within the papal entourage to a young woman necessitated the concession of a cardinal's hat to the bride's brother. Weber cites numerous examples, of which only a few that refer to the period under consideration will be mentioned. Francesco Sforza was made a cardinal by Gregory XIII in 1583 after his sister married Giacomo Boncompagni in 1576. Ascanio Colonna was promoted in 1586 after his nephew Marco Antonio married Sixtus V's great-niece. Alessandro Orsini was created cardinal by Paul V in 1615 following the match between Marco Antonio Borghese and Camilla Orsini. Gerolamo Colonna was made a cardinal in 1628 after his sister Anna married Taddeo Barberini. Anthropologically speaking, we can say that the mechanism had a precise function; it tended to strengthen the bond created by the marriage and to give it an immediate profile in the curia, but it also emphasized, in a way, the superiority of the family who 'made the gift'. This phenomenon also plays its part in the wider context of the complex policy of marriage alliances by papal families in the sixteenth and seventeenth centuries, which will now be analysed.

During the pontificate of Alexander VII, an anonymous author compiled a manuscript history of the 'famiglie papali moderne',[64] producing a

[63] C. Weber, *Senatus Divinus. Verborgene Strukturen im Kardinalskollegium der frühen Neuzeit (1500–1800)* (Frankfurt, 1996), pp. 92ff.
[64] Biblioteca apostolica vaticana (BAV), Barb. lat. 4910, 'Discorso sopra le famiglie papali moderne che hano fondato le loro habitationi in Roma dal regno di Paolo III di casa Farnese sino al presente tempo' (1665).

profile of each family, from Ghislieri to Chigi, with systematic details of honours received, positions taken up, patrimonial vicissitudes and marriages. From the accumulation of data in the text emerges an image of a very unified group, characterized by common forms of behaviour and united by reciprocal ties.

The papal nobility carved out a special place for itself within the elite hierarchy of Italy. To trace its marriage strategies involves above all ascertaining how radically elevation to the papacy changed the matrimonial policy of the family, and how, at the same time, marriage, even after the death of a pontiff, could be a formidable instrument for consolidating positions gained. The change in status from cardinal's family to ruling family, even if only temporary, was accompanied, because of nepotism and the 'spoils system', by a great extension of available economic resources. The Borghese enjoyed income of only 4,900 *scudi* in 1592,[65] whereas in 1610 the cardinal nephew received 153,000 *scudi* per annum from pensions, offices and abbacies.[66] At the same time, the monetary sums destined for dowries increased enormously. Ortensia and Margherita Borghese were married to Francesco Caffarelli (1576) and Orazio Vettori (1579) respectively, each with a dowry of 8,500 *scudi* and 500 *scudi* for weddings and trousseaux.[67] The dowry of Maria Barberini, daughter of Carlo and of Costanza Magalotti, was 9,000 *scudi*, which was returned in 1621 after her death to Carlo Barberini by her widower Tolomeo Duglioli.[68] However, the standard dowry of a 'papal' marriage in the early seventeenth century was around 100,000 *scudi* and could be considerably more. Naturally, the social level of alliances changed completely when a member of the family became pope. As Wolfgang Reinhard has written, 'elevation of rank and entail were not the last steps a rising papal family had to climb. To complete their success they had to be accepted by the established nobility through marriage.'[69]

The ultimate aspiration for all papal families was an alliance with a ruling family, an objective only rarely achieved and always accompanied by considerable difficulties. The relationship between ruling princes and papal families was markedly unequal, above all when the latter were dependent on princes for their fiefs. The negotiations and the fixing of the dowry reveal the papal family operating at a disadvantage, a reflection of the transitory nature of the individual pope's power. Thus, in 1556, the

---

[65] Archivio segreto vaticano (ASV), Archivio Borghese 22.
[66] See V. Reinhardt, *Kardinal Scipione Borghese (1605–1633). Vermögen, Finanzen und sozialer Aufstieg eines Papstnepoten* (Tübingen, 1984), p. 48.
[67] ASV, Archivio Borghese 26.   [68] ASV, Archivio Barberini, Indice IV, 602.
[69] W. Reinhard, 'Papal power and family strategy in the sixteenth and seventeenth centuries', in *Princes, Patronage and Nobility. The Court at the Beginning of the Modern Age*, ed. R. G. Asch and A. M. Birke (Oxford, 1991), p. 339.

marriage negotiations concerning Fabiano del Monte, nephew of Julius III, and Lucrezia de' Medici (two children aged eight and ten years respectively) make it clear that the 'nature and quantity' of Lucrezia's dowry were to be fixed solely by Duke Cosimo, 'since the Holy Father and the Illustrious *Signor* Balduino [father of the proposed groom] were more concerned with the union and mutual goodwill of the families than with the dowry, and did not wish to claim a role, preferring rather that the matter should be in the hands of the duke'.[70]

The efforts of Cardinal Pietro Aldobrandini to arrange marriages for his nieces, the daughters of Giovanni Francesco and Olimpia, were directed to two ruling houses, the Farnese and the Savoy. Margherita Aldobrandini was married to Ranuccio Farnese, duke of Parma, but at the price of opposition and humiliation for the cardinal during the negotiations.[71] The negotiation with Carlo Emanuele I of Savoy was not crowned by success despite the political agreement of 1601 between the cardinal nephew and the duke which offered papal support for Savoy designs on Vaud and Geneva, even though the Calvinist city was under the protection of France.[72] No other Aldobrandini married a reigning prince. Elena was married to Antonio Carafa, duke of Mondragone, and Maria to Gianpaolo Sforza, marquis of Caravaggio. This last marriage was the result of negotiations conducted in 1623 between the Cardinals Ippolito Aldobrandini and Alessandro Montalto, the latter the maternal uncle of the marquis of Caravaggio, and involved the payment of a dowry of 100,000 *scudi*.[73]

The Borghese long aspired to a princely marriage and in particular to intermarriage with the Medici, but without success. The Barberini sought to open negotiations between Taddeo and the princess of Urbino in anticipation of the coming recovery of Urbino. The hostility and negative outcome of these marriage negotiations led to strained feelings within the sacred college between Cardinal Medici and the Barberini, which had serious implications for the alliances and factions of the 1644 conclave. It was only in the following generation that the family of Urban VIII succeeded in negotiating a princely match. Lucrezia, Taddeo's daughter, who did not wish to marry, but 'inspired by God' was 'obstinately

[70] BAV, Vat. lat. 6532, fol. 93r. The promise of marriage was not upheld and in 1588 Lucrezia married Alfonso II d'Este, duke of Ferrara.
[71] P. Litta, *Famiglie celebri italiane* (Milan, 1819–74; Naples, 1902–23), Aldobrandini, tav. II. See also R. Zapperi, *Eros e controriforma: preistoria della Galleria Farnese* (Turin, 1994).
[72] E. Fasano Guarini, 'Aldobrandini, Pietro', in *Dizionario biografico degli italiani*, I, pp. 107–12.
[73] BAV, Fondo Ottoboni 2476, p. 501. Of the 100,000 *scudi*, 43,000 were paid out at the time of the marriage, and the remaining 70,000 in three annual instalments. The marriage followed Roman statutes.

resolved in her desire to become a nun', was at the centre of complex marriage negotiations conducted by her uncle, Cardinal Francesco, first at the French court and then with the Este.[74]

In 1654, an agreement was at last formalized between Lucrezia and Francesco, duke of Modena, and the dowry was set at 200,000 *scudi*. This figure, which exceeded the highest Roman dowries, was made up of 150,000 *scudi* interest from the trust-fund set up by Pope Barberini to establish general succession provisions for the family, including this dowry for his great-niece, 10,000 *scudi* from Cardinal Francesco, and 40,000 *scudi* to be paid by her brothers in annual instalments of 5,000.[75]

Marriage into a reigning family was always pursued, but was realized only rarely and at great monetary expense. This was symptomatic of the uneasy position of papal families in the hierarchy of the Italian nobility. The protocol of the papal court placed the nephew of the ruling pope among the lesser princes, a little below sovereign princes and the Orsini and Colonna, who were considered to have the same status, but above all other Roman and non-Roman nobles.[76] Marriage strategy reflected this ambiguous position.

What were the other choices and to what kind of social identity did they contribute? From the second half of the sixteenth century to the baroque period, the acquisition of a great feudal title was the usual road down which papal families went on the death of a pope in the family. But the great reserve of feudal titles and resources was in southern Italy and was used by Spain in an attempt to draw nobles, courtiers and powerful financiers into its orbit.[77] Feudalization and marriage with a Spanish or Neapolitan heiress were therefore two stages in a single journey. The Boncompagni were made dukes of Sora by Philip II in 1579, and, at the beginning of the seventeenth century, appear completely Neapolitanized: Giulia married Giovanni de Guevara, duke of Bovino, and Gregorio, the heir to the ducal title, married Eleonora Zappata, daughter of Giovanni, postmaster general (*corriere maggiore*) of the kingdom of Naples. In the following generation, a double marriage confirmed the alliance with the Ruffo of Bagnara: Ugo married Maria Ruffo; Costanza married Carlo Ruffo, duke of Bagnara; the unmarried daughters became nuns.

In 1605, Michele Peretti, Sixtus V's great-nephew, was granted the title of prince of Venafro by Philip III and his first marriage was to Margherita di Somaglia, heiress of a feudal line in Spain. Nicolò Ludovisi, nephew of

[74] BAV, Archivio Barberini, Indice IV, 1067. [75] *Ibid.*, 1078.
[76] M. A. Visceglia, 'Il cerimoniale come linguaggio politico. I conflitti di precedenza alla corte di Roma tra XVI e XVII secolo', in *Cérémonial et rituel à Rome (XVIe–XXe siècles)* ed. M. A. Visceglia and C. Brice (Rome, 1997).
[77] A. Spagnoletti, *Principi italiani e Spagna nell'età barocca* (Milan, 1996).

Gregory XV, spent his whole life under the protection of the Spanish Habsburgs. From his marriage to Isabella Gesualdo, negotiated at the court of Madrid by Cardinal Caetani,[78] he inherited the principality of Venosa, a great feudal estate of forty villages and castles in the kingdom of Naples, and following his second marriage to Polissena de Mendoza, heiress of the Appiani, he received the investiture of Piombino from Ferdinand II, having paid a million florins to the imperial *camera*; he became knight of the Golden Fleece in 1657, viceroy of Aragon in 1660 and of Sardinia in 1662.

These experiences are rich in political significance. It would, however, be a considerable oversimplification to reduce the complex affairs of papal families to the single issue of alignment with Spain. The inclination towards Spain, certainly dominant in the early baroque period, does not explain everything, nor does it make the papal families synonymous with the feudal nobility of the kingdom of Naples. The specific nature of the Roman experience resides in the relations that were established even at this highest level between matrimony and curial politics.

The tendency to form alliances through marriages outside Rome, with princely families in central and northern Italy and with great Neapolitan feudal barons well established at the court of Madrid, was in each generation balanced against marriages that united papal families with the highest levels of the Roman nobility. Intermarriage with the Orsini or the Colonna or with both was a recurring option of matrimonial politics among papal families, as is evident from the marriages arranged by the Peretti at the end of the sixteenth century, when the two sisters of Cardinal Alessandro Montalto, Felicia Orsina and Flavia, married respectively Marco Antonio Colonna, duke of Paliano, and Virginio Orsini, duke of Bracciano. In the rivalry between the two houses, diluted in comparison to that of the early sixteenth century although still in force, especially over honours and public recognition, such intermarriage led to a temporary strengthening of one side to the detriment of the other.

Often significant increases in wealth resulted from these marriages. For instance, the agreement drawn up on 27 November 1627 relating to the marriage of Taddeo Barberini and Anna Colonna envisaged a dowry of 180,000 *scudi* which consisted in part of cash, in part of credits in the Colonna *Monte*, and in part of the value of the castle of Anticoli, ceded by the constable on 24 August of the same year to the Barberini. The negotiations were also closely linked with the transfer of Palestrina from one family to the other.[79] Between the sixteenth and seventeenth centu-

---

[78] Simancas, Archivo General, Estado, legajo 1868.
[79] BAV, Archivio Barberini, Indice IV/8, Clauses of the marriage agreement between Anna Colonna and Taddeo Barberini, 27 November 1627, and *ibid.*, Indice IV/11, 'Relatione sopra la dote et heredità dell'Ecc.ma Sig.ra Anna Colonna Barberini'.

ries, under the pressure of dramatic indebtedness incurred through marriages and the consequent sales of possessions, a landslide of wealth passed from old to new nobility, and the papal nobility was the principal beneficiary in this process.[80]

However, financial motives were only one aspect of marriage alliances within the restricted circle of great families of the Roman nobility. As has been mentioned, the most powerful drive came from political motives, from the need to create the widest possible political fronts in order to influence the factions in the conclaves. A study of the factions within the sacred college reveals precise mechanisms at work. In general, the family of a ruling pope adopted a stance of opposition, if not of open hostility, to the faction of the cardinal nephew of the previous pope, while tending to ally with the faction of the pope before that.[81] Thus, the Ludovisi allied themselves with the Aldobrandini when Ippolita, niece of Gregory XV married Giorgio Aldobrandini, bringing a dowry comprising 100,000 *scudi* and jewels worth 150,000 *scudi*.[82] When Innocent X became pope, the Pamfili, in their turn, allied themselves with the Ludovisi–Aldobrandini through the double marriage between Costanza Pamfili and Prince Nicolò Ludovisi[83] and between Olimpia Aldobrandini, widow of Paolo Borghese,[84] and Camillo Pamfili.[85] The motivation behind this intermarriage was closely linked to the events of the conclave at which Innocent X was elected, originating at the court in Madrid, which was anxious to see the defeat of the Barberini party and manoeuvred to ensure that no marriage of importance for the internal factions of the sacred college was concluded by them.[86]

A chain of interlinked alliances, some motivated by the need to mark out political alignments, others by an endogamous tradition which, in any event, characterized this section of the nobility, bound together the papal families who intermarried with one another so that in some cases, by the second half of the seventeenth century, they were on the edge of premature extinction. Thus, the Peretti were absorbed in 1655 by the Savelli; the Aldobrandini, at around the same time, by the Borghese and the Pamfili; the Ludovisi in 1699 by the Boncompagni; and the Facchinetti, who in

---

[80] The fundamental treatment of the problem of noble indebtedness remains J. Delumeau, *Vie économique et sociale de Rome*.

[81] W. Reinhard, 'Papal power and family strategy'.

[82] R. Lefevre, 'Il patrimonio romano degli Aldobrandini nel Seicento', *Archivio della Società romana di storia patria*, 82 (1959), p. 18.

[83] Rome, Archivio Doria Pamfilj, Archiviolo 117, Strumento di matrimonio tra Costanza Pamfili e Nicolò Ludovisi, principe di Piombino. Costanza's dowry was 100,000 *scudi*.

[84] See Lefevre, 'Il patrimonio romano degli Aldobrandini', p. 22.

[85] Olimpia's dowry consisted of the inheritance from Cardinal Ippolito Aldobrandini, though heavily indebted: ASV, Archivio Borghese 26.

[86] M. A. Visceglia, 'Le fazioni nel sacro collegio durante la prima metà del Seicento', in *Roma centro della politica europea (secoli XVI e XVII)*, forthcoming.

any event had a minor role limited to Bologna, by the Pamfili at the beginning of the eighteenth century.

Our aim has been to show how the stereotyped image of the court of Rome as dominated by the principle of celibacy concealed a more complex reality in which marriage played a central role. Marriage to a member of a curial family opened the way into the curia, but, once inside, the choice of alliances was made in relation to the balance of forces within the group of origin. Analysis of marriage policy among the families of cardinals and popes does not simply show how a close tie was established between marriage alliance and the obtaining of curial appointments. At the more comprehensive level of the whole functioning of a political system based on the election of a sovereign by a 'senate', it also shows how women and the marriage alliances in which they were instrumental were fundamental in the coming together of factions to form united electoral fronts. For this reason, from top to bottom of the curial pyramid, over a marriage market divided by social groupings, in different ways and to different degrees, the ruling popes exercised patronage and kept control.

Part IV

Consequences and endings

11 Bending the rules: marriage in Renaissance collections of biographies of famous women

Stephen Kolsky

It is a remarkable paradox of northern and central Italian courts in the later fifteenth and the early sixteenth centuries that although the wedding was the object of so many cultural and political energies, there appears to be a paucity of literature produced in court circles that deals specifically with marriage. The rarity of such texts is intriguing, especially because women at court seem to have more space than elsewhere to perform in the public domain, compared to elite women living under a republican regime.[1] It is doubly ironic that in the court system it was precisely marriage and its dynastic politics that allowed a few women to exercise some power and patronage.[2] In some cases, it was perhaps because of the possibilities of fulfilling a more public role that a few women were in a position to underplay or revise the traditional part of the wife, attracted by the prospect of taking an active role in the administration of the state and/or in the patronage of the arts.[3]

[1] I. Maclean, *The Renaissance Notion of Woman* (Cambridge, 1980), pp. 5, 20–23, 56; J. Kelly, 'Did women have a Renaissance?', in *Women, History and Theory: The Essays of Joan Kelly* (Chicago and London, 1984); D. Herlihy, 'Did women have a Renaissance? A reconsideration', *Medievalia et humanistica*, new ser., 13 (1985); M. Zancan, 'La donna', in *Letteratura italiana*, v: *Le questioni* (Turin, 1986), pp. 788–92; B. S. Anderson and J. P. Zinsser, *A History of Their Own: Women in Europe from Prehistory to the Present*, (2 vols., New York, 1988), II, pp. 26–61; M. L. King, *Women of the Renaissance* (Chicago and London, 1991), pp. 160–4, 181–5; M. E. Wiesner, *Women and Gender in Early Modern Europe* (Cambridge, 1993), pp. 68–75.
[2] E. Ward Swain, 'Il potere di un'amicizia. Iniziative e competenze di due nobildonne rinascimentali', *Memoria: Rivista di storia di donne*, 21 (1987), pp. 7–8; Ward Swain, '"My excellent and most singular lord": marriage in a noble family of fifteenth-century Italy', *Journal of Medieval and Renaissance Studies*, 16 (1986).
[3] The case of Isabella d'Este is perhaps the best documented for the period. See G. R. Marek, *The Bed and the Throne: The Life of Isabella d'Este* (New York, 1976); M. Bregoli-Russo, 'Isabella d'Este nella critica moderna', *Critica letteraria*, 75 (1992), pp. 234–5; J. Cartwright, *Isabella d'Este, Marchioness of Mantua, 1474–1539* (2 vols., London, 1903); M. Bellonci, 'Beatrice and Isabella d'Este', in *Renaissance Profiles*, ed. J. H. Plumb (New York, 1965), pp. 139–56; S. Kolsky, 'Images of Isabella d'Este', *Italian Studies*, 39 (1984). For other women, see J. Cartwright, *Beatrice d'Este, 1475–1497: A Study of the Renaissance* (New York and London, 1905; repr. New York, 1973); W. L. Gundersheimer, 'Women, learning and power: Eleonora of Aragon', in *Beyond Their Sex: Learned Women of the European Past*, ed P. H. Labalme (New York and London, 1980).

It is in this context that the circulation of discourses on women acquires considerable significance in late fifteenth- and early sixteenth-century Italian courts. One can note the multiplication of discourses on women, not limited to any particular genre and connected to each other by the intensity of court discussion on the role of women in that institution. Thus, it is possible to find debate on women in the Renaissance epic, most notably, Lodovico Ariosto's *Orlando furioso* where, apart from the notable appearance of female knights, there is discursive treatment of the 'woman question'.[4] The treatise on love, in vogue in the period, had intimate connections with texts on women, and invoked questions regarding the social function of women and their place in society. One of the writers to be discussed in this essay, Mario Equicola (1470–1525), was the author of a *Libro de natura de amore* (published in 1525, but the history of its composition can be traced back at least twenty-five years). Although the theme of love might seem to limit female behaviour, it did offer the possibility of redefining female nature in relation to the stereotypical view of woman as an instinctual, sexually uncontrolled creature. Other texts too, particularly those on behaviour, the most celebrated being Baldassare Castiglione's *Il libro del cortegiano*, dealt at length with the problem.[5]

Another textual form found favour in the courts: the collection of biographies of famous women. The number of such collections is relatively small, but they do form a conspicuous group dealing expressly with the 'woman question' in a court context. The majority of these collections were not printed and have few manuscript witnesses, suggestive of their elite nature. Three of these texts were brought to light in Conor Fahy's groundbreaking article,[6] which discusses Agostino Strozzi's *Defensio mulierum*, Bartolommeo Gogio's *De laudibus mulierum* and Mario Equicola's *De mulieribus*. To these three texts others can be added: Sabadino degli Arienti's *Gynevera de le clare donne* (1489–90; with some material added in 1492); Vespasiano da Bisticci's *Il libro delle lodi e commendazione delle donne* (composed in the early 1480s); Bernardino Cacciante's *Libro apologetico delle donne* (1504); Galeazzo Flavio Capra's *Della eccellenza e dignità delle donne* (1525); and Iacobo Foresti's *De plurimis claris selectisque mulieribus* (1497). The last-mentioned collection had a new lease of life when it was

---

4 See P. J. Benson, 'An unrecognized defender of women in the *Orlando furioso*', *Italica*, 57 (1980), pp. 268–70; J. C. McLucas, 'Amazon, sorceress, and queen: women and war in the aristocratic literature of sixteenth-century Italy', *Italianist*, 8 (1988), pp. 33–4, 38–45; D. Shemek, 'Of women, knights, arms, and love: the *Querelle des Femmes* in Ariosto's poem', *Modern Language Notes* (1989).

5 See C. Dionisotti, 'Appunti su Leone ebreo', *Italia medioevale e umanistica*, 2 (1959); and G. Bárberi Squarotti, 'L'amante cortigiano', in Bárberi Squarotti, *L'onore in corte. Dal Castiglione al Tasso* (Milan, 1986).

6 C. Fahy, 'Three early Renaissance treatises on women', *Italian Studies*, 11 (1956).

included in an anthology put together by Ravisius Textor, *De memor-abilibus et claris mulieribus aliquot diversorum scriptorum opera*, published in Paris in 1521. The genre achieved its greatest reach through the publication of Cornelius Agrippa's *De nobilitate et praecellentia foeminei sexus*, published for the first time in 1529, but actually written twenty years previously, and, within the same time frame, the third book of Castiglione's *Il libro del cortegiano*, published in 1528, but begun about twenty-five years earlier. Some of these texts have received substantial treatment from scholars, in particular those by Goggio, Foresti and Capra;[7] the focus of this essay will be on those texts that convey a strong sense of views on marriage and that, at the same time, have not been the object of sustained critical analysis.

The court writers certainly did not invent the genre: its founding text is Giovanni Boccaccio's *De mulieribus claris* ('Concerning Famous Women') composed around 1361–2.[8] The original text provided only the most basic sketch for court writers. There is not one who did not effect changes in both its structure and content. *De mulieribus claris* traces the history of women from mythical times up to the present (represented by Queen Giovanna of Naples); it privileges exemplary women, mainly pagan, and places them in approximate chronological order. The text consists of a series of biographies, sometimes followed by moralistic commentary, in which thematic ordering is almost totally subordinated to chronology. Rather than offer a coherent view of women, Boccaccio seems more concerned with producing an encyclopaedic view of different historical women.

In the later fifteenth century the genre underwent a revival and metamorphosed into a more complex, discursive genre, allowing compilers to reflect on what constituted a woman in theological, philosophical and social terms, while retaining the biographical element. The flexibility of the archetype was not regarded as an altogether positive asset by later writers, judging by their efforts to group the women thematically, not chronologically. Indeed, not one of the writers considered here took up Boccaccio's approach: all preferred to reduce the number of exemplary women and to produce a more coherent discourse on women, generally at court.

[7] W. L. Gundersheimer, 'Bartolommeo Goggio: a feminist in Renaissance Ferrara', *Renaissance Quarterly*, 33 (1980); P. J. Benson, *The Invention of the Renaissance Woman: The Challenge of Female Independence in the Literature and Thought of Italy and England* (University Park, Pennsylvania, 1992), pp. 52–64; V. Zaccaria, 'La fortuna del *De mulieribus claris* del Boccaccio nel secolo XV: Giovanni Sabadino degli Arienti, Iacopo Filippo Foresti e le loro biografie femminili', in *Il Boccaccio nelle culture e nelle letterature nazionali*, ed. F. Mazzoni (Florence, 1978); B. Collina, 'L'esemplarità delle donne illustri fra umanesimo e controriforma', in *Donna, disciplina, creanza cristiana dal XV al XVII secolo*, ed. G. Zarri (Rome, 1996).
[8] V. Zaccaria, 'Le fasi redazionali del *De mulieribus*', *Studi sul Boccaccio*, 1 (1963).

Within this discussion at court on the role of women one can read a subtext that breaks with traditional views on marriage. It is true that such texts are often more interested in contesting theoretical positions, and in vaunting new domains of action for women, but nevertheless the reality of court life ensures that they have to make a stand on the issue of marriage. These writers have before them the public role of court wives, and this is frequently confronted in the texts. The court collections of illustrious women often support the intervention of court wives in the public domain, but not without ambiguity. Other writers, in reaction to the 'liberties' of these wives, affirm the more conservative view of the house-bound woman (Vespasiano da Bisticci and Galeazzo Flavio Capra are representative of this trend).

Perhaps the most outspoken of these writers on women is Mario Equicola. His Latin treatise *De mulieribus* ('On Women') of 1501, known to Castiglione, expresses an openly radical view of women. Equicola was trying to establish his position in the court circles of Ferrara and Mantua at this time, and the composition of *De mulierbus* can be interpreted as part of his effort to win the patronage of Isabella d'Este, marchioness of Mantua. Although the text was commissioned by Margherita Cantelmo, a high-ranking court lady, and aimed at Isabella d'Este, no mention is made in the text of the fact of their both being married.[9] Indeed, it is understood that marriage is the principal institution that serves to control women: 'Almost as soon as she reaches puberty, she is given into the dominion of a husband. If she aims higher or raises her sights, just like some workhouse foreman she is declared unfit for household management, as if this is a top occupation or high profession'.[10] Equicola systematically unmasks the system of double standards, which ensures that marriage, as it is understood in contemporary society, is condemned. He talks in terms of liberation from a concept of marriage that does not allow the wife access to the public arena. By the use of carefully selected *exempla*, the writer points to the possibility that things could be different: he adduces the Cantabrians, an ancient tribe of Spain, whose women controlled the dowry system and could normally be designated as heirs. Equicola also reworked a Boccaccian *exemplum* from *De mulieribus claris*, that of the Roman Gaia, which is used to stress a different version of matrimonial relations: 'It was prohibited for the husband to accept anything as a gift from the wife, or the wife from the husband, in order that they might understand it to be a communal matter, that to be loved and to return love was not mercenary, but entirely free and spontaneous.'[11] By implication, the entire text of *De mulieribus* rejects the stereotype of the

[9] For background: S. Kolsky, *Mario Equicola: The Real Courtier* (Geneva, 1991), pp. 67–70.
[10] *De mulieribus* (Ferrara, after 8 May 1501), fol. a6r.   [11] *De mulieribus*, fol. b6r.

wife confined to household duties, an object to be negotiated over in the marriage market; its wide range of exemplary figures demonstrates the potentiality of all women in a wide range of activities which include acting, singing, philosophy and politics. Equicola implicitly takes issue with the view that women will be able to achieve their full potential within the social framework as it exists.

In contrast stands the Bolognese writer Giovanni Sabadino degli Arienti whose *Gynevera de le clare donne*[12] reflects the writer's need to engage with the court as a relatively privileged place for women, against the background of a more conservative notion of woman as home-maker that would have been the norm in Bologna with its strong republican tradition.[13] Arienti worked as secretary for Andrea Bentivoglio – a member of the newly dominant dynasty in Bologna – until the latter's death in 1491.[14] After that date Arienti's life is a continual, and increasingly desperate, search for patronage. Arienti had already had some contact, before Andrea Bentivoglio's death, with Ercole d'Este, duke of Ferrara. The composition of the *Gynevera* marks an awareness on Arienti's part of the importance of the dynastic system of the northern and central Italian states, in particular the role played in it by women. Arienti seems to be preparing the ground for his later hunt for patronage from court ladies, such as Isabella d'Este.[15] The *Gynevera* is a collection of female biographies which, while having a superficial resemblance to the Boccaccian archetype, breaks with the 'rules' of the genre by presenting a series of near-contemporary biographies, often of Bolognese women, whose status is enhanced by their being compared to Boccaccian 'heroines'.[16] It is interesting to note that his first female-focused text, a *Trattato di pudicizia*, written in 1487, appears not to have been affected by court ideology in

12 C. James, *Giovanni Sabadino degli Arienti: A Literary Career* (Florence, 1996), pp. 73–85; S. D. Kolsky, 'Men framing women: Sabadino degli Arienti's *Gynevera de le clare donne* reexamined', in *Visions and Revisions: Women in Italian Culture*, ed. M. Cicioni and N. Prunster (Providence and Oxford, 1993); P. J. Benson, *The Invention of the Renaissance Woman* (University Park, Pennsylvania, 1992), pp. 40–4; S. B. Chandler, '*La Gynevera de le clare donne* di Sabadino degli Arienti', *Giornale storico della letteratura italiana*, 158 (1981), pp. 222–34; G. Zarri, *Le sante vive: Cultura e religiosità femminile nella prima età moderna* (Turin, 1990), pp. 32–3.

13 C. M. Ady, *The Bentivoglio of Bologna: A Study in Despotism* (London, 1937), pp. 89–117, 166–8; A. De Benedictis, 'Quale "corte" per quale "signoria"? A proposito di organizzazione e immagine del potere durante la preminenza di Giovanni II Bentivoglio', in *Bentivolorum magnificentia: principe e cultura a Bologna nel Rinascimento*, ed. B. Basile (Rome, 1984), pp. 28–9; James, *Giovanni Sabadino degli Arienti*, pp. 1–2, 11–24.

14 James, *Arienti*, pp. 21–4; G. Ghinassi in *Dizionario biografico degli italiani* (Rome, 1962), IV, pp. 154–6. For Arienti's *Vita di Andrea Bentivoglio*, see R. Ambrosini, 'Un codice autografo di G. Sabadino degli Arienti', *Atti e memorie della Deputazione di storia patria per le provincie di Romagna*, third ser., 27 (1909), pp. 40–61.

15 James, *Arienti*, pp. 70, 74–5.

16 Kolsky, 'Men framing women', p. 32; James, *Arienti*, p. 73.

that it is situated in Arienti's own family milieu (his sister-in-law is the subject of the exemplary discourses on the defence of sexual purity) and has no visible aspirations to a court audience, unlike the *Gynevera*.[17]

What distinguishes Arienti's collection of biographies is the personal note that enters the text, amplifying other descriptions of married life found in the *Gynevera*. Arienti did not hesitate to introduce a chapter on his own marriage and the exemplary part played in it by his wife, Francesca Bruni. Indeed, impetus may have been given to its composition by her death.[18] He notes, for example, that in spite of the family pressures placed on her to find a richer husband, she wanted to marry only Arienti, 'without regard for my lack of resources', and that she considered him 'a good, virtuous man'.[19] The representation of Arienti's wife points to some of the themes associated with wives in the *Gynevera*, in particular their role in creating a united and harmonious household. Francesca Bruni is described as 'a careful supervisor of the household who was cheerful and gracious in welcoming relatives and friends'.[20] This role she has in common with a number of the other women of the *Gynevera*, not least among them Diana Saliceto Bentivoglio,[21] though the political and dynastic implications of a woman's role in marriage are absent in the depiction of Francesca Bruni.

It is obvious that Arienti's representation of his wife's qualities stresses those traditionally associated with the wifely function. The most extensive part of Francesca Bruni's biography refers to her works of charity, something that Arienti highlights for many of the women included in the *Gynevera* in order to emphasize the role of the woman as donor or helper. Such acts of charity, however, also assist in breaking down stereotypes of women as grasping and avaricious ('there existed in her a generosity which went beyond the bounds of the female sex').[22] Yet, the writer is at pains to point out that his wife's interests were not only in those usual areas of female concern. She consumed devotional literature ('spiritual and holy texts'), but also other kinds of texts: 'she would gladly read Pliny's *Natural History*',[23] an evident indication that husband and wife had a shared culture in common, an interest in humanism through the vernacular.

The portrait of Francesca Bruni does not by any means present a radical revision of the figure of the wife. At first sight, she might appear to

---

[17] Kolsky, 'Men framing women', p. 35.   [18] James, *Arienti*, pp. 69–70.
[19] G. Sabadino degli Arienti, *Gynevera de le clare donne*, ed. C. Ricci and A. Bacchi Della Lega, in *Scelta di curiosità letterarie inedite o rare*, 223 (Bologna, 1887, repr. Bologna, 1968), p. 364. All references are to this edition.
[20] *Gynevera*, p. 365.
[21] James, *Arienti*, pp. 77, 83; Kolsky, 'Men framing women', pp. 29–31.
[22] *Gynevera*, p. 365.   [23] *Ibid.*

offer nothing new.[24] However, she is presented with a certain nobility, compared with exemplary women from *De mulieribus claris*, such as Pompeia Paulina, the wife of Seneca, and Artemisia, the wife of Mausoleus. Arienti sets up a model of the relationship that should exist between a man and a woman defined by 'the most sacred laws of holy matrimony', based on his own personal experience.[25] It is telling that most of the features of Francesca's behaviour will be re-used by Arienti to describe the actions and attitudes of women with a greater role in the public domain.

The *Gynevera* is dedicated to Ginevra Sforza, wife of Giovanni II Bentivoglio, ruler of Bologna. The dedication lacks those personal touches that characterized Arienti's portrait of his wife and instead it becomes the site of conventional court wisdom. Specifics are abandoned in favour of generalizations which seem to anchor the text firmly in the world of courtly compliment. Arienti focuses on Ginevra solely as the wife of Giovanni II Bentivoglio. She can be seen as an alternative means of gaining access to the world of seigniorial politics, able to fulfil this role because marriage lends her a certain authority:[26] 'therefore, as a woman, you do not in any way detract from the incredible virtues of your dynasty and of your illustrious consort'.[27] The reality of her presence in the dedication is circumscribed by the praise of her husband which virtually overshadows that of the wife.[28] In contrast to *his* multifarious activities of state, the wife is pinpointed in one of the most traditional activities for a woman, childbearing: 'angelic bearer of sixteen children'.[29] There is little personal detail, so little that the text portrays Ginevra as a rather passive figure whose main function is to produce children. Her children are enumerated, and usually the only detail given is whom they married. Ginevra appears almost irrelevant at this stage, even the fact of childbirth being passed over in favour of her husband's capacity to produce politically useful children: 'the birth of your children is indeed no less joyful for us because of their future greatness and of the increased prestige of the happy Bentivoglio name'.[30]

However, the text subtly suggests her own role in forging dynastic connections, both personally and through the careful marriages of her children. If the dedication tends to downplay the politically active role of Ginevra Sforza, the text proper underlines her key function of organizing family alliances. Though not stated directly, Ginevra's place at the centre of dynastic politics is made clear by the choice of women in the collection. A group of women represent a network of Bentivoglio interests in north-

---

[24] Benson, *Invention of Renaissance Woman*, p. 42.
[25] *Gynevera*, p. 361.   [26] Kolsky, 'Men framing women', p. 34.   [27] *Gynevera*, p. 7.
[28] *Ibid.*, pp. 2–3.   [29] *Ibid.*, p. 4.   [30] *Ibid.*, p. 6.

ern Italy which is closely associated with Sforza power or with the earlier Visconti dynasty (Battista, Elissa and Ippolita Sforza). The *Gynevera* presents a picture of Ginevra bringing unity to a seemingly disparate collection of women through her own Sforza connections and those of her offspring. In this way, the text gives some sense of how her own influence could operate in the political sphere. Ginevra Sforza is a contradictory figure in the context of the work as a whole. Unlike most of the other women in the *Gynevera*, she is not recorded for any particular achievement. She remains a rather shadowy figure whose claim on the writer is both encomiastic and practical – she represents one of the possible means by which the writer might improve his chances of survival and advancement in Bologna.

Another group of women appear in counterpoint to those of the northern courts. They are Bolognese women, often connected to the senatorial branch of the Bentivoglio, who sometimes present a contrasting mode of behaviour, based on 'republican' values, to that of their courtly sisters. Arienti's description of Diana Saliceto Bentivoglio functions as a model of married behaviour. She was, according to the text, a model wife in all respects: loving to her husband, producing male offspring and 'careful at all times and in all circumstances'.[31] She also knew how to manage family affairs properly: she is indirectly praised for her skill in looking after her husband's property, guarding against 'senseless profligacy'.[32] These 'domestic' qualities are exercised within a circumscribed area, the home, and may appear quite traditional. Although Diana bears some resemblance to the wife in Leon Battista Alberti's *Della famiglia*, in her domestic arrangements there is a noticeable difference from the emphasis given to Arienti's wife. She is described in terms that underline her economic activity within the marriage – she is certainly allowed much more scope for important tasks, something that does not fall into the domain of Alberti's wife.[33] The household of Diana Bentivoglio was an example of good economic management which could be extended to the state.

The other quality for which she receives praise is her ability to unify the extended family of which she is an integral part: 'From her husband, brothers-in-law, brothers, sons, nephews, cousins, daughters-in-law, familiars, servants, and the great rush of visiting relatives and friends, we can even say that, through the offices of such a woman, never was there heard a single word that contradicted the peace and union of the family'.[34] Here is a family network with a woman at its centre and extending

---

[31] *Ibid.*, p. 329.   [32] *Ibid.*, p. 330.
[33] E.g. her 'discreta misura', that is, a rationalist economics that eschews waste (*ibid.*, pp. 330–1).
[34] *Ibid.*, p. 331.

outwards from the nuclear family to include all supporters of the clan. The image could have been applied to the entire state as an ideal of political and social cohesiveness. Thus, the ideal of harmony replaces factionalism. 'Feminine' virtues associated with good and virtuous government are subtly conveyed to the wife of the ruler of Bologna. The feminine therefore becomes associated with a politics of social harmonization and peaceful coexistence.

Arienti introduces a number of wives who utilize these same qualities on the level of the organization of the state. Margaret, queen of Scotland, offers a slightly different variation on the theme of women's political capabilities. She is considered much more positively than her husband: 'She was loved and respected by her people much more than the king because she was more suited to rule the kingdom than he was. She governed the people and the state justly and piously as if she had been a Numa Pompilius.'[35] She attempts to impose a moral framework on her relationship with the king. Because of her lack of success, on her deathbed she makes every effort to inspire the principles of good government in her son: 'you will strive to keep your subjects united and safeguard the peace and tranquillity of the kingdom' – advice that recalls Diana Bentivoglio's household.[36] If husband and wife cannot work together – the ideal of the *Gynevera* where the wife is not excluded from any of the husband's activities and indeed aids the state in his absence – then she is shown to have her husband's and the state's interests at heart.

Arienti, therefore, recognizes the crucial importance of marriage in a city-state. In fact, he makes it the centre of his preoccupations in the *Gynevera* in that it provides a model of behaviour that can be extended to the public sphere – a form of union in which the married woman can work towards political goals in conjunction with her husband. *Gynevera* has been called 'one of the most radically pro-feminist books of the Renaissance', due to the fact that Arienti revises the concept of marriage so that it does not exclude women from political action.[37] Thus, stereotyped female attributes are shown in a completely different light from those employed in a passive depiction of the wife. Theodolinda, for example, a Longobard queen, felt her compassion so much stimulated by Saint Gregory that she converted herself, her husband and their people to Christianity, turning them away from war to the pursuit of peace.[38] This example illustrates how conventional virtues associated with women, such as tenderness and pity, can be used for positive political purposes. Herein lies the force of Arienti's analyses. They do not at all suggest that marriage perforce enslaves women, but that it can be used to provide a

[35] *Ibid.*, p. 313.   [36] *Ibid.*, p. 318.
[37] Benson, *Invention of Renaissance Woman*, p. 44.   [38] *Gynevera*, p. 13.

space for action outside the home. Therefore, for Arienti, marriage can be seen as both personally satisfying for the couple and offering the possibility of bringing about a more harmonious and just society.

Bernardino Cacciante in his *Libretto apologetico delle donne*, written in 1504 at the court of Urbino and dedicated to Elisabetta Gonzaga, duchess of Urbino, sister-in-law of Isabella d'Este and one of the interlocutors of Castiglione's *Il libro del cortegiano*, managed to place marriage in a court perspective without being overtly polemical. Little is known of Cacciante's life. He was associated with the court of Urbino, as is clear from the *Libretto apologetico*, and later with the court of Mantua. To judge from this text, he was in close touch with the intellectual currents of court life.

The book's structure follows a series of virtues, each defined and then illustrated by a number of female figures, who are treated in such a way as to give maximum exposure to those parts of their lives that relate to the virtue under discussion. In the first five chapters Cacciante deals with rather traditional themes that firmly set women in stereotypical roles.[39] The first chapter sets up chastity as the basis of all female action and development. The second and third chapters discuss women as faithful wives.[40] There is a dramatic shift in emphasis when the text moves on to discuss public virtues necessary to a ruler or quasi-prince (chapters VI to X). These later chapter titles seem borrowed from the mirror-of-prince literature and concern subjects such as justice and military valour. This shift only emphasizes the radical nature of the work, which has no difficulty in transferring values and functions from men to women. In the midst of 'new' roles for women, particularly their part in stimulating court culture, their function as wives is not forgotten, but is integrated into this diverse context. In a Boccaccio-type tale, the husband of Euthimia, queen of Cyprus, after her capture by pirates, 'could do nothing but sigh and weep, nor could anything cheer him up even a little'.[41] The telling point in this otherwise unextraordinary tale is that, on her rescue, the man who treated Euthimia with respect during her period of slavery is rewarded by her and not by the husband.[42] This seemingly small detail emphasizes the relative autonomy of Euthimia in the context of her own court.

The structure of the treatise seems to suggest that family relationships, particularly between husband and wife, need not necessarily stifle female action. Marriage plays a rather subdued role in the text as the author puts on display virtues other than those normally associated with the wife. In the crucial case of his patron Elisabetta Gonzaga, Cacciante is resolutely silent about her marriage to the ailing duke, Guidubaldo Montefeltro.

---

[39] The text is in M. Martini, *Bernardino Cacciante Aletrinate. Contributo alla storia dell' umanesimo* (Sora, 1982), pp. 59–179.

[40] *Libretto apologetico*, pp. 72–81.   [41] *Ibid.*, p. 154.   [42] *Ibid.*, p. 155.

The writer depicts her as the perfect prince whose chief characteristic is *clementia*: 'With how much moderation, fairness and compassion does she settle disputes and put an end to or ease disagreements'.[43] And the other aspect of the ruler as patron is highlighted in order to show Elisabetta as a keen cultivator of the arts. These are the sole virtues to be commented upon by the writer. One can detect here a certain similarity to Equicola's description of Isabella d'Este in that the Mantuan writer too makes no mention of her husband. The form of these texts, principally *exempla* of illustrious women, allowed these writers to ignore the basic fact of marriage and to emphasize other activities. The life of the court exercised a strong influence on the writer: the ordering of the *exempla* into public and intellectual life suggested that women could participate in these aspects of court life. It is important to stress that Cacciante is not writing for all women; the court ambience did not recognize women outside its ranks. He was supporting and perhaps advocating female activity in various areas of the court, as were the other court writers discussed.

The problem of integrating married life into analyses of the role of women at court is nowhere more acute than in Castiglione's *Il libro del cortegiano*. Whereas Cacciante and Equicola had simply ignored the roles expected of a wife – obedience owed to her husband, child bearing and rearing – as if their omission were not problematic, Castiglione attempts to deal with the potential conflict between the private and public in the figure of the *donna di palazzo* (court lady), who may also be a wife. It is significant that, although *Il libro del cortegiano* acknowledges the role of women at court, it does so without completely accepting traditional stereotyping. It is implicitly accepted that the *donna di palazzo* may be married, but her traditional role as wife and mother is not given much weight: the *palazzo* stands in contrast to the home, place of confinement and subalternity. Of the total space explicitly given over to the 'woman question' in Book III, there are only passing remarks to marriage: wifely duties are dismissed in the space of a couple of lines in order to concentrate on the woman's role at court. Castiglione purposely puts married life right into the background. His description of essential female qualities as 'those qualities that are common to all women, such as being good and discreet, and, if she is married, knowing how to look after her husband's affairs, managing his house and looking after the children, and all those skills that are required of a good mother of the family',[44] reveals the norm against which the novelty and social dynamism of the court lady is to be judged. Thus the roles of wife and mother, which to a degree allowed her

---

[43] *Ibid.*, p. 152.
[44] B. Castiglione, *Il libro del cortegiano*, ed. E. Bonora (Milan, 1984), III.v, p. 212.

the function of manager in the home, are *subordinated* to another role, the antithesis of the first one: the 'court lady' who can mix with men (other than her husband if she is married – the marital status of the *donna di palazzo* is never made quite clear, and this ambiguity suits the text's purpose of proposing a 'new' social role to noble women). Although Castiglione has made every effort to avoid accusations of sexual promiscuity being levelled against the *donna di palazzo*, the reader is nevertheless left with the impression that social tensions are contained in the text by downplaying the significance of married life in court society. The functions exercised by the *donna di palazzo* negate some of the basic tenets of married life as understood in the period.

If Arienti valorizes marriage as a basic unit of the state, Castiglione in *Il libro del cortegiano* attempts to write out the notion of the wife. But he does not completely succeed. It may be an ill-defined shadow that follows Castiglione's court lady around; she is certainly not entirely free of the shackles of domestic duties: 'household management' is not entirely dismissed, rather it is placed within a broader view of female behaviour so that it is not 'her first profession'.[45] However, it is pushed into the background so that her 'duties' at court are the focus of her activities. Such a situation is exemplified in the fictionalized narrative of the text through the presentation of Elisabetta Gonzaga, duchess of Urbino. She is married, but we never see her husband who is sick and does not join in the evening entertainments. Thus, the figure of Elisabetta Gonzaga can be said to represent all the ambiguities of Castiglione's discourse on married life. The physical separation from the husband because of the structures of court life is emphasized in the text so that Elisabetta does not appear in the stereotyped role of wife – the court has transformed her into a player of its games. Her position is rendered all the more interesting since she is referred to as a widow, in spite of the fact that her husband is still alive, suggestive of her independence assured by the court environment.[46] Though married, a certain degree of liberty is afforded her, the ideal situation to which other court women are seen to aspire both practically and theoretically.

The institution of marriage also comes in for some quite acerbic, though sporadic, criticism which underlies and explains some of the advice proffered to the court lady. The most intriguing discussion involves the woman-hater Federico Fregoso and the defender of women, Giuliano de' Medici. The fact that the trenchant criticisms of marriage are spoken 'laughingly' by the misogynist may appear to underline the speciousness of his argumentation.[47] Yet, two points would seem to

---

[45] *Ibid.*, III.vii, p. 214.   [46] *Ibid.*, III.xlix, p. 256.   [47] *Ibid.*, III.lvi, p. 263.

militate against this interpretation. The first is that Fregoso's critique of marriage is serious and in no way frivolous. It introduces a note of harsh realism into the 'light' discussions of the text, highlighting the inequalities and oppression of marriage for women: 'If it were permitted those women to divorce and separate from those with whom they are badly matched, it would not perhaps be acceptable that they loved others beside their husband.'[48] The picture created of marriage by Fregoso is one of unmitigated unhappiness for women, replete with images of imprisonment and punishment.[49] In one of the rare moments of direct social criticism, *Il libro del cortegiano* condemns a patriarchal system whereby daughters are sacrificed by their fathers for social or pecuniary advantage.[50] The second point is the surprising nature of Giuliano's reply, which does not make the slightest attempt to rebut Fregoso's comments on the nature of marriage. All he does is to render more respectable Fregoso's suggestion about the acceptability of unhappily married women taking lovers. This should be read as an admission that Fregoso's analysis of marriage is considered to be correct and that Giuliano is only concerned with toning down what are taken to be its more exaggerated elements. Thus, he concludes: 'I desire that she concedes to her lover nothing except her soul'.[51] This extremely moral position is modified in the text in one of the rare, lengthy speeches by a woman, Emilia Pia, who, while emphasizing the need for chaste behaviour, allows for greater informal contact between men and women at court.[52] In spite of his earlier declaration that many women found marriage an 'inferno',[53] Giuliano does not propose any solutions that might disturb the delicate balance that Castiglione has set up in the dialogues, so that rather than 'seriously' suggest change he tends to paper over the rifts between the various female roles. The conflict between public and private is superficially resolved by making the court a site of chaste love. Furthermore, even if the *donna di palazzo* is unmarried, she is enjoined to love someone whom she can marry.[54] The repercussions of this statement are enormous given the negative picture of contemporary marriage in the text. The injunction limits the court lady's field of action to the socially acceptable and, more importantly, to the continuation of practices of social oppression. The court offers a different, but preferable kind of social imprisonment from that depicted in married life.

In common with a number of court texts of the period which deal with the 'woman question', Castiglione illustrates his argument with reference

[48] *Ibid.*   [49] *Ibid.*, p. 264.   [50] *Ibid.*, p. 263.   [51] *Ibid.*, III.lvii, p. 264.
[52] *Ibid.*, III.lxiii.   [53] *Ibid.*, III.xxv, p. 231.
[54] *Ibid.*, III.lvii, p. 264. See C. Freccero, 'Politics and aesthetics in Castiglione's *Il cortegiano*: Book III and the discourse on women', in *Creative Imitation: New Essays on Renaissance Literature in Honor of Thomas M. Greene*, ed. D. Quint et al. (Binghamton, 1992), pp. 275–7.

to *exempla* taken from a variety of sources (mostly Boccaccio's *De mulieribus claris*, also classical texts such as Plutarch's *Mulierum virtutes*). Exemplary women are meant to bolster the discussion and to underline its principal points. Their messages, however, are not always straightforward. *Exempla* regarding wives are limited to only a few cases. Exemplary women who were the subject of the biographies in *De mulieribus claris* are mentioned, but usually only in passing.[55] The longer narratives present a much more ambiguous picture of married life. The story of Camma, taken from Plutarch's *Mulierum virtutes*, deals with the murder of her husband by a suitor and her subsequent revenge on the murderer, which also brings about her own death.[56] As an example of married love it does not show the relationship in progress – Camma is only reunited with her husband in death. Similarly, the *exemplum* of the wife who died through the excitement caused by the shock of her husband's imminent return after a long absence, constructs the husband as an absence, perhaps an ambiguous absence, as in the case of Elisabetta Gonzaga. Thus, marriage offers no security from the terrors or changes of the world.

It is not an accident that the last part of the third book of *Il libro del cortegiano* is almost wholly concerned with the conditions and practices under which love is governed in court society. Though married women are not specifically targeted it is clear that they can be involved in amorous activities as long as they do not break the basic rule regarding physical contact, that is, that none should occur. Castiglione responds to the negative criticism of the court as an immoral place, not by prohibiting love-making altogether, but by placing limits on its actuation.

Hence, *Il libro del cortegiano* subtly sets up a definition of love which attempts to ennoble the concept and which offers a safety-valve for married women, who have no alternative to an unhappy marriage. For these women the court acts as a kind of escape route and a place of refuge from oppressive home life. It allows women to develop certain capabilities in areas excluded by traditional married life, especially skills that increase their sociability. Importantly, the solution is seen to be different from that presented by Boccaccio's *Decameron* which allows intelligent women to outwit their husbands and take lovers. In spite of certain similarities between the two texts, *Il libro del cortegiano* denies sexual satisfaction to married women, who instead channel their unused energies into the rituals of court life. Marriage, therefore, is the great understatement of Castiglione's book. It may not receive much specific attention, but it accounts for a large part of the court lady's behaviour and social role. *Il libro del cortegiano* constitutes a confutation of Alberti's *Della famiglia* by

---

[55] *Il libro del cortegiano*, III.xxii, pp. 227–8.   [56] *Ibid.*, III.xxvi.

refusing to accept that the function of wife fulfils all the needs of a woman and all her social possibilities.

In order to evaluate the radical nature of the court texts that have been analysed in this essay it is necessary to examine other works that deal with married life. I shall take two Florentine examples: the first is Alberti's *Della famiglia*, chosen because of its extended discussion of the married couple and its seminal importance in the development of ideas on marriage. The date of composition of the first three books is 1433–4,[57] and in Book III of the treatise, Alberti laid the ground rules for a subservient wife.[58] Perhaps more crucially, he devised a theoretical position which was cogently opposed by the thinking that underpinned court treatises on women. The second is Vespasiano da Bisticci's *Libro delle lodi e commendazione delle donne*, the greater part of which was probably written in the early 1480s.

In order to gauge the difference from the court texts, comparison can be made with Alberti's treatment of the wife in the third book of *Della famiglia*. It is true that it was written well over half a century earlier than the texts we have discussed so far, but it is a useful touchstone by which to gauge the more 'progressive' positions of the texts previously analysed in this paper.

Alberti usually refers to his wife as 'my lady'.[59] The absence of a title that grants the wife a degree of authority and dignity only underlines the differences between husband and wife in their responsibilities both inside and outside the household. It is true that in Book II Alberti had put forward as an *exemplum* of the ideal wife Cornelia, Pompey's wife, who was 'a beautiful woman, learned, skilled in music, geometry and philosophy',[60] but such a wife was more the result of wishful thinking than a model to be proposed. Nor does the text seem to betray any nostalgia for this rare *exemplum* of female exceptionality, which only serves to highlight the practical functions of the wife, stated a few lines later: 'one primarily takes a wife to raise children'.[61]

The basic difference between husband and wife, taken directly from the Pseudo-Aristotelian *Economics*, lies in the space in which each is permitted to move: the house is more or less the limit for the woman, with no such restriction for the man. Alberti writes with contempt for 'those

[57] L. B. Alberti, *Opere volgari*, ed. C. Grayson (3 vols., Bari, 1960–73), I, pp. 378–80; C. Grayson, 'Alberti, Leon Battista', *Dizionario biografico degli italiani*, I, pp. 702–4.
[58] S. K. Cohn Jr., 'Donne in piazza e donne in tribunale a Firenze nel Rinascimento', *Studi storici*, 22 (1981), pp. 517, 527, 533; F. Furlan, 'Pour une histoire de la famille et de l'amour à l'époque de l'humanisme', *Revue des études italiennes*, 36 (1990), pp. 93–4.
[59] L. B. Alberti, *I libri della famiglia*, ed. R. Romano and A. Tenenti, third edn (Turin, 1980), p. 264; p. 266 (for 'madre di famiglia').
[60] *Ibid.*, p. 137.   [61] *Ibid.*, p. 138.

bold and brazen women who are too interested in knowing what is going on outside the home, in relation either to their husbands or to other men'.[62] Confusion between gender roles is the unspoken enemy whereby gendered functions might be 'mis-taken', resulting in social chaos: 'as it would be hardly honourable if the wife busied herself amongst men in the town square, in public, so it would be even more blameworthy to keep me shut up in the house amongst women, when my place is amongst men doing manly things'.[63]

Della famiglia allows no deviation from a black-and-white view of husband and wife. Aristotelian assumptions about women are never far from the surface of the dialogues: 'In contrast [to men] almost all women seem to be timid by nature, feeble, and slow to learn'.[64] The phrase 'almost all women' is in *Della famiglia* a negligible comment, having no strong resonance in the text. This is a strategy opposite to that pursued by court writers of biographical collections and pro-female treatises, where the exceptional woman, in past times and diverse societies, ambiguously points to the possibilities open to contemporary women. The question of exceptional women has no currency for Alberti. The wife is expected to be limited to very ordinary routines – reproduction and housekeeping. Moreover, there is little doubt in the text that the domestic sphere is inferior to the public one, and it is viewed as a sign of weakness on the man's part to show excessive interest in housekeeping.[65] Alberti unambiguously declares that the wife is condemned to 'the management of minor matters'.[66] And even this activity is illuminated by male intelligence because it is suggested that the wife would be quite unable to take up her duties without her husband's guidance.[67] The dialogue structure – a discussion amongst men, written for men with women as the passive objects of the debate – ensures that rhetorical discourse is seen by the reader as the exclusive domain of men. This emphasizes the inequality of the relationship in which there is little possibility of intimacy between husband and wife.

The reader sees the husband and wife together on only two occasions in Book III. Once they are praying. Their prayers bring them together only in one aspect of their existence: 'grant us the grace of living many happy years together in peace and harmony and with many male children'.[68] They also both pray that 'she be granted uprightness, chastity and the virtue of being a good housewife'.[69] Thus, 'religious' ideals shared in common are seen to serve male interests.

---

[62] *Ibid.*, pp. 267–8.   [63] *Ibid.*, p. 264.   [64] *Ibid.*, p. 265.
[65] See C. Freccero, 'Economy, woman, and Renaissance discourse', in *Refiguring Woman: Perspectives on Gender and the Italian Renaissance*, ed M. Migiel and J. Schiesari (Ithaca and London, 1991), pp. 197–201.
[66] *Della famiglia*, p. 266.   [67] *Ibid.*, p. 266.   [68] *Ibid.*, p. 272.   [69] *Ibid.*

The most poignant moment of intimacy described in Book III is when the *padre di famiglia* appears to have let the wife into his confidence; there is a moment when she seems to be on the point of penetrating his externality. The scene is set in the husband's bedroom: 'I desired that none of my precious things were hidden from my wife.'[70] Yet that sentiment is immediately contradicted. Giannozzo *does* exclude his wife from the most important part of himself: his writings. The text is absolutely categorical about this prohibition: 'It was my wish then and henceforth that my books and writings and those of my forebears were always locked up, so that my wife not only could not read them, but not even see them.'[71]

This prohibition demonstrates clearly the limitations of the wife–husband relationship as perceived by Alberti, and equally importantly it underscores the powers associated with writing and the fear of contamination arising from contact with a lesser being. The papers referred to here could be the business accounts and transactions of the husband and the *ricordanze* of himself and his family. The woman is confronted with a dual exclusion: from external business affairs and from the sense of meaning that is conferred on family members by sharing a common history. The *ricordanze* granted a sense of historical place to the male members of a family. In Alberti's view the women of the family should have no access to this sense of selfhood, otherwise it might mean questioning the institutionalized roles imposed on them by men or involve sharing in some real sense. The *studio* is the inner male sanctum (the writings are referred to as 'sacred and religious objects') where the ideal of the family, as it is outlined in Book III, is kept safe.[72] It is clear that the only source of instruction for a wife is her husband. Books of any kind are not available to her, since the knowledge they might provide could be used to undermine the husband's authority or to demand a greater share in family affairs.

On the one hand, *Della famiglia* presents women as unreliable, bereft of 'any real intelligence or proper understanding';[73] on the other, they are considered a possible source of danger. The elaborate precautions and training procedures that are described in the course of the book are a response to a perceived threat from women who might wish to break away from the mould created for them. Exclusion entails apparent female management of some details of family life that the husband does not wish to control directly.

It is of considerable importance that in *Della famiglia* the dowry brought by the wife is reduced in significance by using the ploy of

[70] *Ibid.*, p. 267.
[71] *Ibid.*; and see Freccero, 'Economy, woman, and Renaissance discourse', pp. 202–7.
[72] *Della famiglia*, p. 267.   [73] *Ibid.*, p. 268.

communality, so absent from all the discourse on the wife. It has a hollow ring about it: the rapidity of its treatment carries the suggestion that it should not have a high priority in married life, whereas in reality it might be an instrument of considerable leverage for the wife.[74] Working together signifies the wife's acceptance of the parameters drawn for her by the husband. She has to listen to male discourse, but she is not a completely absent figure. Her presence, conjured up by Giannozzo, is certainly subordinate to the web of talk in which her husband enmeshes her. She rarely speaks in the first person, and when she does her speech usually takes the form of broken phrases, hardly ever constructing a sentence as evidence of thought. Her broken, whispered words form the smallest units of discourse and contrast all too obviously with the lengthy prescriptions of her husband. More frequently, Giannozzo reports indirectly what his wife said, thus taking over her speech and making it part of his own ideologically laden discourse. In most cases too Giannozzo reports the body language of his wife, emphasizing her inferiority and natural indiscipline.[75] The husband aims to control the female body through his words.

Transgression of these boundaries is the underlying theme/fear of the text. Fear of a reversal of roles, even if in carnivalesque fashion, ensures that the text emphasizes the subalternity of the wife. Virility is seen as keeping women in their place, literally. Alberti puts the matter succinctly:

And thus all wives obey their husbands when the latter know how to behave as husbands. But I see a few who are unwise and think they can make themselves obeyed and respected by their wives whom they openly serve as slaves. These husbands show by their words and gestures that their soul is too libidinous and effeminate, so they make the wife no less unchaste than stubborn. It was never my desire to submit to my wife, wherever we were, in the slightest matter, neither in words or action.[76]

This fear of disorder has to be beaten back, because it might mean loss of power and surrender to a different set of (female) values. Behaviour, therefore, not only needs to be controlled, but it has to be recognizable and classifiable, otherwise the larger political disorder (the exile of the Alberti clan against which the *Della famiglia* is set),[77] will lead to even greater disruptions in the familial fabric: '"Wife, order and organization are essential in all matters. It's not done for you to carry a sword nor to do other virile things like men do, nor should women always and everywhere do those things that are allowed to women."'[78] There is no suggestion, however, that the wife can stray from the territory marked out for her. Only one role is allowed woman, that of wife. Her life is mapped out in its

[74] *Ibid.*, p. 270.   [75] *Ibid.*, p. 285.   [76] *Ibid.*, pp. 277–8.
[77] G. Mancini, *Vita di Leon Battista Alberti* (Rome, 1967, repr. of 1911 edn), pp. 8–10.
[78] *Della famiglia*, p. 291.

finest detail by the husband, who acts out his power over her in the vacuum left by exile from Florence and from the political system that gave him his place in the social order. Alberti's treatise seems to be written as a defence and *encomium* of traditional values. It looks back in order to look forward – Giannozzo's wife is dead at the time of the dialogues and he looks back on her nostalgically as the model wife, implicitly criticizing contemporary trends. She has the power of an *exemplum*, but, unlike Boccaccio's or his successors' version of female activity, she accomplishes nothing extraordinary. Indeed, Alberti's wife is a celebration of ordinariness: not only does she not break out of the domestic cycle into which she has been thrust, but the desire to do so is coaxed out of her. The division of labour, which is so central to Alberti's vision of woman, can be read in part as a reaction against the confusion of roles engendered by the emergence of a strong court society in which elite women do not feel as constrained by traditional role models. In fact, some court women entered into domains that are heavily marked as male.

Conversely, one can detect a determination in court society to rewrite Alberti's version of married life. In all cases the court writers needed to come to terms with the figure of the wife: she could simply be re-inscribed and reappropriated in a courtly context with some adjustment, or she could be neglected and written over in favour of more radical and dynamic models of female behaviour. In this context, Vespasiano da Bisticci's collection of female biographies is particularly interesting in that it reappropriates a genre that was in danger of becoming too closely associated with the more radical positions assumed by court writers. It confirms a line of thought about women which might be described as Florento-centric. Bisticci had obviously read Boccaccio's *De mulieribus claris*, although he included very few women from that source. His principal type of woman was the female martyr, normally a virgin – she, rather than the wife, appears to be his model woman, in spite of the fact that the manuscript is dedicated to the wife of Pierfilippo Pandolfini, Mona Maria. The bulk of the work is devoted to female martyrs and even when it deals with married women, such as Esther, the same values of religious faith and constancy are transferred to them. Bisticci's remarks on Christian martyrs make clear his view on women in general: 'The Christian religion is marvellous in that their [the martyrs'] constancy and faith was so great that of their own free will they desired to die for the love of God.'[79] The exemplary women are essentially viewed as religious beings whose lives are conducted wholly according to the dictates of Christian-defined virtues. This is reflected in Bisticci's choice of near-contemporary

[79] *Libro delle lodi*, fol. 52v. For brief discussion of the work, see G. M. Cagni, *Vespasiano da Bisticci e il suo epistolario* (Rome, 1969), pp. 105–8.

women who, although married, are generally discussed without much reference to their husbands. The case of Battista Malatesta is instructive. The sole reference to her husband is the fact that during his life she was allowed to enter a convent and distribute money to the needy.[80] It is difficult to reconcile the fact that this woman was the same one to whom Bruni dedicated his *De studiis et litteris* ('On the Study of Literature'), composed in 1424.[81] Bisticci makes only a passing reference to Battista's literary skills, but he is careful to relate them to her religious calling: 'Her eloquence was accompanied by the holiness of her life'.[82] The same process is at work in the other biographies of 'modern' women. The daughter of Paola Gonzaga, Cecilia, rejects marriage in favour of the enclosed life: 'The girl had made up her mind to abandon the world completely and serve God.'[83] His choice of court women and their treatment is a challenge to other court women to lead a Christian life. He purposely ignores the secular achievements of such women, to emphasize exclusively their devotion to Christian ideals.

The most detailed accounts of married life in the *Libro delle lodi e commendazione delle donne* are to be found in the biographies of the Florentine women chosen by Bisticci to function as models in that urban context. All Bisticci's recent women are married, except for Cecilia Gonzaga. Taking the example of Madonna Nanna, wife of Giannozzo Pandolfini, one can see the social conditions that are necessitated by Bisticci's adherence to his model. He praises her in terms that underline her limited field of action: 'serious, of few words, modest, calm, generous when necessary, completely devoted to the worship of God'.[84] Particular features of her life are picked out for comment. It should be noted that they include no reference to her husband. Her main role is in the home, where she brings up the children in a responsible Christian fashion so that the house becomes the lay equivalent of a monastery. Bisticci conjures up the image of the children praying alongside their mother. Although the religious element far outweighs all other considerations, Bisticci does insist on her role as household manager, much in the same way as Arienti's Diana Saliceto: 'The responsibility for the running of the house was all hers, and it was so well organized that nothing was lacking in the general order of the household. And everything was done in the greatest peace and tranquillity of the entire house, in which never was there heard the slightest cross word'.[85] It is interesting to note that in the case of Checcha Acciaiuoli her political activity, of preserving her husband's

---

[80] *Libro delle lodi*, fols. 84v–85r.
[81] Translated in *The Humanism of Leonardo Bruni: Selected Texts*, ed G. Griffiths, J. Hankins and D. Thompson (Binghampton, 1987).
[82] *Libro delle lodi*, fol. 85r.   [83] *Ibid.*, fol. 86r.   [84] *Ibid.*, fol. 91v.   [85] *Ibid.*, fol. 92v.

property and fortune, is mentioned only after his death, to suggest a more active role for her as a widow. The instructions given to wives at the end of the text do not in any way mention the relationship between them and their husbands. They rather formalize the thrust of the *exempla*, stressing the necessity for individual female probity and sexual continence, the obligation of wives to bring up their children in a Christian manner, and to run the household. Bisticci manages to recreate, using the illustrious-women genre, a model of the wife that does not transgress any of the traditional boundaries.

These two Florentine texts allow us to demonstrate that the court biographies represent an attempt to re-think the role of women in society. Whereas Alberti and Bisticci circumscribe the role of the wife, the re-evaluation of female lives and marriage found in Equicola, Arienti, Cacciante, and Castiglione is refigured and reproportioned. The centrality of legitimacy is recognized, as is that of dynastic alliance, by all writers who are really concerned with a minuscule elite of women. Thus, the attraction of the biographies of famous women for these writers resides in the fact that such women were exceptional, as were those with whom they came into contact in court circles. In some ways, the exemplary women are fantasy figures that allow the court to sublimate feminine desire for public achievement. However, manipulation of these figures is evident in so far as particular texts favour particular typologies or adapt them to the situation of the courts. Therefore, such collections of female biographies take pleasure in projecting images of a female 'other', far removed from the traditional stereotype of the wife. Female warriors, Amazons and queens all put pressure on the image of the obedient and meek wife, the 'patient Griselda' (who paradoxically appears in some collections). She is not completely displaced or submerged, but one can note a shift in emphasis or rather an opening out of female potential.

The impact of these collections is hard to measure and it would be all too easy to dismiss them as having little or no consequence, especially since the majority were never printed and some are now extant in only one or two manuscripts. I would argue that within court circles they were instrumental in shifting the boundaries of how a woman could be defined. The limitations of being solely a wife were either made into virtues in more conservative re-evaluations, or the role of wife was questioned directly or by implication in the more radical treatises. For the highest placed women at court the appearance of such texts in this period could not have been more apposite: it allowed them to claim lineage with some of the most illustrious women known to humanists, permitting a validation of their public performance without denying the facts of their social existence. These texts allow us to gauge the fluctuations in the image of the wife in those courts that were at the centre of a new discourse on woman. The wife, as understood by the traditional Christian paradigm, for a brief historical moment has her discursive authority curtailed and is the occasion for a search for a new identity.

12 Separations and separated couples in fourteenth-century Venice

Linda Guzzetti

In making her will in 1303, the noblewoman Filippa Grioni provided that her husband, Filippo Grioni, should be allowed to live rent-free in her house in the parish of S. Giovanni Crisostomo, Venice, either for the rest of his life or until the house was sold.[1] As she declared, she had bought the house with her dowry, but she herself lived in the parish of S. Gimignano, where other relatives from her birth-family, the Bragadin, also lived. In addition, her husband was to receive a cash legacy of L. 100, if her son and heir died without male or female issue. This last provision was subject to the consent of Filippa's executors who were members of her natal family. This case brings forth a surprising constellation of kin. Filippa lived apart from her husband, and had recovered her dowry. On the other hand, the relations between the separated couple were apparently peaceful, and Filippa expected no basic hostility on the part of her kin to her husband; otherwise it would have been meaningless to leave to them the last decision over the legacy.

Marriages in the Middle Ages did not originate in the free choice of the partners, but their conclusion was a concern of their families, albeit in varying degrees according to social group. However, the influence of the natal kin was not the same in all phases of married life. Through a study of church-court sentences in Ely in the late fourteenth century, Michael Sheehan came to the conclusion that family and feudal constraints, which might be expected in the Middle Ages, were not in evidence in the records: rather, the couple displayed individualistic behaviour regarding marriage.[2] This is one of the issues that will be addressed in what follows:

[1] The following essay has grown out of research for my doctorate, but is not part of it. I would like to take this opportunity to thank the *Förderprogramm für Frauenforschung* of the Senate of Berlin for a two-and-a-half-year grant which made possible my doctoral research.
The sources for all the cases presented here are listed in the appendix.
[2] M. M. Sheehan, 'The formation and stability of marriage in fourteenth-century England: evidence of an Ely register', *Mediaeval Studies*, 33 (1971), p. 263.

to what extent in Venetian examples of marriage crisis was the couple alone involved, and to what extent did their families play a role? In the course of conjugal life, some couples developed a partnership, as shown in Stanley Chojnacki's investigations for Venetian noblewomen of the fourteenth and fifteenth centuries;[3] but others must have lived together grudgingly and unfeelingly. Though the vast majority of marriages ended with the death of one of the spouses, other couples separated either for a limited time or definitively. In the course of marriage, relations between spouses cannot have been as static as they seem when the conclusion of marriage alone is examined: Chojnacki also remarks that it is an error to regard women only as objects of family marriage strategies, and to disregard their development in the decades following the conclusion of marriage. The development of some marriages, as proposed here, can contribute to an insight into the possible course of married relations. It will also be asked what the consequences were, for marriage crises, of the inequality of the sexes, which characterized medieval marriage, and what kind of legal and financial advantages the husband had in separations. Finally, matrimonial matters offer the possibility of examining the relations between secular and ecclesiastical authorities by analysing some concrete examples.

The present study is based on sixteen examples of separation and breakdown. It is concerned with the presentation of individual cases, which do not allow any quantitative analysis.[4] All the cases refer to marriage crisis and separation, except for two which involve annulment and bigamy.

In the course of the Middle Ages, the church tried to call a halt to divorce, and to transfer to its own courts decisions on the legitimacy of separations. The unity and indissolubility of marriage were based by the church on the theological grounds that marriage was a sacrament and copied the union of Christ with the church. Departures from this morality of marriage were, however, widespread in the early Middle Ages, because the indissolubility of marriage was not recognized by either Germanic customs or Roman law. From the time of the systematization of canon law in the twelfth century, the dissolution of a valid marriage became, in theology and law, absolutely impermissible. As a consequence of this development, the term *divortium* is misleading in the Middle Ages and will not be used here: though it was used in the early Middle Ages to mean the end of marriage, it later acquired different meanings, either annul-

---

[3] S. Chojnacki, 'The power of love: wives and husbands in late medieval Venice', in *Women and Power in the Middle Ages*, ed. M. Erler and M. Kowaleski (Athens, Ga., and London, 1992), pp. 127–8.
[4] Cf. Sheehan, 'Formation and stability of marriage', pp. 232–3.

ment (*divortium a sacramento*) or the termination of conjugal cohabitation (*divortium a mensa et thoro*).[5] In the former, the church courts could decide that a marriage had been invalid from the beginning, and thus dissolve it; in the latter, judges could put an end to the cohabitation of the couple. However, whereas both parties could re-marry after an annulment, the ending of conjugal cohabitation by judicial separation left the sacramental bond intact, with the consequence that neither partner could remarry while the other remained alive.

The acts of the church courts have proved in many places a fertile source for the study of separations and annulments.[6] However, the archives of the patriarch of Grado and of the bishop of Castello, who had jurisdiction over Venice until 1451, have not survived.[7] Without these records, it is hard to find petitions for the recognition of contested marriages, even though these are probably present in Venice. Not all secular governments, however, accepted in like degree that control over marriage should be left to the church, especially where this concerned matters of property and finance. The Italian communes are one example, among others, of successful resistance to complete subordination to the church, and their records, as at Venice, provide a rich fund of evidence for separations.

Moreover, some couples did actually separate. It is not possible to know how widespread this phenomenon was. However, there is evidence for it in Venice in some notarial acts of separation, and in casual references in notarial acts or court records to the state of separation. For example, it is evident from the will of Garita Barbarigo in 1398 that, while she lived in the parish of S. Antonino, her husband, Franceschino Lovatino, lived in Murano. Indeed, she mentioned him only in order to inform her daughter and her two sons-in-law, who had the charge of executing the will, from whom they should claim her dowry. In another

---

[5] For a detailed treatment of the word, see S. Nelli, *Lo scioglimento del matrimonio nella storia del diritto italiano* (Milan, 1976).

[6] See J. P. Levy, 'L'officialité de Paris et les questions familiales à la fin du XIVe siècle', in *Etudes d'histoire du droit canonique dédiées à Gabriel Le Bras* (2 vols., Paris, 1965), II; Sheehan, 'Formation and stability of marriage'; A. Lefebvre-Teillard, *Les officialités à la veille du Concile de Trente* (Paris, 1973); R. H. Helmholz, *Marital Litigation in Medieval England* (Cambridge, 1974); R. Weigand, 'Zur mittelalterlichen kirchlichen Gerichtsbarkeit. Rechtsvergleichende Untersuchung', *Zeitschrift der Savigny-Stiftung für Rechtsgeschichte*, 98 (1981), Kanonische Abteilung.

[7] Only from the foundation of the patriarchate of Venice in 1451 was the relevant material kept in the Archivio della Curia patriarcale; there the series Causae matrimoniales provides resources for study of this topic. See G. Ruggiero, *The Boundaries of Eros: Sex Crime and Sexuality in Renaissance Venice* (New York, 1985); A. Rigo, 'Giudici del Procuratore e donne "malmaritate". Interventi della giustizia secolare in materia matrimoniale a Venezia in epoca tridentina', *Atti dell'Istituto veneto di scienze, lettere ed arti*, 151 (1993).

will, that of Francesca Daledople, the notary wrote, alongside their names, that Francesca lived in the parish of S. Sofia, and that her husband, a tailor named Daniel, lived in S. Giacomo dell'Orio; but of him there is no further mention in the text of the will. It is by chance here that the wills record the testators and their husbands living apart, as it was not obligatory to give exact family circumstances in wills.

The first stage in our examination of this problem is to investigate some parts of canon law and of Venetian statute law with regard to the following issues: the demarcation between the secular and ecclesiastical authorities in matrimonial matters, the arguments used by both sides, and the unequal position of the partners in marriage. Canon law regulated the circumstances in which the termination of marriage was permitted. First, separation was permissible on account of culpable behaviour by one of the parties on the following grounds: adultery, heresy (*fornicatio spiritualis*) and use of violence against the other party (*saevitia*). Separation on the basis of mutual agreement was possible only when both parties wished to dedicate their lives entirely to the church.[8] Second, the grounds in canon law for an annulment were numerous. Most frequently marriages were declared null either because there existed another valid union before the marriage; because the couple were related within the fourth degree;[9] because the man or the woman was impotent; or because force, or the fear of force, had been used at the wedding.

From studying church-court records, it appears that in matrimonial matters they dealt mostly not with annulments and separations, but with the recognition of contested marriages (when one party denied that a marriage had taken place).[10] These pleas were much more often entered by women than by men, and had little chance of success. Marriages were declared null by the church courts mainly if they were concluded when one party was already married. In such cases of bigamy, either the first

---

[8] A. Esmein, *Mariage en droit canonique* (Paris, 1891), II, pp. 21–9.
[9] The medieval conception of kinship included relationships by marriage and by godparent-hood (Esmein, *Mariage*, I, pp. 335–83). For a discussion of the significance of this prohibition on marriage, see Helmholz, *Marital Litigation*, pp. 77–87; D. Herlihy, 'Making sense of incest: women and marriage rules of the early Middle Ages', in *Law, Custom and the Social Fabric in Medieval Europe. Essays in Honor of Bryce Lyon*, ed. B. S. Bachrach and D. Nicholas (Kalamazoo, 1990).
[10] Weigand remarks that historical research on medieval marriage law has until recently considered mainly the texts of canon law and only exceptionally the records of the church courts (Weigand, 'Zur mittelalterlichen kirchlichen Gerichtsbarkeit', p. 213). On the frequency of the various pleas before these courts, see *ibid.*, pp. 217–20; Lefebvre-Teillard, *Les officialités*, p. 108; Helmholz, *Marital Litigation*, p. 25. In France, however, almost no proceedings concerned the recognition of contested marriages, but rather the betrothal proceedings (Weigand, 'Zur mittelalterlichen kirchlichen Gerichtsbarkeit', p. 223). Weigand (*ibid.*, p. 230) estimates that on average 10 per cent of church-court proceedings were matrimonial matters.

marriage had to be declared invalid or the second was dissolved. Annulment on the grounds of marriage within the prohibited degrees of kinship was, in all courts that have been studied, only a small portion of the cases. The patriarchate of Grado, within whose territory Venice belonged, issued some orders regarding marriage in the thirteenth century.[11] Banns were declared obligatory, and vicars were instructed to investigate whether fiancé(e)s from outside the city were indeed unmarried. Moreover, the existing prohibitions of marrying a second time while the first partner lived, and of marrying within the prohibited degrees of kinship, were repeated.

The Venetian councils adapted themselves only partly to the wishes of the church authorities. On 2 October 1323, the Great Council decided that the announcement of intent to marry must be made through the banns (*strida*) in the bride's parish on four separate days. Indeed, the banns were not left to the priest, but a public crier was charged with this task by order of the *giudici dell'esaminatore*. The consequences for those men who did not publicize their intention to marry are illuminating: they were made liable for the debts that their brides had incurred before the wedding. Thus it becomes clear that this measure was essentially financial, with the aim of protecting the creditors of women about to marry. The immediate intention of this deliberation was thus not to combat bigamy or to prevent secret marriages.[12]

Further decisions of the Great Council dealt with bigamy.[13] Bigamists were punished by having to pay to the second wife a sum equal to her dowry, which also had to be returned. If she had married without a

[11] The decisions were confirmed at a provincial council in Grado on 13 July 1296 (see *Italia sacra*, ed. F. Ughelli and N. Coleti, second edn (10 vols., Venice, 1720), V, pp. 1143–4, art. XXIV–XXIX; G. Gallicciolli, *Delle memorie venete antiche profane ed ecclesiastiche libri tre* (7 vols., Venice, 1795), II, pt 12, pp. 38–9).

[12] *Statuta veneta* (Venice, 1548), Consulta, fols. 230v–1. Gallicciolli, *Delle memorie venete*, II, pt 12, p. 27, mentions this deliberation, and interprets it as part of the local enforcement of the decree on marriage of the fourth Lateran Council. B. Cecchetti, *La Repubblica di Venezia e la corte di Roma nei rapporti della religione* (2 vols., Venice, 1874), I, p. 58, n. 4, ranks this deliberation with decisions which, though regulating marriage, had a political, not a religious character.

[13] *Deliberazioni del Maggior Consiglio*, ed. R. Cessi (3 vols., Bologna, 1931–50; repr. 1970), III, pp. 220–1, 27 Sept. 1288. This deliberation is also in *Magistrature giudiziarie veneziane e i loro capitolari fino al 1300*, ed. M. Roberti, 3 vols. (I: Padua, 1906; II–III: Venice, 1909–11), II, p. 45, as an element of the standing orders of the *Signori di notte*. On 22 May and 19 Aug. 1292 the Great Council altered the penalties, taking away banishment, which was foreseen in the first deliberation, if the convict paid the fine and served the imprisonment (*Deliberazioni del Maggior Consiglio*, III, pp. 317, 322). The very small fine for bigamy was raised in a further deliberation on 21 Sept. 1359, which laid down that at least L. 100 *parvorum* be paid, even when the second wife's dowry was less than that (Maggior consiglio, Novella=reg. 20). See also Cecchetti, *La Repubblica di Venezia e la corte di Roma*, I, p. 60; and cf. G. Ruggiero, *Violence in Early Renaissance Venice* (Brunswick, 1980), p. 44.

dowry, a fixed sum of L. 100 was appointed. According to this council decision, only men could be bigamists. The second wife appeared only as a deceived party, so that compensation was due to her, to facilitate a new marriage. However, in the early fourteenth century the Venetian jurist and chancellor Jacobus Bertaldus wrote that a woman who married, knowing her husband to be married already, should lose her dowry.[14]

Separation by agreement was regulated by one clause in the Venetian statutes, when (as provided for in canon law) both partners aspired to a religious life: in such an event, the wife recovered her dowry.[15] Only in two further clauses was marriage separation mentioned.[16] One of them dealt with the restitution of dowry. This was provided for not only in the case of widows, but also in that of separated wives.[17] The other clause was concerned with separation owing to adultery.[18] According to Roman law, as also to Venetian legislation, the situation of women varied according to whether they or their husbands were found guilty of adultery by the court. For their own adulterous behaviour, wives lost their dowries; if the husband was found guilty, the deceived wife had to demand in court maintenance or restitution of dowry.

As adulteresses were at great risk of losing their dowries, they could be tempted to compensate themselves with goods taken from the matrimonial household. Therefore, the Great Council was concerned for the goods of the deceived husband, as is shown in a deliberation of 4 August 1306: it made it a duty of the *Signori di notte* to prosecute those women who, in leaving their husbands, also made off with their property. According to Guido Ruggiero, the Council of Forty was very attentive to the

[14] J. Bertaldus, *Splendor venetorum civitatis consuetudinum*, ed. F. Schupfer (Bologna, 1895), p. 36.
[15] *Statuta veneta. Statuti veneziani di Jacopo Tiepolo del 1242 e le loro glosse*, ed. R. Cessi (Venice, 1938), I.59. When only one spouse wished to enter a convent, the other had to consent and pledge him or herself to chastity. This was not always so easily achieved, as the case of the blessed Maria of Venice shows: *La santità imitabile: La 'Leggenda di Maria da Venezia' di Tommaso da Siena*, ed. F. Sorelli (Venice, 1984), pp. 157, 171–5.
[16] Italian statutes gave little attention to separation: G. Di Renzo Villata, 'Separazione (storia)', *Enciclopedia del diritto* (Milan, 1989), XLI, p. 1359.
[17] *Statuta veneta*, I.62 ('Qualiter mulier post obitum viri vel separationem possit petere dotem suam'). According to the *Corpus iuris civilis* (Novellae 117, 9:4–5), the wife recovered her dowry if the husband was guilty of causing the separation.
[18] *Statuta veneta*, IV.32 ('Mulier per adulterium iudicio ecclesie a viro separata non audiatur super exigenda sua repromissa. Si qua mulier iudicio ecclesie a viro suo per adulterium separata fuerit et a nostris iudicibus super repromissa sua petierit iustitiam exhiberi, volumus quod super hoc nullatenus audiatur. Verum, si vir post talem separationem eam sibi adiunxerit *tamquam uxorem eam tractandum, secundum quod potest publice apparere*, ius dotis ad ipsam redeat, sicut ante separationem habebat'). Bertaldus, 'Splendor', p. 35, observed that adulteresses lost their dowries only after a judicial sentence: it was therefore not sufficient that adultery by the wife be publicly known.

prosecution and punishment of such removal of valuables from the matrimonial home by wives and their lovers.[19]

The statutes (IV.32) also foresaw the possibility that the separation could be limited in time and that the couple could be reconciled. However, this was expressed only from the standpoint of the husband, and only in the event of the wife's guilt. If he took her back again and treated her as his spouse, she kept the rights to her dowry as before the separation.

In some of these provisions, the inequality of the sexes in marriage is clearly reflected. An adulteress was, with regard to her property, dependent on the generosity of her husband to forgive her, while an adulterer had at most to pay maintenance, but suffered no loss of property.[20] Moreover, something different, for men and for women, was understood as adultery in Roman law and in judicial practice.[21] In bigamy, the possibility was overlooked by the legislators that a woman could marry twice without one of her partners being deceased. As a result, no punishment was provided for female bigamists. But Bertaldus' remark shows that women were not treated as guiltless as a matter of course. It is not without significance that the statutes and the deliberations of the Great Council were written in a language that envisaged only the men as active subjects.[22] But judicial practice did not treat women only as victims, and, compared to the statutes, overlooked their deeds and rights less.

In considering relations between secular and ecclesiastical jurisdiction in Venice, the following petition of the bishop of Castello shows how restricted the bishop's power was in fact. Around 1310, he asked the Venetian commune for help in exercising his jurisdiction over marriage. Thereupon, the Senate, according to a deliberation of 8 June 1310, charged two official bodies (the *Signori di notte* and the *Avogadori di comun*) to prosecute those witnesses who made false statements in matrimonial cases in the bishop's court. The bishop complained that, as the witnesses were lay people, he was not able to combat their lies, because his court could take no proceedings against them for false statements.[23] Elsewhere, bishops carried out their administration of justice in matrimonial matters with the help of ecclesiastical penalties;[24] but in Venice, it emerges from judicial practice and from a later deliberation of the Great Council that, at

---

[19] Ruggiero, *The Boundaries of Eros*, pp. 51–3. The decision is published in *Capitolare dei signori di notte*, ed. F. Nani Mocenigo (Venice, 1877), p. 99.

[20] The maintenance was mostly paid from the dowry: see below.

[21] *Corpus iuris civilis*, Novellae, 117, 8–9.

[22] Ruggiero, *The Boundaries of Eros*, pp. 47–8.

[23] Gallicciolli, *Delle memorie venete*, II, pt 12, p. 39. The corresponding Senate record is burnt.

[24] Helmholz, *Marital Litigation*, pp. 114–18, gives details on the effectiveness of ecclesiastical courts in England.

least over maintenance payments, it was the secular councils, not the ecclesiastical courts, that decided. By this later deliberation, of August 1374, questions over the maintenance of separated women were transferred to the court of the *giudici del procuratore*.²⁵ The deliberation did not demand that the separation be effected through an ecclesiastical judgement, but only that the wife raise an action against her husband for payment of maintenance. It is true that in the judges' standing orders the rubric mentioned the husband's guilt, but the text of the deliberation presupposes only the plea for maintenance. The latter was possible also in separations by mutual agreement, and was not completely excluded in those which were a result of the wife's guilty behaviour.²⁶

Before, various courts had dealt with maintenance payments, and the deliberation of 1374 did not mean that wives previously had had no claim for maintenance. On 31 December 1274, for example, the Great Council resolved that the wife of Marino di Tebaldino 'de Galeto' had to receive upkeep contributions of L. 60 *parvorum* each year from the government bonds belonging to her husband. In this decision, her name was not given, but it was stressed that her husband was 'going wrong' (*in mala via*). It is not clear what he had done, but, whatever it was, this expression refers to his responsibility for the separation.

However, the jurisdiction of the communal courts in marriage disputes went beyond the financial consequences of separation. For the period following the Council of Trent, Antonio Rigo has analysed the activity of the church and secular courts regarding marriage disputes, and has established that the *giudici del procuratore* also pronounced judgements on separations.²⁷ This activity, which shows an extension of their jurisdiction, was probably current practice already in the fourteenth century, though it is visible in only one of the cases studied here.

In the dispute between Caterina and Micheletto Morosini, the *giudici del procuratore* not only decided the level of the annual payments he had to make to his wife, but also instituted a full separation hearing. There is no mention, in the record of their sentence, of a previous ecclesiastical decision authorizing the separation. The complaint was raised before the court by Caterina because of the wickedness (*duricia et asperitas et*

---

²⁵ *Statuta veneta* 1548, Consulta, fols. 191v–2 ('Iudices procuratorum audiant uxores de viro conquerentes et iustitiam ministrent'). This decision was copied into the standing orders of the appointed judge (*Magistrature giudiziarie veneziane*, III, p. 182) under the rubric 'De provisione danda mulieri que stare non potest cum viro suo ex defectu viri'; the text states: 'Et si alique mulier fuerit que non steterit cum eius viro et ipsa de suprascripto eius viro conquesa fuerit quod vir eius de victu et vestitu sibi providere debeat, ipsam audiam et rationem sibi faciam secundum quod mee disretioni vel maiori parte nostrorum bonum videtur bona fide sine fraude'.
²⁶ See footnote 63.   ²⁷ Rigo, 'Giudici del Procuratore', p. 249.

nequicia) of her husband. She told the court that he had expelled her from the house, and that she no longer wished to live with him, unless he left off his wickedness and treated her decently. Micheletto replied with unfair and malicious words, and refused to live with her again. The judge awarded to Caterina an annual maintenance payment of L. 3 *grossorum*. This sentence was explicitly justified by the great freedom allowed to the judges, in their standing orders, in making decisions over maintenance.[28]

Matrimonial cases can also be unravelled through notarial acts. In the Italian cities a widespread notarial culture offered the possibility of drawing up before the notary agreements on many matters, including marriage crisis and separation. A bigamist in 1289 put her situation in order through a notarial act, without any court becoming involved. She and her second husband reciprocally bound each other neither to treat each other as spouses, nor to marry in the future.[29]

Nor was a court decision mentioned in the maintenance agreement between the noble partners Coletta and Nicoletto da Pesaro, which was drawn up before a notary. As grounds for the separation it was specified that the couple, because of their different characters (*propter diversitates animorum*), were no longer compatible, especially if they were obliged to live together. Following this agreement, Nicoletto paid to Coletta for thirty years the stipulated 10 ducats every six months.[30] In two other cases in which the couple made notarial settlements, no court proceedings were referred to. In both cases it was a question of the husband undertaking, for the future, neither to beat his wife, nor to abuse her, but to treat her well.[31] The promises were made with the aim that the wives accept living again with the husbands from whom they had fled. These reconciliation agreements contained formulas similar to those in all other notarial contracts: for non-fulfilment of promise a financial penalty was envisaged, and each party could take the other to court.

In medieval separations only the women received maintenance. Men had at their disposal their own assets independently of their matrimonial

---

[28] 'Habito eciam respectu ad plenum et liberum arbitrium quod habent in huius modi placitis provisionum per suum capitularem': Procuratores Sancti Marci, Citra, busta 179, decision of *iudices procuratorum* (9 June 1343).

[29] 'Qua de causa dictus Tomaxinus eidem Chaterine solempni stipulacione promisit numquam eam petere neque requirere seu requiri facere in uxorem et per sacramentum juravit tactis scripturis . . . et ex adversso dicta Chaterina iuravit per sacramentum tactis scripturis solempni stipulacione promisit numquam eum petere neque requirere seu requiri facere in marittum suum seu mollestare in aliquo predictorum seu de predictis': Cecchetti, *La Repubblica di Venezia*, p. 58. For non-compliance with this oath, a penalty of L. 100 was imposed on both.

[30] Payments ceased when Nicoletto died, as he had stated 'et hoc duret donec nos vivemus in hoc seculo'.

[31] The cases of Biancafiore and Nicoleto Rosso, and of Maddalena and Leonardo Michiel.

status; women, on the other hand, or their families for them, consigned dowries to their husbands on marriage. The purpose of the dowry was explicitly established in Roman law and in legal doctrine: to meet the costs of matrimony. If the husband kept the dowry for himself, without providing for the upkeep of his wife, it was not used in accordance with its purpose. With the exception of women guilty of adultery, all wives had a claim to receive maintenance through their dowry. In a separation, this could happen in two ways: through restitution of dowry or through payment of maintenance. Medieval jurists regarded the dowry profits (*fructus dotales*) as a privileged source of maintenance for a separated wife. In the event that no or insufficient dowry was available, the jurists proposed various solutions: some made the husband liable only up to the value of the dowry; others required him to provide adequately for his wife from his own means.[32]

In their agreement to separate, Nicoletto da Pesaro acknowledged to his wife that 'I, Nicoletto da Pesaro am obliged and am your debtor, Nicoletta my wife, in providing for your necessary expenses, and we have agreed thereon that I should give you every year as provision . . .' Because this was a private agreement, the undertaking appears as a statement by the husband; by it the wife undertook to demand nothing in addition. In judicial cases, sentences obliged the husbands to maintenance payments.

Marco Ferro, who in the late eighteenth century recorded Venetian law and judicial practice, reported that at that time, by order of the court, 6 per cent of the dowry was the rate for yearly maintenance.[33] In the fourteenth century, the statutes of, for example, Rome, provided that the maintenance should be 7.5 per cent of the dowry.[34] Only in four of the cases studied here is the level of both dowry and maintenance known. In three cases, maintenance amounted roughly to 8 per cent of dowry, and in one case to 25 per cent. In this last case, that of Moreta and Stefano, it is possible that maintenance represented an additional penalty for the husband, though he had already paid a judicial fine on account of his violence against his wife. In the other three cases, the amount of maintenance equated to expected rates of return from good investment of the dowry.

Though the statutes provided that women who were separated could

---

[32] A. Marongiu, 'Alimenti. Diritto intermedio', *Enciclopedia del diritto* (Milan, 1958), II, p. 22; J. Kirshner, 'Wives' claims against insolvent husbands in late medieval Italy', in *Women in the Medieval World*, ed. J. Kirshner and S. W. Wempel (Oxford, 1985), p. 278, n. 50; G. S. Pene Vidari, 'Ricerche sul diritto degli alimenti. L'obbligo "ex lege" dei familiari nei giuristi dei secc. XII–XIV', *Memorie dell'Istituto giuridico dell'Università di Torino*, 144:II (1972), pp. 438–504.
[33] M. Ferro, *Dizionario del diritto comune e veneto* (Venice, 1778–81), I, p. 212.
[34] F. Ciccaglione, 'Alimenti', *Enciclopedia giuridica italiana* (Milan, 1892), I, pt 2, sctn ii, p. 1269.

recover their dowries, this can be established in only one of the cases studied here (that of Filippa Grioni). Possibly the term *separata* in the statutes meant essentially the declaration of nullity of marriage (*separatio a vinculo/sacramento*) and not the termination of cohabitation (*separatio a mensa et thoro, separatio quod ad corpus*). Considering the vagueness of the term, this confusion in a text of the thirteenth century is not surprising.[35]

Two reasons might explain why the Venetian courts obliged the husband to pay maintenance and did not order return of dowry. On the one hand, separation could possibly be a temporary state of affairs. On the other, there was a widespread preference to pay women yearly rents, rather than to make their capital available to them. Many wills of men and women prove this practice. Of course, this does not mean that Venetian married women were excluded from owning property and possessions. The court could, however, take into consideration the security of the dowry, and this happened, for example, in the proceedings against Beligno Signolo. He was convicted because of his grievous bodily harm to his wife, Marina Volpe. The court imposed on him as condition of leaving jail that he not only pay the judicial fine, but also furnish his wife with surety for her maintenance and dowry.[36] In another hearing concerning a less serious bodily assault, the husband Stefano was sentenced, in addition to a fine, to give his wife Moreta a guarantee for the maintenance alone.

Almost all the couples studied here belonged to the privileged social strata. Their good social standing is clear from the level of dowry and maintenance payments, from their family names and from the use of honorific forms of address. Presumably this collection of cases is not representative of separated couples from the whole range of social groups.[37] An indication of this is that some Venetian women, who at the beginning of their wills are defined as married, do not mention their husbands in the text of their wills.[38] We need not suppose that all these women lived apart from their husbands, but probably many did. And the

---

[35] *Statuta veneta* I.62. The statutes of Brescia also forbad marrying twice, with the exception of those who were separated 'iudicio ecclesie' (evidently meaning separated *quod ad vinculum*: see Di Renzo Villata, 'Separazione', p. 1360).

[36] See appendix, no. 9. In the sentence of 17 Dec. 1324 it was laid down: 'De quo [carcere] non exeat nisi primo solveret dictas libras 50 grossorum [the fine] et nisi primo fecerit securam dictam eius uxorem, sororem viri nobilis ser Nicolai Volpe, de libris quatuor grossorum dandis . . . et nisi fecerit eius uxorem securam de sua repromissa'. The following sessions of this court case (10 and 26 June 1325) dealt mainly with the sureties provided by other noblemen for Beligno.

[37] Sheehan, 'The formation and stability of marriage', p. 234, has established that the socially well positioned in the Ely church-court register of 1374–82 are underrepresented.

[38] From a group of 1,000 Venetian women's wills of the fourteenth century, collected for my dissertation, it emerges that these cases represent roughly 8 per cent of all female testators.

majority of them were from the lower classes. The conjecture therefore suggests itself that many ordinary people ended conjugal cohabitation without recourse to written records. A reason for this was that the lower the social level, the slighter the formalities of marriage were. *De facto* cohabitation and clandestine marriage were more widespread among the common people than among the better-off.[39] In addition, poor women, who had only a meagre dowry, and whose husbands were insolvent, had little to look forward to from a maintenance agreement.

From the effort at reconciliation of Maddalena and Leonardo Michiel, on the one hand, and of Biancafiore 'de Tarvisio' and Nicoletto Rosso, on the other, emerge the different conceptions of marriage among noblemen and craftsmen.[40] Dennis Romano observes that the nobleman Leonardo Michiel wanted above all that the formal marriage contract with his wife Maddalena should remain in force. In the craft milieu, conversely, a self-contained, functioning work- and living-community was the decisive issue, and so the *popolano* Nicoletto Rosso, as Romano stresses, insisted that his wife made common cause with him and accepted him as head of the family.

What influence did original families have on marriage separation? With the exception of the case of Vito Lion and the Morosini (which we shall come to shortly), the cases studied here give no reason to attribute a significant role to the couple's original families in marriage crises and separations. An example from thirteenth-century Genoa contrasts with the situation in fourteenth-century Venice. Giovanna Embrone was married into a family to which her brothers had been hostile. The peace, that came about through this marriage, did not hold, and Giovanna was abducted by her brothers from her husband's house in 1226; her husband was shortly afterwards murdered. She was forced to make a will in favour of her brothers and against the interests of her daughter.[41] This story is told by Diane Owen Hughes in order to portray the tragic situation in which noblewomen got caught, if peace between the families, which had found expression in the conclusion of their marriages, broke up.

In Venice, colliding political and business interests, as represented by

[39] Ruggiero, *The Boundaries of Eros*, p. 100: 'the authorities [meaning the Venetian councils] found the custom not particularly objectionable'. As the church-court records for the fourteenth century are lacking, we cannot know whether the bishop of Castello actively sought out irregular couples and compelled them to marry, though this seems unlikely. Sheehan, 'The formation and stability of marriage', p. 250, relates that the church court of Ely did.

[40] D. Romano, *Patricians and Popolani: The Social Foundations of the Venetian Renaissance State* (Baltimore, 1987), pp. 39–40.

[41] D. O. Hughes, 'Domestic ideals and social behaviour: evidence from medieval Genoa', in *Family in History*, ed. C. Rosenberg (Philadelphia, 1975), p. 137; S. Epstein, *Wills and Wealth in Medieval Genoa, 1150–1250* (Cambridge, Mass., 1984), pp. 91–6.

noble families, did not come to open conflict. In contrast to many other Italian cities, disputes in Venice were largely unarmed.[42] This peculiarity of Venetian politics was of great importance for Venetian noble wives. They were symbols of the conclusion of peace or the victims of dispute much less than were Giovanna Embrone, or the women referred to by Christiane Klapisch-Zuber in the peace settlements of Florentine family conflicts.[43]

A number of cases show the slighter ways in which kin were involved in resolving tensions between husbands and wives in Venice. In the agreement with which Leonardo Michiel wanted to end the dispute with his wife, it was established that it had been negotiated by the 'propinquos pariter et amicos'. Thus kindred and friends strove for the preservation of the marriage, but they seem not to have influenced the events that led to the marriage crisis.[44] In another case, in 1312–13, the noblewoman Marchisina, wife of Niccolò Badoer, received court costs and maintenance not from her husband but from Marino Badoer. A decision of the *giudici di petitizione* allowed her to claim the corresponding sums either from the property of the Badoer or from that of Marino. In all probability Marchisina's dowry had been taken charge of not by her husband, but by his father, or one of his other relatives, who for that reason was obliged to pay maintenance. In this case the Badoer acted as a unit at the financial level.

It also emerges that wives or widows were sometimes represented in court against their husbands by men belonging to their original families. Marina Volpe's brother appeared for her in a hearing before the Council of Forty in 1325 between her and her husband; Caterina Gradonico was partly represented by her father; and Zaccaria Contarini represented his sister. Often, however, one comes across the woman's direct participation in the court hearings.

From the will of Madaluza, daughter of a deceased weaver, it emerges that she received assistance from her brother. She made her will in 1400, during an awful plague epidemic, in the house of her brother, Marco Lambardo, in the *contrada* of S. Luca: he wrote her will for her and was

---

[42] See G. Fasoli, 'Nascita di un mito', in *Studi storici in onore di Gioacchino Volpe* (Florence, 1958); G. Cracco, *Società e stato nel medioevo veneziano (secoli XII–XIV)* (Florence, 1967); F. C. Lane, 'The enlargement of the Great Council of Venice', in *Florilegium historiale: Essays presented to Wallace K. Ferguson*, ed. J. G. Rowe and W. H. Stockdale (Toronto, 1971); S. Chojnacki, 'In search of the Venetian patriciate', in *Renaissance Venice*, ed. J. Hale (London, 1973); D. E. Queller, *The Venetian Patriciate: Reality versus Myth* (Urbana, 1986); G. Rösch, *Der venezianische Adel bis zur Schliessung des Grossen Rates. Zur Genese einer Führungsschicht* (Sigmaringen, 1989).

[43] C. Klapisch-Zuber, 'Les femmes et la famille', in *L'homme médiéval*, ed. J. Le Goff (Paris, 1989), p. 318.

[44] In the agreement that Nicoletto Rosso proposed to his wife, the heirs and successors are mentioned as part of the fixed formulae in financial obligations.

named as executor. She declared that she lived in the *contrada* of S. Giovanni Evangelista, while her husband, Tomasino da Mantova, lived in Canareggio. The will expressed her situation clearly and vividly, which for this period is unusual.[45] She claimed that her husband had thrown her out of the house, so that she had had to go to a hospital, while he and a bad woman enjoyed what was rightfully hers.[46] Evidently Madaluza thought she had no possibility of recovering her dowry or of receiving maintenance from her adulterous husband. No judicial or notarial settlement of separation was mentioned in her will, and probably there was none. Madaluza was also afraid to die in 'la cha' dele puovere di madona Lucia Dolfin', that is, in a hospital.[47] In addition, she wanted her brother to fetch back her deceased mother's household objects, which were still in her husband's house. Evidently, Madaluza's brother did give her some support, but this did not go so far as allowing her to live with him.[48]

The separation of Coletta Contarini and Nicoletto da Pesaro apparently did not spoil the relations between Nicoletto and Coletta's brother, Zaccaria Contarini. When Nicoletto made his will in 1396, that is thirty years after the separation, he named Zaccaria as his executor, together with the *Procuratori* of San Marco, his adopted son Gotardo, and his servant of many years, Agnola. In the following year, Zaccaria appeared for Coletta in the court proceedings over restitution of her dowry, while he was at the same time co-executor of the property from which the dowry was to be paid. Nicoletto bequeathed a significant sum for the dowries of Zaccaria's daughters. This points to a conflict-free situation.

These cases show that, on the one hand, wives in difficulties in their married lives could find support in their original families, but on the other hand that, even among nobles, the separation of a married couple did not necessarily have consequences for the families.

An exceptional case is that of the Morosini versus Vito Lion. The Morosini, who were a noble family, behaved differently from Zaccaria Contarini or Filippa Grioni's brothers, in acting aggressively against the husband of their kinswoman. Vito, a noble and rich man, had married Franceschina Morosini, and after the conclusion of marriage, but before

[45] Cf. F. Ambrosini, '"Da mia manu propria"'. Donna, scrittura e prassi testamentaria nella Venezia del Cinquecento', in *Non uno itinere. Studi storici offerti dagli allievi a Federico Seneca* (Venice, 1993), pp. 43, 51–2, who maintains that the will was for women a favourite place in which to express anxieties.
[46] 'Tomaxin y che me stensada e lasada sença ben alo spedal goldando el mio chon una mala femina e chazada de cha' alo ospedal': Not. test., Notary Servadeus Maçor, busta 993 (24 Aug. 1400).
[47] She meant the Hospital of S. Giobbe in Canareggio founded by Giovanni Contarini in 1380. Lucia Dolfin, his daughter, was proprietress of the hospital after his death in 1407. See F. Semi, *Gli 'ospizi' di Venezia* (Venice, 1983), p. 189.
[48] Filippa Grioni and Biancafiore also found help in their natal families.

its consummation, the Morosini let Vito know that he and Franceschina were related (in the third and fourth degrees). Accordingly, Vito Lion sent to the cardinal of Ancona for a dispensation on grounds of kinship. His action was justified in the court proceedings on the grounds that the Morosini had wanted to give him Franceschina. The court notary, unusually, did not specify the forenames of these Morosini. Nor did he refer to Franceschina's wishes.

The story went further, because Vito fell into discord with Franceschina and asserted that the dispensation was invalid. To compel Vito to obtain a further, valid dispensation from the pope, the doge and Small Council threatened him with a very high fine of 2,000 ducats. As he still did nothing, he was taken to prison, and the money for the fine was confiscated from his property. Under this harsh treatment, Vito eventually procured the papal letter of dispensation, and married Franceschina a second time, with all due formality, in the presence of the bishop of Torcello and of the highest Venetian civil authorities. However, he did not live with her, but with another woman, Agnesina Coco, whom he also married, though in the presence of her parents only, pretending that his previous marriage had been annulled by a papal order. For this reason, he was charged with bigamy, and convicted. This does not seem to have changed the actual situation, however, for there was a second trial against him in 1380, to invalidate his will in favour of Agnesina and his son by her, Zanino.

This exceptional case shows the heavy hand of aristocrats attempting to preserve their family strategy. Kinship was certainly sufficient grounds for the annulment of a marriage, but for rich and powerful people like the Lion and the Morosini, there was no difficulty in obtaining papal dispensation beyond the second degree of kinship.[49] These unnamed Morosini were very determined in their family strategy, perhaps because Vito Lion was rich. The Morosini at this time were a powerful family,[50] and it seems likely that they exercised influence on the decisions of the councils that were involved in this story. However, the situation might have ended differently: because this marriage was both invalid on grounds of kinship, and unconsummated, it could just as well have been declared null by the papal court. In fact, Vito Lion pretended that this had happened, but the decision of the judges (the Council of Forty) confirmed the version of the Morosini, although by a slim majority. The Morosini wanted the marriage to take place, and if it did not, they were intent on doing Vito Lion harm.

---

[49] B. Cecchetti, 'La donna nel medioevo a Venezia', *Archivio veneto*, 31 (1886), pp. 316–17, relates that in the course of forty years in the fourteenth century, Venetian noble families received seventy marriage dispensations for kinship from the pope or cardinals.
[50] Chojnacki, 'In search of the Venetian patriciate', pp. 60–2.

According to the trial record, the cause of the dispute between Vito Lion and the Morosini lay in the discord between Vito and Franceschina, that is, in the relationship between the two of them, but the conflict extended to the family of the bride. In this regard, this case resembles that of Giovanna Embrone, but the differences are also striking: on the one hand, Giovanna's brothers, not she herself, created the conflict, and on the other, the dispute in fourteenth-century Venice was resolved not through a feud but through the organs of the commune. What emerges from this case is that some noblemen perceived the marriage of a woman of their family as a matter for the whole group. Beside that, something else was perhaps at stake here (political objectives?) that does not emerge in the trial records. Least evident of all were the views and wishes of Franceschina Morosini.[51]

Violence in Venetian separation cases was limited to the couple and did not spread to the wider kin. Moderate use of force by the husband against the wife, if she would not obey him, was regarded as wholly legitimate, and was so pronounced by legal doctrine. On the other hand, excessive force was grounds for termination of cohabitation. From today's standpoint, it is not easy to establish where the limits lay.[52] According to Justinian's *Corpus juris civilis*, intention to kill the partner was grounds for separation.[53] In the Middle Ages, violence (*saevitia*) was considered sufficient grounds even without direct danger to life. Helmholz maintains that a very high degree of violence in fourteenth-century England had to be proved before the bishops' courts would allow a separation; the French church courts too, in the early sixteenth century, allowed separation on these grounds only exceptionally.[54] In general, judges favoured a search for reconciliation: the wife had to return to the husband's house, and he had to bind himself in a pledge to treat her well. According to Rudolf Weigand, most separation cases in France and England happened because of *saevitia*, and all cases of violence known to him were pleas of the wife against the husband.[55]

The use of force is at the heart of several of the cases studied here. From the work of Guido Ruggiero it is known not only that force was wide-

---

[51] However, the wishes of Vito's second wife, Agnesina Coco, are clearly expressed in the second trial of this case.

[52] In the agreement of reconciliation of Nicoletto with his wife can be seen his attitude to this limit: it should again be permissible for him to 'corrigere et castigare moderate et decenter', while he confessed his guilt that 'verberassem te Blançaflorem uxorem meam inordinate et malo modo'.

[53] *Corpus iuris civilis*, Novellae 117, 8:3 and 9:2.

[54] Helmholz, *Marital Litigation*, pp. 101–5; Lefebvre-Teillard, *Les officialités*, p. 181.

[55] Weigand, 'Zur mittelalterlichen kirchlichen Gerichtsbarkeit', pp. 241–3. He also observes that in Germany most separations were pronounced for adultery, though he adds that court practice varied more from place to place than has been supposed hitherto (*ibid.*, p. 247).

spread in Venetian society, but also that the nobles committed more acts of violence than corresponded to their share of the population.[56] Thus, Beligno Signolo, a nobleman, cut off the nose and lips of his wife Marina Volpe, as well as four fingers of her right hand. As explanation he claimed to have been led by a devilish impulse.[57] Perhaps Beligno wanted to punish his wife in the same way as a court. Not only were these mutilations cruel, but they also corresponded to judicial punishment of thieves (amputation of nose and lips in the case of females, and of a hand in the case of males).[58] In any case, the Council of Forty did not approve of his private justice. After it became clear that Marina had a good reputation, Beligno received a heavy, but not corporal, punishment. This hard punishment of a nobleman was presumably intended as a warning example to his peers, lest they take justice into their own hands. For the court it was certainly also important that Marina was a noble and honour-worthy woman.

Such a degree of cruelty represents an exception, but use of force is also visible in other cases of separation.[59] Two wives, Biancafiore and Maddalena, left the matrimonial home in order to escape their husbands' violence. The husbands admitted, in reconciliation proposals, that their use of force had been excessive: notarial record of this could offer the wives a certain protection, provided that, if need be, they made use of it. In the face of violence in the matrimonial home, flight to their own parents could for some wives offer a possibility of escape – one that Biancafiore used, for example. Violence in marriage also arises in the cases of the noblewoman Catarina Gradonico, who successfully prosecuted her husband on account of his 'duricia, asperitas ac nequicia', and of Madaluza, who was chased out of the house by her husband.

Especially noteworthy is an act of violence to which the victim, Moreta, was exposed because she observed a judicial order by the doge and the Small Council. Following a sentence of the *giudici del proprio*, Moreta received maintenance from her husband, which she regarded as too small. She lodged an appeal against the court's award, but the doge and Small Council, instead of increasing her maintenance, ordered her to return to her husband's house. The terse description in the records of the *Avogadori di comun* do not reveal whether Moreta herself proposed this, or

[56] Ruggiero, *Violence*, pp. 65–81.
[57] 'amputaverit uxori sue Marine nasum et labrum incidendo eciam sibi quatuor digitos manus eius dextre non ultra diabolico spiritu ductus ut proprio suo ore dixit': Avogaria de comun, Raspe 1, fol. 11v (17 Dec. 1324).
[58] *Statuta veneta* 1548, Liber prommissionis maleficii 4 and liber VI.79. S. Chojnacki, 'Patrician women in early Renaissance Venice', *Renaissance Studies*, 21 (1974), pp. 186–7, describes some examples of the use of these punishments and discusses their meaning.
[59] 'A fair amount of violence against women may have been typical of sexuality': Ruggiero, *Boundaries of Eros*, p. 31. Though Ruggiero refers to pre- and extra-marital sexuality, the cases here show that a similar use of violence occurred also in marriage.

whether the governing council worked for a reconciliation between the separated couple. In either case, the decision in the event turned out to be extremely unwise. When Moreta returned to Stefano the tailor, he seized her by the hair, pulled her down, and hit her hard with his fists all over her body, shouting meanwhile that the doge had let her come, and that he wanted to see whether the doge would protect her, adding 'Take that for the lord doge'.[60] This insult to authority is, in the record, especially emphasized, and it is probably due to this that in the second hearing the maintenance was set at a high figure. The decision about living with her husband was this time left to Moreta.

In the case of Margarita and Giovanni Ravagnano, mention is made of *iniuriae* (injustices, violence or insult), which could have been bodily as well as merely verbal. This couple was separated, and the husband must have felt guilty, as in his will of 1319 he bequeathed to his wife L. 1 *grossorum* and all her clothing, as compensation for the *iniuriae* that she had had to endure.[61] He at once added that he was not seeking thereby to evade repaying her dowry. Given the circumstances of the testator, L. 1 seems actually only a moderate legacy (about 10 ducats). He was a well-to-do merchant and a pious person, who left almost all his possessions for the support and enlargement of the hospital of Santo Spirito, and who sought to provide for his daughter, about to become a nun in Padua.

According to canon law, only culpable behaviour (adultery, *fornicatio spiritualis* or *saevitia*) could lead to a separation. Unwillingness to live together, on one or both sides, was seen by the church as insufficient grounds to end conjugal cohabitation. Instead, it was demanded of the couple that they exercise compassion towards each other. This ecclesiastical view could not, however, prevent agreement between couples who no longer wished to live together, especially in places where secular government did not acknowledge complete church jurisdiction in matrimonial matters.[62] Coletta and Nicoletto da Pesaro are one example of separation by mutual consent.

[60] 'Eunte dicta Moreta ad domum eiusdem viri sui, secundum quod dominatio ordinaverat, cepit ipsam Moretam [uxorem] suam, statim cum fuit in domo, per treçias straxinando et eam per totam personam cum pugilis acriter verberando dicens: dominus dux fecit te venire, sed ego volo videre si dominus dux tanssabit te, subiungendo: accipe nunc hoc pro domino duce': Avogaria de comun, Raspe 3, fol. 100v.

[61] 'Item dimitto solidos 20 grossorum Margarite uxori mee et omnes suos pannos de lana, lino et velamina et omnia sibi pertinencia pro suo portare pro satisfactione omnium iniuriarum, quas a me passa fuit': Procuratores Sancti Marci, Misti, busta 90.

[62] Helmholz, *Marital Litigation*, p. 103, reports some cases in which even the church courts accepted, as grounds for separation, a declaration by the couple that they no longer wished to live together. The church court of Cambrai in the first half of the sixteenth century allowed separations on the grounds of *morum incompatibilitas* or *morum discrepantia et difficultas*: a justification that did not exist in canon law (Lefebvre-Teillard, *Les officialités*, p. 202).

In the other cases studied here, how the separation came about is either unrecorded, or the guilt clearly lay with the husband. Though these cases are not representative, the explanation for this point is obvious: violence was the grounds for many separations, and husbands were exclusively guilty of this. It is, of course, true that adultery and bigamy could be committed by either partner. Vito Lion was accused of bigamy, and Caterina declared herself a bigamist. Adultery was explicitly mentioned in only one of the cases: that of Madaluza's husband, Tomasino da Mantova, who lived with another woman. It is possible that the causes of some of these separations lay in extra-marital sexual relations, but this is mentioned neither in the separation agreements, nor in reconciliations or wills (with the exception of Madaluza). Nor does the fact of maintenance payment by itself indicate guilt. Separated wives who received maintenance were not adjudged as guilty, for otherwise the husband's obligation to provide for their upkeep would in principle have been extinguished.[63] But separations could in practice come about not only on grounds of the husband's guilt, but also by mutual consent.

For some of the couples under scrutiny here, it is possible to find information about what happened after the separation. Only from wills do we happen to learn that some couples had children, who had not been mentioned in the marriage breakdown and separation.

For example, after two judgements over separation and a bodily assault, Moreta reconciled herself with her husband Stefano, and in 1382 she named him as executor of her will, together with two unrelated men, and bequeathed him a quarter of her possessions. This occurred fourteen years after the assault that she had suffered. At the time of her will she had two sons, who were not yet eighteen years old, and a deceased daughter, whose executor she was. Her will depicts a situation wholly different from that at the time of the hearings, but does not give enough clues to explain this change. She was living again with her husband, and must have felt trust in him once more.

The story of the marriage crisis of Caterina and Micheletto Morosini also had a happy ending, as Chojnacki remarks.[64] The sentence of separation on account of Micheletto's wickedness left open a possibility of reconciliation: Caterina was willing to live with Micheletto, if he treated her well. When Micheletto made his will in May 1348, that is during the Black Death, he named Caterina as executor together with the *Procuratori*

---

[63] This point was disputed: some communal statutes ruled out the right to maintenance of guilty wives, but some jurists were of other mind (Marongiu, 'Alimenti', p. 23). Venetian judicial practice seems to award no maintenance to guilty wives. Ruggiero, however, reports a case of 1476, in which the Council of Forty obliged a husband to pay maintenance to his adulterous wife (*Boundaries of Eros*, p. 56).

[64] Chojnacki, 'Patrician women', p. 188.

of San Marco and his deceased father's second wife, who however soon died. Caterina survived the plague epidemic and took an active part in administering the will. Micheletto had foreseen the case that Caterina might be pregnant, and had made provision for a posthumous child. From the administration it is clear that she was not pregnant, but she had had a daughter, Filippa, who had died before Micheletto. Micheletto left Caterina further legacies in addition to her dowry: most of these were tied to the precondition that she remain a widow. From the *commissaria*, that is from Micheletto's estate, she also received L. 3 *grossorum*, which represented the remainder of maintenance due under the court order of 1343.[65]

In the case of Coletta and Nicoletto da Pesaro, the lives of this couple can be partially reconstructed for thirty years after the separation. Although neither was allowed to have another legitimate family, sexual abstinence applied only to the woman. In his will, Nicoletto left to his nephew Franceschino, son of his deceased brother Marino, a house from the family patrimony ('la mia parte de la chassa de Senta Fosca'), but probably mainly out of a sense of class duty. His other houses he left to his illegitimate son Andrea ('le chasse de Sen Samuer') and his adopted son Gotardo ('la mia chasa granda de Canareglio'). To his illegitimate son and his nephew he threatened loss of legacy if they desired more from his estate than was specified in the will. Conversely, Nicoletto had full trust in Gotardo, his adopted son, who was living with him, and in his servant Agnola, who had lived with him for twenty-six years. These two were among his executors, and were favoured most of all in the will (though the will also reflects the usual preference for granting women annual rents, but men property in full possession).

Coletta survived her husband, recovered her dowry after his death, and made her own will ten years later. She seems to have had no children and had become a Franciscan tertiary. This evidently offered noblewomen the possibility of building up social networks. Since Coletta had married around 1350, she must at the time of her will have been about seventy years old. She was living with three other lay sisters, Beta Vigustino, Magdalucia and Francesca, who belonged to a lower social stratum. Beta, Magdalucia and the noblewomen Beruzia Foscarini and Marina de Mezzo, were the executors of Coletta's will. Beruzia Foscarini and another noblewoman friend, Antonia Ghisi, also lived together with lay sisters. Magdalucia was given most of all, as she received the right to live in Coletta's dwelling, and all her belongings. For her salvation, Coletta also willed that a poor person go on pilgrimage to Rome and Assisi, and

[65] This payment was acknowledged on 27 May 1351 by Caterina herself and the Procurators of San Marco. It was normal for executors to acknowledge bequests paid to themselves, but it seldom happened that a separated wife acted as executor of her husband's will.

Magdalucia was supposed to undertake this task. She made many pious bequests to, among others, the Franciscan order. Furthermore she left small cash sums to various lay sisters and other women. Her residual property was to go to her two nephews, sons of her brother Zaccaria Contarini. Thereby she took a decision, which her family probably expected from her. Yet she insisted on the condition that the nephews lose the legacy if they opposed the executors.

In separations in the Middle Ages, children seem to have played only a slight role. Canon law provided that the non-guilty party had to bring up the children.[66] But from judicial practice and from agreed separations it is seldom possible to learn how these decisions turned out. Though the church courts as a rule in extra-marital relations obliged fathers to provide for their children, in church-court records the judges did not mention the children in hearings for separation.[67] The will of Giovanni Ravagnano provides an example of a caring father. He looked after his daughter, Nicolota, with whom he did not live (she was about to be consecrated at her convent in Padua): at the beginning of his will, he made many detailed directions for her provision. He stressed twice that his executors (the *Procuratori* of San Marco) should carry out his legacies to his daughter and to her nunnery first of all.

The depiction of these separated Venetian couples shows a great variety of situations and fates. Nevertheless, it is possible to draw some conclusions and to stress some common features. By directing attention onto separation, we can reveal the women studied here to be neither so silent nor so lacking in rights as at the point of marriage: on their own initiative they went against their husbands before the court. This was assured to them as a right by Venetian legislation, but it cannot have come easily. Nevertheless, the pleas of wives against their husbands can certainly not have been rare, otherwise no conciliar deliberation to determine the competence of judges would have been necessary.

Despite differences between the phases of married life, the inequality of spouses on the legal and material level in marriage breakdown is easily discovered. In a separation the woman was the weaker party: when the separation was only *de facto*, the dowry could be kept by the husband, as in the case of Madaluza. In the case of a legal separation because of adultery, wives had to do more than men to satisfy the court of their

[66] I. Riedel-Spangenberger, *Die Trennung von Tisch, Bett und Wohnung (cc. 1128–1132 CIC) und das Herrenwort Mk 10.9. Eine Untersuchung zur Theologie und Geschichte des kirchlichen Ehetrennungsrechts* (Frankfurt, 1978), p. 100 and n. 41 (p. 184).

[67] M. Sheehan, 'The formation and stability of marriage', p. 263; Lefebvre-Teillard, *Les officialités*, p. 197; Helmholz, *Marital Litigation*, p. 174. Weigand knows of no case in which a late medieval court decided on meetings of children with the parent with whom they did not live ('Zur mittelalterlichen kirchlichen Gerichtsbarkeit', p. 245).

respectability and risked losing their dowries. The financial risk for husbands was thus limited to having to pay maintenance, possibly out of the wife's dowry.

Regarding relations within marriage, separation shows on the one hand that some wives were confronted with verbal and physical abuse on the part of their husbands, on the other that some fought against this, and through pleas before the court or agreements before the notary improved their position in the household. By arguing and defending themselves against the violence of their husbands, but without separating from them, other women too probably escaped from the full subordination to their husbands in which they found themselves at the beginning of marriage. Wives who left their husbands on account of their violence had the possibility of putting conditions in place for their return to the matrimonial home. But not all could do this, as the case of Madaluza and Tomasino da Mantova shows. Nor was this wholly dependent on personal character traits, but also on financial and family safeguards which women had at their disposal in varying degrees.

Some of the crises studied here did prove to be severe, but temporary. Despite the violence that some wives had suffered from their husbands, they reconciled themselves with them. In order to understand this, we must remember that marriage was indissoluble and that for adult women it was the only fully acceptable social position.

The families of the couple remain in the background in most of the cases studied here, even though they do mainly involve socially well-placed people. The only exception is the case of Vito Lion: against him some members of the Morosini used their political influence. In the other cases, the couple seem to have acted individually. Some women did receive help from relatives, but separations and agreements were not conducted through the families. Though the Venetian upper-class paterfamilias played a central role in the conclusion of his daughters' marriages, no influence on his part is evident in the development of marriage relations.

Court records and notarial acts, which mention separations, were written in a language that hardly makes visible the feelings and experiences of the people concerned (though showing the attitudes of the authorities). Wills in the fourteenth century were only in slight measure a means of personal expression: the experiences of marriage breakdown cannot be reconstructed from them. Nevertheless, it is possible to conclude that some incidents were unbearable or unacceptable: when the husband threw the wife out of their home, when he lived on her dowry with another woman, when he maltreated or injured her. But in addition to these cases, there were also separations based on mutual agreement, in which no wrong was mentioned.

Beside separations through court proceedings there were private agreements before the notary, which settled not only a marriage crisis, but also provided for separation. These notarial acts prove that in Venice too the view was widespread that marriage was a private contract which could be controlled privately, despite the efforts of the church to the contrary. Certainly the influence of the ecclesiastical view meant that by the fourteenth century a valid marriage could no longer be dissolved by private agreement of the couple. Nevertheless, the competence of the church authorities in matrimonial matters in Venice must have been slight. The deliberation of the Great Council, which transferred to the *giudici del procuratore* decisions over the payment of maintenance to estranged women, induced these judges to hold proceedings over separation too. In none of the cases studied here was it specified that the decision over separation had been taken by an ecclesiastical court. The bishop's appeal for help in 1310 shows that he certainly had a matrimonial court, but as its records have not survived, it cannot be ascertained whether only a few hearings were held there or whether the secular courts and the notaries merely failed to mention church-court decisions in drawing up their own acts on the same matters. In either case, the subordination in this field of the church authorities to the secular is confirmed in late medieval Venice.

Appendix: Sources, and amounts of dowry and maintenance

The sequence of couples is arranged chronologically according to the first evidence of their separation. All unpublished sources are in Venice, Archivio di Stato. Noble surnames are normalized according to the Italian form; all other names appear as in the sources, but variants have been standardized. The amount of maintenance per year is given for each couple, if available. When the amount of dowry is also known, it appears in brackets, together with the percentage relation of maintenance to dowry. At the beginning of the fourteenth century, the rates of exchange among the various units of Venetian money were as follows: L. 1 *grossorum* = L. 32 *parvorum* = L. 26 8s *ad grossos* = 10 ducats. The last rate remained constant, but the other two lost relative value.

  1. 1274 – Marinus filius Thebaldini de Galeto
    A deliberation of the Great Council over payment of maintenance to his wife is published in *Deliberazioni del Maggior Consiglio*, ed. R. Cessi, (3 vols., Bologna, 1931–50), II, p. 161 (no. 104), and also in *Magistrature giudiziarie veneziane*, III, p. 182. Maintenance: L. 60 *parvorum*.

2. 1289 – Chatarina filia quondam magistri Egydii de Mantua, Thomaxinus filius quondam Donati and Blaxius murarius filius quondam Bertaldi murarii
   The obligation of 17 July of Chatarina and Tomaxinus, to treat their marriage as invalid, because of her previous marriage with Blaxius, is published in Cecchetti, *La Repubblica di Venezia*, p. 58, citing only 'Archivio notarile di Venezia, Miscellanea'.

3. 1303 – Phylippa and Phylippus Grion
   Filippa's will of 21 May is in Cancelleria inferiore, busta 9, notary Almerico de Blanco, no. 5.

4. 1312 – Blançaflor de Tarvisio and Nicoletus Rosso
   The agreement between them is published in *Domenico prete di S. Maurizio notaio di Venezia, 1309–1316*, ed. M. F. Tiepolo (Venice, 1970), no. 204. This case is discussed by Romano, *Patricians and Popolani*, p. 39.

5. 1312 – Marchisina and Nicolaus Badoer
   Some receipts from 1312–13 for maintenance and court costs are published in *Domenico prete*, nos. 264, 275, 283, 350. Marchisina's will of 2 June 1320 (varied on the same sheet on 23 July 1324) is in Notarile testamenti, busta 55, notary Amiçus, cedola no. 265. Maintenance: L. 60 *ad grossos*.

6. 1314 – Margarita and Johannes Ravagnano
   A receipt for maintenance, given by Margarita on 12 Feb. 1314, is published in *Domenico prete*, no. 371. The execution of Johannes' will is in Procuratores Sancti Marci, Misti, busta 90, which contains, *inter alia*, his will of 20 Oct. 1319. Maintenance: L. 45 *ad grossos*.

7. 1317 – Beriola and Marcus Erizzo
   This case is described by Chojnacki, 'Patrician women', p. 188. The sentence of separation was pronounced in 1317. In the records of the notary Marinus (Canc. inf., busta 114, 1335–50) are included some receipts for maintenance that Beriola made in the years 1335–42. Maintenance: L. 1 5s *grossorum*.

8. 1323 – Francisca Daledople and Daniel sartor
   Her will of 14 Nov. 1323 is in Not. test., notary Egydius S. Sophie, busta 926, fol. 188.

9. 1324 – Marina Volpe and Belignus Signolo
   Stefano Piasentini drew this case to my attention. Sessions of the trial for severe physical injury to Marina by Belignus took place on 17 Dec. 1324, 10 and 25 June 1325. The decision is in Avogaria de comun 3641 (=raspe 1), fols. 11v–12, 16–v, 17. Maintenance: L.4 *grossorum* (dowry: L. 50 *grossorum*; 8 per cent).

10. 1339 – Magdalena and Leonardus Michiel
    The agreement between them is published in *Felice de Merlis prete e notaio in Venezia ed Ayas (1315–1348)*, ed. A. Bondi Sabellico (2 vols., Venice, 1973–8), no. 971. This case is discussed by Romano, *Patricians and Popolani*, p. 39.

11. 1343 – Catarina filia Johannis Gradonico and Michaletus Morosini
    This case is described by Chojnacki, 'Patrician women', p. 188. Execution of Michaletus' will survives in Procuratores Sancti Marci, Citra, busta 179. There are also to be found, *inter alia*, his will, a document of agreement to separate, Caterina's *diiudicatus carta*, a copy of the administration of the will, and further documents of court proceedings. Caterina's will, written on 20 June 1352 and delivered on 23 June, is in Not. test., busta 1123, Notary Arianus Passamonte, cedola no. 17. Delivery of dowry was in 1328. Maintenance: L. 3 *grossorum* (dowry: L. 1,000 *ad grossos* [= L. 37 18s *grossorum*]; 8 per cent).

12. 1366 – Coletta Contarini and Nicholetus da Pesaro
    Luca Molà has drawn this case to my attention. Nicholetus' *commissaria* is in Procuratores Sancti Marci, Misti, busta 150, and contains his will of 2 Feb. 1396, two agreements over separation (1367 and 1374), many receipts for payment of maintenance, Coletta's *diiudicatus carta*, copy of administration of the *commissaria*, and further interesting material regarding Nicholetus' private life. For Coletta, only her will has come to light (Canc. inf., busta 55, notary Campisano, no. 100). Delivery of dowry: 1351. Maintenance: 20 ducats and interest ('prode 300 librarum parvorum') (dowry: L. 1,000 *ad grossos*; 8.75 per cent).

13. 1368 – Vitus Lion, Francischina Morosini and Agnesina Coco
    Stefano Piasentini has drawn my attention to this case. The trial for bigamy which took place on 26 June 1368 is in Avogaria de comun 3643 (=raspe 3), fols. 107v, 108–v. The second trial is in Avogaria de comun 3644 (=raspe 4), fols. 20v–21v (23 Aug. 1380). A shorter version of the decisions in this case (not mentioning the Morosini) is to be found in a register of the Council of Forty: *Deliberazioni del consiglio dei XL*, ed. A. Lombardo (3 vols., Venice, 1957–67), III, pp. 201–3, nos. 553–6. Vitus' will is not known to me, but it can be largely reconstructed through quotations made from it in the second trial and through the will of his son, Çanotus Lion, on 1 Nov. 1387 (Not. test., busta 1039, Notary Petrus de Corazatiis, cedola no. 177). A will of Agnesina has survived, consigned to the notary on 23 June 1371 (Not. test., busta 921, notary Nicoletus Sajablancha, cedola no. 212).

14. 1368 – Moreta and Stephanus sartor
    Stefano Piasentini has drawn my attention to this case. The separation of Moreta and Stefano was at an unknown time settled by the *giudici del proprio*. A later hearing between them on account of physical injury, which took place on 26 Aug. 1368, is in Avogaria de comun, 3643 (=raspe 3), fol. 100v. Moreta's will of 9 Nov. 1382 is in Canc. inf., busta 69, Notary Damianus, no. 119. Maintenance: 20 ducats (dowry around 80 ducats; 25 per cent).

15. 1398 – Garita Barbarigo and Franceschinus Lovatino
    Garita's will of 21 Nov. 1398 is in Not. test., Notary Thomas de Malumbra, busta 731, cedola no. 71.

16. 1400 – Madaluza filia che fo de Menego tesier and Tomaxin de Mantoa dai Zaloni
    Madaluza's will of 24 Aug. 1400 is in Not. test., Notary Servadeus Maçor, busta 993, unnumbered cedola.

13 Reconstructing the family: widowhood and remarriage in Tuscany in the early modern period

Giulia Calvi

The question of remarriage of widowers and widows is a complex one. Quantitative information from before the statistical age is minimal and the difficulties in the way of a scientific survey are considerable, owing to the absence of relevant data (age, marriage status, frequency of remarriage, presence or otherwise of children). The phenomenon of remarriage was presumably relatively extensive, above all in rural areas, and more frequent in north-western than in Mediterranean, Catholic Europe, despite the climate of disapproval emanating from both the church and society at large. Whereas the stance of the church authorities and clergy oscillated between prejudice and considerable tolerance, thus reflecting the attitude of the Tridentine church, popular mentality seems to have persisted in derision and criticism, above all of the remarriage of widows. Throughout Europe, the controversial practice of *charivari*, a symbolic mock ritual on the occasion of a second marriage, was a noisy, vulgar expression of society's unease at such an event.[1]

Late twentieth-century historians have seen the remarriage of the surviving spouse as a sign of the lack of affective bonding typical of *ancien régime* family relationships. According to this view, remarriages, particularly by widowers, celebrated less than a year after the death of the wife, or by widows on average two years after the death of the husband, point beyond economic and domestic issues to the fragility of the emotional bond that had united the couple in life. To remarry after such brief intervals implies having already forgotten the previous partner. Conversely, the dramatic fall in remarriage in nineteenth-century England (from 25–30 per cent in the sixteenth century to 10 per cent) suggests, besides demographic considerations, a changed sensibility among

[1] See C. Klapisch-Zuber, 'The mattinata in medieval Italy', in Klapisch-Zuber, *Women, Family and Ritual in Renaissance Italy* (Chicago, 1985).

spouses.[2] The establishment, it is claimed, during the nineteenth century of a model of marriage based on equality of the spouses, bound by
class, age and elective affinity, reduced the frequency of remarriage,
emphasizing the drama of losing the spouse to whom one was bound by
profound affection. In short, to remarry less frequently and at longer
intervals of time meant greater love.[3]

Historians have stressed the essential asymmetry of remarriage.
Widowers remarried at all ages and in much greater numbers than
widows, on average more than twice as often, and at shorter intervals,
preferring women who were single and much younger. For widows, often
hindered in any event by the presence of young children, the age of forty
marked the impossibility of remarrying. Besides demographic constraints, the asymmetry between the sexes was linked to economic, social
and cultural factors among which the position of women in marriage and
the system of inheritance were the determining elements. 'Widows did
not have the same chances as widowers to remarry: they also proliferated
after the age of forty, especially in towns', concludes Christiane Klapisch-
Zuber in her classic study of the Florentine *catasto* of 1427, citing inheritance law and religion as the main factors impeding the remarriage of
women.[4] In fifteenth-century Tuscany 'widows were much more numerous in the general population than widowers (13.6 per cent and 2.4 per
cent, respectively). In Florence these percentages doubled (25 per cent
and 4 per cent)'.[5] However, 'many women certainly appreciated their
new-found independence', she stresses, confirming what contemporary
Renaissance theorists believed, that some women 'rejoice at the death of
their husbands as if they had been freed from the heavy yoke of servi-
tude'.[6]

Yet, the essential asymmetry of remarriage patterns still characterized

[2] For a comprehensive discussion of remarriage, see *Marriage and Remarriage in Populations of the Past*, ed. J. Dupâquier et al. (New York and London, 1981), especially S. Sogner and J. Dupâquier, 'Introduction', E. A. Wrigley, 'Remarriage intervals and the effect of marriage order on fertility', A. Burguière, 'Réticences théoriques et intégration pratiques du remariage dans la France d'Ancien Régime' and M. Segalen, 'Mentalité populaire et remariage en Europe occidentale'; also V. Brodsky, 'Widows in late Elizabethan London. Remarriage, economic opportunity and family orientations', in *The World We Have Gained*, ed. L. Bonfield, R. M. Smith and K. Wrightson (Oxford, 1986); J. Boulton, 'London widowhood revisited: the decline of female remarriage in the seventeenth and early eighteenth centuries', *Continuity and Change*, 5 (1990).
[3] P. Ariès, 'Introduction to Part I', in *Marriage and Remarriage*, ed. Dupâquier et al., pp. 27–33; but contrast Introduction to this volume.
[4] D. Herlihy and C. Klapisch-Zuber, *Les Toscans et leurs familles* (Paris, 1978), p. 610.
[5] C. Klapisch-Zuber, 'The "cruel mother": maternity, widowhood and dowry in Florence in the fourteenth and fifteenth centuries', in *Women, Family and Ritual*, p. 120.
[6] 'S'allegrano della morte de' loro mariti non altramente, che se fosse loro scosso dal collo un grave giogo di servitù': L. Dolce, *Dialogo della istituzione delle donne*, fourth edn (Venice, 1560), p. 68, quoted in Herlihy and Klapisch-Zuber, *Les Toscans*, p. 610.

the lives of Florentines in the eighteenth century. A survey of the population in 1767 provides some figures related to the marital status of the city's population, allowing us to measure the difference in the ways the marriage market operated for men and women. In 1767 Florence had a total population of 78,635 resident within the walls. The overall sex ratio measured 90.89 men to 100 women, but the sex ratio among the age group between fourteen and fifty-nine ranked somewhat lower at 88.3 to 100.[7] Of the total male population of 36,026, those who were or had been married numbered 11,947, that is, 33.1 per cent. Of these, 8.6 per cent – 1,032 in total – were widowers. By comparison, the data on the female population presents a significant imbalance. The total female population was 41,135. Of these, 12,035 were or had been married, that is, 29.2 per cent. Among these were 4,383 widows, constituting 36.4 per cent of married women and 10.6 per cent of the whole female population, as against widowers who made up only 2.8 per cent of the male population. These figures, allowing for the surplus female population, seem to suggest a different pattern of life for men and women. The difference between the number of widowers (8.6 per cent of men who were or had been married) and of widows (36.4 per cent of women who were or had been married) points to different opportunities for rebuilding life after the death of a spouse.[8] Indeed, it is likely that the number of remarried widowers greatly exceeded that of remarried widows, suggesting a situation of greater fluidity between the conditions of widower and married man. Men, that is to say, moved with greater ease and frequency from one state to the other.

For a greater percentage of women, however, the isolation of widowhood was envisaged as permanent, and the hiatus between marriage and widowhood appeared more marked. In addition to the factors already mentioned, the possibilities of remarriage for widows were also influenced by a more general condemnation of women's remarriage present in almost all cultures and probably rooted in a similarly universal concept of marriage as the husband's possession of the wife not only in life but also after death. This idea is found in the Counter-Reformation treatises for widows, and is still present today in some eastern societies which identify the wife's love of her husband with annihilation of self, to the point of preventing the wife surviving the death of her husband. In the second half of the sixteenth century, praise was explicitly given to models of conjugal love in which wives, at the death of the husband, renounced life and were

---

[7] A. Contini and F. Martelli, 'Il censimento del 1767: una fonte per lo studio della struttura professionale della popolazione di Firenze', in *Fonti archivistiche e ricerca demografica*, ed. F. Grispi (Rome, 1996), p. 368.

[8] Florence, Archivio di Stato (hereafter ASF), Regio Diritto, 6133 bis, fol. 2. See also A. Zobi, *Storia civile della Toscana dal MDCCXXXVII al MDCCCXLVIII* (5 vols., Florence, 1850–2), ii, p. 53.

burnt in the flames of the funeral pyre, buried alive, or even put to death on his tomb. 'To marry more than once is the sign of an almost libidinous intemperance', chorus the late sixteenth-century tractarians, pointing as examples to the women of ancient Rome such as the virtuous Antonia, widow of Drusus, who always slept with her mother-in-law, so that the bed 'on which the young husband died enfolded the old age of his wife'. For the Counter-Reformation theorists, therefore, the examples of Penelope, Alceste and Lucretia were the starting points of a genealogy extending from the classical period to the contemporary, in which widows who had ruled – Catherine de' Medici, Margaret of Navarre, Battista Sforza – were, together with learned women, examples of exceptional achievement by virtue of their indestructible loyalty to the memory of their dead husbands.[9] Power and visibility, in other words, were ideologically linked to continence and singleness.

However, theoretical positions, the experience of mourning and the reality of widowhood could show many variations. Urged by their own families, driven by their own inclinations or by necessity, many women did not follow these illustrious and heroic paradigms. Other than the few and denigratory observations in *libri di ricordi*, which describe the behaviour of the urban patriciate, we know very little of this phase in the family life of the past. Folk tradition throws a negative light on the figure of the step-mother, but ignores that of the step-father, so confirming the picture that demography gives us of the quantity and frequency of remarriage among widowers. Of remarriage of widows, their changing roles and personal relationships, there are, however, very few traces.

To condemn the entry of a widow into a new marriage, there arose the image, alive in family journals, of the 'cruel mother' who abandoned the children of the first marriage to their deceased father's kin, in order to unite herself to her new husband.[10] Popular writing also exploited the theme of desertion, dramatizing it as the destruction, widely and acutely experienced, of an affective bond, broken only from the female, maternal side. Giovanni Gherardi of Prato in his *Paradiso degli Alberti* (1426), when introducing the story of Madonna Cosa, writes, 'Every day we see little children whose father has died, abandoned and almost forgotten by their mothers, who have taken a new husband. No man has ever done such a thing. From this I form the opinion that a father's love for his children is greater than the mother's.' It is for the woman to disprove this

[9] G. C. Cabei, *Ornamenti della gentil donna vedova* (Venice, 1574); G. Trissino, *Epistola della vita che dee tenere una donna vedova* (Rome, 1523); C. Lanci, *Essempi della virtù delle donne* (Florence, 1590); L. Dolce, *Dialogo della institution delle donne* (Venice, 1545). For the church's negative attitude towards the remarriage of widows, see G. B. de Luca, *Il cavaliere e la dama* (Rome, 1675).
[10] Klapisch-Zuber, 'The "cruel mother"'.

assumption, to reassert the value of maternal love. Wives, Gherardi maintains, must obey their husbands and be under a master. They cannot take care of their own children because 'the female sex cannot without great hardship, particularly in youth, be without the protection of a man'. They are therefore forced to act in this way – to separate themselves from their children – because they must place themselves under the control of a new husband. 'But there is no doubt', Madonna Cosa bitterly concludes, 'that, despite being separated from her children, they are constantly in her mind and most surely will always remain there'.[11]

The provisional nature of the mother's presence, the impending threat of desertion described by Renaissance diarists in their *libri di famiglia*,[12] bear witness to the fact that matrimonial strategies remained in the hands of the woman's family, of the fathers and brothers who took back widowed daughters and sisters, along with their dowries, in order to marry them to new husbands. However, these decision-making processes took place in a field shot through with opposing tensions – the pain and longing of mothers and children, the testamentary wishes of the dead husbands and the intervention of institutions, specifically in Florence, the *Magistrato dei pupilli et adulti* (the court of wards). By becoming visible and active in this critical phase of the family's life-cycle, the mother's kin also undermined the juridical coherence of patrilinearity.[13] It is important to note, however, that the new role which widowed mothers and their kin assumed *vis-à-vis* the wards and their paternal agnates was by no means an informal one, but rather was enhanced and officially legitimated by the institutional framework of the grand-duchy of Tuscany. There, the prestige of widows in the family was closely connected to the administrative and therefore public supervision of the

[11] G. Gherardi da Prato, *Il Paradiso degli Alberti*, ed. A. Lanza (Rome, 1975), p. 181.
[12] There is a rich bibliography on Florentine family memoirs. See, mainly, C. Bec, *Les marchands écrivains. Affaires et humanisme à Florence, 1375–1430* (Paris and The Hague, 1975); F. Pezzarossa, 'La memorialistica fiorentina tra Medioevo e Rinascimento. Rassegna di studi e testi', *Lettere italiane*, 1 (1979); Pezzarossa, 'La tradizione fiorentina della memorialistica', in La *"memoria" dei mercatores*, ed. G. M. Anselmi, F. Pezzarossa and F. Avellini (Bologna, 1980); F. W. Kent, *Household and Lineage in Renaissance Florence* (Princeton, 1977); Klapisch-Zuber, *Women, Family and Ritual*; G. Calvi, 'Maddalena Nerli and Cosimo Tornabuoni: a couple's narrative of family history in early modern Florence', *Renaissance Quarterly*, 45 (1992); A. Molho, R. Barducci, G. Battista and F. Donnini, 'Genealogia e parentado. Memorie del potere nella Firenze tardo medievale. Il caso di Giovanni Rucellai', *Quaderni storici*, 2 (1994); C. Klapisch-Zuber, 'Albero genealogico e costruzione della parentela nel Rinascimento', *ibid.*
[13] See S. Chojnacki, 'Kinship ties and young patricians in fifteenth-century Venice', *Renaissance Quarterly*, 38 (1985); R. Ago, 'Giochi di squadra: uomini e donne nelle famiglie nobili del XVII secolo', in *Signori, patrizi, cavalieri nell'età moderna*, ed. M. A. Visceglia (Rome and Bari, 1992); R. Ago, 'Maria Spada Veralli, la buona moglie', in *Barocco al femminile*, ed. G. Calvi (Rome and Bari, 1992), pp. 51–70.

Magistrato dei pupilli over family affairs: the empowerment of women and state intervention in the realm of parental relations went, as it were, hand in hand.

Founded in 1393, the *Magistrato dei pupilli et adulti*[14] was concerned with guardianship of orphans and widows in cases where heads of family died intestate (*post mortem* guardianship) or where the guardians nominated in the will of the deceased disagreed. Operating throughout the grand-duchy, the Magistracy had the power to intervene in such situations, to assume the guardianship of minors often left to themselves or to the neglect of relatives charged with their care. The guardian administered the estate, and took care of the minors and their education until they married, entered religious life or came of age (at eighteen for boys and twenty-five for girls). The Magistracy thus resolved family conflicts, essentially to guarantee to children who had lost their father a stable prospect of life suitable to their status. It also exercised control over the remarriage of widows who were guardians of their own children but who, on remarrying, were forced to relinquish that role, as Roman law dictated. The archive of the Magistracy contains numerous files dealing with the remarriage of widows with children. What concerns us here is the effect such an event had on the life of the orphans, who left their mother's guardianship and often changed dwelling and life-style. Only occasionally do these texts reveal events of greater relevance to demography, such as the birth of new children, the age of the spouses or the marital status of the second husband. On the other hand, the records of the Magistracy allow us to sample the diverse motivations, effects and reactions among mothers, children, husbands and relatives as regards the mother's remarriage. In some lucky cases we can see the complex texture of often conflicting interests and ties that determined the decision-making processes of the domestic group.

By law, as well as by established custom, a remarried widow automatically and irrevocably lost the guardianship of her own children. This involved giving up the privileges she enjoyed as *donna et madonna* and consequently the usufruct of the estate left by her first husband, as well as the right to live with her children in their common home. However, within this legal framework there existed an element of flexibility, deriving from the possibility of separating legal guardianship from the practical

---

[14] ASF, Magistrato dei pupilli et adulti avanti il principato, 248, 'Statuti et ordini della corte et magistrato delli offitiali de' pupilli et adulti della città di Firenze riformati il XX Agosto 1565'. For an edition of the medieval statutes, see F. Morandini, 'Statuti e ordinamenti dei pupilli et adulti nel periodo della Repubblica fiorentina (1388–1534)', *Archivio storico italiano*, 113 (1955); ASF, Miscellanea Medicea, 413, Niccolò Arrighi, 'Teatro di grazia e di giustizia ovvero formulario de' rescritti a tutte le cariche che conferisce il Ser. Granduca di Toscana per via dell'Uffizio delle Tratte e dedicato al Ser. Cosimo III' (1695).

care of the minors over which the Magistracy had discretionary powers. While delegating to others the administration of the minors' estate, the mother, even when remarrying, could, with the agreement of the Magistracy, care for them in her new home and provide for their education. There was thus a possibility of reconstituting a family unit around the new couple, who could keep with them, besides the children of the new husband's previous marriages (that, of course, was obvious), those of the widow's first marriage too.

An important question is whether the Magistracy continued to give weight to the presence and role of the mother and her family at the delicate and critical moment of constituting a new family unit. In other words, did the empowerment of the *donna et madonna* which had taken place after her husband's death continue in the remarriage process? Did the relationship of mutual trust which progressively linked magistrates and widows produce a pattern of family reconstruction that overcame the traditional ideological hostility towards remarrying widows inspired by Roman law and the church?

From the period 1580 to 1750, I have identified 150 cases of remarriage of which the outcome is known, including the destination of the wards, their sex and age, the economic transactions that determined the arrangements for their care (restitution of dowry to the mother, provision of food). The remarriage of a widow with guardianship of children is among the less frequent reasons for reviewing the guardianship and care of orphans. Identifying the documentation for these cases is thus laborious; the material is often fragmentary, incomplete and condensed, particularly in those cases dealing with wards distant from Florence of whom little was known because of the state of abandonment in which they lived. The documentation does not contain any information regarding surviving relatives (investigation on this front was referred to local officials), nor, when the children were entrusted to paternal relatives or to strangers, regarding the fate of the mother – though sometimes her death is recorded. Frequent revision of decrees gives a glimpse of implacable quarrelling among the guardians, or of firm refusal to accept the responsibility of guardianship and care. All this is reflected in the movements of minors who passed from one carer to another, or from one institution to another (convent, monastery, tutor, owner of a *bottega*, prison).

This first sample of 150 cases is valuable in starting to form a picture of how children were cared for when their mother–guardian remarried. In 68 cases (45 per cent), the orphans were entrusted to their remarried mothers and in 27 cases (18 per cent) to the paternal family. In the remaining 55 cases (37 per cent), the administration of the estate and the care of the minors were assigned to third parties nominated by the

Magistracy (23 cases) or the whole question was referred to Florence's representatives in the localities, such as *commissari* and *vicari*, who would screen and nominate suitable administrators and carers (32 cases). In this situation, depending on the specific context, the mother and her family could re-enter the arena, although, unfortunately, we lose all trace of them.

Once again, as in the case of *post mortem* guardianship, the role played by the father's family was less important than that of the mother's. The mother was placed first in the list of potential carers. The powers of the Magistracy take on central importance in nominating responsible persons or referring the solution of the problem to local functionaries, thus determining the entire process. The remarriage of widows thus constitutes a good observation point from which to survey the tangled web of the private and public spheres, of personal motivation and the ability of institutions to listen, intervene and offer guarantees.

The data from this first sample provides further information about the age and sex of the children entrusted to one or other branch of the family, recording also, in the majority of cases, the length of time between the death of the husband and the remarriage of the widow. We will now look in detail at this picture.

Of the 115 minors entrusted to the mother or her family, 60 were male and 55 female (table 1). The most numerous group is made up of children aged between four and seven, followed at some distance by those between eight and twelve. There is a substantial fall after the age of twelve. Seventeen children in this category were given in care to the mother. Generally, girls over the age of twelve were sent to a convent to be educated. We should note the higher number of male children above the age of infancy assigned to the mother or her family (44 out of 60), twice as many as assigned to the father's family (22 out of 32). In this context, we should bear in mind that the Magistracy had a statutory obligation not to entrust a minor to somebody who could become a direct heir in the event of the minor's death. Male heirs, in general bound by patrilineal succession, were thus most exposed to the risk of maltreatment or even extinction for reasons of interest, if entrusted to a paternal grandfather or uncle. Giving them, however, into the care of the mother and step-father – who did not stand to gain from their death – provided a strong guarantee of their safety.

Closeness of mothers and children was considered essential to the latters' well-being according to Roman law, which decreed that, until the age of three, offspring should be left in their mothers' care. The Magistracy's juridical practice was that this deadline could be prolonged for widows, and children were entrusted to them, even when remarried, until

Table I. *Minors entrusted to the mother or to the maternal family (1580–1750)*

Males:	60				
Age	0/3	4/7	8/12	13/18	not specified
	11	22	13	9	5
	(18.3%)	(36.6%)	(21.6%)	(15%)	(8.3%)
Females:	55				
Age	0/3	4/7	8/12	13/18	not specified
	6	17	17	8	7
	(10.9%)	(30.9%)	(30.9%)	(14.5%)	(12.5%)

the age of five if boys and seven if girls. In the absence of a father, a prolonged closeness to the one remaining parent was required, and this situation could be extended even further, depending on individual cases. Therefore, the Magistracy checked the wards' health, physical growth and emotional development before deciding about education or changes in custody. Decrees were moreover revised if a sudden illness broke out or general unhappiness was expressed by the children themselves: in such delicate situations mothers were often entrusted with custody up to adolescence. The physical and emotional well-being of sons and daughters thus became a flexible matter, which mothers could negotiate and perhaps manipulate in order to keep their children with them.

Table 2 deals with minors entrusted to the father's family, usually to uncles. In this case also, of the 32 males in question, the largest group is that of boys between seven years and puberty. The relatively high number of wards whose age is not shown means that it is not possible to form a complete picture. As regards female children, the data are slightly different, showing a concentration in the age-range of four to seven years, the numbers diminishing as the age for entering a convent arrived. One should note the small number of infants entrusted to the paternal family (indeed, one case only among the females, a three-year-old). This confirms the conclusions reached from other sources (wills, *libri di famiglia*) which reveal the explicit wish of the father to entrust female children to the mother, as well as the trend that emerges in the decisions of the Magistracy which, above all in the case of only daughters, entrusts them to the mother.

The relative rarity of male children entrusted to the paternal family (18 per cent) is to be attributed, in my view, to the concern to keep entirely separate the two areas of care and inheritance, since male relatives inherited from minors. In short, as I have shown elsewhere,[15] the paternal

---

[15] G. Calvi, *Il contratto morale. Madri e figli nella Toscana moderna* (Rome and Bari, 1994).

Table 2. *Minors entrusted to the paternal family (1580–1750)*

Males:	32				
Age	0/3	4/7	8/12	13/18	not specified
	3	9	10	3	7
	(9.3%)	(28.1%)	(31.2%)	(9.3%)	(21.8%)
Females:	23				
Age	0/3	4/7	8/12	13/18	not specified
	1	8	7	2	5
	(4.3%)	(34.7%)	(30.4%)	(8.6%)	(21.7%)

family was a truly ambiguous and risky environment for minors, bound as they were by patrilineal succession, their physical safety thus endangered. This concern regarding the paternal family is confirmed in table 3, which deals with minors entrusted by the Magistracy to third parties. Unfortunately, the documentation of these cases does not specify whether the mother also was dead, nor which members of the two families were living and what therefore persuaded the Magistracy to choose care outside the family group. This category of ward, comprising 121 individuals (68 males and 53 females) had as its largest group children on the threshold of puberty (32). We should, however, note the high number of cases in which the age is not recorded, a common omission in cases of third-party care and probably indicative of the neglect in which these minors languished. Their precarious position, lacking close relatives and for the most part a long way from Florence, was probably not notified for some time to the Florentine officials, whose first step was to delegate the gathering of information to Florence's representatives. Most of the female children were assigned to convents and, while the age of entrance was normally around eleven to twelve years, in these situations it tended to fall below seven and even, if seldom, to three. The convent was usually chosen because there were relatives there who had taken the veil, and the female wards were thus entrusted to the care of paternal aunts resident as nuns.

Comparing the data of table 3 with those of table 2, we should note the imbalance in numbers: eleven infants entrusted to third parties, as against four given in care to the paternal family. This underlines yet again the extreme reluctance with which defenceless wards were entrusted to the care of those who could have every interest in eliminating them. It was better to entrust such wards to strangers nominated by the Magistracy than to place them in a situation of danger.

As is well known, a series of severe disasters invaded the cycle of family life between the end of the sixteenth century and the middle of the

Table 3. *Minors entrusted to third parties (1580–1750)*

Males:	68				
Age	0/3	4/7	8/12	13/18	not specified
	7	12	19	13	17
	(10.2%)	(17.6%)	(27.9%)	(19.1%)	(25%)
Females:	53				
Age	0/3	4/7	8/12	13/18	not specified
	4	14	13	8	14
	(7.5%)	(26.4%)	(24.5%)	(15%)	(26.4%)

seventeenth. Families were dispersed and reformed in the devastation brought by famine, typhus and plague, which increased the numbers of abandoned children and of cases of institutional guardianship in the absence of both parents and often also of living relatives able to bring up a minor. Significant for this is table 4, which shows, for a total of 113 cases, the interval between the death of the husband and the remarriage of the widow. The largest category (27 per cent) consists of second marriages celebrated within the first year of widowhood, which coincide, in the great majority of cases, with a period of epidemic: between 1620 and 1622, during an outbreak of typhus; between 1630 and 1633, during plague; and finally, though to a lesser degree, between 1648 and 1649, when a new and terrible wave of typhus devastated the whole of Tuscany.

Remarriage decreases as the period of widowhood increases. Lacking additional data (above all the age of the women), we must assume that the prerogatives associated with the status of guardian tended with time to act as a disincentive to remarriage. However, the high number of remarriages in the category headed 'several years' should also be noted. From related material, I would conclude that these occurred after more than five years of widowhood, involving moreover family units resident outside Florence, and deaths, presumably of intestate husbands, a long time earlier.

The practical possibility of rebuilding a family after the husband's death seems to have coalesced at two points in time: first, when the choice was made within the first year of widowhood, accelerated by events which threatened the very survival of the family unit; and second – spread over a longer period – presumably when the responsibility of bringing up children in earliest childhood had already been accomplished and the new life in common was organized around a unit of fewer people.

Several considerations emerge from the documentation studied. In the first place, there is the question of the identity of the informer notifying the *Magistrato dei pupilli* of the remarriage of a widow and the consequent

Table 4. *Interval between the death of the husband and the widow's remarriage (1580–1750)*

Total number of cases: 113					
Years	0/1	1/3	4/6	7/9	10 and over	'several years'
	31	120	17	12	9	24
	(27.4	(17.6%)	(15%)	(10.6%)	(7.9)	(21.2%)

'unprotected' status of the minors, threatened with a reduction in inheritance because of the need to restore the mother's dowry to her, or subject to a change of residence or life-style through the presence of the new step-father. Through their sympathetic concern for, and close participation in, the family unit, these informers initially entered into an informal relationship with the grand-ducal functionaries, heeded and trusted by them. By taking pen and paper to draw up a statement, such attentive observers (rarely women) often also made themselves available to administer the inheritance and to assume a role of legal responsibility towards the orphans. We see this happening in the following events involving a family of modest social background.

Bartolomeo di Gualtieri from Modena, resident in Florence, died in 1571 leaving a six-year-old daughter, Lucrezia, in the guardianship of her mother. Four years later the mother remarried. A spinner who drew up the statement to the Magistracy was nominated administrator of the inheritance, with a coachman as his guarantor. The Magistracy ordered them to realize the whole inheritance and invest it in the *Monte di pietà* to provide a dowry for Lucrezia. The income was to be collected by the coachman for use in feeding and clothing the child.[16]

A similar picture emerges for the estate of Giovanbattista di Piero del Mancino, a Florentine notary, who, dying in 1576, had made a will leaving his widow Oretta as guardian of seven-year-old Maria, their only daughter. In a situation of this kind, set up by a man of the law, one may suppose that the statement regarding Oretta's second marriage, drawn up by a doctor, Antonio di Marco Pacini, set the scene for the restructuring of the new family, whereby the administration of the child's inheritance was removed from the mother and granted to the doctor who put himself forward as administrator.[17]

A second consideration involves the frequent and systematic removal of daughters from the house, particularly in situations where the family unit was reconstructed under a step-father. In the remarriage of a widow

---

[16] ASF, Magistero dei pupilli et adulti del principato (hereafter MPAP), Campione di partiti, 17, fol. 136, 27 Apr. 1575.
[17] *Ibid.*, 17, fol. 203, 18 May 1576.

who succeeded in keeping with her the sons of her first marriage, it was assumed that daughters approaching adolescence would enter a convent. This was clearly intended to avoid their living under one roof with a male adult from outside the family and, unlike the natural father, not bound by the taboo of incest. On the other hand, when the widow brought with her a daughter who was still a child, the latter was normally entrusted to the new couple. As we have seen, the removal of daughters to a convent was not for them an experience of unqualified exclusion, since it often led to closer ties being developed with the paternal side of the family. The girls were generally welcomed by paternal aunts who had taken the veil in the same convent. In this way, the women of the paternal family were not alienated and the girls' potential marriage prospects would be controlled by their aunts and the paternal family, who were responsible for paying their dowry.

Being shut up in a convent, away from home and from younger brothers and sisters after the marriage of one's own mother, could prove to be a traumatic experience, and some daughters did express resentment against their mothers, accusing them of abandonment and betrayal. These episodes offer a glimpse of what the remarriage of a widow might mean for a young daughter. The following story allows us a rare reconstruction of the experience of such a child.

Camilla Rossermini, a wealthy girl from Pisa, was born in 1608, five months after her father's death. A few months passed and her mother Ginevra remarried, was again left a widow, and, by the time Camilla was three, had taken a third husband: a Rossermini cousin (so as not to separate her large dowry of 6,000 *scudi* from the family patrimony). The baby was entrusted to the Magistracy who named her paternal uncle Odoardo administrator of Camilla's goods. He was also given custody of the child who, reaching the age of *serbanza*, was put in the convent of S. Matteo in Pisa, under the care of her paternal aunt, who was a nun.

More time went by: Ginevra bore her third husband a son, but in 1619 was again left a widow. She appealed to the Magistracy and asked to be again entrusted with the custody of her first child Camilla, as she was the only one who could 'lovingly take care of her'. But Camilla refused to go and live with her mother, arguing vehemently that 'she had been abandoned when she was only two months old, because her mother had chosen to remarry'. She preferred to stay in the convent where she felt 'safe'.

Summoned by the Magistracy, Ginevra insisted that her daughter had been influenced by the Rossermini and was refusing to leave the convent because she had been spoiled and influenced by her aunt. The girl verged on adolescence and was entitled to a patrimony of 12,000 *scudi* and

Ginevra wanted to find an appropriate husband for her daughter, without yielding to a match exclusively chosen by the Rossermini. The Magistracy promptly charged the commissary of Pisa with visiting Camilla in the convent. Standing in front of him, the girl repeated all the charges she had already made against her mother: she would never go to live in her mother's house. Ginevra had not only remarried once, but twice, abandoning her daughter to a servant when she was only a few months old. Her mother never paid any attention to Camilla and the only place where she felt at home was her uncle Rossermini's family. Since his death, she had lived in the convent where good care had been taken of her and she had been given an education. Until her future was decided, she refused to leave.

Summoned again, Ginevra protested her right: she was a widow and wanted her daughter. But, confronted by Camilla's stubbornness, the Magistracy postponed all decisions, allowing her to stay where she was. Suddenly, one year later, news reached the Magistracy that Ginevra was dead. She had written a will in which, out of her own dowry of 6,000 *scudi*, she had left her daughter, 'once and for all', only 10 *scudi*. Contrary to Pisan statute, Ginevra had disinherited her child, carrying her hostility and revenge into the grave. One month went by, and in July 1620, Camilla married her cousin, the son of her uncle Odoardo, in whose family she felt at home. This was probably the match Ginevra had wanted to avoid, and all the Rossermini, aided by the aunt in the convent, manoeuvred in order to keep family wealth united under their name.[18]

A third point of interest is the division of the children on the reconstruction of a family following remarriage. There was a general tendency to separate brothers from sisters, and the children of the first marriage from those of the second. Various sources, in particular collections of family papers, show the strength of ties between brothers and sisters even when born from different marriages.[19] The *Magistrato dei pupilli*, however, concerned above all to protect the financial interests of the minors, only rarely considered the possibility of horizontal bonding in a family group divided by an inheritance system that placed in conflict the interests of male and female children not born to the same couple. Children were often put in care on a temporary basis and the arrangements for this did not follow a set pattern, but were subject to less clear-cut and more complex variables. The readiness to take on a ward without payment was instrumental in determining the child's placing with the mother's new

---

[18]   *Ibid.*, Campione di sottoposti, 35, fol. 186; 40, fol. 60; *ibid.*, Suppliche con informazione, 2289, fols. 21, 90r–v; *ibid.*, Atti e sentenze, 758, fol. 735.

[19]   G. Calvi, 'Maddalena Nerli e Cosimo Tornabuoni: comportamenti domestici e affettivi (XVI–XVII secolo)', in *Signori, patrizi, cavalieri*, ed. Visceglia, pp. 275–6.

husband who, on declaring his willingness to assume the entire burden of upbringing and education, received the child in care. Similarly, looking after children in illness was regarded as a good qualification for being awarded care. Another determining factor was class. High-ranking step-fathers, functionaries of the grand-ducal administration, were assigned to act as the guarantors of their wives, who administered the children's inheritance and obtained care of them also. There was one exceptional case in which Count Pecori, a patrician in high public office, was actually nominated guardian of his new step-children.

At the other end of the social scale, in the artisan and working class, a remarried widow's freedom of action to obtain management of her children's estate and care of them was guaranteed by the Magistracy's lack of interest in wards without substantial inheritances. Where the estate was very small, freedom to manage what little there was was even given to the step-father without any control over him. The reconstruction of these family units was thus left to the initiative of the single members and to the strength of the bonds that united them. Thus, in distant Barga, the step-father of Cristofano and Giustina, orphan children of Jacopo di Cristofano, was allowed to make use of the wards' funds to feed and clothe them without being accountable to the Magistracy, given the poverty of the little family.[20]

To be able to offer a child a home in an urban environment that would include nearness to a school was a strong recommendation for being awarded care. Clothing, shoes, personal hygiene and health, vouched for by doctors with increasing frequency, as well as participation in the rites of the church, certified by the priest, became essential requisites for evaluating the living standards of wards and the reliability of those to whom their care was entrusted.

In coming to a decision about including a minor in the family unit reconstructed around the new marriage, particular weight was given to the wishes of the dead husband who, if he so specified in his will, could agree to derogate from the legal requirement which excluded the mother from guardianship. Thus, the Florentine Niccolò Fagni, who died in 1598, left his wife Margherita the guardianship of their children, whether she remained a widow or remarried. Remarrying two years after her husband's death, she was able to retain the guardianship of their only son of three years.[21] It is possible that these exceptions are attributable to rather particular situations in which, after taking into consideration all the relatives of both branches or in their absence, the only practical solution was to concentrate all authoritative functions and powers in one family

[20] ASF, MPAP, Campione di partiti, 30, fol. 104v, 21 Nov. 1600.
[21] Ibid., 30, fol. 39, 28 June 1600.

member. However, even if the husbands' wills usually placed less emphasis on maternal guardianship, they were nonetheless decisive in strengthening the role of the widow. The differing outcomes of the following series of events are essentially to be explained by the presence or absence of the dead husband's will, which was all-important in determining the subsequent restructuring of the family.

Niccolò di Girolamo Tomassi of Cortona died in 1572, the event being notified by one of his brothers. Intestate, he left three daughters – Faustina aged ten, Doralice aged six and Lucrezia aged three. Two years later, in 1574, his widow, Caterina, remarried and the Magistracy assumed the guardianship of the children, nominating a paternal uncle as administrator of the estate. He was to make an inventory and nominate as guarantor the paternal uncle who drew up the statement for the Magistracy. We can assume that the two elder girls entered a convent and that Lucrezia was entrusted to her mother, although the brevity of the text, the absence of a will and a mother whom we barely glimpse, emphasize the central importance of the paternal family in deciding the course of events.[22]

A very different situation followed the death of Piero di Stefano, a miller of Montecarlo, who left an only daughter aged two. By the spring of 1575, a few months after his death, his widow, who had been left guardianship of the child in his will, had already remarried and the guardianship passed to the Magistracy. The mother, however, was nominated as administrator and the step-father as guarantor. All the ward's 'incomes, interest and rents' were to go to her mother and the second husband, who was to collect money owing to the estate and invest as advantageously as possible the proceeds of the sale of certain household goods 'in order to increase the income of the said ward'.[23]

Widows named as guardians – *donne et madonne* – in their husbands' wills were often entrusted with the administration of the estate and the care of the children even on remarriage, provided they did not voluntarily relinquish this responsibility. The Magistracy paid particular attention to step-fathers, whose economic position, stable way of life and trustworthiness were evaluated before they were allowed to become part of a new family. Even the presence of sons from the new husband's first marriage was carefully considered, with the intention of preventing possible matrimonial strategies involving them and female wards.

A very detailed example of the careful attention given to a child at the centre of one of these family reconstructions is the story of Giovanni, son and heir of Domenico di Luca di Girotto of Pescia who died intestate in

[22] *Ibid.*, 17, fol. 127, 18 Mar. 1574.   [23] *Ibid.*, 17, fol. 133v, 15 Apr. 1575.

1577. Nobody took on the guardianship of the child, who was then seven years old, and when the mother, Dorotea, remarried, the Magistracy intervened to arrange matters. It entrusted the administration of the ward's estate to a certain Antonio di Domenico Berti

on condition that the said Antonio keep the boy at his home, feed and clothe him, and teach him his trade. Antonio shall use and enjoy all the ward's estate, but shall not be able to ask the said ward to cover any expenses he may incur over the income of the ward's estate, except, however, if the said ward, Giovanni, should die while still a ward. In this case, the said Antonio may claim from the heirs of the said ward what he had spent on food, clothing and education, as above, in excess of the income he received from the estate. And as for his role as administrator, he promises to the said officials and to me, the notary, to carry out such administration free of charge.

However, Antonio, administrator of the estate, was sentenced to exile outside Pescia for six months; we do not know why. The care arrangements were therefore reviewed and Giovanni was transferred to the house of his mother and her new husband, on condition, however, 'that the said step-father and Madonna Dorotea provide adequate guarantees that they will keep the said boy and look after him well and responsibly, and feed and clothe him, and meet any other need of his at their own expense, and send him to school to learn moral values, and not use him for servile tasks or those performed by peasants'. Madonna Dorotea and her second husband, Francesco, formally pledged themselves before the Magistracy, while the administration of the estate – separated from the issue of care – remained the responsibility of Antonio, the previous nominee.[24]

The dynamics of constructing a new family unit involved a series of adjustments and stages, aiming at permanent solutions and able to satisfy differing needs. The attention given by the Magistracy was flexible, sensitively related to actual situations and to the relations between the two families and the new couple, as in the case that follows. At Lucignano in 1569, Bartolomeo di Giovanni Grandi died, leaving as his only heir Francesco, a child of two years. Nobody took on the guardianship of the boy, who was looked after for eight years in the home of paternal uncles until the mother, on remarrying, re-opened the matter. The Magistracy assumed guardianship of the child and nominated as administrator of the estate the step-father, Andrea, who undertook to make an inventory of the ward's estate and to produce a guarantor.[25] A month later, the differences of opinion between the new couple and the relatives of the dead husband were smoothed over by a timely agreement submitted to the Florentine Magistracy. The text starts by saying that the minor 'spent

[24] *Ibid.*, 19, fol. 102v, 3, 7 and 17 July 1579.   [25] *Ibid.*, 19, fol. 79v, 15 Apr. 1579.

the past year at the house of the said Andrea, his step-father, together with his mother'. This meant that the question of the estate was to be reviewed, leading to the division of some assets which the ward held 'in common with his uncles, as well as produce owing to them'. The parties – the step-father, Andrea, and the uncle, Menico – presented themselves before the Magistracy, where they signed

the following agreement, according to which the said Francesco ought and was to remain with his mother at the house of the said Andrea, his step-father, while the administration of the estate was to be given to the said Menico and Mariano, his uncles, who were to provide adequate guarantees and undertake the inventory in a correct form of all the remaining assets Francesco inherited from his father, and were obliged every year at harvest time to give and consign to the said Andrea the amount of fruit, grain, fodder, oil and wine owing to the said Francesco for his sustenance, and, in the event that they were not sufficient, the said Andrea was obliged to feed, clothe and look after him in an appropriate manner from his own resources, and the two parties were to come to an agreement about the expenses incurred up to the present regarding the present law-suit and provision of food.[26]

What stands out here is the consensus between the maternal and paternal branches of the family that was encouraged by the separation, sanctioned by the Magistracy, between the administration of the estate and the care of the boy. By delegating responsibilities and different roles to the relatives, orchestrating, so to speak, a 'team event' that emphasized the co-functioning of the maternal and paternal branches, the points of disagreement were smoothed out.

A dense tangle of conflict, on the other hand, often surrounded the question of the restitution of the mother's dowry – this was the really thorny issue that could impede the rebuilding of the family around the new couple. In cases where repaying the mother's dowry necessitated the division of the ward's inheritance and the sale at auction of real estate, the parties were, unsurprisingly, drawn up on opposing sides, the mother and her new husband ranged against the orphans.

In the summer of 1579 Lucia, the widow of Bernardo di Francesco della Casa, remarried and left the guardianship of her four children – the eldest seventeen years old and the youngest, Isabella, six – to the Magistracy. Lucia was a mature widow, presumably over thirty-five, and her decision to remarry led to bitter economic arguments and opposition between the new couple and the children of the first marriage. In order to repay the mother's dowry, the wards' inheritance was broken up by the sale at auction of a house in Florence which was valued, because of the disagreement between the parties, by two assessors, one for the children, the other

[26] ASF, MPAP, Atti e sentenze, 624, fol. 639r–v. The agreement was approved on 6 May.

for the widow. A third assessor could be called in, were disagreement to ensue. Furniture was also sold.[27]

The Magistracy was concerned at the sale of part of an orphan's inheritance and, whenever feasible, tended to propose an arrangement analogous to that customary for the payment of the dowry at marriage: that is to say, repayment in instalments on which 5 per cent interest was calculated periodically, rather than resort to the sale of unencumbered assets.

The entry of daughters into a convent could also burden the inheritance, particularly if the dowry paid to the convent was added to the payment to the mother and the entry of the daughters coincided with their mother's remarriage. This happened in Florence in 1579, when the widow of Niccolò di Francesco Santini remarried. Mother of three children – Francesco, sixteen years old, Isabella eleven and Virginia six – she asked for the restitution of her dowry. At the same time, coinciding with the restructuring of the family group after the new husband's arrival, the Magistracy ordered the two girls into a convent, San Matteo at Arcetri, where they had to pay the customary dowry. Thus the orphans' estate was burdened by three substantial payments, and to meet them the officials of the Magistracy held an auction of some of the estate's goods. For two houses two offers of 900 and 600 *scudi* each were received; 200 *scudi* were withdrawn from the *Monte di pietà* to pay the nuns at Arcetri; a further 50 *scudi* came from the sale at auction of furniture and furnishings. This, however, was not sufficient, and, to complete what was owing to the mother and the convent, 'a piece of agricultural land of twenty *staia* and a piece of vineyard of five *staia*' remained to be sold at auction.[28]

Despite the difficulties and tensions caused by repayment of the mother's dowry, the Florentine officials were flexible and, in addition to their respect for the rules of inheritance, sought to reconstruct family groups united by bonds of affection. The *Magistrato dei pupilli* ordered an inventory to be made of the property in the house of the poor heirs of Bernardino del Palagio, which was visited on 27 April 1591. The rooms of the house however were empty and desolate because the mother of the wards, 'Madonna Baccia, had taken the few pieces of furniture remaining there to repay her dowry'. The officials' initial dismay did not prevent them, however, from nominating the remarried mother administrator of the remaining property 'provided the said mother fed her three children and carried out this administration without payment, as she offered to do, without being obliged to produce a guarantor'.[29]

The conflicts typical of this critical phase in the cycle of family life

[27] ASF, MPAP, Campione di partiti, 19, fol. 99, 19 June 1579; fol. 143v.
[28] *Ibid.*, 19, fol. 148, 15 Jan. 1579; fol. 151r–v.   [29] *Ibid.*, 24, fol. 57, 26 Mar. 1591.

diminished, however, to the point of disappearing when the step-father offered to take on the administration of the estate and the care of the orphans 'free of charge and for the love of God'. This is what happened in February 1589 when Madonna Piera, daughter of Luca Landucci, mother of seven children (the last a boy born four months after the death of his father), remarried only six months after she was widowed, and two after the youngest child was born. Luca Torni, the new husband, was granted the administration of the estate and the care of the children, offering his services free of charge, and he was therefore granted the management of the family's affairs.

Licence was given to Luca Torni, the step-father and administrator of the children of Ridolfo di Francesco Giamberti, citizen of Florence, to sell such furniture and household goods belonging to the said estate as he thinks best for the benefit of the wards, and from the proceeds he is to pay the convent and nuns on behalf of Lucrezia, daughter of the said Ridolfo, when she takes the veil.

All seven wards, male and female, were to live for a year with the mother and the step-father, who was to 'take all their income and for that year was not required to be accountable for his use of it'.[30] Such an assumption of responsibility evidently deserved trust.

In the same year, Buonromeo di Bernardo Buonromei, a goldsmith from Pistoia and second husband of the widow Nanna, offered to administer without payment the estate of his two step-children, twelve-year-old Lisabetta and ten-year-old Ambrogio. While the girl was to be placed in a convent of her choice, the boy was to live 'and receive food at the house of his mother Madonna Nanna and his step-father Buonromeo', with the financial arrangements to be agreed and 'on condition the boy attend the school of the priest Messer Achille Baroni, his maternal uncle, morning and afternoon, with whatever payment was usual from such pupils'.[31]

In some cases, the construction of these new families took place in the house of the dead husband, which had been left to the wards. In the following instance, the mother–child unit exerted a kind of centripetal attraction for the step-father, who was joining the existing household. In 1590, Benedetto Ziti married the widow Lisabetta Lanfranchi, mother of four children: Gherardo aged fourteen, Giovan Battista aged ten, Gostanza aged thirteen and Olivia aged eight. As was usual, by order of the Magistracy, the family unit was divided and reorganized observing a gender division between brothers and sisters. The two girls, 'with all their furniture and necessary utensils', were placed in the convent of Monticelli, entrusted to the care of a paternal aunt who had taken the veil there, while the new couple kept the two boys with them. Following an agreement with the dead husband's relatives, the new family dwelt in the house belonging to the wards, 'rented' by the step-father for 40 *scudi* a year. To bring up the two boys, he was to receive yearly the same sum in florins to cover 'food and clothing', thus balancing the family budget.[32]

The even-handed solutions seen in similar situations were the result either of a series of negotiations between the parties or of a readiness on the part of the officials to suggest temporary and experimental measures (periods of custody of a few months or a year) until it became possible to identify more permanent solutions based on a thorough examination of the living arrangements of those concerned. A similar flexibility is evident in the Magistracy's dealings with those who were willing to save money for the wards' estate by administering and managing it free of charge. Their willingness, which presupposes, of course, a solid financial position and a far-sighted sense of responsibility, opened a relationship of trust between the institution and the new couple, in which the step-father assumed a role of complex and delicate mediation. Sometimes, the relationship of trust between them is underpinned by an implicit pact of exchange. This occurred in 1601, when Antonia, widow of Giovanni di Lorenzo Berardi, remarried to the *cavaliere*, Giovannantonio Popoleschi, was nominated administrator and carer of her daughters, together with her second husband, to serve 'without payment and for love'. In exchange she requested a substantial administrative freedom, 'to be able to manage at will the gains from the farms of the said estate without being accountable year by year'.[33]

The step-father of the three children of the widow of Bartolomeo di Matteo also offered to feed the wards, on condition that he was assigned 'their household goods and linen and woollen cloth', which would bring him enough to pay for their food and clothing. Having obtained the agreement and trust of the Magistracy through his good character, he was also allowed to collect the rent from a house in Borgo Ognissanti belonging to the three young wards, in order to provide for expenses 'that would occur from time to time in addition to the food and clothing of the said children, without having to be accountable for what he would spend on them to the Magistracy, who had trust in the benevolence and generosity of the said Giovanni'.[34]

Various types of agreement existed, moreover, between the widow and her new husband to avoid the development of conflicts once they were living together. Thus, in 1589, Margherita Cenni, a widow for many years and mother of two adolescent daughters, included in the marriage contract with her second husband precise agreements about the feeding and

[32] *Ibid.*, 23, fols. 204v, 206, 6 July 1590.   [33] *Ibid.*, 30, fol. 191, 2 Nov. 1601.
[34] *Ibid.*, 24, fol. 115v, 23 Oct. 1591.

care of the minors, setting it down in black and white that the new husband would cover the cost of food for the step-daughters from the income of their inheritance, while living together in their house.[35] Cases in which the second marriage was negotiated on the basis of the widow's explicit wish not to be separated from the children of her first marriage were relatively rare in the early modern period, but became a frequent practice during the eighteenth century. In time, widows' remarriage tended to be based on formal agreements that made the incorporation of the children of the first marriage into the new household a *sine qua non* for the celebration of the wedding.

On balance, it would appear that widowed mothers and the Florentine *Magistrato dei pupilli* had substantially, in their actual dealings, agreed a common interpretation, based on interaction and communication, of what a family was (and therefore on how it could be reconstructed). Both increasingly stressed its narrow definition as a nuclear unit, and gave pride of place on the one hand to the guarantees of inheritance and the well-being of the wards, and on the other hand to a code of family relationships based on ethics and natural feeling. Progressively, in the course of the eighteenth century, the language of affective bonding and morality, by defining the territory of maternal care, was to give new possibilities to women who, from the safeguard of their new position of strength, were increasingly able to impose an extensive network of controls over the nuclear family itself: through negotiations about care arrangements, on which the remarriage would come to depend; through the education of daughters, opposing their transfer to far-away convents; and through the request for measures of control over spendthrift and dissolute sons.

[35] *Ibid.*, 24, fols. 102v, 204, 14 Nov. 1600.

Index